YORKSHIRE TEXTILE MILLS

1770 - 1930

YORKSHIRE TEXTILE MILLS

The Buildings of the Yorkshire Textile Industry 1770 – 1930

Colum Giles
Ian H Goodall

LONDON: HMSO

First published 1992

ISBN 0 11 300038 3

British Library Cataloguing in
Publication Data
A CIP catalogue record for this book
is available from the British Library

This publication has been assisted by a grant from the
West Yorkshire Archives and Archaeology Joint
Committee

COVER PHOTOGRAPH:
Armitage Bridge Mills, South Crosland, near Huddersfield

FRONTISPIECE:
Firth Street Mills (62) and, beyond, Larchfield Mills (64), Huddersfield, two steam-powered textile mills built next to the Huddersfield Canal in the mid 1860s

Printed in the United Kingdom for HMSO
Dd 295261 6/92 C30 531/3 12521

Contents

Commissioners

Chairman
The Rt Hon The Baroness Park of Monmouth CMG OBE

Maurice Warwick Beresford
Martin Biddle
Richard Bradley
Robert Angus Buchanan
Bridget Katherine Cherry
John Kerry Downes
John Davies Evans
Richard David Harvey Gem
Derek John Keene
Peter Erik Lasko CBE
Trevor Longman
Geoffrey Haward Martin CBE
Gwyn Idris Meirion-Jones
Antony Charles Thomas CBE DL
Malcolm Todd

Secretary
Tom Grafton Hassall

Forewords

Textiles were once one of England's major manufacturing industries, and they continue to be important today, particularly in Yorkshire. The development of the industry is closely reflected in its buildings, as much in its recent decline as in former periods of prosperity. Its decline in the 20th century has presented a considerable threat to its monuments, and many mills have been demolished or lie vacant or underused. The Royal Commission has responded to this threat and to the increasing interest in industrial buildings by conducting a survey of Yorkshire textile mills, continuing the fruitful association which it has enjoyed with the West Yorkshire Archaeology Service. The Service has helped to fund both the survey itself and the present publication; we acknowledge this with gratitude. The Royal Commission has also supported surveys of textile mills in two further areas, Greater Manchester and East Cheshire, and it is hoped that publication will result from both these initiatives.

The survey of Yorkshire textile mills has had two products, an archive and this book. The complete archive resulting from the programme of fieldwork and documentary research is publicly accessible in the National Buildings Record at the Royal Commission's head office, which is currently at Fortress House, 23 Savile Row, London W1X 2JQ; copies of detailed reports on selected West Yorkshire textile mills, and an index to the complete archive, are also held by the West Yorkshire Archaeology Service at 14 St John's North, Wakefield WF1 3QA. The book which draws on this archive presents an analysis of buildings and complexes connected with the textile industry, and it is hoped that both will increase the understanding of the industry's architecture and help those whose work or research encompasses this field.

Commissioners would like to thank all owners of mill property and custodians of relevant documentation who gave assistance during the survey. They would also like to acknowledge the work of the staff involved in the survey and publication: Dr Ian Goodall and Colum Giles investigated the buildings and wrote the archive reports and text for the book; Gillian Cookson and Dr Bridgett Jones undertook documentary research; Tony Berry and Paul Clayton produced archive drawings and Tony Berry prepared illustrations for publication; Bob Skingle, Terry Buchanan, Tony Perry, Roger Thomas, Peter Williams and Keith Buck took archive and publication photographs; Roger Featherstone supervised aerial photography; Davina Turner typed reports and the book text, and carried out editorial work on the latter; Jean Craven and Helen James provided secretarial and clerical support; and Kate Owen, Jane Butcher and Fran Brown undertook editorial work.

PARK OF MONMOUTH
Chairman, Royal Commission on the Historical Monuments of England

The West Yorkshire Archaeology Service and the Royal Commission on the Historical Monuments of England have already collaborated successfully on two county-wide building surveys. Previous RCHME publications, on *Rural Houses of West Yorkshire 1400–1830* (1986) and *Workers' Housing in West Yorkshire 1750–1920* (1986), have been well received not only by specialist readers but also by a much wider audience. There is every reason to suppose that the present volume, dealing with a class of building which has traditionally been seen to typify the county, will attract a similarly wide readership.

West Yorkshire has a remarkably rich heritage of historic buildings, a heritage which reflects the county's prosperity – much of it textile based – from the later Middle Ages down to the present century. Textile mills themselves form the most prominent element of this heritage. The 1960s and 1970s witnessed large-scale demolition of mills throughout West Yorkshire. However, there developed a slowly changing attitude from the belief that the mills were an eye-sore that had to be removed as rapidly as possible to a recognition that this industrial heritage portrayed a true regional identity and a valuable potential asset that could be utilised for the service industry and light industrial uses. These new uses were accompanied by conversions and alterations which, unless carried out in a sympathetic manner, could present another threat to their fabric, albeit of a less conclusive nature than wholesale demolition. Recognising these losses and continuing threats to the county's dramatic architectural heritage, John Hedges, the newly appointed County Archaeologist, in 1983 approached Dr Peter Fowler, Secretary of the Royal Commission at that time, with a proposal to implement a survey to record a representative sample of surviving mills. The Commission had independently identified mills as a class of threatened building requiring further study so was very happy to collaborate on this venture. A rapid survey of all the textile mills in the county was followed by detailed investigation of a representative sample of the most important examples. This publication presents the main findings of the survey. It is hoped that it will increase awareness of the importance of these buildings and encourage a positive approach towards finding a secure and appropriate future for those which are redundant.

The Archaeology Service is devoting an increasing proportion of its resources towards the recording and management of the county's industrial remains. It would welcome further information on these or other mills to supplement its county-wide records housed at 14 St John's North, Wakefield WF1 3QA. Although this may be the last in the recent series of jointly funded surveys, the Archaeology Service will continue to take a leading role in recording the county's historic buildings.

COUNCILLOR KEITH RHODES
Chairman, West Yorkshire Archives and Archaeology Joint Committee

Acknowledgements

This study was carried out with the support of two successive Secretaries of the RCHME, Professor P J Fowler and T G Hassall, and with the encouragement and advice of J T Smith, Dr J Bold, D W Black and Keith Falconer of the RCHME. Commissioners maintained a continuing interest in the project, but particular thanks are due to Professor M W Beresford and Professor R A Buchanan who read the complete text and made valuable comments. Thanks are also due to Dr D T Jenkins, Dr D A Farnie and Negley Harte who commented on individual parts of the text. The RCHME greatly appreciates the co-operation of the West Yorkshire Archaeology Service and the County Archaeologist, John Hedges, throughout the survey.

The Royal Commission owes a great debt to the many individuals who made available the results of their own historical research, in particular Peter Brears, Alan J Brooke, Mrs E Burgess, Ron Fitzgerald, John Goodchild, Dr Roger N Holden, Griff Hollingshead, Cyril Pearce, David Scriven, George Sheeran, Harold Taylor, Dr Philip Townhill, Mrs S J Wade and Mark Watson. The staff of many archive offices and libraries have given much help, as have the Building Control Departments of the various Councils which still retain their Building Plans. Particular thanks must also be given to the many millowners who readily allowed the RCHME to examine their buildings, and who frequently made available their company records.

Illustration credits

All illustrations are copyright of the RCHME, with the exception of the following which are reproduced by permission: Leeds City Libraries, 6, 14, 102, 108; Calderdale Museums and Arts, 18; John Goodchild Loan MSS, Wakefield Library Headquarters, 27; G C Barber, 38; J G Collins, General Manager, Estates Division, Illingworth Morris plc, 49, 201, 241, 258, 269; George Lumb (Spinners) Ltd, 66; Grattan plc, 71; Robert Glew and Co Ltd, 72, 97; S Lyles, Sons and Co Ltd, 76; Bradford Libraries and Information Service, 85, 299; West Yorkshire Archive Service, 86, 87, 143, 199; R Gaunt, 103, 227a; Metropolitan Borough of Calderdale, Planning Department, 107; Council of the Yorkshire Archaeological Society, 133; West Yorkshire Archaeology Service, 144; J I Case Europe Ltd, 157; C G Hobson, 168, 190, 200; Trustees of the Allendale Settled Estates, 186; Mrs H Aldridge, 187; Bradford Industrial Museum, 208; Mrs T M Cree, 210; Birmingham Library Services, 222; Trustees of the Science Museum, 226; Kingsley Cards (1980) Ltd, 231; Ian Holden, 233; Laycock International Ltd, 263, 271; J Maude, 272; Leeds City Museum, 273; Woods of Bradford, 274, 300; Kirklees Cultural Services, 279, 298; Automatic Components (Stanningley) Ltd, 338.

Editorial notes

The structure of this book is explained in the Introduction. The numbers in brackets throughout the text refer to the Selective Inventory which gives brief accounts of the buildings recorded in detail during the Royal Commission's survey of Yorkshire textile mills. Unless otherwise indicated, plans of buildings are of the ground floor and are to the scale of 1:750. Drawings follow the conventions outlined in *Recording Historic Buildings: A Descriptive Specification* (RCHME, 1990), 6–8. A few conventions specific to industrial buildings have been used, namely:

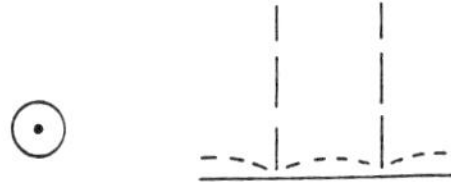

upright shaft fireproof arches

The following abbreviations have been used on some plans:

B/H Boiler house
Ch Chimney
Ec/H Economiser house
E/H Engine house
H Hoist
r/r rope race
tr trapdoor
w/c water closet
w/w waterwheel
W/H Wheelhouse

On most block plans, the position of the engine house or engine houses is indicated by a darker tone. Exceptions occur where the position of some engine houses is uncertain.

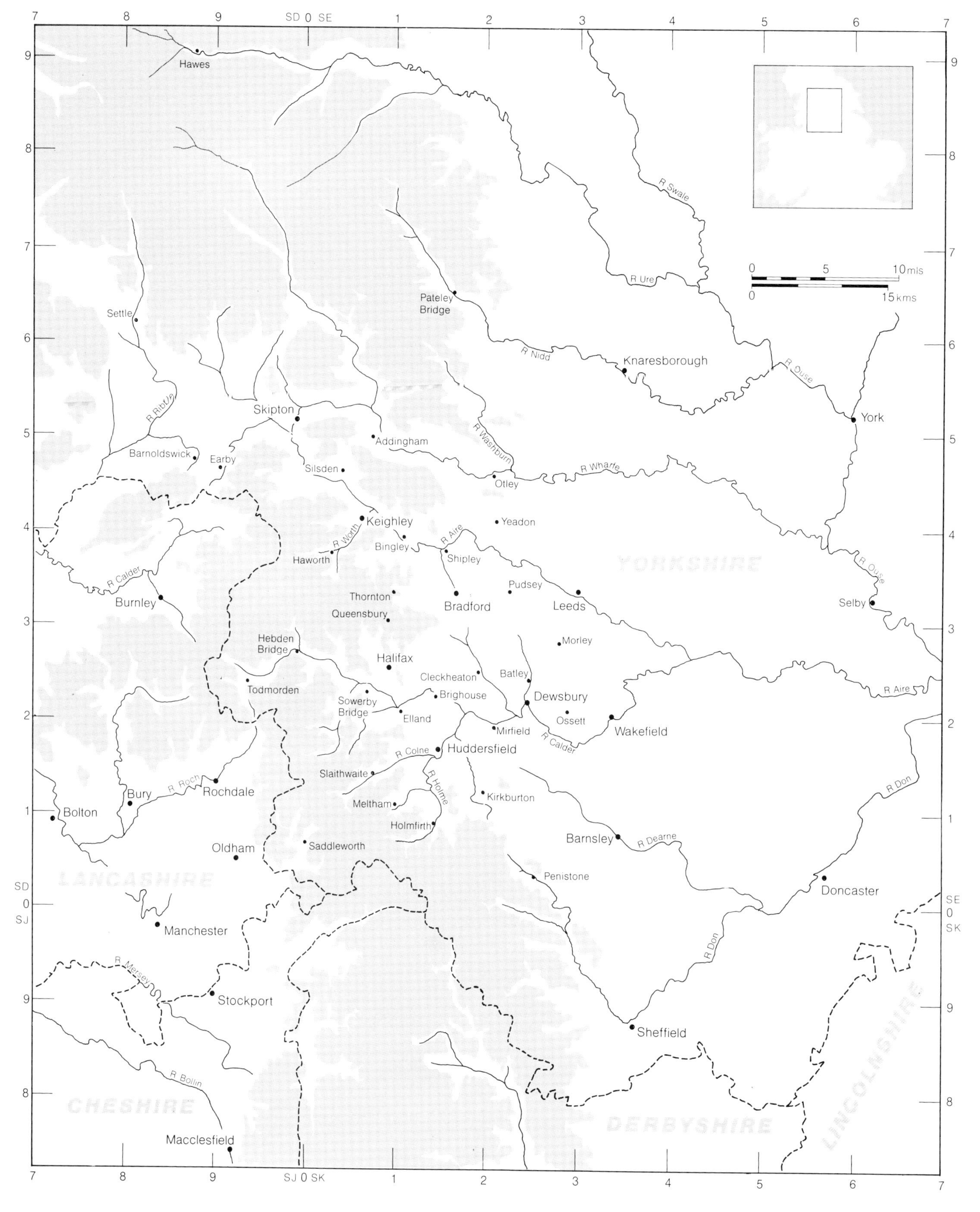
Hawes
Settle
Skipton
Pateley Bridge
Knaresborough
York
Barnoldswick
Earby
Addingham
Silsden
Otley
Keighley
Yeadon
Bingley
Shipley
Haworth
Burnley
Thornton
Bradford
Pudsey
Leeds
Selby
Queensbury
Morley
Hebden Bridge
Halifax
Cleckheaton
Batley
Todmorden
Brighouse
Dewsbury
Sowerby Bridge
Elland
Ossett
Wakefield
Mirfield
Huddersfield
Slaithwaite
Rochdale
Bury
Bolton
Meltham
Kirkburton
Holmfirth
Barnsley
Oldham
Saddleworth
Penistone
Doncaster
Manchester
Stockport
Sheffield
Macclesfield
R Swale
R Ure
R Nidd
R Ouse
R Ribble
R Washburn
R Wharfe
R Aire
R Worth
R Calder
R Colne
R Holme
R Roch
R Dearne
R Don
R Mersey
R Bollin
YORKSHIRE
LANCASHIRE
CHESHIRE
DERBYSHIRE
LINCOLNSHIRE
0 5 10 mls
0 15 kms
SD 0 SE
SJ 0 SK
SE 0 SK
SD 0 SJ

Introduction

This book examines the development of the buildings of the Yorkshire textile industry, in particular its mills, between the late 18th century, when new developments in machines and in power generation permitted a rapid expansion of production, and the 1930s, when the industry retracted and the age of new mill building ended. The scope is thus broad, since the period included the transition from domestic production to the factory system, the mechanisation of all major processes, and the development of new building types and techniques of construction. The book adds to the literature on the history of the industry, but seeks to use architectural evidence to illustrate how the textile sector developed.

Although nominally a study of textile mills in the historical county of Yorkshire, this volume in fact concentrates almost entirely upon the former West Riding. Fig 1 shows the area of survey and adjacent counties. Saddleworth, formerly in the West Riding and an important woollen and cotton manufacturing area, was excluded because since 1974 it has formed part of Greater Manchester where a similar mills survey has been conducted. The rest of Yorkshire, where the textile industry was of only local importance, was not covered systematically in the survey.

The methodology adopted in the Yorkshire textile mills survey has been described in print already.[1] Briefly, early 20th-century Ordnance Survey maps and other sources were used to identify sites connected with the textile industry, giving a total of about 2,000. An initial survey, involving a visit to each site, established the survival of *c*1,750 mills and other complexes, and produced a short record of each, comprising brief notes and one or more ground-level photographs, to which aerial photographs were subsequently added. These records were used as a basis for selecting sites for more detailed recording, and the aim in selection was to produce a sample reflecting the range of material in terms of date, textile branch, structural form, organisational type and power source. Ultimately about 150 sites were recorded in detail, representing a sample of slightly under ten per cent of those extant at the time of the initial survey. The mills were investigated through architectural examination and by the consultation of documents, thereby allowing the compilation of reports giving detailed accounts of historical and architectural evolution. The importance of using both architectural and documentary evidence in the study of buildings of this type cannot be overstated, since while the architecture alone might have yielded a reliable picture of evolution, documents including title deeds, insurance policies, plans, maps, company archives and many other sources often provided precision in terms of date and the function of individual structures. In addition,

Fig 1 Map showing the area of the Yorkshire Textile Mills survey and adjacent counties. The county boundary of Yorkshire is that of the former West Riding; ground above 244m is shaded.

documents often gave information about the nature of a site at different periods, an essential consideration when the architectural evidence is so ephemeral, as is the case in mills which evolved over many years and where early structures were often demolished to make way for new and larger buildings. The survey archive, therefore, has a large and important documentary element, and indeed many of the survey's most interesting discoveries were of documents in private or company ownership. All unreferenced statements in this book relating to the history and evolution of individual mill sites are based on evidence gathered during the survey and are contained in the reports which form part of the archive, which is publicly accessible (see p224).

This book has three principal parts. The main part comprises five chapters. The first chapter gives a brief introduction to the history of the Yorkshire textile industry and describes the different processes involved. The second chapter examines the evolution of the different building types adapted to or developed by the textile industry, and looks at both their design and structure. The third chapter studies how sites, whether isolated loomshops or large mill complexes, reflect the changing methods by which production was organised. The fourth chapter describes the buildings and features associated with the generation and transmission of power, and the last chapter adopts a wider perspective to look beyond the mill, showing how the textile industry affected the landscape and communities. The second part of the book is the Selective Inventory, which contains brief descriptions of the sites either recorded in detail in the survey or otherwise used as evidence in the book. The third part is a Gazetteer listing all sites recorded in the survey. It is hoped that these contents will allow the reader easy access to the archive which provides the basis for the account given in this book.

1

The Yorkshire textile industry 1770–1930

The Yorkshire textile industry has a long history. Cloth was already being produced in the Middle Ages, by the 17th century the industry was an important part of the rural and urban economy, and in the late 18th and 19th centuries mechanisation brought an era of mass production. The industry was also diverse, far more so than is often realised. Justly famous for its woollen and worsted products, the county developed a flax and linen industry in the 17th century, a cotton sector in the late 18th century, and silk and recovered wool branches in the 19th century. The buildings of the industry fully reflect its long history and varied character, and this chapter provides a brief historical and technical introduction to assist the understanding of the architectural developments which form the subject of this book.[1]

The branches of the Yorkshire textile industry

In the pre-industrial period, virtually all areas of England were involved in textile production; woollen cloth was made in Worcester and the south-west, worsteds were produced in Norfolk, fustians in Lancashire, and so on. Few areas, however, could match the diversity and scale of the Yorkshire industry. Before 1770 there were three deeply entrenched branches. The largest was the woollen branch, oldest established and spread over the widest area. Second in rank was worsted production, introduced to the county in the 17th century, and flax and linen, the third branch, was important over a wide area by the late 18th century. There was even a short-lived attempt to introduce silk production to Sheffield in 1760.[2] Each of the main branches had an organisational structure which involved participation by significant numbers of the population, both urban and rural. Profits from the textile industry made fortunes for the great clothier and merchant families, while the poorer levels of society gained a more secure livelihood through combining an agricultural interest with employment in textiles.

After 1770 the Yorkshire industry became still more diverse. To the three established branches were added cotton production in the late 18th century, silk manufacturing, growing slowly in the 19th century, and, finally, recovered wool production. By the mid 19th century, carpet manufacturing, not studied in this volume, was important in some areas, in particular in Halifax where John Crossley's Dean Clough Mills grew into a massive complex employing 5,000 people.[3] The balance between the branches in terms of size and importance can be assessed through study of the Factory Returns, produced periodically from the 1830s to assist governmental regulation of the industry.[4] The woollen sector remained the largest before 1900: in the mid 19th century half of all Yorkshire's mills were woollen mills and, at the end of the century, the 925 woollen mills represented forty-four per cent of textile establishments. Worsted was the second largest branch before 1900, having between one quarter and one third of Yorkshire mills between 1835 and 1889. The flax and linen branch, one of the sectors established before 1770, experienced widespread growth before 1850, with Leeds and Barnsley developing as major new centres of production. By the 1830s, however, it had been supplanted as the third-ranking branch by cotton, introduced to Yorkshire in the 1780s. Parts of the traditional woollen and worsted producing areas switched to cotton manufacturing and, despite early setbacks, the branch maintained a strong presence in the county. Between 1835 and 1903, thirteen to twenty per cent of Yorkshire mills were cotton mills, compared to at most five per cent in the flax and linen branch. Post-1850 decline in the face of competition from cotton products was such that hemp and jute production took over in some parts of the flax and linen area.

Silk, including both pure and waste-silk processing, was always a numerically small branch in Yorkshire. Although the first silk mill in the county had been established in Sheffield in 1760, subsequent growth was slow and limited. The greatest number of silk mills – forty-five, recorded in 1889 – represented only two per cent of all mills. The recovered wool industry, established only in the early 19th century with the development of shoddy grinding *c*1809 and of mungo grinding in the 1830s, was never a major branch but was important in some localities. It may be under-represented in the Factory Returns, since it was first recognised as a separate category only in the 1867 Returns. For the rest of the century, however, it had between three and five per cent of Yorkshire's mills, and by 1903 this figure had increased to nine per cent (156 shoddy and mungo mills).

Twentieth-century trends are difficult to quantify with precision since the Factory Returns cease in 1905. One of the major changes of the late 19th century, however, is revealed in the Returns for 1903–4: worsted mills (746) outnumbered woollen mills (569) for the first time, reflecting the diversification of parts of the traditional woollen-manufacturing zone, particularly Huddersfield, into worsted production. By 1919–20, wool textiles – woollen, worsted and recovered wool – accounted for over seventy-five per cent of Yorkshire textile companies, roughly the same proportion that it had enjoyed over much of the 19th century. Within that broad category, however, the increasing strength of worsted and of mixed production was apparent, for nearly 500 firms were involved in worsted spinning or manufacturing, nearly 500 were involved in both worsted and woollen production, but only 200 firms concentrated on woollen spinning or manufacturing. Cotton companies (329) were strongly represented and there were about 180 firms involved in various aspects of the recovered wool industry. The seventeen flax and linen companies and the twenty-six silk firms together represented only two and a half per cent of concerns.[5] An important development, particularly in the Leeds area, in the late 19th and early 20th centuries was the growth of the clothing industry producing ready-to-wear articles. The Burtons' Hudson Road Mills in east Leeds was probably the largest employer, but many other large and small clothing firms existed. Clothing works lie outside the scope of this volume, although sites are listed in the Gazetteer.

Fig 2 The distribution of the Yorkshire textile industry, c1850.

The geography of the Yorkshire textile industry

Although present at different times over much of the historic county of Yorkshire, the textile industry was concentrated in the former West Riding, in a belt west of Leeds and Wakefield and between Skipton in the north and Barnsley in the south (Fig 1). The geographical character of the area is varied. In the west are the Pennines, where the landscape shows a pattern of scattered settlement on the valley sides, with small towns like Sowerby Bridge and Pateley Bridge at old bridging points across the major rivers. Mills are found in both tributary and principal valleys. Most of the remote mills were sited to take advantage of water power, but many of the mills in the valley bottoms originated as steam-powered factories and enjoyed proximity to the transport systems – turnpikes, canals and railways – which ran along the valley floors. The old market towns on the Pennine fringes – Bradford, Halifax and Huddersfield – developed into major industrial centres in the 19th century as their mills and associated housing spread out along the valley bottoms and over the surrounding hills.

To the east of the Pennines the textile area is one of undulating landscape with a varied settlement pattern of isolated farms, hamlets, villages and towns. In the early 18th century Daniel Defoe described it as 'in a hurry of work', 'infinitely populous' and 'a noble scene of industry'.[6] The exploitation of its coal resources gave the area advantages in the 19th century, and towns like Batley, Cleckheaton and Morley rose to new prominence with large numbers of steam-powered mills. Dominating the local economy were the major towns of Wakefield, an ancient administrative centre and important wool exchange, and Leeds, the largest industrial town and a regional market sited at the meeting point of manufacturing and agricultural zones.[7]

The branches making up the Yorkshire textile industry were each concentrated in different and often overlapping zones. The growing diversity of the industry after 1770 and the differing fortunes of the branches meant that distribution altered over time. In the 1770s, the three principal branches – woollen, worsted, and flax and linen – had more or less clearly defined zones. The woollen branch was dominant over a broad belt of territory from Saddleworth in the far west, through the Colne, Holme, Dearne and Upper Don valleys, in the mid Calder valley from Sowerby Bridge to Wakefield, in most of the area between the Aire and Calder east of Bradford and west of Leeds and Wakefield, and in the mid Aire valley in the Yeadon and Guiseley areas. Leeds, Wakefield and Huddersfield were the main marketing centres, and Leeds dominated the finishing trades. Many of the woollen zones had their own specialities: narrow cloths were made around Huddersfield, white cloths and blankets in a central zone including Dewsbury, and coloured cloths in the north and east around Leeds. Worsted production was important in the hinterland of Bradford, in the Worth and upper Aire valleys around Keighley, and in the upper Calder valley where Halifax was the principal marketing centre. Flax and linen production was split between two areas. In the north, Cleveland and the North York Moors were involved to a limited extent, but the major centre was Nidderdale, including the important manufacturing town of Knaresborough. In the south, Barnsley and its immediate environs developed as a linen-weaving area, using principally imported yarn.

By 1850, the three traditional branches had altered little in their location. Some minor adjustments had taken place, accommodating, for example, the decline of the woollen industry in the Penistone area, the spread of flax spinning into Nidderdale's tributary valleys, and the rise of Leeds to pre-eminence as a flax-spinning centre (Fig 2). The major geographical changes were caused by the adoption of steam power, allowing development away from the rivers, and the irruption of cotton production into the Yorkshire industry. The first cotton mill in Yorkshire, Low Mill, Keighley (74), was established in 1780 and the following two or three decades saw a rapid expansion, with over 200 new mills being built. Cotton production was centred first on the upper Calder valley west of Halifax, in the Bradford and Keighley areas, in Leeds, and in the northern dales. In the early 19th century the cotton boom ended, and many mills, especially in the Bradford and Keighley areas, were converted to worsted production. Even so, cotton remained dominant in 1850 in the upper Calder valley, in Craven and in the northern dales, Todmorden and Skipton being important centres. Elsewhere, cotton flourished in the heartland of the woollen and worsted zones, in, for example, the Colne valley and Brighouse, where cotton-spinning mills were well placed to supply warps to mixed-cloth manufacturers. Brighouse was also a centre of silk production, and Halifax, Bradford and the Huddersfield area all had small numbers of silk spinners and weavers. The final branch of the industry, recovered wool, was concentrated in the Dewsbury–Ossett–Morley triangle, where it supplied shoddy and mungo for low-grade woollen production in the local mills. This area came to be known as the 'Heavy Woollen' area because of the nature of its products, mainly thick coatings and blankets.

Geographical change after 1850 was caused mainly by economic conditions. The Yorkshire flax industry declined progressively after 1850: mills in Nidderdale and Knaresborough were severely affected, many turning to rope making; Leeds ceased to be an important spinning town, its last flax mill, Balm Road Mills, Hunslet (66), being built *c*1880; and Barnsley ultimately declined as a linen-weaving town. In contrast the cotton branch not only maintained its position in the upper Calder valley and Craven but expanded through the development of Barnoldswick and Earby (now in Lancashire) as weaving towns and by the construction of further mills, especially in the Colne valley and Huddersfield, to supply the local woollen and worsted industry with warps. The textile zone thus shifted after 1850, but in a core area it was of great significance well into the 20th century. Within that core area, roughly bounded by Leeds, Skipton, Todmorden, Holmfirth and Wakefield, the most important geographical change was perhaps the blurring of the demarcation between woollen and worsted zones. By the early 20th century the Bradford area and the Worth valley were still dominated by worsted production, even if increasingly of yarn rather than cloth, but parts of the former woollen zone, in particular Huddersfield and Leeds and their hinterlands, were involved in the manufacture of both worsted and woollen cloth. Even with this change, however, there was little overlap in product between the old and new worsted zones, for Huddersfield especially became renowned as the producer of fine-quality worsted cloth, in contrast to the low-cost, low-quality article which had raised Bradford to pre-eminence before 1875.

Raw materials

The Yorkshire textile industry used four principal raw materials: two animal fibres (wool and silk) and two vegetable fibres (cotton and flax). In addition, hair (mohair, alpaca, angora, vicuna) was used in the wool sector. The wool sector was divided into three branches according to the material processed: short-staple wool was used for woollens, long-staple wool for worsted, and wool waste material in the recovered wool branch. As long-stapled fibres, mohair and alpaca were treated as worsted wools and therefore belonged to the worsted branch. To a large extent, most Yorkshire mills dealt exclusively with one type of material. Woollen mills often had their own recovered wool plant by the mid 19th century, but otherwise even those mills which produced mixed-fibre cloths – with, say, a cotton warp and a worsted weft – appear to have restricted their production to a single material by buying in the warps, manufacturing their own weft, and then combining the two at the weaving stage.

Products

The diversity of Yorkshire's textile industry was possible because the products of the different branches were more complementary than mutually competitive. There were close links between the branches, and the industry should be seen more as a number of interrelated sectors than as a series of separate ones. The woollen branch, the largest branch over much of the period from 1770 to 1930, traditionally produced plain heavy cloth for use in uniforms, coats and blankets, but fancy patterned cloth was made in the Huddersfield area and Yorkshire tweeds came to rival the products of the Scottish woollen industry. The woollen branch also used recovered wool – shoddy, mungo and extract (see p14) – in the production of cheap heavy cloth. Worsted cloths, known early in the period as stuffs, shalloons, or by other specialist terms, were generally lighter than woollens and had a smooth finish with a visible weave which contrasted with the dense felted nature of most woollens. Linen was originally used for a variety of products from fine-quality cloth for clothing to coarse household ware and sailcloth but, in one of the principal instances of competition in the Yorkshire industry, the introduction of light, cheap cottons led linen manufacturers to concentrate on coarser products and some ultimately to switch to rope-making using hemp. Silk was a high-quality fabric produced in limited quantities in Yorkshire, and the products – chiefly velvets and plush fabrics – were aimed at a specialist luxury market.

During the 19th century, mixed-fibre cloths came to play an important role in the Yorkshire industry, emphasising the links between the branches. Cotton warps were used widely in the worsted branch from the 1830s, and the typical product of the Bradford area became a cotton warp/worsted weft cloth. Cotton/woollen mixes became common too, and Morley union cloth and mixed-fibre blankets were important products. In addition, the woollen branch used recovered wool and silk, the latter for use especially in the manufacture of waistcoats and striped materials. The worsted industry also used a limited amount of silk in combination with alpaca. Alpaca and mohair increased the range of the worsted branch in the middle decades of the 19th century and 'lustre cloths', combining alpaca or mohair with cotton warps, brought huge success to firms like Salts of Saltaire Mills, Shipley (116).

As well as producing finished cloth, the Yorkshire industry sold large quantities of yarn. Worsted yarns were produced in mills for local consumption in the early 19th century and were increasingly sold abroad as Europe and the United States of America developed their own manufacturing sectors, often behind a tariff shield. Cotton and silk yarns were produced in Yorkshire mills for the local woollen and worsted industry, and cotton, linen and silk sewing threads were also made to serve a specialised market.

Processes and mechanisation

The five branches of the industry which dealt with raw materials strictly defined (recovered wool being the exception) employed a range of processes which may be grouped into four stages of production: preparatory, spinning, weaving and finishing. Within this broad picture, however, there were significant differences, each raw material requiring a particular method of treatment, especially in the first and last stages. These differences applied in the pre-mechanised period and were perpetuated by mechanisation.

The preparatory stage of production

A lengthy sequence of processes was required before textile fibres could be spun. Wool had first to be sorted

Fig 3 Cotton breaking by hand (Tomlinson nd, The Manufacture of Cotton Yarn, *Part 2, 7).*

into different qualities, since a single fleece contained many different grades. It was then scoured to remove dirt and grease before being washed and dried. Cotton was cleaned by beating or scutching to remove dust and vegetable particles, in a process which was at first a hand operation (Fig 3). Wool and cotton were each then willeyed or willowed, involving further beating and therefore cleaning and also the separation of the mass of fibres to assist later processing. Willeying machines were introduced in the late 18th century to perform this operation, which had the further effect of blending the fibres to give a consistent character to a batch.

The early stages of production in the flax industry were very different, for they involved the extraction of the useful part of the flax plant from the rest of the vegetable matter. This was achieved by prolonged steeping, or retting, in water, which caused the unwanted part of the plant to decompose, and then, after drying, by breaking, beating or scutching, which removed the straw leaving the raw flax ready for processing. Mechanically powered scutching machines were introduced in the 18th century, but most of the flax used in Yorkshire mills appears to have been imported ready-scutched.

Pure and waste-silk preparation was done by different means. Pure silk had first to be washed and dried before it was wound and knots removed by passing the thread through a gauge. Mechanically powered winding machines replaced hand-powered methods in the 19th century. Waste silk, packed in bales, had to be opened and the mass of fibres torn apart before cleaning by scutching.

Willowed cotton and wool and scutched flax and waste silk were at the same stage of preparation. Before spinning could take place, the various fibres had to be further disentangled and straightened out. In the cotton and woollen branches this was achieved by carding, which involved drawing wire teeth through the fibres to produce a roll or sliver in a process which was originally hand-powered and used hand cards. In 1775, however, Richard Arkwright introduced his carding engine (Fig 4) which accelerated production and had the advantage of making a continuous sliver ready for spinning. Carding engines were introduced rapidly into the cotton industry and, together with the similar but coarser scribbling engine, into the woollen industry.

Worsted wool and flax required a different treatment, for they contained both long and short-staple fibres. Worsted wool was first carded, but then the long fibres, 'tops' in the worsted industry and 'line' in the flax industry, had to be separated from the short ('noils' and 'tow' respectively) by combing or heckling, involving passing the fibres through combs, heated in the worsted industry (Fig 5). The process also straightened the fibres in preparation for spinning. Worsted noils were then sent to the woollen branch of the industry, in which they were treated like normal short-staple wool and carded before being spun. The flax tow was also carded and used for poorer-quality products than the superior line fibre. Waste silk was also combed and carded, and then boiled to remove the natural gum which had held the cocoon together.

Fig 4 Carding machines (Baines 1835, pl 6).

Fig 5 Hand combing, shown in a panel on Samuel Cunliffe Lister's statue in Lister Park, Bradford.

*Fig 6 Flax-heckling machine (*The Penny Magazine, *30 December 1843, 505).*

Combing and heckling proved difficult to mechanise. Successful flax-heckling machines were first developed in 1808 and were soon adopted by the industry (Fig 6), but combing machines for worsted wool were not successfully made until the 1840s, following developments by Lister, Holden, Heilmann and others (Fig 7). In the silk industry, Lister introduced a machine comb as late as 1859, but it was not a great success and further progress in the preparatory processing of silk was delayed until he produced a silk-dressing machine in 1877.

Dyeing was undertaken as part of the preparatory stage of production in some circumstances. Where patterned cloth was required, wool was either dyed in the raw state, for woollen-cloth production, or in the combed state for worsted-cloth production (dyeing at this stage was called slubbing dyeing).

Fig 7 Combing machine, shown in a panel on Samuel Cunliffe Lister's statue in Lister Park, Bradford.

The spinning stage of production

Methods of spinning, especially mechanised spinning, varied according to the nature of raw material, since textile fibres differ considerably in natural strength. The easiest to process, and the first to be mechanised, was pure silk which as a strong continuous filament required only twisting to give yarn. This process, called throwing in the silk industry, was first performed by hand but in 1721 Thomas Lombe introduced large throwing machines of Italian design to England, working them in his mill in Derby.

Two operations were required to produce yarn in other branches. First, a sliver of material had to be drawn out to produce an increasingly fine thread, and secondly, the thread had to be twisted to give strength to the yarn. For centuries flax, woollen and worsted yarns were produced on the hand-powered spinning wheel (Fig 8), and cotton too was at first spun on the wheel. This method of production was, however, slow and the great expansion of the textile industry in the late 18th century was initially made possible by the development of mechanically powered spinning machines. The cotton branch pioneered the introduction of machinery: in 1764 James Hargreaves introduced the hand-powered spinning jenny, the first machine to spin more than a single thread at one time (Fig 9); in 1769, Richard Arkwright patented the water frame, which spun thread on the different principle of roller drawing and which was operated by animal or mechanical power (Fig 10); and in 1779 Samuel Crompton introduced his spinning mule, which was hand-powered until the 1790s. The different machines produced different types of yarn: the jenny gave soft yarns suitable for weft, the water frame gave a strong yarn used for warps, and the mule was capable of producing finer yarns. The machines were improved over the years: power was applied to part of the action of the mule in the 1790s, Richard Roberts developed a fully automatic self-acting mule in the 1820s (Fig 11), and in *c*1800 the water frame was enlarged and made to run at higher speeds, the improved machine being called the throstle.

These machines – jenny, frame, throstle and mule – were adapted with varying degrees of success to the other branches of the industry. By 1784 worsted spinning was possible on the water frame and in 1787 Kendrew and Porthouse were granted a patent on a similar frame for spinning flax (Fig 12). In both these branches the quality of the yarn produced on machines was low, but later improvements in flax spinning, involving the introduction of wet spinning after 1825, allowed finer counts of yarn to be spun. The water frame proved too severe in its action for the tender, short-stapled woollen fibres. Instead from the 1770s the

Fig 8 Hand spinning (Walker 1814, pl 29).

Fig 9 Hargreaves' spinning jenny (Baines 1835, pl 4).

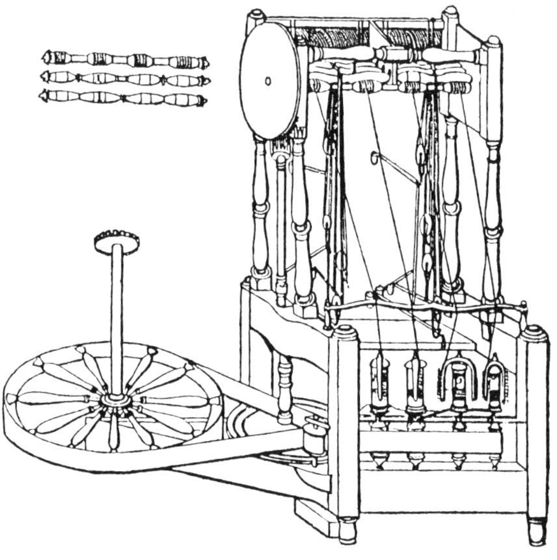

Fig 10 Arkwright's water frame (Ure 1836, Vol 1, 232, fig 18).

woollen branch used the hand-powered spinning jenny. Only in the 1820s, with the adoption of the automatic mule, was mechanised spinning introduced to woollen production. Both mules and throstles were used in waste-silk spinning.

Frame spinning and mule spinning dominated yarn production in Britain throughout the 19th century and even into the early 20th century. In the early and mid 19th century, however, two new methods – cap and ring spinning – were developed in the United States of America. They used modified methods of introducing twist to the yarn and of winding the yarn on to bobbins, and operated at much higher spindle speeds, giving, therefore, more rapid production. Cap and ring spinning were adopted to a limited extent by the Yorkshire cotton and worsted branches after 1870, but never replaced other methods of yarn production.

In some branches yarn underwent further treatment before weaving. Doubling of two or more threads to

Fig 11 Powered mules in a cotton mill (Baines 1835, pl 11).

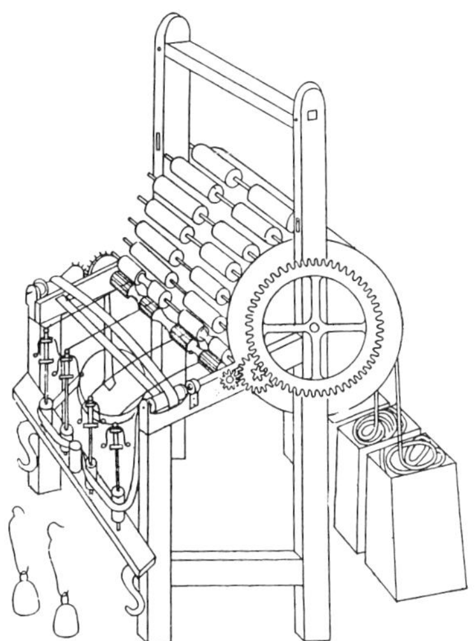

Fig 12 Kendrew and Porthouse's flax-spinning machine, patented in 1787 (drawing based on 1787 Patent No. 1613).

Fig 13 A simple traditional handloom (Ure 1836, Vol 2, 262, fig 97).

produce a stronger, more even yarn was common in the cotton and silk branches, and waste silk and some worsted yarns were gassed by passing them through a flame to singe off loose fibres.

The weaving stage of production

The method of weaving did not differ fundamentally from branch to branch. After the warp thread had been wound on to a warp beam and then strengthened by the application of a size paste, the loom was set up in a laborious operation which required each warp thread to be passed through the 'eyes' in two or more wire 'healds'. In the action of weaving, the healds rose and fell, creating a gate through which the shuttle, containing the weft thread, was passed. Plain cloths required a limited number of healds and a simple operation, but patterned cloths, such as linen damasks and fancy woollens, demanded a large number.

Weaving was traditionally performed on different types of handloom (Fig 13). The development of a successful powerloom proved an obstacle for many decades. Progress depended in part upon the nature of the different yarns, for cotton and worsted proved much easier to work by power than woollen and flax. Edmund Cartwright developed a powerloom in the 1780s, and his Doncaster factory, which ran from 1786 to 1793, contained small numbers of cotton and linen looms. There were further experiments with powerlooms, in the cotton branch in Scotland in the 1790s and in Preston and Stockport in the early 19th century, and in the linen branch in John Marshall's Leeds and Shrewsbury mills in the same period. Successful powerloom weaving was not, however, achieved in the cotton and worsted branches until the 1820s (Fig 14) and in the linen, silk and woollen branches until the 1830s. The introduction of the Jacquard mechanism, at first to handlooms in the 1820s and later to powerlooms, allowed intricately patterned cloth to be woven automatically.

The finishing stage of production

Finishing processes played a very important part in giving each type of cloth its particular character. Linen

*Fig 14 Powerlooms in a Yorkshire worsted mill (*The Penny Magazine*, 27 January 1844, 33).*

and cotton cloth was finished by a similar range of processes, but wool textiles required very different methods. Even within the wool sector, woollen and worsted finishing differed considerably.

The principal stages in finishing the vegetable-fibre cloths (linen and cotton) were bleaching, dyeing and printing. Bleaching was an extremely protracted operation before the late 18th century, involving prolonged exposure to sunlight ('crofting'), 'souring' in buttermilk or weak acid, and washing (Fig 187): often more than six months was required to complete the whitening process. According to whether plain or patterned cloth was required, the material was then dyed or printed. In the linen branch, beetling and calendering, involving, respectively, pounding the cloth with heavy weights and rolling it between cylinders, gave a smooth, glossy finish. Water-powered beetling machines were developed in the early 18th century,[8] and in the second half of the century acid and chlorine bleaching were introduced to speed up the lengthy process. In the cotton branch, waterproofing and mercerisation were developed in the early to mid 19th century to provide new types of cloth. Chemical dyes were also introduced as a substitute for traditional natural dyes.

Wool textiles required different treatment, the nature and extent of which were determined by the character of the finished product. The aim in most woollen-cloth production was to produce a finish in which the actual weave was disguised beneath a smooth nap, whereas in worsted-cloth production, by contrast, the object was to expose the weave, the pattern being the chief character of the material. The stages involved in finishing both types of cloth included wet and dry processes.

Fig 15 Fulling stocks (Tomlinson nd, The Manufacture of Woven Goods, *Part 4, Woollen Cloth).*

Fig 16 Rotary milling machine (Schofield and Schofield 1927, 307, fig 77).

Woollen cloth first required scouring, a washing process undertaken in fulling stocks and traditionally using fullers' earth, the action of stocks and earth serving to remove the oil, size and other dirt. The cloth was then washed and fulled in the stocks, involving prolonged pounding in a soapy solution (Fig 15). Fulling, often called milling, gave a dense felted finish to the cloth. Both scouring and fulling had been mechanised in the Middle Ages. Fulling stocks continued in use up to and beyond the mid 19th century, when rotary scouring and milling machines were introduced for some types of cloth (Fig 16).

After washing, the cloth was stretched and dried. The traditional method was open-air tentering, with cloth hung on racks under tension and pulled to the correct width (Fig 143). Indoor tentering using heated dryhouses was developed in the early 19th century but in the mid 19th century tentering machines began to replace earlier methods (Fig 17): although expensive, the machines performed the operation quickly. The next processes were raising, traditionally employing teazels to raise the nap of the cloth, and shearing, which cut the raised fibres to the required even finish (Fig 18). Hand raising and hand shearing were gradually replaced, particularly from the early 19th century, by mechanically powered 'gig' mills and shearing frames,

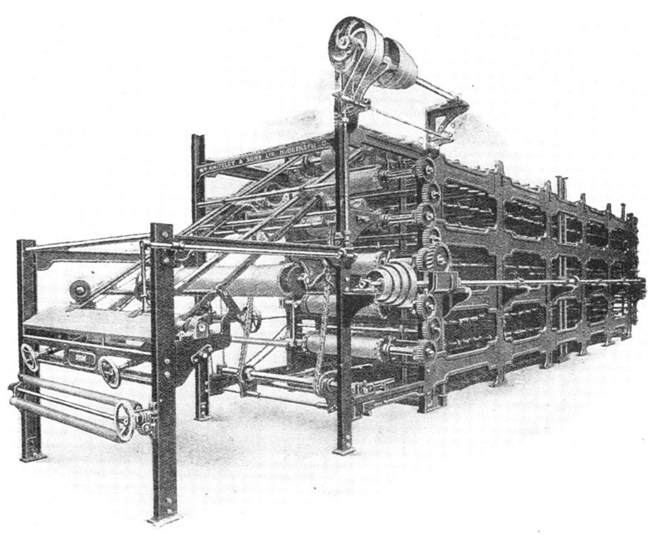

Fig 17 *Tentering machine (Schofield and Schofield 1927, 437, fig 132).*

some of the latter working on a rotary cutting principle (Figs 19, 20). The introduction of these machines was extremely erratic geographically. Gig mills had been used since the 17th century in the Gloucestershire woollen industry, but in Yorkshire their use by mill-owners and cloth finishers sparked the Luddite riots of 1812. After shearing, minor processes such as checking for faults, pressing and packing gave the woollen industry its final product.

Finishing worsteds was simpler, generally involving scouring, tentering and shearing, the intention of the last being to expose the weave of the cloth rather than produce a smooth, even nap. In both woollen and worsted production, dyeing was performed 'in the piece' when plain cloths were required (Fig 21). Dyeing gained in complexity where mixed fibres (silk and cotton combined with woollen and worsted) were concerned, since the fibres reacted in different ways to treatment. Chemical dyeing solved many problems in this area.

Fig 18 *A 19th-century view of a cropping shop showing hand raising and hand shearing.*

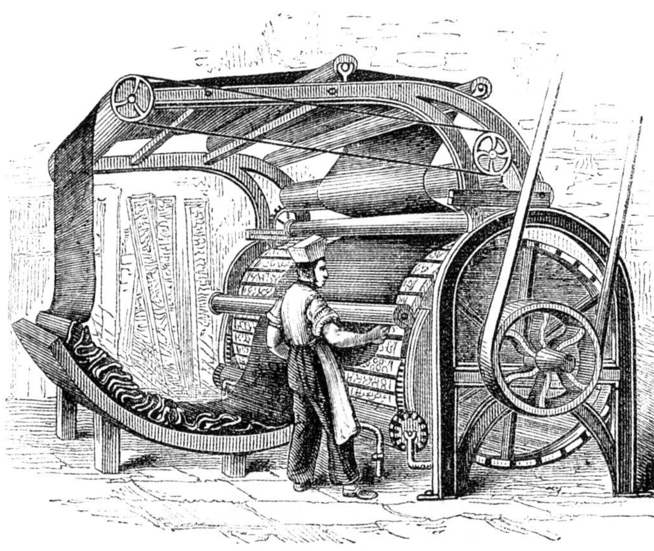

Fig 19 A 19th-century 'gig mill' used for raising the nap of woollen cloth (Tomlinson nd, The Manufacture of Woven Goods, *Part 4, Woollen Cloth, 11).*

Fig 20 A rotary shearing machine of the mid 19th century (Tomlinson nd, The Manufacture of Woven Goods, *Part 4, Woollen Cloth, 13).*

The finishing of silk cloth demanded a different sequence of processes. The cloth was boiled to remove residual natural gum, and then dyed, rinsed and dried before being printed. Chemical treatment improved resistance to decay. Pressing and drying, followed by calendering to give a sheen and 'breaking' to give pliability, completed the sequence.

Processes in the recovered wool industry

The recovered wool branch had an entirely different range of processes from other textile branches. It began its sequence not with a raw material but largely with a finished article from other branches, from which the useful, re-usable content had to be extracted. Rags, tailors' clippings and other waste material were first sorted by colour and quality, since it was important to segregate the loosely woven 'soft rags' used in shoddy production from the tightly woven 'hard rags' used to make mungo. After sorting, the rags were 'seamed' to remove non-wool thread, ripped and cut. After blending and the application of warm oil, the rags were then ready for the main operation in shoddy and mungo production, rag grinding or pulling, which involved feeding the rags into a machine which tore them up so effectively that they emerged as a fibrous material akin to raw wool (Fig 22). A further process, garnetting, took the shoddy and mungo to a more refined state by further eliminating cotton or other threads and preparing the material for scribbling and carding. The development of carbonising in the mid 19th century allowed mixed woollen or worsted and cotton cloth to be processed. Hitherto, mixed-cloth rags had not been supplied to the recovered wool industry, for the cotton content could not easily be separated from the wool fibres and, as a harder material, damaged the rag-pulling machines. Acid or acid gas, however, acted on the materials in different ways: the cotton was destroyed but the wool content remained largely unaffected, permitting its easy recovery. This wool content – called 'extract' when recovered – was used in the lowest-quality products. Wet and dry carbonising, therefore, became increasingly important as mixed-cloth production rose in both the woollen and worsted sectors.

Fig 21 Piece dyeing in the mid 19th century (Tomlinson nd, The Manufacture of Woven Goods, *Part 2, Bleaching, Calendering and Dyeing, 38).*

*Fig 22 A late 19th-century rag-pulling machine (*Textile Manufacturer, *15 July 1889, 344).*

The progress of mechanisation

The different fibres and the different machines which were developed to work them at the various stages of production gave each branch a unique history of mechanisation. The cotton branch was fully mechanised first, by *c*1825, a few years ahead of the woollen and flax and linen branches, and twenty years and more ahead of worsted and silk. One branch, recovered wool, was entirely a product of mechanisation.

Mechanisation was not a once-and-for-all matter. Some of the most important new machines amounted to little more than adaptions of earlier equipment: Arkwright's water frame, for example, was closely modelled on machines developed over twenty years earlier by John Wyatt and Lewis Paul. Furthermore, each new device was subjected to a process of continual improvement, making it work faster, more automatically or more sensitively to allow cheaper production methods and a more varied range of products.

It is one thing to outline the stages in the mechanisation of the industry, but quite another to describe the extent to which each machine actually replaced earlier methods. There was frequently only a limited application for a new machine and equally frequently there was a considerable interval between its first use and the obsolescence of traditional ways of working. One example will illustrate the point. A successful worsted powerloom was developed in the 1820s, but in the mid 1830s fewer than 3,000 were in operation in Yorkshire. By 1841 the number had risen to over 11,000 and by 1850 to over 30,000. Take-up of the new machines was even slower in the woollen branch. Powerlooms were first recorded in Yorkshire woollen mills in the 1830s, but less than 4,000 were in use by 1850. Ten years earlier it had been estimated that 10,000 handlooms were in operation in the Leeds district alone. After 1850 expansion was rapid, for by 1874 over 30,000 woollen powerlooms were in operation. Even late in the 19th century the handloom still played a part in the woollen industry, specifically in the fancy woollen sector where the production of complex patterned cloths gave an advantage to traditional production methods. The linen branch showed a similar pattern, with a slow increase in numbers of powerlooms after their first use in the mid 1830s. There were, for example, still over 1,100 handloom weavers in Barnsley in 1871 and only about 3,500 linen powerlooms in operation in Yorkshire in 1874.

Whether or not new inventions were applied quickly and widely depended upon a number of circumstances. The principal consideration was usually financial: savings from new machinery, resulting from lower labour costs or greater speed of production, had to be balanced against the cost of purchase and installation. Even when new machinery offered medium and long-term benefits, smaller manufacturers in particular might find the initial outlay beyond their means, especially if costs of necessary new buildings were added to those of the machinery itself. Foreign competition in the world market also influenced the decision on whether or not to re-equip. The advantages given by the British industry's early start were slowly eroded by the development of rival foreign manufacturing industries, often using more modern production techniques. The dilemma for the British manufacturer was whether low capital outlay and old equipment offered a better prospect of competitiveness in the market than high outlay on new machinery. The degree to which the Yorkshire industry has been successful may be gauged by its continual adaptation to new materials, changing fashions and different economic climates, for it remains today an important part of the local manufacturing scene.

2

The buildings of the textile mill

The Yorkshire textile industry gave rise to a wide variety of building types which reflect the differing needs and changing methods and scales of work of the industry's six main branches in the period 1770–1930. The trend towards mechanised production, which led to the concentration of activity on mill sites, created the need for new building types, some with a general purpose, others with a specific use. Batley Carr Mills, Dewsbury (29), with its mixture of multi-storeyed mills and loomshop, single-storeyed dryhouse, dyehouse and weaving sheds, and its steam-power plant, shows something of the diversity of buildings (Fig 23). The full range of buildings is discussed below, the origin and evolution of each type being examined before common aspects of their structure are considered.

Building types

Buildings for hand processes

Heckling and combing shops

Carding, heckling and combing were the principal preparatory processes in textile production (see pp

Fig 23 A view of Batley Carr Mills, Dewsbury (29), showing something of the range of building types that appeared on textile mill sites during the 19th century (Pike c1895, 18).

6–8). Carding, which ordered the short fibres, was mechanised in the late 18th century and its machinery was usually housed in multi-storeyed mills, but since it took longer to develop machines to heckle the long fibres of flax and to comb those of worsted and of waste silk, accommodation for these hand processes was initially provided both on mill sites and away from them.

Heckling or dressing flax was dusty, but as a hand process it did not make major demands on a building, requiring only adequate light, some storage space, and room for the wooden benches which supported the iron-toothed heckles through which bundles of flax were drawn. Specialist flax-dressing shops, such as one used by the Metcalfes in late 18th-century Pateley Bridge,[1] were a feature of the domestic flax industry in Yorkshire even before the introduction of mill working, and off-site working continued after the construction of flax mills. The best architectural evidence survives in Knaresborough, where a three-storeyed building in Green Dragon Yard (79) (Fig 24), built in or shortly after 1808 by John Robinson, a flax dresser, was probably used as a heckling shop with other space devoted to the storage of both raw and heckled flax. The building, of traditional construction with timber beams and joists, was never powered. The rooms on each floor offered uninterrupted working space, and were well lit from both long walls.

The form and situation of heckling rooms on flax mill sites varied. William Brown[2] noted in 1821 that the heckling rooms in some Leeds mills were awkwardly situated in an outhouse or a distant wing: those at a mill in Hunslet in 1823 were over the stables,[3] whilst at West House Mill, Fewston (40), heckling was carried out in a former loomshop in 1831 and in 1847 in part of a former warehouse (Fig 153).

No recognisable purpose-built heckling shop has survived on a mill site, but historical evidence indicates that on some of the larger mill sites they were quite large buildings. At Marshall's Mill, Holbeck (57), the heckling shop rebuilt after a fire in 1796 was a long, narrow building set apart from the spinning mills (Fig 142). Its height is unknown, but it may have resembled a similarly proportioned heckling shop at John Maberley's Broadford Mill, Aberdeen, which in 1814 was of one storey and attics.[4] At Benyons' Mill, Holbeck (56), heckling was carried out in a four-storeyed, 8 metre wide wing of 1802–3 whose principal use was probably as a warehouse (Fig 152). A powered heckling machine was developed in 1808, and though machines displaced hand hecklers in some of the largest flax mills within a decade, the hand process continued in use elsewhere, principally off rather than on mill sites, well into the 19th century.

Fig 24 Hand-heckling shop and warehouse in Green Dragon Yard, Knaresborough (79), built c1808.

Combing machines, of varying efficiency, were introduced into a number of worsted mills in the early 19th century, but it was not until after the development of a fully successful machine in the 1840s that hand working was rapidly displaced.[5] Until machine combing became usual, it was customary either to put wool out for hand combing or to comb it on mill premises, the wool being drawn through the heated iron teeth of a comb. Wool which was put out was usually combed on commission by a master comber employing from three to six men who generally worked together in a combing shop. Such shops were concentrated in Halifax and Bradford and the villages surrounding them, but the buildings have rarely survived in recognisable form, having been abandoned in the mid 19th century and either converted to new uses or swept away in urban improvements. Many combing shops were probably contrived out of existing buildings, in the manner of a 17th-century house in Bowling used as a combshop in the early 19th century.[6] Reach noted in 1849 that the general aspect of a combing room was of a bare chamber, heated to nearly 85°F, with masses of wool heaped about and a round fire-pot in the centre which heated the iron combs. When coals were burned the pot could be a fixed apparatus like a stove, with a funnel to carry away the smoke, but when charcoal was used the pot was a movable vessel without a funnel, and noxious fumes spread freely in often ill-ventilated spaces.[7]

Before the advent of the spinning mill, some manufacturers undertook combing in shops attached to their place of business,[8] but subsequently it was not uncommon for worsted spinners to have woolcombers at their mills. Despite the risk of fire from the pots, combing was sometimes housed in a spinning mill or, more usually, as at Aireworth Mills, Keighley (69), in a warehouse. Such arrangements sometimes preceded the construction of a combshop, as at Greengate Mill in Keighley where the Marriners used part of a warehouse as a combshop[9] before providing a purpose-built shop in 1822. Such combshops would have been detached or at least distinct buildings, since two combshops with combs and comb pots formed part of Charles Mill, Haworth (48), as early as 1808. Combshops were doubtless at first small rooms or buildings, but the expansion in the number of combs at Marriners', from three pairs in 1818 to seventy pairs in 1836–7, suggests that in some mills at least generous provision had to be made in the era of hand combing.[10]

Spinning shops

The mechanisation of spinning in the 18th century, which created the need for buildings with space and power for the new machines, was the reason for the construction of many multi-storeyed mills. Hand spinning, however, was not immediately superseded since the jenny and the early mule both remained hand powered and continued in use in the cotton and woollen industries. Domestic production for these branches, from spinners working in their own homes (see p9 and Fig 8), has left little architectural evidence because it was generally a fireside occupation, but a number of manufacturers sought to control their yarn supply by gathering hand spinners together to work in supervised conditions for a wage. Most of the early cotton manufacturers in Yorkshire who used jennies and hand mules installed them in small factories which also ran powered carding engines and drawing and roving frames,[11] and a number of woollen manufacturers undertook hand spinning in mills which were also used for powered scribbling and fulling. Largely because of the late date at which mechanised spinning was introduced into the woollen industry, most of the evidence for hand spinning on mill sites comes from this branch. On those sites where only a limited amount of hand spinning was carried out, spinners were housed in domestic-scale buildings of the type built in the early 19th century at Stone Bridge Mills, Wortley (151) (Fig 147), but taller and longer buildings were required for work on a larger scale. At Bean Ing Mills, Leeds (85) (Fig 150), the spinning rooms occupied an 11.4 metres wide, three-storeyed wing built against the 1799 multi-storeyed mill;[12] a longer, 9 metres wide, four-storeyed building at

Fig 25 Front elevation and internal view of second floor of hand-spinning and weaving shop built in late 1820s at Winker Green Mill, Armley (8).

Sowerby Bridge Mills, Warley (143), was probably similarly used (Fig 151). The width of these buildings contrasts with that of the hand-spinning and hand-weaving shops built at Armitage Bridge Mills, South Crosland (127), between *c*1815–16 and 1825, which form a long, narrow building, four storeys high, internally 5.6 metres wide, and built in two stages of fifteen and eleven bays (Fig 165). Neither stage can be specifically identified as just for spinning; different use by floor is likely, the wider windows of some upper floors perhaps implying weaving for which light was more important. At Winker Green Mill, Armley (8), a pair of similar four-storeyed workshops, only one of which survives, was built in the late 1820s and may have been used for both spinning and weaving (Fig 25). They were 5.8 metres wide internally, and like the other workshops had internal timber beams and floors, and provision for heating from fireplaces or stoves.

Loomshops

The introduction of powerloom weaving to the various branches of the Yorkshire textile industry during and after the 1820s and 1830s inevitably led to weaving becoming a mill-based industry, although it was many decades before weaving by hand, particularly in the woollen and linen branches, was completely superseded. Handloom weaving had been a domestic industry for generations, and in the 17th and 18th centuries clothiers, who were frequently also farmers, often provided a textiles workshop within their own dwelling for use in the various stages of cloth production, or for the storage of raw materials or finished pieces.[13] Such workshops were not necessarily architecturally distinctive, although some had first-floor piece doors to ease the handling of bulky materials such as wool, yarn and cloth.

Clothiers working on the domestic system of production had small workforces, frequently just members of their family and perhaps a few journeymen, but during the late 18th and early 19th centuries increased demand for cloth combined with the growth of mill-based spinning led to changes in the organisation, scale and place of handloom weaving. The most noticeable effect of these changes was the appearance of the loomshop, either in association with domestic accommodation or as a special-purpose building on or off a textile mill site.

Loomshops associated with domestic accommodation took a variety of forms, some of them in cellars or on ground floors, others on top floors, some in individual buildings, others in terraces. The two principal vegetable fibres, cotton and flax, were best woven in damp conditions, and if domestic cotton handloom weaving in Yorkshire followed the practice in Lancashire,[14] cellar or ground-floor cotton loomshops must generally have been favoured. The cotton-weaving areas of Yorkshire, like the linen-weaving areas, have few top-floor domestic loomshops, and it seems evident that this practice was followed, even if few buildings of the type have been identified. Domestic linen weaving is better represented by buildings, and dwellings with cellar loomshops were a characteristic building type in Barnsley, the principal linen-weaving town in Yorkshire in the 19th century. Such houses were built in and near Barnsley during the late 18th and early 19th centuries, many of them by linen manufacturers such as the Dearmans who, in partnership from 1801 to 1806, built sixteen weavers' cottages with 'arched Weavers' Shops . . . with the Looms fixed in the Shops'.[15] The cellar loomshops, which varied in size to accommodate from one to six handlooms,[16] were either vaulted in stone or ceiled with timber. They were generally poorly lit and ill ventilated, with floors about 1.2 metres below the surface of the street, as described and illustrated in a Sanitary Report of 1852[17] (Fig 26). Although few buildings now stand, photographs of Taylor Row in Barnsley (Fig 27) confirm this description. Few other cellar loomshops seem to have been built outside Barnsley and its immediate environs, although a pair of cottages behind Fringill Mill, Menwith with Darley (100), in Nidderdale, an early 19th-century flax-spinning mill, both have two-room cellars almost certainly used for linen weaving. Knaresborough, an 18th-century linen-weaving centre which was increasingly overshadowed by Barnsley in the 19th century, has few houses with suitable cellars, and above-ground loomshops must have been found adequate.

The most distinctive domestic loomshops were those which occupied the top floors of cottages and were lit by long rows of mullioned windows (Fig 28). Such weavers' cottages, built between 1770 and 1850, were almost entirely restricted to the woollen-cloth producing areas

Fig 26 Cellar loomshop in Barnsley, used for weaving linen (Frontispiece to Ranger 1852).

Fig 27 Taylor Row, Barnsley, an early 19th-century terrace of linen-weavers' houses with pavement-level windows lighting cellar loomshops.

Fig 28 Weavers' cottages with top-floor loomshops in Cliffe Ash, Golcar.

of Yorkshire where they occur in their hundreds, for example, in the Colne, Holme and Calder valleys. This correlation between branch and building type reflected the requirements of woollen weaving, which did not need a damp atmosphere, and for which a top-floor loomshop afforded sufficient space and light with only minimal disruption to normal domestic planning. The frequent grouping of these weavers' cottages in pairs or terraces of three or more suggests that they were built either as a speculation or by manufacturers providing housing and working accommodation for a wage labour force. Internally the loomshops were open rooms with a fireplace or some other source of heat; some had internal access to the cottages below, while others had their own external doors enabling domestic and industrial functions to be totally separate.[18] In some cottages shared workrooms extending over two or more dwellings offer strong evidence for control by an employer. Coffin Row, Linthwaite, built *c*1820–40 with a loomshop over a terrace of four, two-storeyed cottages,[19] is a notable example; another is the four-storeyed loomshop in Ramsden Mill Lane, Golcar (43) (Fig 145), built *c*1840, which has two floors of loomshops over a pair of dwellings and some storage space.

An alternative but rarely used way of providing shared weaving accommodation in close association with domestic accommodation is shown at The Rookery, Addingham (2) (Fig 29). The first-floor loomshop here, built in or shortly after 1805, and originally one of a pair, is long and narrow, lit from just one side, and has a distinctive single-pitched roof. It is 13 metres long by 2 metres wide internally, and in 1829 housed eight pairs of looms.

Shared loomshops allowed control over materials and the quality of work, as well as supervision of the workforce, but this was most effectively achieved by the construction of non-domestic loomshops on and off textile mill sites. Such loomshops were built in Yorkshire between the late 18th and mid 19th centuries, and their form was influenced by a number of factors, among them the size of the workforce and the number of looms required, the need for good lighting, particularly for weaving fancy cloths, and site restrictions. Those which were built varied considerably in length and height, but the inability to provide satisfactory artificial light in deep buildings meant that they were characteristically both narrow and well lit. At Bean Ing Mills, Leeds (85), and Benyons' Mill, Holbeck (56), site constriction was not a serious problem; the former site had two, two-storeyed loomshops (Fig 150), the larger over 100 metres long with a ground-floor storage area and only the well-lit first floor used for weaving, whereas at the latter site the weaving shops stood along three edges of the perimeter (Fig 152). Elsewhere, and particularly on mill sites, space was usually at a much greater premium, and shorter loomshops of three, four and even five storeys were more usually built. The loomshop at Sowerby Bridge Mills, Warley (143) (Fig 30; see also Fig 151 for context), built shortly before 1792, was four storeys high when first built, and four-storeyed ranges were also built in the first phase at Armitage Bridge Mills, South Crosland (127) (Fig 165), at Winker Green Mill, Armley (8) (Fig 25), and, to an L-shaped plan, at Batley Carr Mills, Dewsbury (29) (Fig 23). Among the tallest loomshops were those added to Armitage Bridge Mills (127) (Fig 148) and Folly Hall Mills, Huddersfield (63) (Fig 178), both of them five storeys high. More modest accommodation was provided at some mills, including the

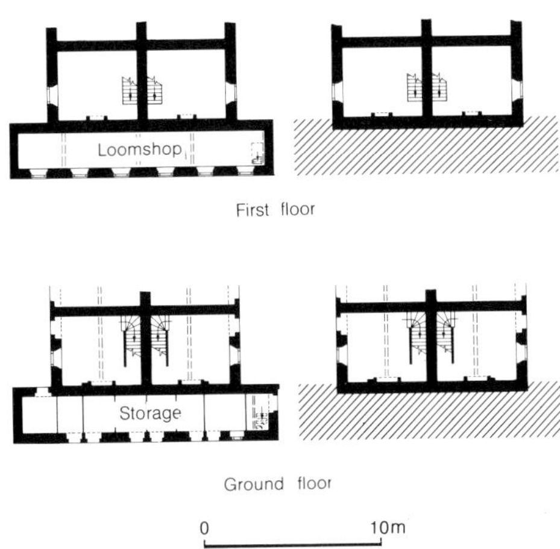

Fig 29 The Rookery, Addingham (2). Two terraces of back-to-back houses built in or shortly after 1805, each originally with an attached first-floor loomshop over ground-floor storage places. The site of the demolished loomshop is indicated by shading on the plan.

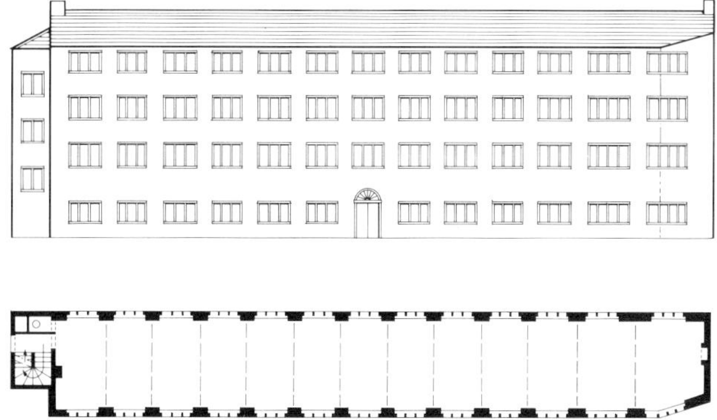

Fig 30 Front elevation and first-floor plan of handloom shop built shortly before 1792 as part of Sowerby Bridge Mills, Warley (143).

short, two-storeyed range at Stone Bridge Mills, Wortley (151), which has a well-lit upper storey giving suitable conditions for weaving (Fig 147). Loomshops away from mill sites were often similarly modest. The early 19th-century linen-weaving shop in Raw Gap in Knaresborough is just two storeys high and four bays long (Fig 31), and other loomshops, including that which forms the core of Green Grove Mills, Kirkburton (78), and one in Wesley Street, Ossett (108) (Fig 32), are only a little larger. The loomshop in Chapel Street, Addingham (3) (Fig 144), which is three storeys high, twelve bays long and housed sixty-two looms in 1829, is nevertheless a reminder that off-site loomshops could be quite large.

Despite variations in overall size, the non-domestic loomshops have many features in common. They were generally between 5 metres and 6 metres wide internally and, except where security or other reasons dictated otherwise, they were generously lit from windows set in both side walls. The windows, though occasionally mullioned (Fig 30), or with the proportions of mullioned windows (Figs 32, 147), were more usually square in shape and set either singly (Figs 23, 144) or in pairs separated by a mullion (Fig 25). These non-domestic loomshops, like the domestic loomshops over cottages, were all of traditional internal construction with timber beams and floors, and with access from floor to floor normally provided by timber stairs set against an end or a side wall. The loomshop at Green Grove Mills (78) is unusual in having an external stone staircase serving its upper floor, although several of the largest loomshops, including that at Sowerby Bridge Mills (143) (Fig 30) and the latest one at Armitage Bridge Mills (Fig 148), had stair towers at one end, in each case combined with a tier of taking-in doors for the receipt of yarn and despatch of cloth. The loomshop at Winker Green Mill (8) is one of the few others to have original taking-in doors (Fig 25), although they serve only the first and

Fig 31 Early 19th-century handloom shop in Raw Gap, Knaresborough.

Fig 32 Loomshop in Wesley Street, Ossett (108), built between 1853 and 1855.

second floors. There was rarely formal provision of sanitation: the loomshop at Sowerby Bridge Mills (143), one of the earliest as well as one of the largest loomshops, had dry closets, but there is otherwise very little evidence of original privies. Most loomshops had fireplaces for heating by open fires or stoves, but steam heating was subsequently introduced to some of those on mill sites.

Multi-storeyed mills

The first multi-storeyed textile mills in England were built in the early and mid 18th century to house the then newly introduced silk-throwing machinery.[20] Their main concentration was in Derbyshire and Cheshire, and although one was built in Sheffield *c*1760, it was not until the late 18th century and the introduction of powered working to various stages in the processing of cotton, woollen, worsted and flax fibres that such buildings became a significant feature of the textile industry, and particularly of that in Yorkshire.

Multi-storeyed mills, 1770–1825

Multi-storeyed mills were built to house mechanically powered processes, and between 1770 and 1825 most of the preparatory and spinning stages of textile production were successfully mechanised (see Chapter 1). Although Yorkshire had hardly any silk-throwing industry in the period before 1770, and so had few mills in this branch, over one hundred fulling mills, many of them long established, were in operation in the 1770s serving the county's woollen industry.[21] Little is known of these mills, but since fulling, with its heavy stocks and plentiful use of water, was exclusively a ground-floor operation, they may have been single-storeyed buildings, some perhaps with an attic for storage. Subsequent expansion led to the rebuilding or replacement of almost all these fulling mills, including those built after 1770, but Little Hebble Mill at Ovenden (112) (Fig 33) appears to incorporate part of a late 18th or early 19th-century fulling mill evidently of one storey with attics. The mill, just 6.9 metres wide internally, retains some original mullioned windows as well as two arched openings in its west wall, the taller for goods access, the lower over the watercourse which fed the internal waterwheel which drove the fulling stocks.

The specialised fulling mill was not typical of mills built after 1770, which were almost invariably multi-storeyed buildings constructed to house the newly developed preparatory and spinning machinery. The rectangular multi-storeyed form, which had established itself as the norm for the first silk-throwing mills, had

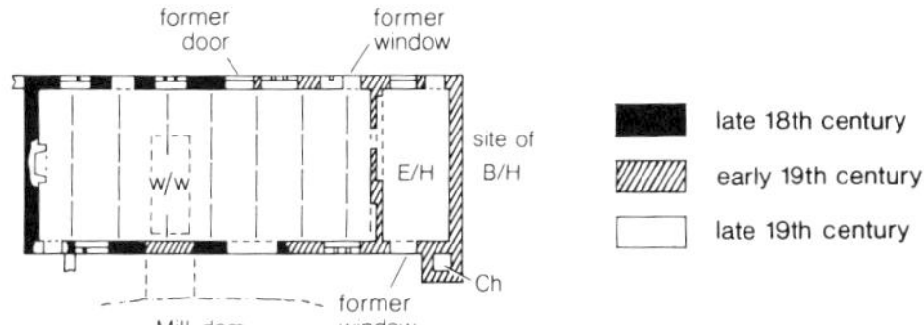

Fig 33 Little Hebble Mill, Ovenden (112), a water-powered fulling mill of probable late 18th-century date heightened by two storeys and converted to steam power in the 19th century.

Fig 34 Runley Bridge Mill, Settle (115), a water-powered cotton-spinning mill built c1783.

taken existing warehouses and corn mills as its precedent and was adopted because it could be adapted to provide adequate space and light, as well as housing the power generation and transmission systems necessary for the new machinery.[22] These early mills varied considerably in size, the smallest generally offering several hundred square metres of working space, the largest over 2,000 square metres. The small mills (Figs 34, 41) were two or three storeys high, three to six bays long and had up to 400 square metres of working space, whereas mills of medium size (Figs 35, 42), three or four storeys high and seven to ten bays long, had between 400 and 1,000 square metres of space, and large mills (Figs 36, 37, 43), four or five storeys high, ten or more bays long, had between 1,000 and 2,500 square metres of space. These variations in size reflect a variety of circumstances, most particularly the availability of capital which determined the equation between the amount of machinery needed or anticipated, the power level required, and therefore the requisite size of building.

The majority of pre-1825 multi-storeyed mills displayed little architectural embellishment. They were built with local materials, generally stone rubble in the Pennine foothills and brick elsewhere, and they took their details from the local vernacular tradition. The doors and windows of most late 18th-century stone-built mills had ashlar surrounds (Fig 42), but these were only occasionally used in the early 19th century when simple, rectangular stone lintels usually sufficed (Fig 40). Brick-built mills rarely had other than segmental-headed openings. Windows, occasionally mullioned

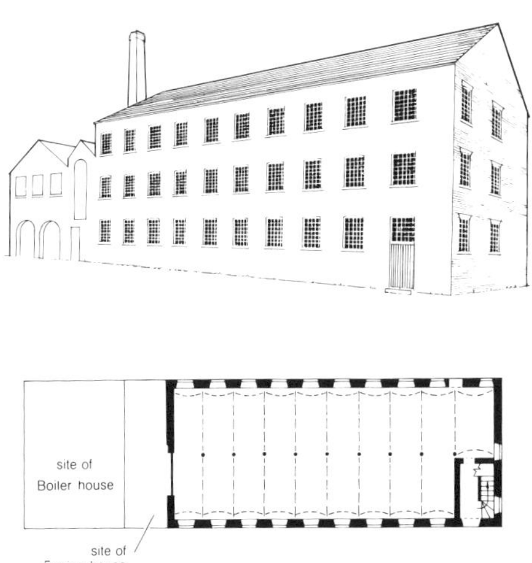

Fig 35 Lawrence Street Flax Mill, York (154), a steam-powered flax-spinning mill as originally built shortly before 1816.

Fig 36 Armley Mills, Armley (7), built in 1805–7 as the first fireproof woollen mill in Yorkshire.

(Figs 33, 38) but otherwise smaller in size, were regularly spaced to give an even light internally. The tall, round-headed window which was later to become a characteristic feature of engine houses, though found on Mill C at Marshall's Mill in Holbeck (57), which was built in 1815–16, was not a common feature at this date, although many water-powered mills had distinctive arched openings through which water was led to feed waterwheels or fulling stocks.

Multi-storeyed mills with multiple rows of regularly spaced windows offered few concessions to decoration or appearance but in Yorkshire, as elsewhere in the country,[23] some builders countered this austerity with the application of such Palladian details as pediments and cornices, Venetian windows, semicircular lunettes, and cupolas. The central bays of the front elevations of three late 18th-century mills, at Sowerby Bridge Mills, Warley (143) (Fig 37), Bean Ing Mills, Leeds (85) (Fig 150), and the smaller Smithies Mill at Birstall,[24] are all surmounted by triangular pediments, whilst at other mills, among them Low Mill at Keighley (74) of 1780, Armley Mills, Armley (7), of 1805–7 (Fig 36) and Mill 1 at Armitage Bridge Mills, South Crosland (127), of *c*1816–17 (Fig 146), the central bays merely break forward, giving some relief to the monotony of the fenestration but not creating the impressive effect given by a pediment. The decorated front elevation has been seen as epitomising the social aspirations of many 18th-century entrepreneurs,[25] and the fact that such detailing was generally restricted to the largest mills of the period lends some support to this theory. Venetian windows and lunettes were never common features of Yorkshire mills, and they were usually restricted to lighting attics, their use at Lumb Mill, Warley (142), and Mill C at Marshall's Mill (57) (Fig 43) being characteristic.

The form of the multi-storeyed mill, rectangular on plan and with two or more storeys, was adopted because it met the requirements for housing, powering and working machinery, as well as providing for any associated storage needs. One of the influences on mill planning was the position of the power source, whether waterwheel, steam engine, or a combination of the two, and there was an initial period of experimentation as these were sited in one of a number of different places. The usual solution was a wheelhouse or engine house attached to either the outer or inner face of the gable of a mill, but waterwheels in particular were also set along side walls and internally close to the centre of mills. Most

Fig 37 'Greenup's Mill', built shortly before 1792 as part of Sowerby Bridge Mills, Warley (143), the earliest known integrated woollen mill in Yorkshire.

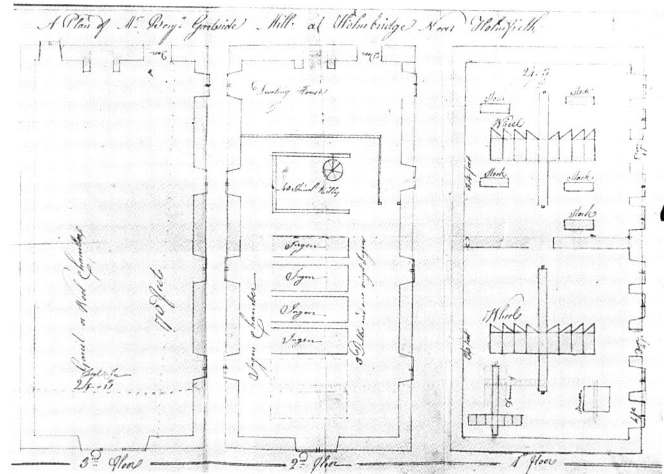

Fig 38 Plan of Holmbridge Mill, Austonley (9), drawn c1800. The ground floor is shown housing two waterwheels, a dressing machine, teazer and five fulling stocks, the second floor a willeying machine, six scribbling or carding engines, and a small dwelling house, while the attic was a wool storage chamber.

mills had just a single power source, but woollen mills, which in this early period generally housed fulling stocks on the ground floor and scribbling and carding engines on the floors above, frequently required more than one power source. Most of these woollen mills were water powered, and the early plan of Holmbridge Mill, Austonley (9) (Fig 38), drawn *c*1800, shows its two waterwheels, the arrangement of its machinery and the use of its floors. The division of functions between floors was maintained in later scribbling and fulling mills, with fulling stocks sometimes occupying all the ground floor and the other machinery the floors over (Fig 39).

The width of multi-storeyed mills was mainly determined by the requirements of the machinery they

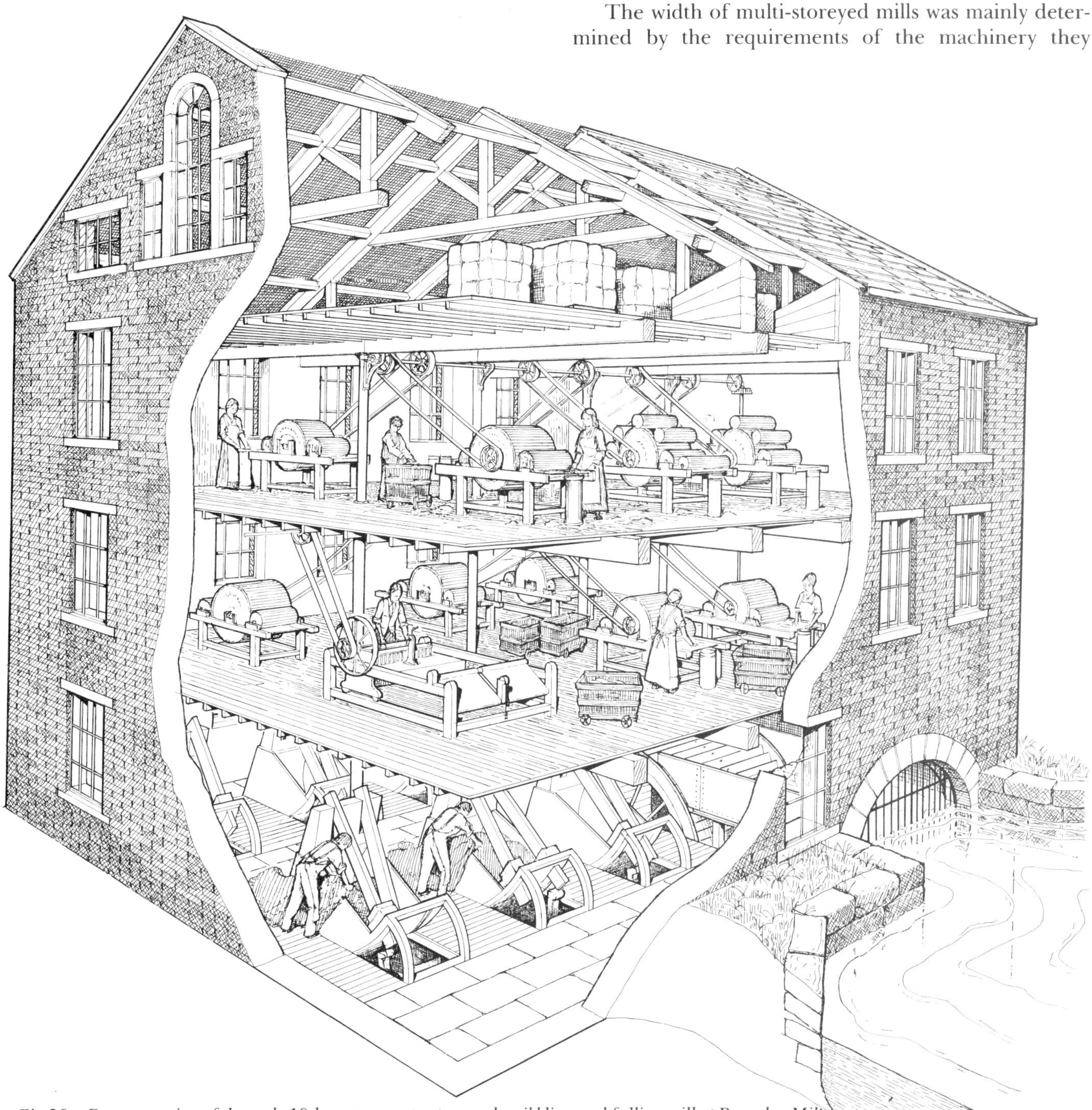

Fig 39 Reconstruction of the early 19th-century water-powered scribbling and fulling mill at Ramsden Mills, Linthwaite (87), showing two rows of fulling stocks on the ground floor, carding engines and a slubbing billy on the first floor, carding and scribbling engines on the second floor, and bales of wool in the attic.

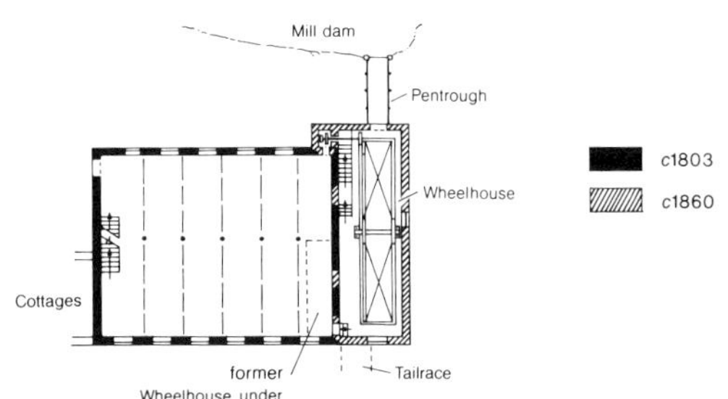

Fig 40 Lumb Mill, Warley (142), built c1803 as a water-powered cotton-spinning mill, heightened and extended after conversion to worsted spinning in 1828.

housed, and it has been proposed that the first generation of cotton mills, built in the late 18th century to house the spinning frames and carding engines patented by Richard Arkwright, were typically three or four storeys high, and mostly about 22 metres long by 9 metres wide externally, longer and higher if 2,000 rather than 1,000 spindles were to be installed.[26] Since the scribbling and carding engines of the woollen and flax industries, as well as the spinning frames of the later industry and of the worsted and waste-silk industries, all had a common ancestry in the same Arkwright machines, the proposition has implications beyond the cotton branch. The widths of the textile mills built in Yorkshire in the 1780s and 1790s coincide well with those of the proposed Arkwright-type mills, but not their lengths or heights. The coincidence of width, however, with internal dimensions showing a marked concentration between 8.2 metres and 9.1 metres, is probably more a reflection of contemporary building technology, in particular the maximum span of an unsupported timber beam, than of machine technology. Length and height, which varied from the small three-storeyed, three-bay Runley Bridge Mill at Settle (115) (Fig 34) to the large four-storeyed, twenty-bay mill at Bank Mills, Leeds (84), and the five-storeyed West House Mill, Fewston (40) (Fig 272), indicate that overall size was dependent more on the availability of capital and the ability to work at different capacities than on set numbers of spindles, particularly after Arkwright's patents had been finally abrogated in 1785.

Textile machinery grew in size throughout the period under review. Arkwright's original 48-spindle frames were superseded by machines with 72 spindles from the late 1780s and by others with 120 spindles at the turn of the century.[27] Late 18th-century multi-storeyed mills were initially able to house most of the larger machinery, but with the introduction of the part-acting mule in the 1790s, and of the throstle, an enlarged and more economic form of Arkwright's spinning frame, shortly after 1800, greater width was frequently required. The internal widths of multi-storeyed mills built in Yorkshire in the twenty years before 1800 ranged from 6.4 metres to 9.45 metres, whereas between 1800 and 1825 it increased to between 7.0 metres and 13.4 metres. Lumb Mill (142) (Fig 40), built *c*1803 and some 11 metres wide, and the 1818 extension to Langcliffe Mill, Langcliffe (81), 13.1 metres wide, are among the wider cotton mills; Ebor Mill at Haworth (50), the Old Mill at Lawrence Street Flax Mill in York (154) (Fig 35) and Mill 1 at Armitage Bridge Mills (127) (Fig 146) are comparable worsted, flax and woollen mills. The greater width of these mills was achieved by the use of cast-iron columns which gave intermediate support to the timber beams of traditionally built mills, or supported the cast-iron beams of mills of fireproof construction. Cast-iron columns had been introduced into textile mill construction outside Yorkshire in the 1790s, initially as a component part of fireproof construction, but they soon gained wider use, frequently incorporating provision for the support of line shafting (see pp67–70, 158–60). Fireproof construction was not used in any Yorkshire mill until the early 19th century, its first use being at Benyons' Mill, Holbeck (56), a flax mill built in 1802–3, but by 1825 it

Fig 41 High Mill at Shaw Mills, Bishop Thornton (23), a water-powered flax-spinning mill as originally built c1804–5.

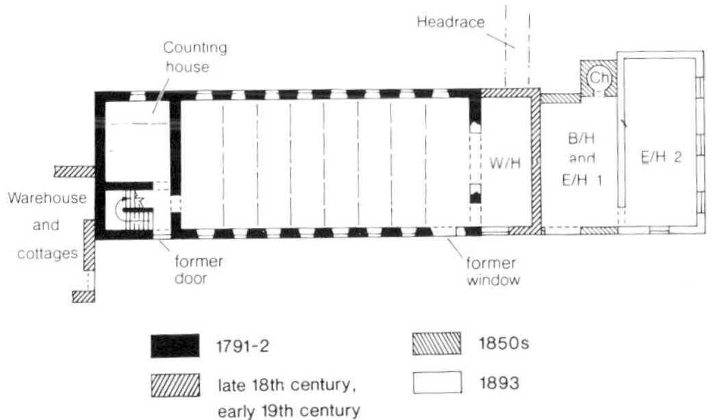

Fig 42 Ponden Mill near Stanbury, Keighley (76), built as a water-powered cotton-spinning mill in 1791–2 and later extended.

had been employed in a number of other woollen, cotton and flax mills, among them Armley Mills (7), Greenholme Mill, Burley, and Marshall's Mill (57), all of them built by firms which were among the largest of their time.

Mills were designed to provide working areas which were as uninterrupted as possible, and as they grew in size the problems of the movement of raw materials and goods, of access for workers, and of sanitary facilities, raised themselves. Goods and raw materials were almost always moved internally between floors in early mills, although a few also had taking-in doors. High Mill at Shaw Mills, Bishop Thornton (23) (Fig 41), and Armley Mills (7) each had them in a gable wall. Staircases for the movement of goods and people were almost invariably internal and of timber, and they were, as such, a potential risk in the event of fire. A few mills, generally the larger ones, had staircases set in their own compartments. Two positions were favoured, either in a tower within the corner of a mill, or in a tower projecting from the outside wall. The former arrangement risked encroaching on the working space of the mill, as it did in the Old Mill at Lawrence Street Flax Mill (154) (Fig 35), but this was usually avoided by setting it in a bay shared with an engine house or wheelhouse or occasionally, as at Ponden Mill near Stanbury, Keighley (76), with a

Fig 43 Mill C at Marshall's Mill, Holbeck (57), built in 1815–16, showing the circular privy windows and, at the far end, the projecting stair tower.

counting house (Fig 42). This last arrangement was also a feature of some other early cotton mills.[28] External stair towers, such as those on the 1792 mill at Bean Ing Mills (85), or on Mill C at Marshall's Mill (57) (Figs 43, 46), provided safe access without interfering with working space. Sanitary facilities were generally rudimentary. Privies were rarely provided within mills at this early date, although a few of the larger mills did make provision. The earliest mill at Barkerend Mills, Bradford (26), had a projecting privy tower, whilst in Mill C at Marshall's Mill (57) the privies were grouped against the gable wall of each floor, each compartment lit and ventilated by small circular windows (Figs 43, 46).

The roof spaces of many mills were used either for storage or for working machinery, and in both cases adequate headroom and sufficient light were required. A number of different types of roof truss, some of timber, others of iron, were used to ensure adequate headroom (see pp70–5), while light usually came from a combination of gable-end windows and skylights. Brown

(1821, 3) noted that 'The garret rooms (of Leeds flax mills) seem mostly in use for machinery for they are served with sky lights.' Better lighting was occasionally obtained by a row of windows rising from the roof slope, an arrangement found in the 1799 mill at Bean Ing Mills (85),[29] as well as in two post-1825 mills, Mill 2 at Armitage Bridge Mills (127) (Fig 146), and Nortonthorpe Mills, Cumberworth. All were woollen mills, and the light may have been required for a hand-finishing process.

Multi-storeyed mills, 1825–1875

Developments in machinery and structural advances influenced the evolution of the multi-storeyed mill in the period before 1825, and continued to be significant in the years 1825–75. The most influential developments in machinery, both of which took place immediately after 1825, were the introduction of the newly patented, fully self-acting mule to the cotton and woollen branches of the industry, and the adoption of the wet spinning of flax which finally enabled all types of linen yarn to be mill spun. Cap and ring spinning

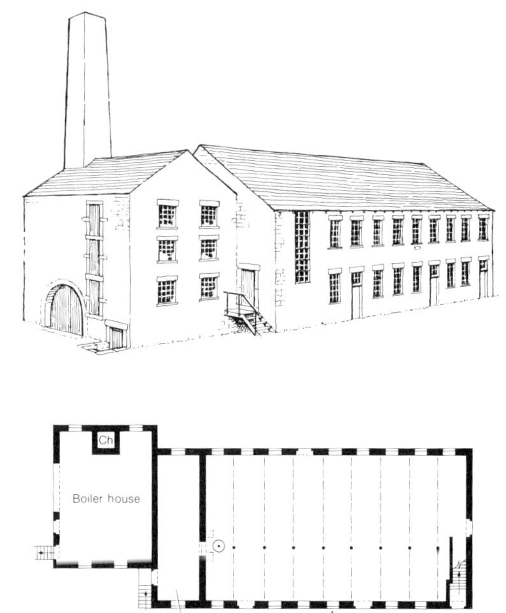

Fig 44 Albion Mill, Batley (15), a steam-powered woollen mill as originally built in 1831.

Fig 45 Winker Green Mill, Armley (8), a woollen mill rebuilt in 1833 and 1836 but incorporating an earlier engine house. The mill dam is in the foreground.

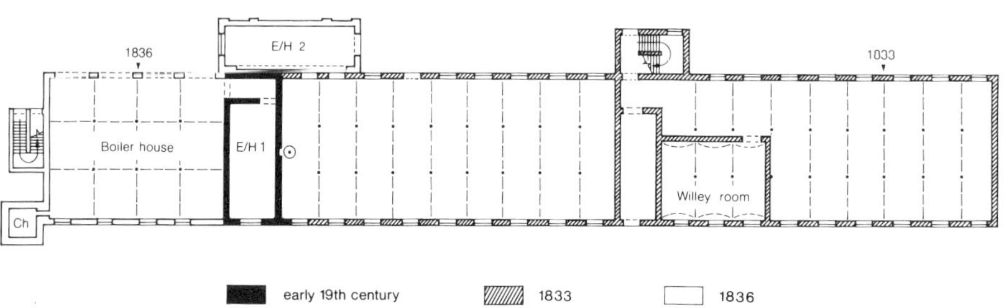

were invented before 1875, but they were not adopted in Yorkshire until after that date.

A feature of multi-storeyed mills in the period 1825–75 was their ever-increasing length, height and width. With the exception of a few mills, mostly in rural situations, among them Fringill Mill, Menwith with Darley (100), and Woodfield Mill, Bishop Thornton (24), in Nidderdale, no mill with less than 500 square metres of working space was built. The small mills of this period, such as Healey New Mill at Ossett (107) and Albion Mill, Batley (15) (Fig 44), had up to 1,000 square metres of working space and were two or three storeys high and up to eleven bays long, but most of the mills were between three and six storeys high, ten to twenty bays long, with working areas of between 1,000 and 4,000 square metres. These mills, which included Old Lane Mill, Northowram (105) (Fig 56), Winker Green Mill, Armley (8) (Fig 45), and Lower Providence Mill, Keighley (75) (Fig 328), were equivalent in size or even larger than the largest pre-1825 mills. The largest mills, exemplified by buildings such as Robinwood Mill, Todmorden and Walsden (140) (Fig 156), Britannia Mills, Lockwood (90) (Fig 179), and Whetley Mills at Manningham (95) (Fig 161), were generally between five and seven storeys high, twenty to thirty bays long, with between 4,000 and 7,000 square metres of working space. These mills were mainly just single, multi-storeyed buildings, but as a result of expansion several sites had as much accommodation in a succession of buildings. By 1831 the working area in Mills C, D and E at Marshall's Mill, Holbeck (57), totalled some 6,000 square metres (Fig 46), at Bank Mills, Leeds (84), three separate mills offered a similar area by *c*1840, and by 1845 Batley Carr Mills, Dewsbury (29), had about 4,000 square metres in a row of three conjoined mills (Fig 23). Over-riding all these were the main buildings at Saltaire Mills, Shipley (116) (Fig 172), and Manningham Mills, Manningham (93) (Fig 47), respectively five and six storeys high, over forty bays long and with more than 10,000 square metres of working space.

Architecturally the majority of mills of the period 1825–75 were, like their predecessors, utilitarian in style and built with local building materials. Healey New Mill (107), built in 1825–7, was one of the last mills built with mullioned windows (Fig 335). Ashlar surrounds were rare too: they occur on the 1831 mill at Belle Vue Mills, Skipton (119), but were subsequently almost entirely restricted to mills in the upper Calder valley, including Woodhouse Mill, Langfield (83), Robinwood Mill (140) and Hollins Mill, Todmorden and Walsden (138), where the availability of local, high-quality stone ensured their continued use. Most other mill windows were plain, with rectangular lintels in stone-built mills and segmental-

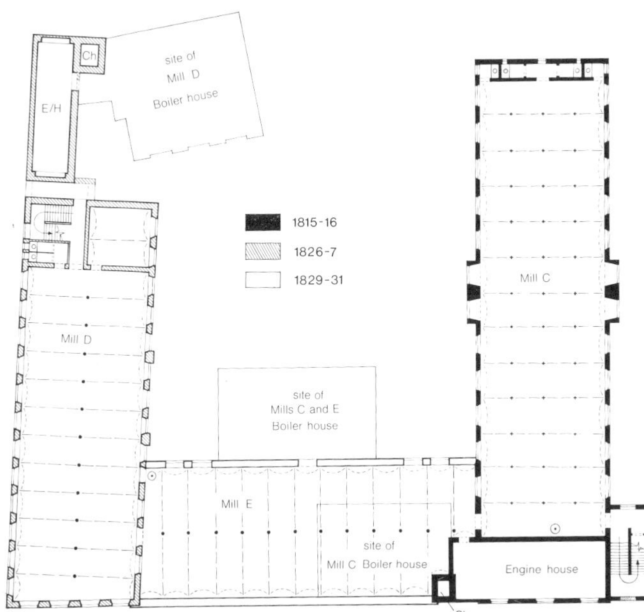

Fig 46 Marshall's Mill, Holbeck (57), showing the main, U-shaped block of flax-spinning mills built between 1815 and 1831 to succeed the original late 18th-century mills elsewhere on the site.

arched lintels in those built of brick. Palladian details had been applied to a number of pre-1825 mills, and this practice continued into the mid 19th century. Its simplest manifestation was in the attic windows of some mills, Venetian in form at Underbank Mill, Wooldale (148), and in the early mill at Britannia Mills (90) (Fig 179), lunettes on Mills D and E at Marshall's Mill (57) (Fig 43), and in the cornices applied to some of the

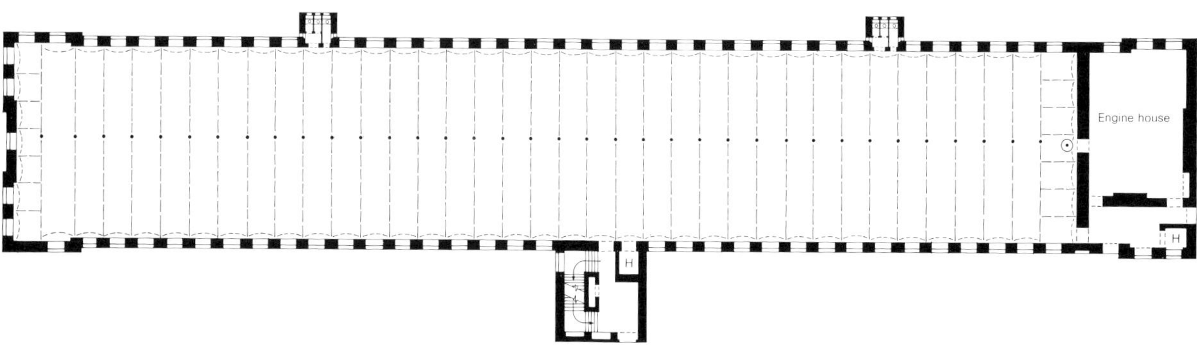

Fig 47 Manningham Mills, Manningham (93). The multi-storeyed mill, the warehouse behind and the shed in front were all built in 1871–3 as part of an extensive, integrated silk mill (plan redrawn from survey held by Lister and Co plc).

major Leeds flax-spinning mills (Fig 53). Pediments were in general restricted to the larger mills, among them Old Lane Mill (105) (Fig 56) and Robinwood Mill (140) (Fig 156), although Woodhouse Mill (83) (Fig 110) shows that such display was not entirely restricted to the larger entrepreneurs. Folly Hall Mills at Huddersfield (63), rebuilt in 1844 but copying the form of its burnt-down predecessor of 1825, was one of the most accomplished designs of its period (Fig 48). The main elevation had a central pediment with a stylised Venetian window, projecting end bays with smaller pediments over tiers of round-headed windows lighting staircases, and an overall parapet. Old Lane Mill (105) (Fig 56) also has a rusticated surround to its engine house window, and this feature, found on otherwise plain mills such as Albert Mills, Lockwood (89), serves as a link with the other notable stylistic development of the period, the adoption of the Italianate style for mill design.

Italianate detailing, like the use of Palladian motifs which preceded it, was frequently applied selectively to mill buildings. One of its earliest and most influential appearances was at Saltaire Mills (116), built in 1850–3 to designs by the Bradford architects, Lockwood and Mawson. The multi-storeyed mill there had rusticated pilasters, voussoired arches, different window forms and an overall moulded cornice, as well as a more elaborately treated centrepiece surmounted by pavilion

Fig 48 The 1844 mill at Folly Hall Mills, Huddersfield (63), which copies the style and incorporates some of the masonry of its burnt-down predecessor of 1825.

towers (Fig 49). By 1875 further large mills, including Cannon Mills, Horton (58), Dalton Mills, Keighley (71) (Fig 50), Legrams Mill, Horton (60), and Manningham Mills (93) (Fig 47), had been built in the same style to the designs of the leading architects Andrews and Delaunay, Sugden, Lockwood and Mawson, and Andrews and Pepper respectively. These great mills made extensive use of the Italianate decorative repertoire, but it was through its more selective and economical use, particularly in the form of rustication, round-headed windows and moulded cornices, that the style gained wider popularity. Even in this restricted use it could still contribute to an impressive effect. At Brookroyd Mills, Stainland (130), the otherwise austere elevation of B Mill was relieved by a cornice and a series of rusticated door and window surrounds (Fig 52), and at Whetley Mills (95) Milnes and France restricted their detail to rustication, round-headed ground-floor windows and a moulded cornice (Fig 161). At other mills, special treatment was given to tiers of windows in privy towers, or to tiers of taking-in doors (Fig 179). At Lower Providence Mill (75), a combination of different window forms created a varied elevation (Fig 328). In the wider field of Victorian architecture, the Italianate style vied with the Gothic, but the latter gained few adherents among Yorkshire mills and was restricted to minor detailing, principally the crenellation on a few stair towers at such mills as New Ing Mills, Batley (19) (Fig 329), and Aireworth Mills, Keighley (69).

The rectangular, multi-storeyed plan which had established itself before 1825 continued throughout the later period, although there were changes in overall size and structural form, as well as some advances associated with the transmission of power. The majority of multi-storeyed mills built between 1825 and 1875 were steam powered, only a few being water powered or having both sources of power, and wheelhouses and engine

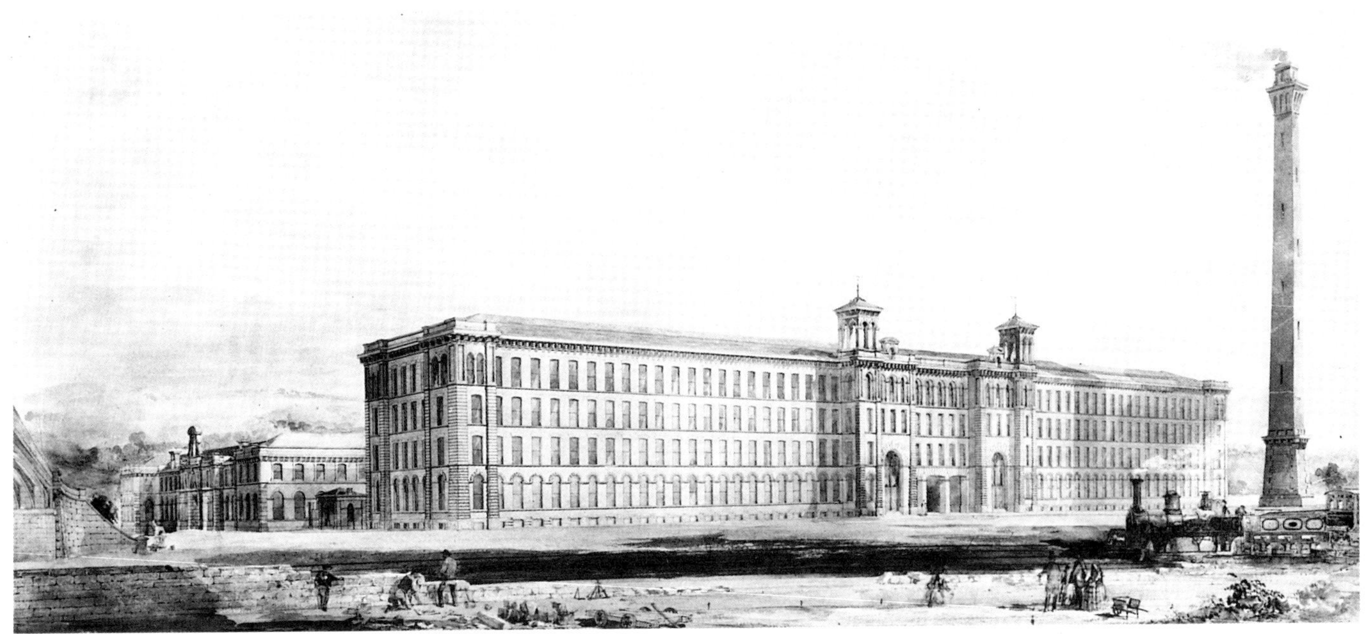

Fig 49 Early watercolour view of the spinning mill and offices at Saltaire Mills, Shipley (116), built in 1850–3 as part of an integrated worsted mill.

Fig 50 Dalton Mills, Keighley (71). Tower Mill in the distance, begun in 1866, and Genappe Mill in the foreground, begun in 1868, form part of a large worsted mill.

houses were in general built in one or other of the positions already adopted in pre-1825 mills. A significant development, however, lay in the construction of double mills in which two halves of a mill were powered from a central power source. Such mills had been built elsewhere in England, though not in great numbers, since the mid 18th century.[30] Zetland Mill in Bradford (27) (Fig 51), built in 1850–1, is the earliest double mill so far identified in Yorkshire, and one of the reasons the plan form was adopted there was probably the intention that the building should house two companies. A few mills evolved as double mills before 1875, among them F and G Mills and B and A Mills at Brookroyd Mills (130) (Fig 52), each of which began as a single conventional mill which was later doubled in size by the addition of a range beyond the original end engine house. The double-mill plan was not fully exploited, however, until after 1875.

The scribbling and fulling mill was the characteristic type of woollen mill in the years before 1825, and even after that date when, as a result of the introduction of the fully self-acting mule, powered woollen spinning was at last possible, a few such mills were still built. As before (Figs 38, 39), the fulling stocks had to be on the ground floor because of their weight, action and need for water, with scribbling and carding engines on the upper floors. A feature of these mills, in contrast to those of other branches, was their tendency to have tall ground floors and more than one doorway: Cape Mills, Bramley (28), had two doorways, Albion Mill (15) (Fig 44), three, and Healey New Mill (107), five. The need for multiple doorways probably reflects the fact that they were public mills where bulky goods were moved around, and where many people, including the head miller and his workforce, as well as some clothiers supervising work or delivering or collecting goods, were going about their business.

The specialised scribbling and fulling mill nevertheless became increasingly anachronistic in the years after 1825 when multi-storeyed mills generally housed the full range of powered preparatory and spinning processes of the main textile fibres. The various fibres were all spun on two basic types of spinning machine, the frame and the mule. Flax and waste silk were spun on the frame, worsteds generally on the frame but occasionally on the mule, cotton on either the frame or mule, and woollens on the mule. The two types of machine differed in form as well as in their demands on buildings: the frame, which was double-sided in operation, could not be set too far from natural light since, as it grew in height, this was increasingly obscured, but the mule, whose headstock and carriage remained low, was more versatile.[31] The increase in the width of mills built between 1825 and 1875, which was not uniform in time nor always within a branch, must nevertheless reflect the influence of the machinery in use. Flax mills show only a modest increase in width. A few small mills, among them Fringill Mill (100) and Woodfield Mill (24) in Nidderdale, were less than 10 metres wide, the width of some pre-1825 flax mills, and although D Mill at Bank Mills (84) in Leeds, built in 1856, was 15.8 metres wide, none of the great series of flax-spinning mills built in Leeds in the late 1820s and 1830s, including D and E Mills at Marshall's Mill (57) (Fig 46) and Hunslet Mills, Hunslet (67) (Fig 53), exceeded 12 metres. Worsted mills built between 1825 and 1850, among them Old Lane Mill (105) (Fig 56), were generally between 12 metres and 15.5 metres wide, while others of the 1860s and early 1870s, including Whetley Mills (95), Dalton Mills (71) and Lower Providence Mill (75) (Figs 161, 50 and 328), were between 17 metres and 22 metres in width. The extreme size of Zetland Mill (27) (Fig 51), built in 1850–1 with a width of 26 metres, is probably explained by a desire to house both spinning and

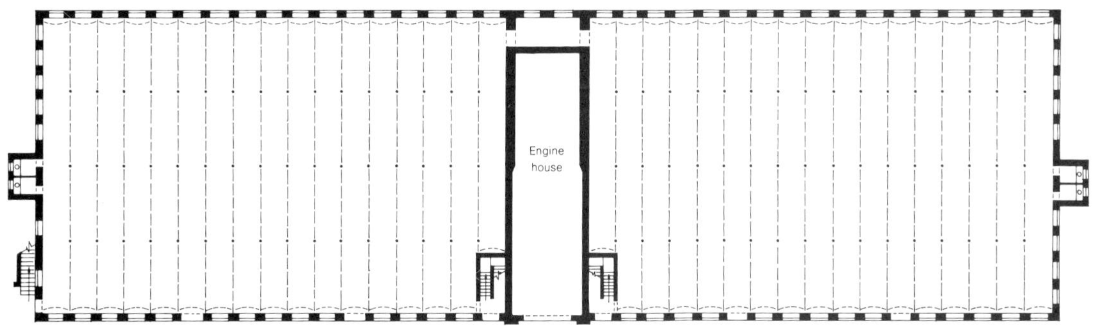

Fig 51 Zetland Mill, Bradford (27), a steam-powered worsted mill built in 1850–1.

weaving. Cotton mills of the 1830s included Woodhouse Mill (83) with a width of 11.9 metres, and Robinwood Mill (140) (Fig 156) at 16 metres, the former only slightly wider than most pre-1825 cotton mills, the latter significantly wider than these but still narrower than some earlier 19th-century Lancashire mills.[32] Lancashire's influence on Yorkshire's cotton mills was more noticeable during and after the mid 19th century, with its wider mills reflected in Hollins Mill (138) (Fig 171), built in 1856–8 and 19.5 metres wide, and Hanson Lane Mill, Halifax (44) (Fig 54), built in 1868–9 and 32.9 metres wide. The ever-increasing length of cotton mules evidently had limited influence on contemporary woollen mules since most woollen mills of the period, including Mill 2 at Armitage Bridge Mills, South Crosland (127) (Fig 146), and Mills B and A at Brookroyd Mills (130) (Fig 52), were between 11 metres

Fig 52 Brookroyd Mills, Stainland (130). B Mill, in the foreground, built in 1860, and A Mill, beyond, added in 1866, are part of a large woollen mill.

and 14 metres wide. Two mills built in the 1860s, Britannia Mills at Lockwood (90) and New Ing Mills (19), each 18.5 metres wide, nevertheless represent some increase in size. The absence of wider woollen mills need not indicate that woollen mules were not at times as long as cotton mules, since they may have been set along, rather than across, a mill, a known arrangement for long mules at a later date (Fig 66). Insufficient silk mills were recorded for their width to be assessed.

Multi-storeyed mills built in the first quarter of the 19th century were predominantly of traditional construction with timber beams and floors, although these were frequently supported by the then newly introduced cast-iron columns. Similarly constructed mills were built between 1825 and 1875, but a feature of this period was the far more common use of fireproof construction, which was no longer restricted to the larger firms with access to greater capital. Fireproof construction, adopted not only because of the resistance it offered to fire but also because it enabled more and heavier machinery to be housed, was usually employed for all the floors of a mill, although in a few instances it was restricted to the lower or lowest floors. Such limited use could have been for both structural and functional reasons. The fireproof basement at West Vale Mills, Elland cum Greetland (39), may have protected the floors above from the dampness of the scouring and milling processes, whereas at Larchfield Mills, Huddersfield (64), as later at North Dean Mill, Elland cum Greetland (36) (Fig 63), the fireproof floors may have been intended to support the weight and vibrations of powerlooms. Fireproofing most frequently took the form of brick arches springing from cast-iron beams, although an alternative system using stone flags and a grid of cast-iron beams and joists was employed on a small scale in the late 1820s and early 1830s, and by 1870 concrete, rather than brick, was being used for some fireproof vaults (see pp63–7). A few mills were

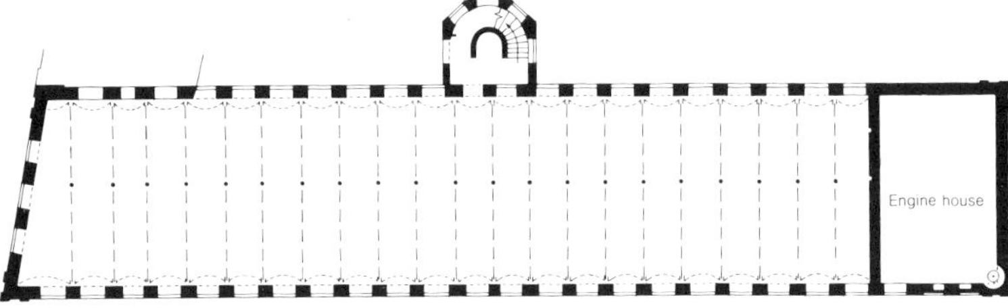

Fig 53 Hunslet Mills, Hunslet (67), built as a steam-powered flax-spinning mill in 1838–40. The three-storeyed warehouse and office range in Goodman Street was remodelled during the 1840s.

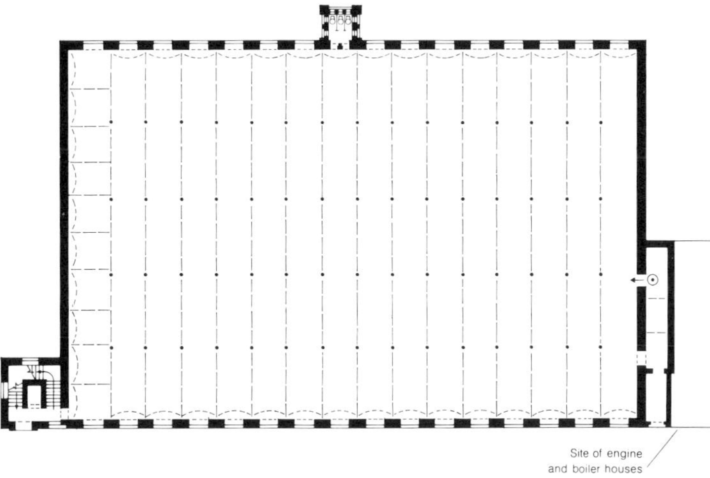

Fig 54 Hanson Lane Mill, Halifax (44), a steam-powered cotton-spinning mill built in 1868–9 (plan based on survey by Ron Fitzgerald).

narrow enough to be spanned by timber beams without any intermediate support, but in most mills, whether with beams of timber or cast iron, one or more rows of cast-iron columns was usual. The columns frequently supported line shafting, and the number of rows was usually related to mill width and structure. The majority of both traditionally built and fireproof mills had a single, central row of columns, an arrangement which sufficed for mills as wide as 17 metres, including Young Street Mills, Manningham (96), and Manningham Mills (93) (Fig 117). A number of mills less than 17 metres wide had two equally spaced rows of columns, perhaps because of structural caution on the part of their builders. Winker Green Mill (8) (Fig 45) and Woodhouse Mill (83), at 11 metres and 11.9 metres, were among the narrowest of these mills, whereas Mill 2 at Belle Vue Mills (119), some 20.1 metres wide, was one of the widest. A few traditionally built mills of the late 1860s and early 1870s, with widths of between 16 metres and 22 metres, and including Lower Providence Mill (75) (Fig 55) and two mills at Dalton Mills (71) (Fig 261e), had a row of closely spaced pairs of columns down their centre, an arrangement which had the benefit of creating unobstructed working areas as well as a secure central passage which also gave sound support to line shafting. The widest pre-1875 mills, all of them of fireproof construction, were supported by greater numbers of rows of columns, three at the 26 metres wide Zetland Mill (27) (Fig 51) and four at the 33 metres wide Hanson Lane Mill (44) (Fig 54).

Roof forms evolved alongside those of other elements of mill structure (see pp70–5), and the greater use of iron is reflected in a number of trusses, some of cast iron, others combining cast and wrought iron, which frequently covered a mill in one span. A variety of timber trusses, most frequently of queen-strut type, some of them raised on timber blocking pieces or cast-iron brackets, were also used, and multiple span roofs became quite common.

Access to mills, the storage and movement of raw materials and finished goods, and the provision of sanitary facilities, became increasingly important aspects of the planning of mills as these buildings grew in size to house ever more machinery and greater numbers of workers. A variety of ways was tried to create the most efficient working environment, one being the addition of a wing to the established rectangular plan of mills. At Old Lane Mill (105), a shallow wing housing the staircase, offices and some storage space enabled unim-

Fig 55 The first floor of the multi-storeyed mill of 1874–5 at Lower Providence Mill, Keighley (75), showing its traditional timber construction and the central passage for access and power transmission.

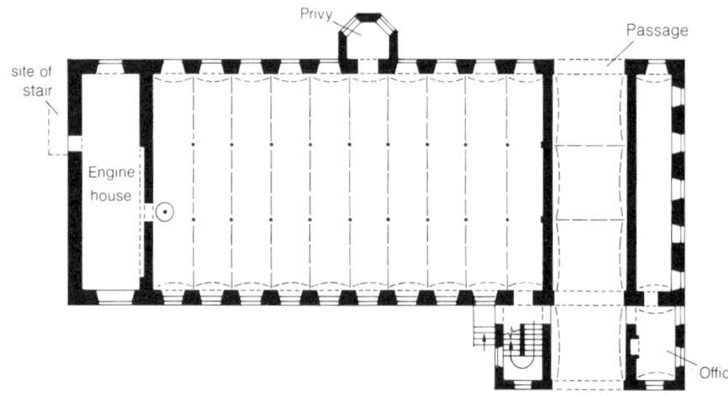

Fig 56 Old Lane Mill, Northowram (105), a steam-powered worsted mill built in 1825–8.

peded working floors to be created (Fig 56). A similar result was achieved at Robinwood Mill (140) where, in a more ambitious U-shaped plan similar to its designer, William Fairbairn's, near-contemporary Orrell's Mill at Stockport,[33] the north wing was used for warehousing and offices while the rest of the mill, apart from the engine and boiler houses in the base of the south wing, was working space (Fig 156). Mills with wings were, however, rare since most builders found it adequate to have stair towers and, if necessary, separate warehouses which frequently also included offices. Stair towers had been restricted mainly to the largest pre-1825 mills, but after 1825 they became almost universal, and were only absent from the smallest, and generally earliest, mills. They were usually sited in order to interfere as little as possible with working space: external stair towers were set against a side or corner (Figs 45, 47, 54), and internal stair towers were usually in the corner of a mill, either in isolation (Figs 44, 51) or more often sharing an end bay with an office (Fig 43) or, more commonly, an engine house (Figs 63, 172).

Fig 57 Sanitary provision in multi-storeyed mills: a) Saltaire Mills, Shipley (116), 1850–3; b) Barkerend Mills, Bradford (26), 1852; c) Manningham Mills, Manningham (93), 1871–3.

The movement of goods was made easier by the more widespread use of taking-in doors serving all floors of mills. The position of these doors varied according to the plan and situation of individual mills, but an efficient arrangement set the taking-in doors as part of the main stair towers (Fig 48). In mills without taking-in doors, raw materials, finished goods and machine parts must have been moved via staircases, although trapdoors were occasionally incorporated. A later alternative was the internal hoist tower, a common feature in post-1875 mills, but already present in the earlier period in mills such as Whetley Mills (95) of 1863 and Young Street Mills (96) of 1874.

Sanitary provision was poor in most pre-1825 mills, and though the smaller mills of the later period rarely have structural evidence for privies, it survives in many other mills. Privies were sometimes set at or close to the corner of mills (Figs 46, 57a), but a more frequent and healthier arrangement involved siting them in projecting towers housing one, two or more closets (Fig 57b, c). These towers were either rectangular or polygonal on plan, and the larger mills often, of necessity, had more than one privy tower.

Multi-storeyed mills, 1875–1930

The principal developments in multi-storeyed mill design after 1875 were associated with the introduction of rope drive, the continuing evolution of machinery, and major structural advances. The increase in the overall size of multi-storeyed mills which characterised earlier periods continued to be a factor in this late period when virtually no mill with less than 1,000 square metres of working space was built. The majority of mills were between two and six storeys high, most commonly of four or five storeys, ten to seventeen bays long and with between 1,000 and 4,000 square metres of working space (Figs 58, 230). The largest mills, some three storeys high but most of five or six storeys, now commonly had between 4,000 and 11,000 square metres of working space (Figs 39, 59, 336). The increasing width of some of these mills, including the construction of some which were nearly square on plan, together with the use of steel and concrete which radically altered their internal structure, makes simple bay counts misleading. A few even larger mills were built: the first and only half of Hare Mill, Stansfield (134), had some 17,700 square metres of working space (Fig 60).

Architecturally there was only limited use of Italianate detailing on these late mills. Balm Road Mills, Hunslet (66), built in the 1880s, was one of the few to make full use of its repertoire (Fig 61), its influence otherwise being represented by such minor features as the paired, round-headed windows of stair towers and privy towers (Fig 230), or more frequently by an overall moulded cornice occasionally coupled with a parapet (Fig 330). The crenellations and mullions of Bridge Street Mill, Slaithwaite (122), built in 1903, are unusual,[34] most mills offering just plain expanses of wall with rows of flat or segmental-headed windows. The early 20th century brought a number of new stylistic influences, some of them from Lancashire, including the Byzantine detailing of Hare Mill (134) (Fig 60)[35] as well as the rational styles of buildings such as Ardsley Mills, East Ardsley (35), and the New Mill at Brookroyd Mills, Stainland (130) (Figs 62, 337), whose outward form reflects their structure.[36] The increased depth of many of these late mills required better lighting, and this was achieved both by building taller storeys and providing larger windows; in some mills the fenestration was almost continuous.

The multi-storeyed mills of the period 1875–1930 were almost all steam powered, a few of the latest ones being powered by electricity. The rectangular plan was still favoured for most mills, usually with an engine house in one or other of the by-then customary positions (Fig 63), although the introduction of rope drive with its associated rope alley led to the construction of engine houses which usually projected either from the side or close to the corner of mills (Figs 64, 65, 330; see Chapter 4). Two variant types of plan, the double mill and the

Fig 58 Wellington Mills, Elland cum Greetland (38). The nearer multi-storeyed mill was built in 1875, the far one in 1912, both for cotton spinning

Fig 59 The latest multi-storeyed mill at Blakeridge Mills, Batley (16), built in 1912–13 for woollen spinning.

Fig 60 Hare Mill, Stansfield (134), a cotton-spinning mill built in 1907–11 and renamed Mons Mill in 1914.

Fig 61 The multi-storeyed flax-spinning mill of c1880 at Balm Road Mills, Hunslet (66).

Fig 62 Ardsley Mills, East Ardsley (35), a worsted-spinning mill built in 1912.

square mill, established themselves as significant in this period. The double mill with its centrally placed engine house, popular among Lancashire cotton-spinning mills in the late 19th and early 20th centuries, had already been used for some Yorkshire mills before 1875, but it was more fully exploited after 1875 because of the economies of power generation and transmission which it offered both in mills of one build and in those planned for completion in two stages. Globe Mills, Slaithwaite (123), of 1887 and Ardsley Mills (35) of 1912 (Fig 62) were both of one build, the former with a central internal engine house, the latter with a projecting central external engine house. Hare Mill (134) and Knowle Mill, Keighley (73) (Figs 60, 64), both also with projecting engine houses, were planned for staged completion, but this was only achieved at the former. The square mill, as deep as it was long, and consequently wider than most double mills, was derived from cotton mills in Lancashire where its plan, which allowed light to penetrate the building from four sides, had been developed to house new and longer spinning machines. Scarr Bottom Mill, Meltham (99), and Spa Mills, Slaithwaite (124) (Figs 65, 336), both had corner engine houses and rope races, whereas the Twist Mill of 1927–8 at Meltham Mills, Meltham (98), was electrically powered. Bridge Street Mill (122), of 1903, unlike the others a woollen mill rather than a cotton mill, utilised the upright shaft of an earlier mill.

Mill widths had increased significantly in the third quarter of the 19th century, particularly among cotton, woollen and worsted mills, and many post-1875 mills did not exceed the limits then established. The principal exceptions were a few mills in the cotton and woollen branches, both of which were dominated by mule spinning. The widest cotton mills, which were between 38 metres and 40 metres wide, were based on prototypes developed by the Lancashire cotton industry, and two of them, Scarr Bottom Mill (99) and Hare Mill (134), were designed by Stott and Sons of Manchester and Oldham, the principal mill architects and engineers of the period. The architect Theodore Sington[37] noted that the width of a cotton mill's spinning floors was dependent on whether it was intended for ring or mule spinning: a width of 31 metres would suffice for ring spinning, but for mule spindles it might be 42 to 44 metres. The widest Yorkshire cotton mills were therefore evidently designed for mule spindles, an observation which gains credence from the fact that the ring spindle was only adopted slowly by British cotton spinners,[38] and accounted for little more than a tenth of Yorkshire's cotton spindleage in 1901.[39] On these statistics, most of the narrower, newly built mills must have housed mules too, but set along rather than across the mill, as in Mill 4 at Wellington Mills, Elland cum Greetland (38) (Fig 66), rebuilt in 1912 to the 20 metre width of its burnt-down predecessor. No woollen mill was built with a width even approaching that of the widest cotton mills: Bridge Street Mill (122), a square mill of 1903, was just 21.3 metres across, although the New Mill at Brookroyd Mills (130), built *c*1920, was 30.8 metres wide.

Many post-1875 mills had fireproof internal structures, traditional timber-construction generally being restricted to smaller mills such as Moor End Mill, Dewsbury (33). The predominant earlier form of fireproof construction, with cast-iron beams and brick arches, was replaced after 1875 by a variety of structural

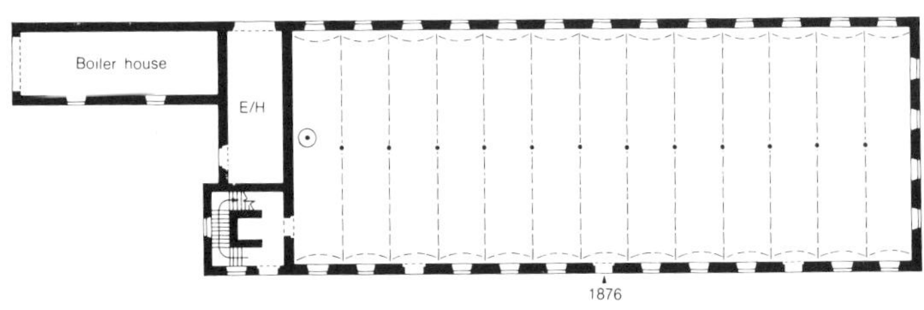

Fig 63 North Dean Mill, Elland cum Greetland (36), a woollen mill as originally built in 1876–7.

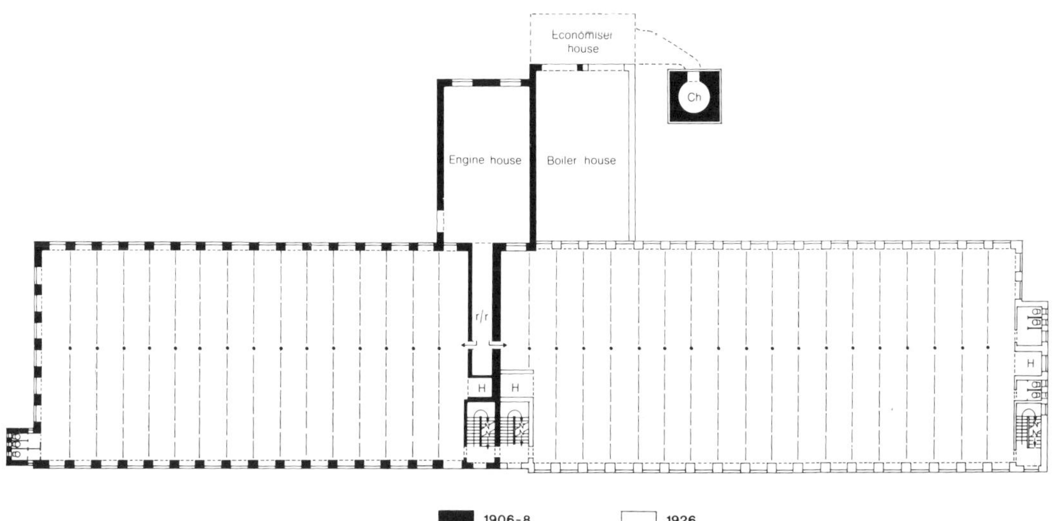

Fig 64 Knowle Mill, Keighley (73). The multi-storeyed worsted-spinning mill was built in two stages in 1906–8 and 1926.

forms using cast iron, steel and concrete in various combinations (see pp65–7). The majority of mills, whether of traditional or fireproof construction, gained intermediate support either from rows of cast-iron columns or, in some early 20th-century mills, from steel stanchions. The number of rows varied with the width of mills: a single row usually sufficed in mills up to 18.5 metres wide; around 20 metres paired columns or two rows of supports were usual; and in mills over 30 metres wide between four and ten rows were employed.

Stair towers, taking-in doors, hoists and privy towers continued to be component parts of many mills. Internal stair towers, usually sharing the same bay as an engine house or rope race, were less common than external towers set against the corners or sides of mills. Taking-in doors were less frequently provided than hoist towers, and projecting privy towers were common features.

Single-storeyed sheds

The single-storeyed shed, usually a building with a series of saw-tooth profile roofs, was a major component of many textile mill sites. The weaving shed at Waterside Mill, Langfield (82) (Fig 67), built in 1829 to house 800 cotton powerlooms, was probably the first such shed to be built on a mill site in Yorkshire, and the construction of sheds over the next two decades or so was largely due to the adoption of powerloom weaving by all branches of the textile industry. The shed was favoured in preference to the multi-storeyed mill because its form was more appropriate to the type and scale of work undertaken. The multi-storeyed mill was able to house the generally small number of looms used in the early phase of powerloom weaving, but once these looms became accepted and put to use in larger numbers, only sheds met all the demands which housing and working

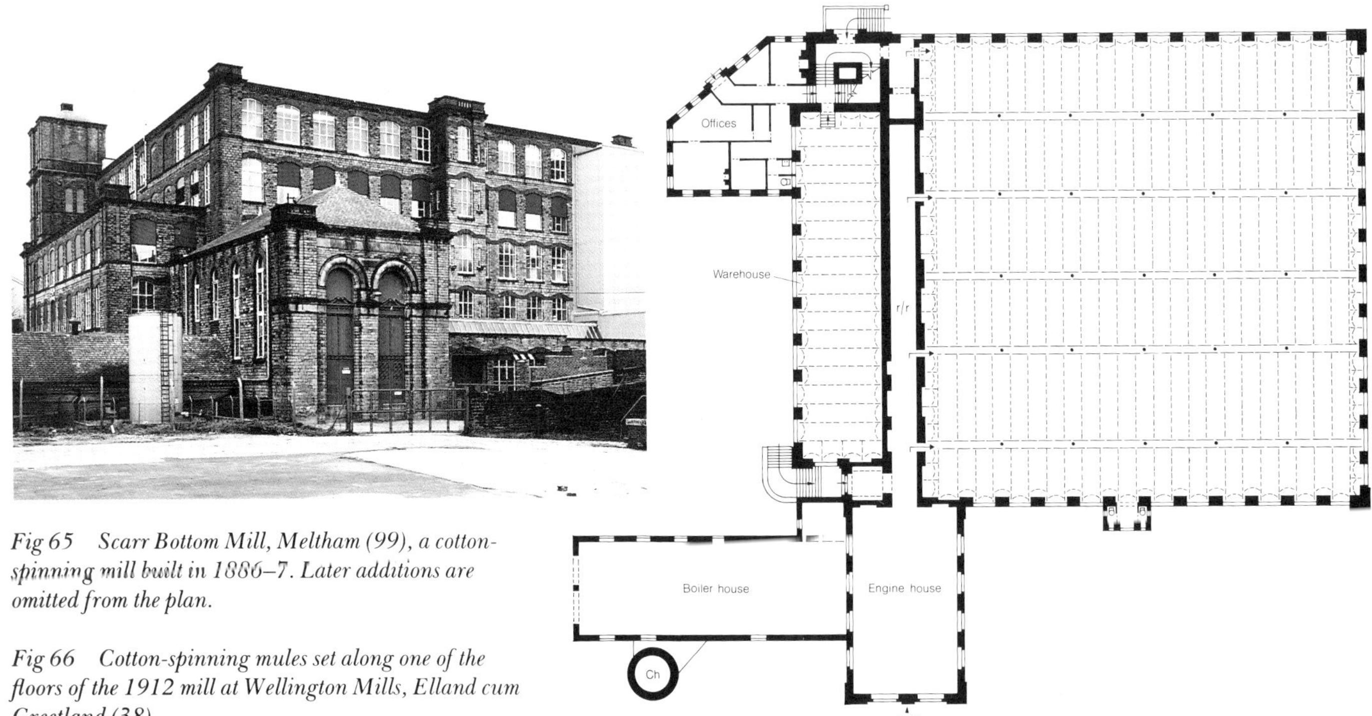

Fig 65 Scarr Bottom Mill, Meltham (99), a cotton-spinning mill built in 1886–7. Later additions are omitted from the plan.

Fig 66 Cotton-spinning mules set along one of the floors of the 1912 mill at Wellington Mills, Elland cum Greetland (38).

Fig 67 Waterside Mill, Langfield (82). The cleared area is the site of the original powerloom shed of 1829; the surviving triangular-shaped shed was built c1840.

them in large numbers posed. The shed was structurally secure since it could withstand the weight and vibration of working looms more easily than a storeyed building, and by virtue of its top lighting it was also freed from the restriction on size imposed by lighting from side walls alone, and so could cover a larger area if required. The need for good, even light was particularly important in a weaving plant since it eliminated shadows which could disguise faults, particularly in complex weaves. Working on a single level was also more efficient, enabling long warp beams and heavy rolls of woven cloth to be moved around with greater ease.

Although commonly used for weaving, single-storeyed sheds also came to house other processes, including silk throwing at Bent Ley Mill, Meltham (97), scutching, breaking and mixing cotton at Robinwood Mill, Todmorden and Walsden (140), wool combing at Saltaire Mills, Shipley (116) (Fig 172), and Cumberland Works, Manningham (92) (Fig 182), cotton spinning at Hope Mill, Todmorden and Walsden (139) (Fig 162), willeying, milling and scouring woollens at Calder Bank Mills, Dewsbury (30) (Fig 175), and dyeing and finishing at Bowling Dyeworks (Fig 85) and Oakwood Dyeworks (Fig 190). They were also used for integrated working: Temple Mill at Marshall's Mill, Holbeck (57) (Fig 168), built between 1838 and 1841, was intended to house flax spinning, thread twisting and linen weaving, and Alverthorpe Mills, Alverthorpe with Thornes (4) (Fig 177), and Westfield Mills, Yeadon (153), are two late 19th-century woollen mills which exploited the advantages of single-storeyed planning (see p107).

Architecturally the vast majority of single-storeyed sheds were plain structures with little, if any, detailing to their walls. The situation of many sheds, against and often behind either a multi-storeyed mill or a warehouse block, or on part of a site away from the entrance, gave little incentive to providing decoration, and the almost invariable use of top lighting meant that most side walls were blind. In such circumstances, builders sometimes chose to emphasize doorways, ventilation openings or the ashlar blocks to which the brackets supporting internal line shafting were attached (Fig 255), or to make a feature of an entrance lodge or privy towers (Figs 68, 69). There were exceptions to the general severity, however, most notably in the Egyptian-style ashlar façade of Temple Mill at Marshall's Mill (57) (Fig 168), and in the sheds at Manningham Mills, Manningham (93) (Fig 47). The windows of these sheds are an unusual feature and may indicate that the areas next to them were used for examining and mending cloth, or as offices.

Shed interiors were occupied by rows of cast-iron columns which supported the roof and frequently also the line shafting, and the evolution of the interior was marked by a steady progress towards creating wider bays and clearing the floor space of obstruction in order to have as unimpeded an area as possible for machinery. Columns were arranged to create either long and

Fig 68 The pavilion at the corner of the 1875 woolcombing shed at Cumberland Works, Manningham (92), houses the time office.

Fig 69 The pavilions attached to the weaving shed of c1882 at Bowers Mill, Barkisland (11), house privies.

narrow bays or square bays, and their dimensions tended to increase as the date of construction grew later. The 1838 shed at Armitage Bridge Mills, South Crosland (127) (Fig 70), had bays 2 metres by 5 metres, those at Bent Ley Mill (97) of 1840 were 4.2 metres square, whereas those in the weaving shed at Saltaire Mills (116) of 1850–3 were 10 metres by 5.8 metres (Fig 172). City Shed, Wyke (152), built in 1899, had bays 7 metres square (Fig 338); at Park View Mills, North Bierley (103), in 1925 they were 15 metres square (Fig 71). The wider spans often required the provision of support for the ends of intermediate roof trusses. Timber or cast-iron beams were generally used in the 19th century, but in the early 20th century steel girders supported by steel stanchions bridged the almost clear interiors (Fig 72).

All single-storeyed sheds were top lit, and for a time a variety of different types and shapes of roof was tried. The groined brick vaults of Temple Mill at Marshall's Mill (57), each lit by a circular lantern (Figs 73, 168), follow the form of a slightly earlier weaving shed built at Deanston Mills, Perthshire.[40] They were unique in Yorkshire and were never copied, no doubt because of the cost of their construction, and instead the roofs of

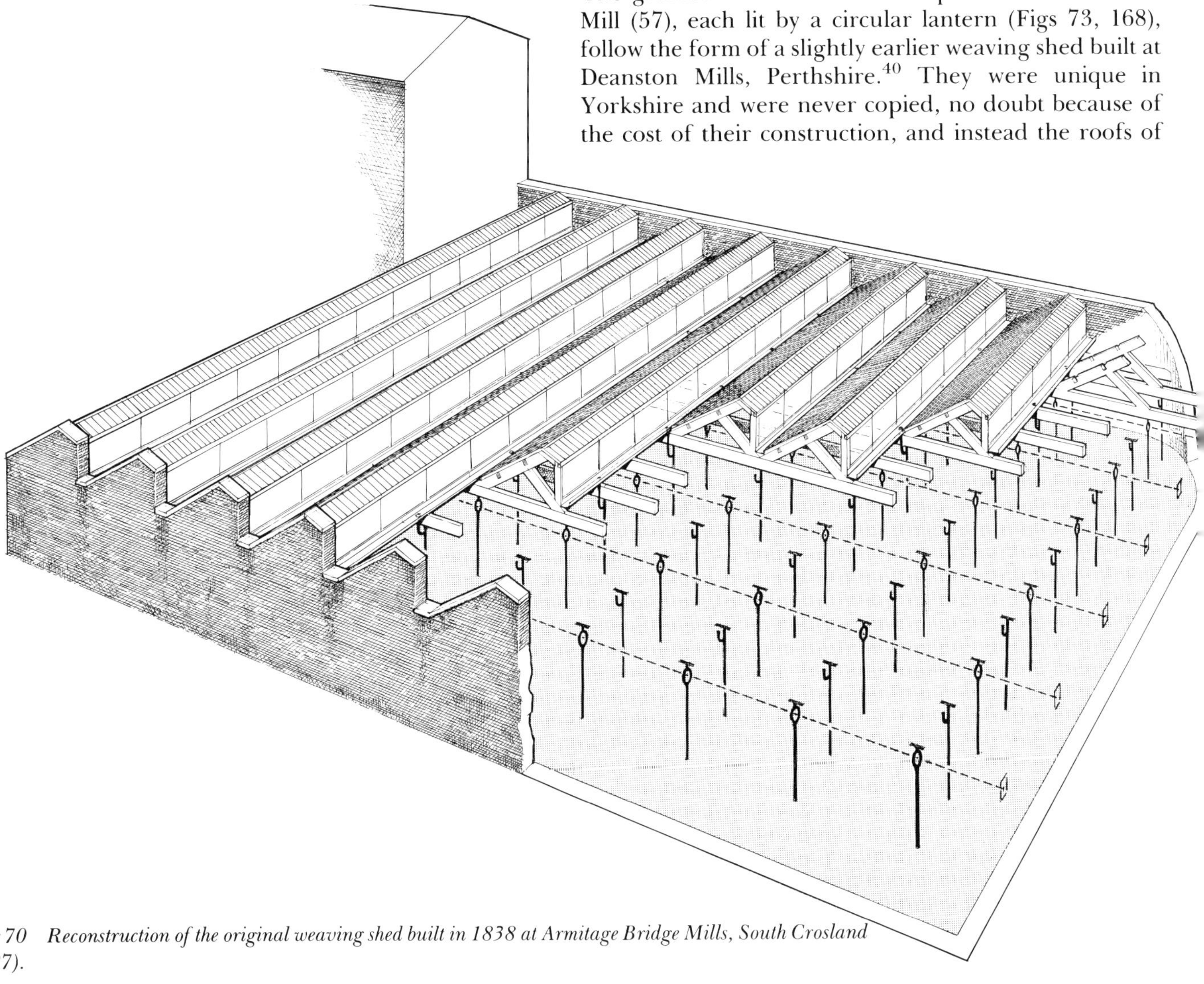

Fig 70 Reconstruction of the original weaving shed built in 1838 at Armitage Bridge Mills, South Crosland (127).

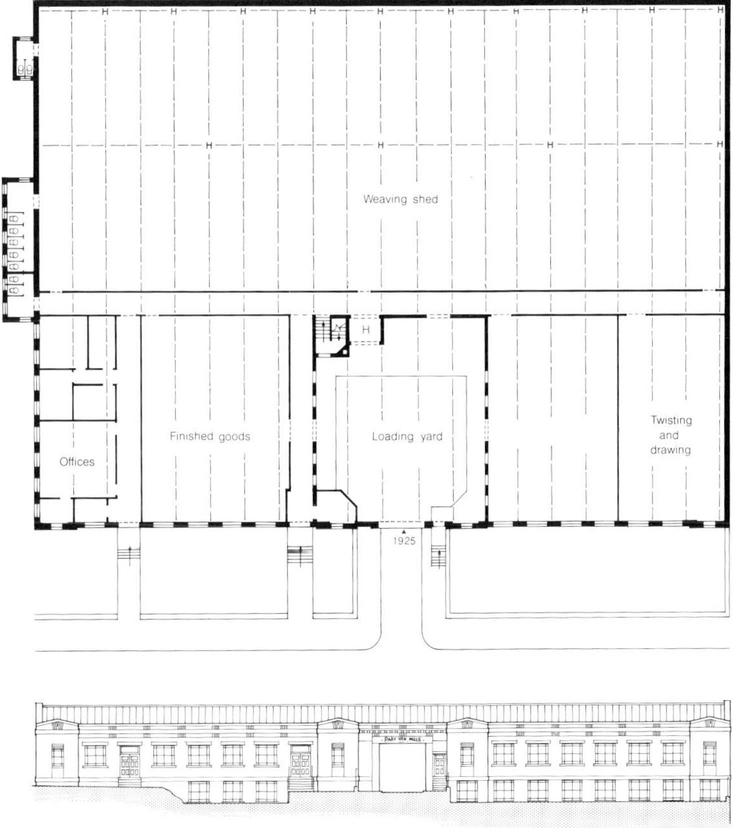

Fig 71 Plan and front elevation of Park View Mills, North Bierley (103). The plan of the main working floor shows the uses noted on the architects' drawing of 1925.

sheds were usually one or other variant of a basic saw-tooth profile which comprised a long, straight, covered slope and a scarp slope which included the glazing but whose profile varied (Fig 74). The 1829 shed at Waterside Mills (82), perhaps because of the narrowness of its bays and its pioneering date, had just a single, vertical, glazed panel (Fig 74a), whereas other early shed roofs either had scarp slopes which were in two planes with the glazed, vertical panel preceding or following the slope, or had just a single, inclined, glazed slope (Fig 74b–d). The double-plane scarp slope continued to be constructed as late as the 1870s, the date of its use at Upper Carr Mills, Liversedge (88), but it was the more practical profile, with its long, single, glazed slope, which established itself as the classic saw-tooth profile shed roof (Fig 74e–n). Introduced to Yorkshire sheds probably during the 1830s, used at Langcliffe Shed, Langcliffe (81), in about 1840, at Bent Ley Mill (97) in 1840, and still in use in the early 20th century at Park View Mills (103) and elsewhere, it was no doubt widely adopted because of its simplicity, effectiveness and ease of maintenance. Shed roofs employed a variety of different types of truss made from a range of different materials. Timber trusses, often but far from always of king-post type, were used at all times, sometimes in conjunction with wrought-iron members (Fig 74e, i, m). Cast-iron trusses, either arched or of king-post type, and occasionally with wrought-iron components, were used in the mid to late 19th century (Fig 74d, e, h, j, l); angle iron was preferred in the early 20th century (Fig 74n). The equal-pitched roof was not entirely abandoned. Bowers Mills, Barkisland (11), was one of the few weaving sheds with such a roof (Fig 69), and it was also used over some non-weaving areas of Calder Bank Mills (30), and certain finishing areas at Oakwood Dyeworks. The glazed sections of almost all these roofs, irrespective of form, faced as near north as possible in order to avoid direct sunlight and so cast an even light on the shed interior.

The single-storeyed shed form was attractive because of its versatility, since it was almost infinitely expandable and could fit any shape of land (Fig 67). A variant type, more restricted in form, was developed to house the process of rag grinding, one of the stages in producing shoddy and mungo. Separate, single-storeyed, rag-grinding sheds, always with equal-pitched

Fig 72 Early 20th-century photograph showing the unobstructed interior of the weaving shed at Devonshire Mills, Keighley (72), built in 1909–10.

*Fig 73 Marshall's Mill, Holbeck (57), showing the interior of Temple Mill, built in 1838–41 (*The Penny Magazine*, 30 December 1843, 501).*

roofs, formed part of some mid 19th-century woollen mills, including Cheapside Mills, Batley (18) (Fig 191), but the development in the late 19th and 20th centuries of specialist mills devoted to the manufacture of shoddy and mungo led to adaptations of the shed form, again always with equal-pitched roofs. Some, including Perseverance Mill (109) and Gedham Mill (106), both at Ossett (Fig 194), were long single-storeyed structures subdivided internally into different working areas by brick walls, but in an alternative arrangement, seen at Runtlings Mill, Ossett (110) (Figs 75, 195), the sheds form a row of six, later seven, bays arranged not as a linear shed but as a series of short, gabled sheds set side by side, each with its own entrance door.

Dryhouses

The Yorkshire textile industry processed a range of fibres which, as raw materials, yarn or cloth, passed through a number of washing, scouring and wet-finishing processes, and which therefore required drying. Natural drying in the open air or in a ventilated building, and drying by heat in a building or in a machine, were all adopted as alternative methods of drying, and since all but the first required use of a building, a number of distinctive building types developed.

Open-air drying

Open-air drying was the traditional method of drying in the textile industry. Wool, which had to be scoured and washed prior to scribbling and carding, was dried at some early mills by being spread out on areas of stone flags. Joseph Rogerson laid down such flags at his woollen mill in Bramley in 1808 (see p81), and 'drying-flags' were included in a survey of Winker Green Mill, Armley (8), in 1821. After the fulling process, woollen cloth was dried and stretched on tenters, outdoor frames with pairs of continuous, horizontal rails set with tenter hooks. Tenters, which had to be long enough to support full lengths of cloth, were frequently found next to woollen mills (Figs 23, 76), and for economic reasons they continued in use in good weather, even when other means of drying were available (Fig 143). Linen yarn and cloth were also dried and bleached in the open air. A number of early 19th-century flax mills, including Benyons' Mill, Holbeck (56) (Fig 152), and Castleton Mill, Wortley (150), had either drying grounds or tenters on their sites, and at times these must have resembled the environs of Crimple Mill, Scriven with Tentergate (Fig 187), or the yard of Hunslet Linen Works, Hunslet, with its linen hung on frames to dry (Fig 77).

Fig 74 Roof trusses from single-storeyed sheds: a) Waterside Mill, Langfield (82), 1829; b) Armitage Bridge Mills, South Crosland (127), 1838; c) Waterside Mill, Langfield (82), c1840; d) Bent Ley Mill, Meltham (97), 1840; e) Saltaire Mills, Shipley (116), 1850–3; f) Low Mill, Dewsbury (31), c1850; g) New Ing Mills, Batley (19), 1860; h) Albert Mills, Lockwood (89), c1866; i) Young Street Mills, Manningham (96), 1871; j) Manningham Mills, Manningham (93), 1871–3; k) Cumberland Works, Manningham (92), 1875; l) Hope Mill, Todmorden and Walsden (139), by 1890; m) Lees Mill, Bingley (22), by 1892; n) Park View Mills, North Bierley (103), 1924–5.

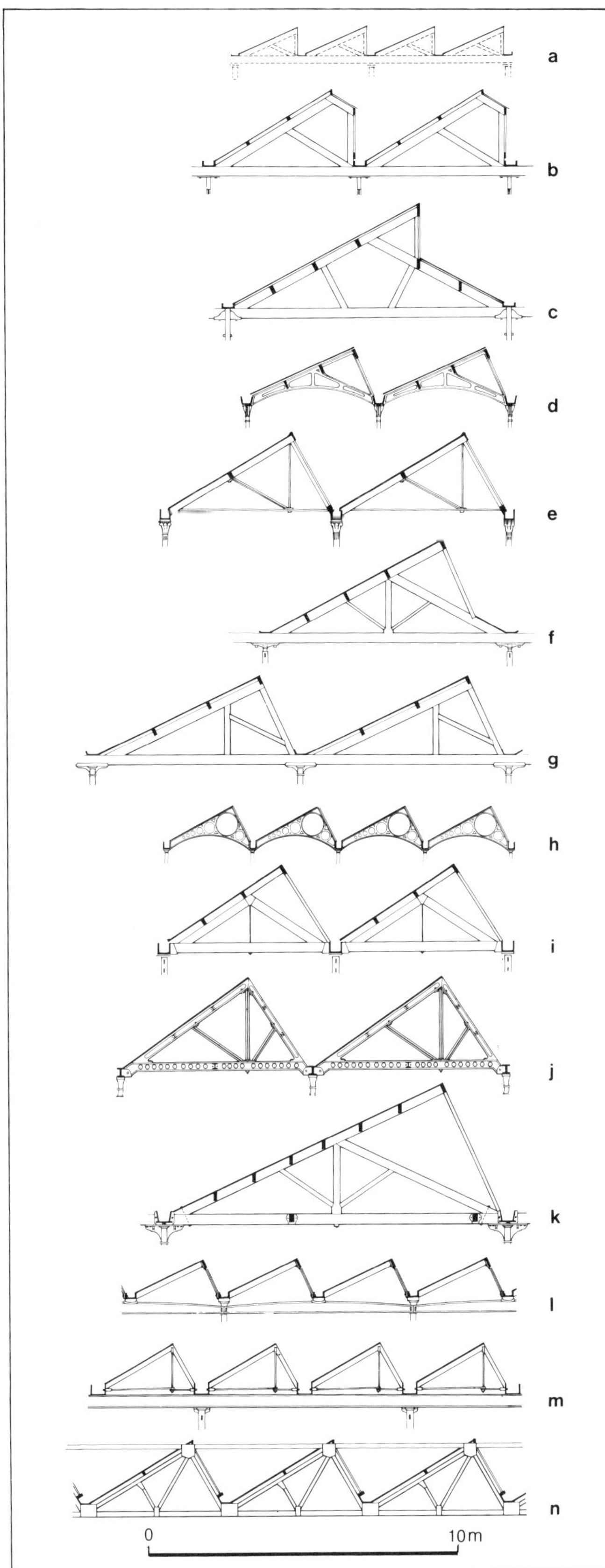

Fig 75 Rag-grinding sheds at Runtlings Mill, Ossett (110), built c1907.

Air dryhouses

The unpredictability of the weather was the major drawback to open-air drying, and from the late 18th century an alternative method of drying was provided by the air dryhouse which made use of natural ventilation. Most air dryhouses were built in the late 18th century, followed by a few in the 19th century, and they are known mainly from documentary sources. Sowerby Bridge Mills, Warley (143), is one of the few woollen mills known to have had one. Built by 1792, it evidently occupied the top floor of a three-storeyed building once ventilated by large openings (Fig 151), and its length suggests that cloth rather than wool was dried. Air dryhouses were more numerous in the flax and linen branch, in which they were probably used to dry both yarn and cloth. One at Marshall's Mill, Holbeck (57), rebuilt in 1796 to replace its burnt-down predecessor, was recorded as being of 'brick, timber and slate'.[41] Its plan, long and narrow (Fig 142), was appropriate for drying cloth. In 1816, West House Mill, Fewston (40), had an air drying room and a 'drying house for warps warranted not to be used for drying by fire heat'.[42] No other details were specified, but in 1843 there were two air drying rooms, each 7.8 metres by 8.9 metres, a size appropriate for drying warp threads, on the two upper floors of a building shown on a letterhead to have conventional window openings (Fig 272; for identification see Fig 153). Since air drying was beneficial for better-quality linen, it persisted in parts of the linen branch well after drying by heat had been introduced. Crimple Mill, Scriven with Tentergate (Fig 187), used for bleaching and finishing linen, had two cloth-drying sheds in *c*1870, each evidently for natural drying. The Low Shed had fifty-five poles each 4.6 metres long, and the Top Shed fifty-two poles each 5 metres long,[43] on which the material to be dried was no doubt hung.

Heated dryhouses and drying rooms

Drying by natural means, with its inherent lack of control, was increasingly inadequate as levels of textile production rose, and from the early 19th century

Fig 76 Tenters at Aldams Mill, Dewsbury, as shown in 1835 sales particulars.

indoor drying by heat, either in heated dryhouses or in drying rooms over boilers, was widely adopted. Cloth required a long building in which it could be stretched out to dry, whereas raw materials and yarn required less space, and although for a short period separate heated dryhouses, sometimes called stoves, were built to meet each of these needs, it was soon accepted that the most efficient way of drying raw materials and yarn was in drying rooms over boilers, whereas cloth was best dried in heated dryhouses.

Wool-drying stoves, circular on plan, several storeys high and heated by a central iron stove, had been built in the west of England since the 17th century,[44] but there is no evidence that such buildings were ever constructed in Yorkshire where the heated dryhouse was a feature of the industrialised phase of the textile industry. The earliest heated dryhouses constructed in Yorkshire to dry raw materials and yarn were built in the first two decades of the 19th century, and included a wool dryhouse of 1809 at Bellisle Mill, Bramley,[45] and a linen-yarn dryhouse built by John Marshall at Marshall's Mill, Holbeck (57), between 1806 and 1815. The size of the Bramley building is not known, although it was storeyed, had iron-plate floors which were almost certainly perforated to allow warm air to circulate, and achieved temperatures of at least 168°F when drying.[46] The stove at Marshall's Mill (57) was three storeys high, measured about 13 metres by 8 metres, and had an internal cast-iron frame which supported floors of perforated iron plates.[47] In size it was similar to the stove at Ditherington Mill, Shrewsbury,[48] which John Marshall had constructed in about 1802 or 1804 and which may have been the model for his Yorkshire building. The heat in these buildings is likely to have come from steam pipes fed by separately housed boilers, but as boilers became more common on mill sites with the spread of steam engines in the early 19th century, it became customary for drying rooms to be built as the upper floors of their boiler houses.

Early mill boilers were often simply set within an outer wall pierced by a firing place: those of the flax mills in Leeds in 1821 were noted as having no house or roof over them.[49] However, during the second decade of the 19th century, in a development represented in other textile districts,[50] boiler houses with drying rooms over were built on a number of mill sites, including Lawrence Street Flax Mill in York (154) (Fig 35) and Stone Bridge Mills, Wortley (151), and they continued to be built in the early 20th century, as at Oak Mills, West Ardsley (144) (Fig 203). Drying rooms were built as part of woollen, flax and linen, and silk mills, serving to dry raw wool and silk which had been scoured and washed before processing, and linen yarn which had undergone wet spinning. They also formed part of dyeworks (Fig 86). The size and number of storeys of drying rooms varied, their floor area being determined by the number of boilers on the ground floor, usually

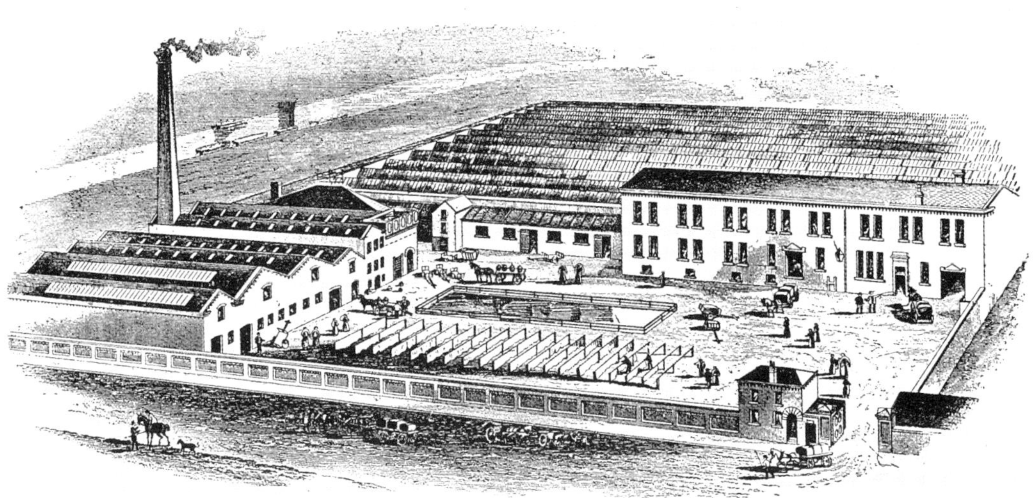

Fig 77 Hunslet Linen Works, Hunslet (Calvert 1910, 242).

Fig 78 Boiler house with drying floor over, attached to the beam-engine house of the multi-storeyed mill at Calder Bank Mills, Dewsbury (30).

a

b

Fig 79 Perforated cast-iron drying floors over boiler houses: a) Bridge Street Mill, Slaithwaite (122); b) Glasshouses Mill, High and Low Bishopside (55).

between one and three, but, as at Manningham Mills, Manningham (93), as many as ten. Boiler houses normally had one or two storeys of drying rooms over them, as at Calder Bank Mills, Dewsbury (30) (Fig 78), and Firth Street Mills, Huddersfield (62), but they were occasionally taller, of three storeys at Albion Mill, Batley (15) (Fig 44), and four at West House Mill, Fewston (40). Goods were sometimes loaded and unloaded through taking-in doors, again as at Albion Mill (15) and Firth Street Mills (62), but more commonly by a staircase which was either external or, more frequently, internal. Fenestration was not generous, in order to limit heat loss, and drying was usually effected by heat which rose through perforated floors and circulated around the rooms. Floors were sometimes of timber, the wool-drying floor over the boiler at Stone Bridge Mills (151) having in 1819 'a wooden trellis worked floor between boiler and racks on which the wool is laid to dry',[51] but, no doubt in order to minimise the fire risk, they were more usually of cast iron with perforated plates and grilles set on a framework of cast-iron beams and joists (Fig 79). It was not uncommon for roofs, as at Firth Street Mills (62), to be of cast iron too.

Woollen cloth, because it had to be stretched and dried to regain its size and shape after fulling, required special drying facilities, as did some silk cloths after dyeing or scouring. Silk was not a major component of the Yorkshire textile industry until the second half of the 19th century, and so much of the early evidence for drying cloth by heat relates to the woollen industry. Drying rooms over boilers were not long enough to take a length of cloth unfolded, although it is possible that some might have been able to take the cloth folded in the manner of the stove at a mill in Melksham, Wiltshire, set up in 1823 to hold 37 metres of cloth 'with four turns'.[52] However, architectural evidence in the form of distinctive long and narrow heated dryhouses on many woollen mill sites indicates that this was the customary method of drying cloth in Yorkshire at this time.

Heated cloth dryhouses were built mainly in the first half of the 19th century: the earliest may have been one at Bean Ing Mills, Leeds (85), first used in 1814, but there were other early examples at Armley Mills, Armley (7) (Fig 80), Stone Bridge Mills (151), and Cape Mills, Bramley (28) (Fig 141). Fewer were built in the second half of the 19th century when manufacturers increasingly adopted tentering machines instead, but post-1850 cloth dryhouses include those built at Calder Bank Mills (30) in 1861 (Fig 175) and at Moor End Mill, Dewsbury (33), in 1876. The length and number of storeys of all these dryhouses varied considerably, in so

Fig 80 Heated dryhouse built in the 1820s at Armley Mills, Armley (7).

doing reflecting the differing capacities and requirements of textile firms. Most, among them those at Aspley Mills (Fig 143) and Armley Mills (7) (Fig 80), were one or two storeys high, but others were taller: of three storeys at Bean Ing Mills (85) and Mill House Mill, Sowerby (128) (Fig 82), and of four storeys at Abbey Mills, Kirkstall (Fig 81). Lengths, generally between 40 metres and 80 metres, were sufficient for one or more pieces of cloth on each tenter, although cloth in the 22 metre long tenter at Green Grove Mills, Kirkburton (78), must have been folded. Widths were usually between 4 metres and 7 metres. Cloth dryhouses had distinctive external appearances: they were lit by small windows which, to conserve heat, were usually set in alternate bays, and they often had ventilators along the ridge of the roof (Figs 141, 143).

Details of the internal arrangement of cloth dryhouses are obscure because many have been altered and had their floors removed. Nevertheless, like drying rooms, they must have had slatted or perforated floors to assist the circulation of warm air. Two Leeds dryhouses noted in 1822,[53] as well as that at Mill House Mill (128) (Fig 82), had slatted timber floors, but perforated cast-iron floors were also installed. Thomas Cook of Dewsbury Mills, having reviewed the latest developments in the design and construction of dryhouses in Leeds in 1822, rejected the use of timber in favour of an 'iron floor'.[54] Cloth in need of drying must have been attached to tenters, which were frames with iron tenter hooks, several of which would have been set upright along each dryhouse floor. The roller mechanisms which survived at one end of the first and second floors of the dryhouse at Mill House Mill (128) (Fig 82), and the pair of vertical rollers set slightly in advance of them, were probably used to draw the pieces of cloth along the building prior to drying and to hold them in tension as they were attached to the tenters. A related feature occurs in the roof of the dryhouse at Armley Mills (7) (Fig 83), which has cast-iron trusses of unusual form with fixing points probably for tenters.

Heat for the actual drying process was provided in several ways. The dryhouse at Cape Mills (28) (Fig 141) had a chimney which may have served a stove or boiler, or have sent heat down flues along the centre of the building, an arrangement noted in some Leeds dryhouses in 1822,[55] but otherwise the absence of chimneys in dryhouses suggests that air was warmed by steam pipes fed from boilers elsewhere on mill sites.

A few mills had boiler houses with fireproof vaults over their boilers, and it seems evident at Manningham Mills (93) that the stove over the boiler house of Heaton Dyehouse, built in 1886 (Fig 174), was used as a heated chamber to dry silk cloth after dyeing.

Drying machines

The introduction of hydro-extractors and drying machines in the second half of the 19th century had a significant impact on the workings of textile mills,

Fig 81 Heated dryhouse at Abbey Mills, Kirkstall, Headingley cum Burley, built in the first quarter of the 19th century.

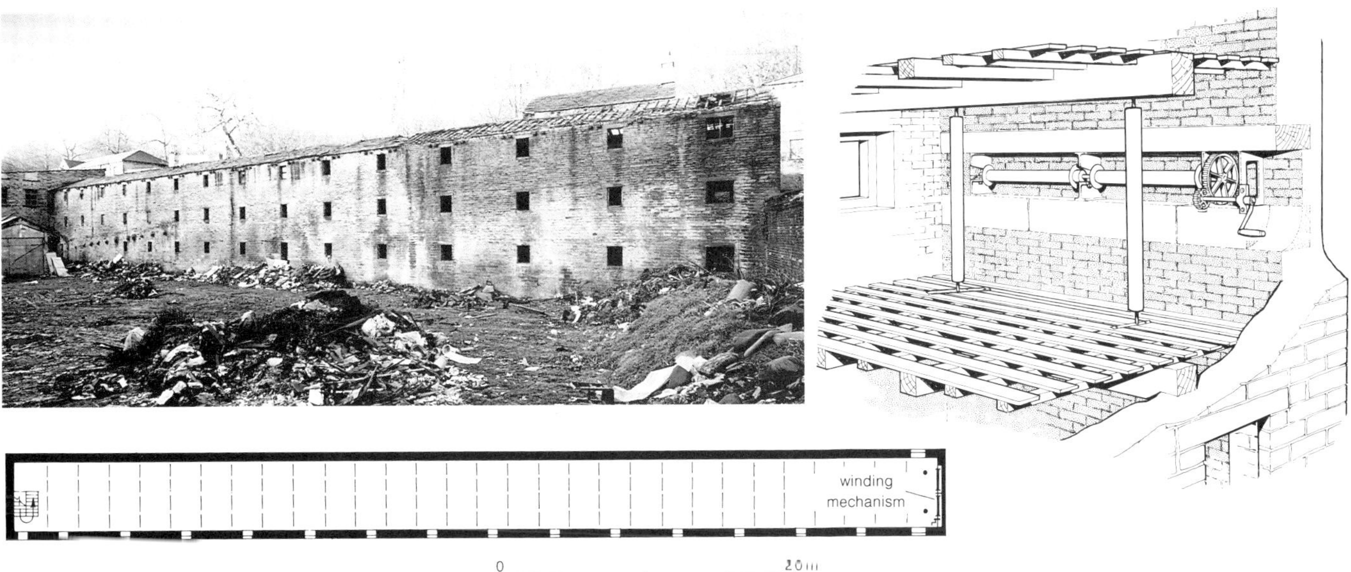

Fig 82 Heated dryhouse at Mill House Mill, Sowerby (128), including first-floor plan and detail of winding mechanism at one end.

speeding up the various drying processes and, if not rendering the earlier specialised buildings redundant, then at least enabling less distinctive buildings to be used to house the new machinery. Heated dryhouses and drying rooms over boilers were still built in the late 19th century, sometimes even in the early 20th century, clearly indicating that established methods of drying still continued despite the introduction of new machinery.

Yarn-drying machines were noted in the sales advertisements of 1869 and 1886 for the two flax-spinning mills of Hunslet Mills, Hunslet (67), and Marshall's Mill, Holbeck (57), those at the former mill evidently being housed in rooms in a single-storeyed building which is unlikely to have had any special characteristics. The use of machines to dry silk after it had been washed no doubt also reduced the need for specialised buildings for drying in silk mills. The greatest impact on the need for these buildings probably came in the second half of the 19th century with the introduction of the tentering machine which both dried and tentered woollen and silk cloth. Although expensive, the machines reduced labour costs and accelerated the finishing process, and could be accommodated in a lofty room of modest size. At West Vale Mills, Elland cum Greetland (39), one was placed in a former two-storeyed heated woollen-cloth dryhouse whose floor was removed to take it, while at Calder Bank Mills, Dewsbury (30), one was placed in its own building, the original, conventional woollen-cloth dryhouse of *c*1861 having by 1883 been superseded by a new 'Tentering Machine Place', also called a 'Tentering Stove', which was 15.4 metres by 7.3 metres. At Manningham Mills, Manningham (93), tentering machines in time superseded the Heaton Dyehouse stove in which silk cloth had once been dried.

Dyehouses

Dyehouses formed part of a number of individual textile mills, almost all of them woollen or silk mills, as well as of specialist dyeworks, and they were variously used to dye raw materials, generally wool, or yarn or cloth. Dyeing required space for dye vats and for the easy movement of dyewares and the materials being

Fig 83 Cast-iron roof trusses of heated dryhouse built in the 1820s at Armley Mills, Armley (7).

Fig 84 Dyehouse of c1872 at Calder Bank Mills, Dewsbury (30), showing the characteristic louvred ridge and open interior with dye vats. The attached boiler house with its water reservoir and chimney are early additions.

dyed, as well as height to allow fumes, steam and heat to dissipate. Demolition has removed the evidence of the form of the earliest dyehouses in Yorkshire, although documentary evidence implies that they were frequently small: one at Ramsden Mills, Linthwaite (87), measured about 11 metres by 4 metres in 1789, and others of 1820 at Crank Mill, Morley (102), and 1831 at Albion Mill, Batley (15), were only a little larger. That at Albion Mill (15) is known from an insurance plan of 1896 to have housed three dye vats and to have been one storey high with a 0.9 metre deep gap under the eaves to provide ventilation.[56] More detail is however known about surviving dyehouses of mid 19th-century and later date, which were typically tall buildings with undivided interiors open from ground to roof. Their roofs were generally of equal pitch with a raised and louvred central section to give the required ventilation; lighting was usually from the side walls, frequently supplemented by windows in the end walls and by skylights (Fig 84).

The size of dyehouses varied with the scale of work undertaken. The majority of mills which carried out their own dyeing had just one dyehouse, generally a single broad bay wide, sometimes two bays wide with a row of cast-iron columns supporting the intermediate valley gutter. Larger mills, including Armitage Bridge Mills, South Crosland (127), and Manningham Mills, Manningham (93), with their greater range of products, sometimes had a number of dyehouses, often several bays wide. In 1856 Armitage Bridge Mills (127) had blue, black and pattern dyehouses, kept separate to prevent any possible contamination of materials. Spec-

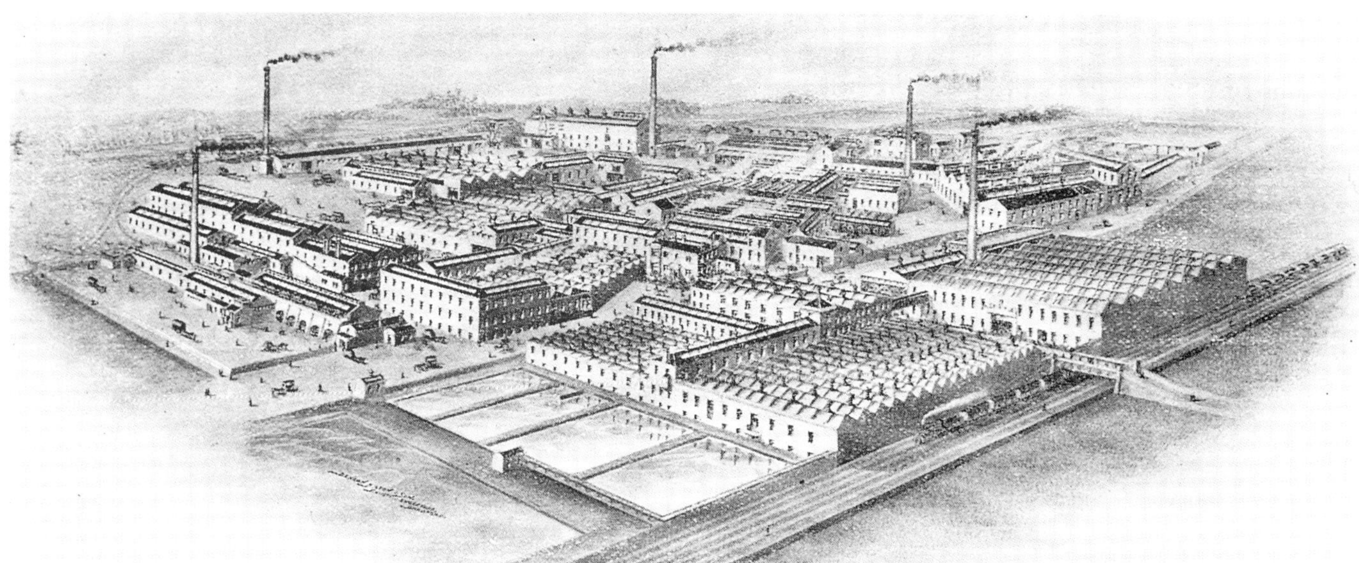

Fig 85 Bowling Dyeworks, Bowling (The Bowling Dye Works, The Warehouseman and Draper, *30 September 1899).*

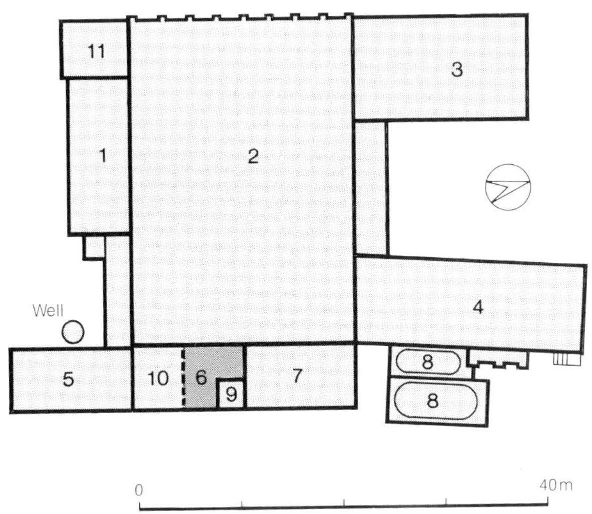

1	Cotton-warp dyehouse	7	Boiler house, drying room over
2	Pattern dyehouse	8	Boiler
3	Black dyehouse	9	Chimney
4	Press shop	10	Cottage
5	Grey room and office	11	Stable, blacksmiths' shop over
6	Engine house		

Fig 86 Bowling New Dyeworks, Bowling, from Sale Plan of 1852 (West Yorkshire Archive Service, Wakefield Headquarters: C325/15).

ialist dyeworks also ranged in size from small sites such as Jesse Street Dyeworks, Horton (59) (Fig 188), through others of medium size such as Bowling New Dyeworks (Fig 86), to the largest, Bowling Dyeworks and Oakwood Dyeworks, Bradford (Figs 85, 190). The scale and range of work at most of these dyeworks led to the construction of separate dyehouses, much as on the larger mill sites. Bowling New Dyeworks had cotton warp, black and pattern dyehouses in 1852 (Fig 86), and in 1888 Bowling Dyeworks had black, blue and pattern dyehouses. Pattern dyehouses dyed any shade of colour required.

Dyeing was a hot-water process, the heat for which was drawn either from the boiler plant which served the whole mill, from one which served just the dyehouse, or from furnaces which gave direct heat. The smaller dyehouses, including those at Albion Mill (15) of 1831 and at Cape Mills, Bramley (28), of *c*1901–2, used the mill boilers, as evidently did that at Alverthorpe Mills, Alverthorpe with Thornes (4) (Fig 177), but otherwise other calls on mill boilers, the situation of a dyehouse or the scale of dyeing resulted in there being specific dyehouse boilers. The pattern dyehouse at Armitage Bridge Mills (127) housed a wagon boiler in 1859, and at Calder Bank Mills, Dewsbury (30), a boiler house and chimney were added against one side of the dyehouse a short time after its construction, evidently replacing a furnace (Fig 84). Manningham Mills (93), the largest silk mill in Yorkshire, ultimately had three separate dyehouses, each the size of a small or medium-sized specialist dyehouse, and the latest, the Heaton Dyehouse, built in 1886, had seven intercommunicating dyehouse bays attached to a large boiler house with a stove over the boilers. Specialist dyeworks all had boiler houses, and the plan of Bowling New Dyeworks in 1852 (Fig 86) clearly indicates both an original boiler house and two further boilers added to meet the demands of expansion. Evidence for furnaces which provided direct heat is best given by the dyehouse at Albert Mills, Lockwood (89), as rebuilt in 1871. The architect's plans (Fig 87) show it to have been designed for eight dye vats set against one wall of the dyehouse, each vat individually heated from a lean-to firing place set along the outside of the building. The timber roof has trusses with queen struts, braces and collars, a form commonly used in dyehouses to support the ventilated structure set along the ridge.

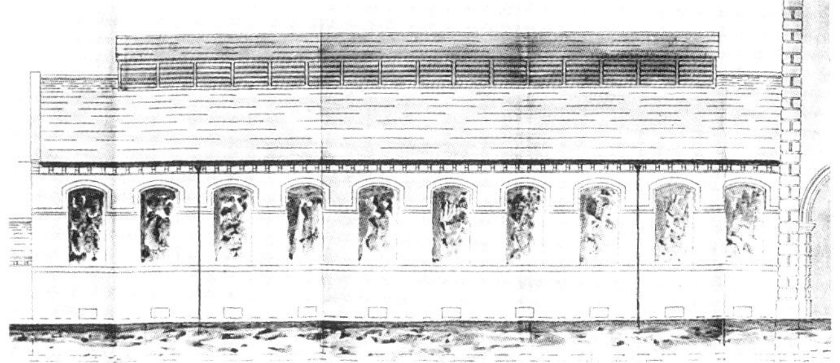

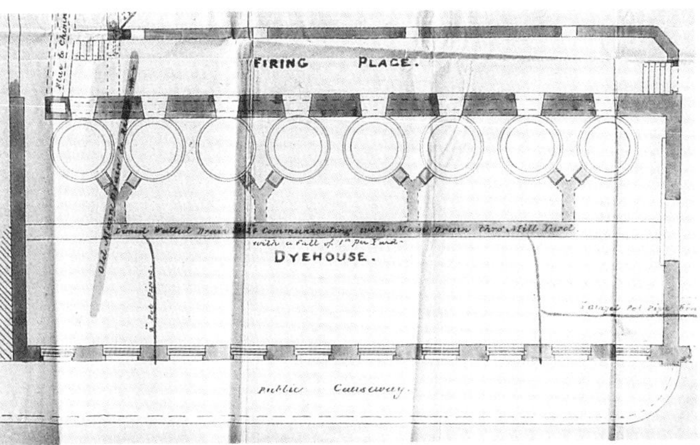

Fig 87 Architect's plan and elevation, dated 1871, for new dyehouse at Albert Mills, Lockwood (89) (West Yorkshire Archive Service, Kirklees: Lockwood Building Plans, no. 61).

Fig 88 Warehouse in St Mary's Place, Barnsley (14). The warehouse, newly built in 1821, overlooks an enclosed yard with a pedimented stable and coach house along one side.

Warehouses

The main function of warehouses was to store raw materials, finished goods, or materials at an intermediate stage in production, and they were built both on mill sites and away from them. Although the majority of warehouses were in fact on mill sites, far from every mill had one, particularly before the mid 19th century, since storage space was frequently contrived within multi-storeyed mills. Warehouses off-site were built for a variety of purposes, some serving the domestic industry (Fig 88), others built close to railheads by some of the larger mill-based manufacturers who often included showrooms in them for prospective purchasers (Figs 89, 276). Merchants, some of whom specialised in yarn or cloth, also built warehouses, among them those in Little Germany in Bradford[57] (Fig 277), as did the rag merchants who served the shoddy and mungo industry (Figs 196, 197).

Warehouses off mill sites, with the exception of some rag warehouses, were almost all large, whereas those on mill sites varied much more in size since they served firms with widely differing requirements. Warehouses were almost invariably multi-storeyed buildings, although when storage needs were limited, one floor of

Fig 89 Rag merchants' warehouses in Station Road, Batley.

Fig 90 Warehouse with cottages over, dated 1820, at Ellar Carr Mills, Bingley (21).

Fig 91 Warehouse of 1863 at Whetley Mills, Manningham (95).

accommodation sufficed. The warehouse at Ellar Carr Mill, Bingley (21), built in 1820, occupies the ground floor of a three-storeyed building whose upper floors were millworkers' cottages (Fig 90), whilst at Oak Mills, West Ardsley (144), the original 1906 warehouse was single storeyed. Warehouses two or three storeys high were not uncommon on many mill sites (Figs 92, 93), but on the largest sites they were frequently four or five storeys high and of considerable length (Figs 91, 98, 149, 185). Most mills had just a single warehouse, although occasionally there were separate warehouses divided by function. Bank Mills in Leeds (84) had individual warehouses for raw flax, for the long (line) and short (tow) fibres of flax (Fig 111), and for the spun yarn. Duplication was usually avoided by building on a sufficiently large scale, or by subdividing interiors. The warehouses at Armitage Bridge Mills, South Crosland (127), and Saltaire Mills, Shipley (116) (Fig 172), were both divided by spine walls which created distinct storage areas, and a similar arrangement was achieved in the 1806 warehouse at Marshall's Mill, Holbeck (57) (Fig 92), which had six separate storage areas, each with its own external taking-in door, but all also reached from a central staircase.

Warehouses reflected the architectural styles of their time. Many, particularly on mill sites, were plain or had the minimum of detailing, but others made a point of display. On mill sites this display was usually restricted to those warehouses which housed an office or an entrance to a mill, areas to which public attention was drawn, and for the same reason many of the off-site warehouses built by merchants and larger manufacturers were also elaborately treated. Detailing was at first

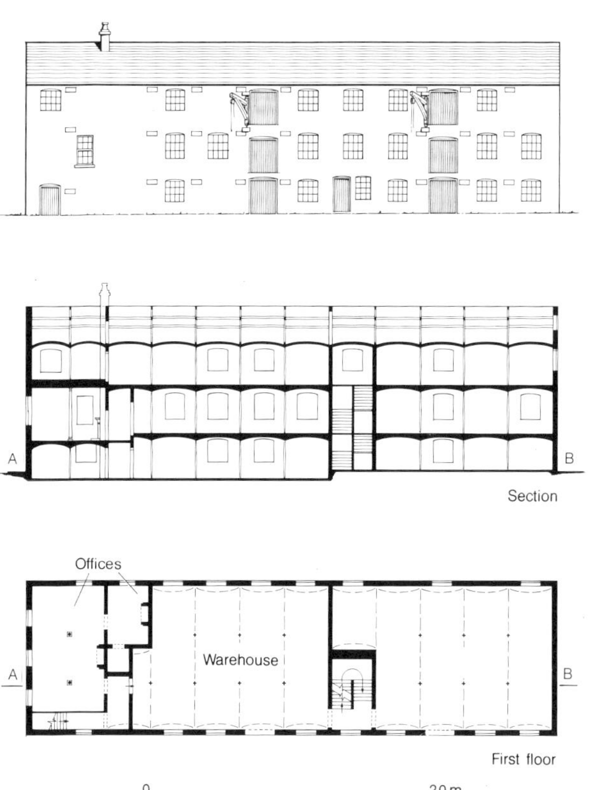

Fig 92 Warehouse and office of 1806 at Marshall's Mill, Holbeck (57), drawn as originally built. See Fig 101 for detailed plan of office.

Fig 93 Mid 19th-century warehouse at Mill House Mill, Sowerby (128).

Fig 96 Interior of 1863 warehouse at Whetley Mills, Manningham (93).

Fig 94 Warehouse and offices built c1865 at Cheapside Mills, Batley (18).

Fig 95 Warehouse of 1914 at Blakeridge Mills, Batley (16).

restrained, as the main warehouse at Hunslet Mills, Hunslet (67) (Fig 53), or one of those at Mill House Mill, Sowerby (128), with its central pediment and gable-end Venetian window (Fig 93), demonstrate. Italianate detailing, as on multi-storeyed mills, was sometimes restricted to the use of round-headed openings, rustication and moulded cornices, but it was sometimes lavishly used, as at Cheapside Mills, Batley (18) (Fig 94), and on some merchants' and manufacturers' warehouses (Figs 89, 276, 277). By the early 20th century this exuberance had been replaced by the more austere design of such warehouses as those at Spinkwell Mills, Dewsbury (34), and Blakeridge Mills, Batley (16) (Fig 95).

The internal structure of warehouses, like their external style, reflected that of contemporary multi-storeyed mills. Despite the value of the materials they housed, most were traditionally built with timber beams and floors (Fig 96), rather than being of fireproof construction. The earliest fireproof warehouses in Yorkshire were all part of flax-spinning mills in Leeds, the earliest almost certainly a building of 1802–3 at Benyons' Mill, Holbeck (56), usually recorded as just a heckling shop, but which by virtue of its size must also have been used as a warehouse (see p17 and Fig 152). Another was built in 1806 at Marshall's Mill (57) to house flax at a time when the French wars were interrupting supplies from the Baltic (Fig 92). A number of mid 19th-century warehouses were built with fireproof ground floors, including those at Bent Ley Mill, Meltham (97), in 1840, Albert Mills, Lockwood (89), in *c*1860, and Legrams Mill, Horton (60), in 1871, but otherwise it was not until the late 19th and early 20th centuries, and again on the sites of the largest mills

Fig 97 Packing room in warehouse at Devonshire Mills, Keighley (72), built in 1909–10.

Fig 98 Warehouse of 1871–3 at Manningham Mills, Manningham (93).

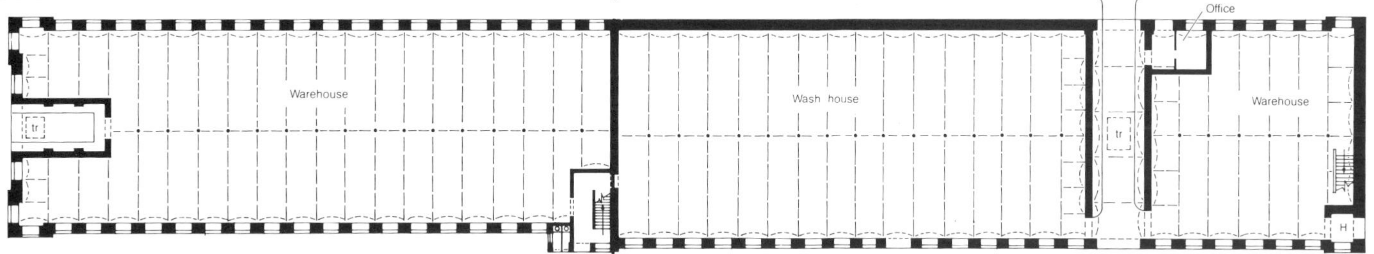

of the period, including Cumberland Works, Manningham (92) (Fig 185), Spinkwell Mills (34) and Manningham Mills, Manningham (93) (Fig 98), that fully fireproof warehouses were again constructed. Even the merchants' warehouses in Little Germany in Bradford were built with timber internal structures until the 20th century.[58]

Warehouses were usually well lit, both for the practical reason of access around floors fully used for storage (Fig 96) and because some of the tasks carried out in them, including the sorting of raw wool, rags or cloth, or the despatch of goods, required good natural light (Figs 97, 198). Storage was usually restricted to the main floors of warehouses, the roof space only occasionally being used. The top floors of a few warehouses, among them those at Manningham Mills (93) (Fig 98) and Spinkwell Mills (34), with their well-lit saw-tooth profile roofs, are likely to have been used for sorting or processing rather than for storage. Planning was influenced by the need to move goods into and out of warehouses, and it was often eased by the provision of tiers of taking-in doors, sometimes on the street front (Fig 140) but more frequently, for security reasons, from a controlled yard (Figs 91, 92). Goods were loaded and unloaded either by an externally mounted crane or from a crane beam projecting centrally over the taking-in doors. A less common alternative was the internal loading bay, found in the warehouse of *c*1816–17 at

Fig 99 Offices of 1870–2 at Alverthorpe Mills, Alverthorpe with Thornes (4).

a

b

d

c

*Fig 100 Offices:
a) Adjacent to Temple Mill at Marshall's Mill, Holbeck (57), 1842–3; b, c) Saltaire Mills, Shipley (116), 1850–3; d) Manningham Mills, Manningham (93), 1870; e) Hare Mill, Stansfield (134), 1907–11; f) Ardsley Mills, East Ardsley (35), shortly after 1915; g) Blakeridge Mills, Batley (16), 1923.*

e

f

g

Armitage Bridge Mills (127) (Fig 149), and in such later warehouses as that at Manningham Mills (93) of 1871–3 (Fig 98) or Law, Russell and Company's warehouse of 1874 in the Little Germany area of Bradford.[59] In warehouses without any of these features, goods are likely to have been man-handled up staircases, although some later buildings had internal hoists for their transport.

Offices and site security

Mills were both busy working environments and the centre of commercial transactions, and offices were frequently provided close to their main entrances to regulate the traffic which they generated. These offices were of two types, administrative offices which dealt with accounts, orders and other matters associated with the running of a business, and time offices which regulated access to a site. Administrative offices, whose size varied with that of the business they served, were often incorporated in other buildings: a few early mills, including Ponden Mill, Keighley (76) (Fig 42), had an office or counting house within a multi-storeyed mill, but they were more usually set within warehouses, close to the goods and materials they monitored. The offices built in 1806 at Marshall's Mill, Holbeck (57) (Fig 92), were on the first floor of a warehouse, as they were on a few other sites, including Armitage Bridge Mills, South Crosland (127) (Fig 149), but elsewhere, when they were within warehouses, they were usually on the ground floor where they were both more accessible and could be combined with a time office. This was so at Hunslet Mills, Hunslet (67) (Fig 102), Cheapside Mills, Batley (18) (Fig 94), and Spinkwell Mills, Dewsbury (34). Freestanding offices were also built, most of them serving the larger mills. A number, including Alverthorpe Mills, Alverthorpe with Thornes (4), combined an administrative office and a time office (Fig 99), but it was more usual for the two to be in separate buildings.

Administrative offices were built in the styles of contemporary multi-storeyed mills. The earliest, among them those at Marshall's Mill (57) (Fig 92) and Hunslet Mills (67) (Fig 53), were externally undemonstrative, but a number of later ones, which were separate buildings and points of contact with the public, were more elaborate. The offices next to Temple Mill at Marshall's Mill (57), at Saltaire Mills, Shipley (116), and Manningham Mills, Manningham (93), were Egyptian or Italianate in style, whereas those of the later Hare Mill, Stansfield (134), Ardsley Mills, East Ardsley (35), and Blakeridge Mills, Batley (16), were Byzantine, Jacobean and Free Style (Fig 100a–g).

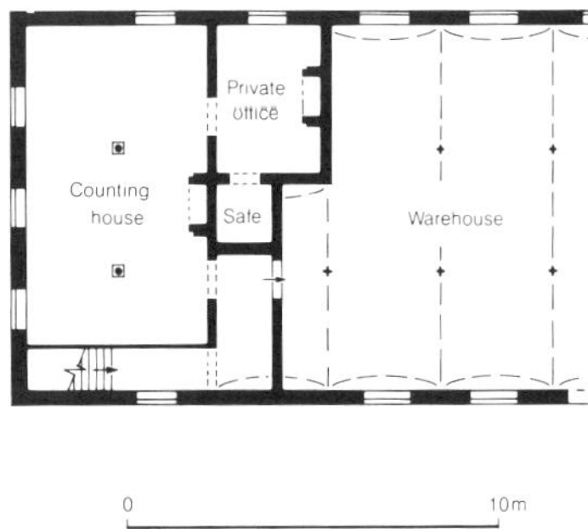

Fig 101 Offices on first floor of 1806 warehouse at Marshall's Mill, Holbeck (57).

Administrative offices varied in their number of rooms and in the decorative detail expended on them. Occasionally a single room sufficed, but it was not unusual for there to be two or more rooms. The offices on the first floor of the 1806 warehouse at Marshall's Mill (57) (Fig 101; see Fig 92 for situation) had two rooms, each with panelled doors, chimneypieces and moulded cornices; the larger room is likely to have been the counting house or clerks' office, the smaller, from which access was gained to the safe, the private office. The offices at Hunslet Mills (67) (Fig 102) had more rooms, namely a large counting house with elaborately carved woodwork and plasterwork and two private offices. The smaller, rear private office was the only room with a fireplace; the others must have been heated by steam pipes fed by the mill boilers. A counting house, private office and lavatory were the main rooms in the original office of 1860 at Whetley Mills, Manningham (95), and much the same accommodation, with the addition of rooms for account books and ledgers, was designed for Cape Mills, Bramley (28), in 1891 (Fig 103). Many of the later offices lacked ostentatious internal detail, but they often had elaborate, partly glazed, wooden partitions subdividing them. A development of the late 19th and early 20th centuries was the

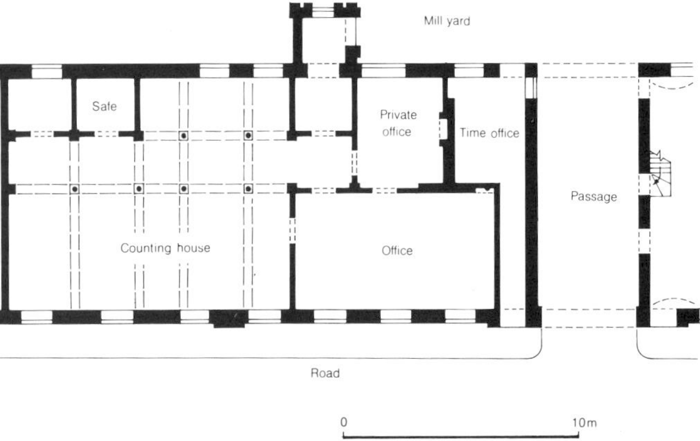

Fig 102 Plan of offices of 1840s at Hunslet Mills, Hunslet (67), and early 20th-century photograph of interior of counting house.

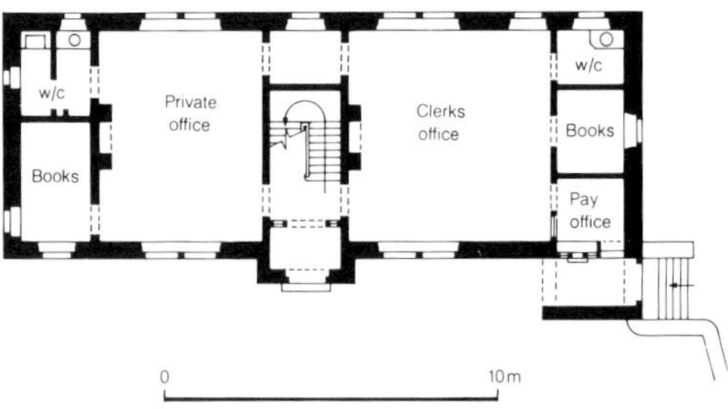

Fig 103 Offices at Cape Mills, Bramley (28), built in 1891 (redrawn from architects' plans).

need for the administrative offices of some of the larger companies, by now limited companies, to include board rooms. Existing offices sometimes sufficed, for example at Saltaire Mills (116) and Manningham Mills (93), but at others, such as Blakeridge Mills (16), they were included in newly built offices.

Time offices were rarely buildings of architectural pretension unless, as at Alverthorpe Mills (4) (Fig 99), they were combined with an administrative office. They were, of necessity, built next to the main entrance to mills, and generally controlled vehicular as well as pedestrian access, having doorways which could be used when the gates were closed. The time office at West Vale Mills, Elland cum Greetland (39), is in many ways typical, having an entrance passage, with lockable doors at each end, overlooked from a heated time-keeper's and watchman's office which also had good views on to the street and down the mill yard (Fig 104). A similar arrangement had been incorporated next to the main entrance to Hunslet Mills (67), where the time office and

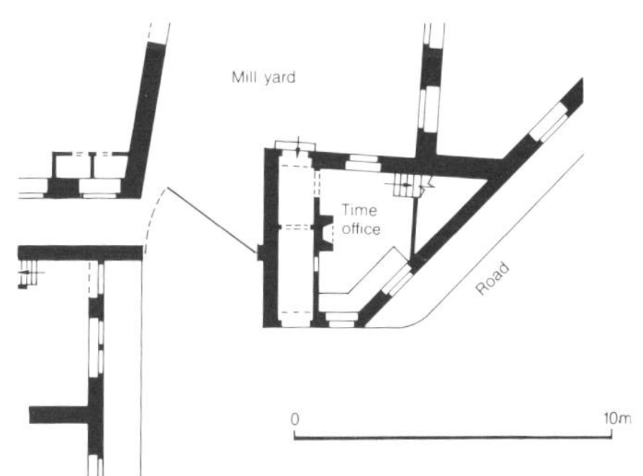

Fig 104 Time office at West Vale Mills, Elland cum Greetland (39).

Fig 105 Entrance and cottages of 1877 at Carlinghow Mills, Batley (17).

administrative office formed part of the same building (Fig 102). At Calder Bank Mills, Dewsbury (30), the two types of office were in separate buildings to either side of the main entrance, the time office and gates overlooked by the bay windows of the administrative offices (Fig 175). On large sites, more than one time office had to be provided; at Manningham Mills (93) there were several, each controlling a different building or part of the site.

Perimeter walls and entrances controlled from time offices provided adequate security on most textile mill sites, but on a few this was reinforced outside working hours by on-site housing provided for night-watchmen and other workers. At Carlinghow Mills, Batley (17), the entrance block built in 1877 controlled both day-time and night-time entry, since its ground-floor passage was flanked on one side by a time office and on the other by a cottage which may have housed a night-watchman (Fig 105). Try Mills, Manningham (94), had a cottage in the mill yard (Fig 160), whereas at Whetley Mills (95) a more imposing foreman's house, built on the opposite side of the entrance to the time office, also assisted security (Fig 106). At an altogether different level, a house at North Dean Mill, Elland cum Greetland (36), originally occupied by the most junior of the five founding partners of the mill, was built in 1878 within the curtilage of the site (Fig 107). It included a time office, and its situation and plan, with access provided from the stair hall either into the mill yard or on to the street, was clearly intended to provide incidental security for the site outside working hours.

Fig 106 Foreman's house at Whetley Mills, Manningham (95).

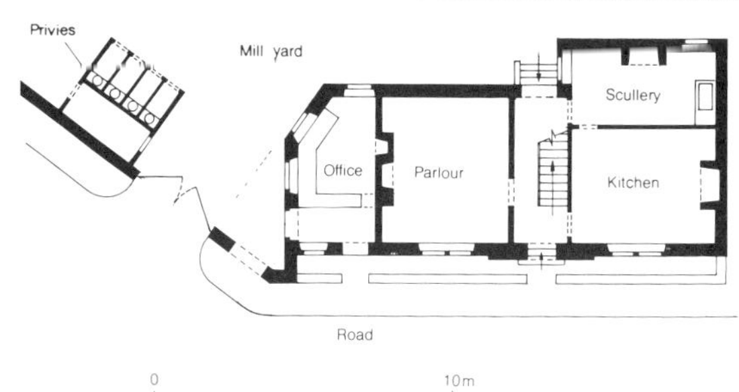

Fig 107 North Dean House, built in 1878 at North Dean Mills, Elland cum Greetland (36) (Metropolitan Borough of Calderdale, Planning Department: Greetland Building Plans, no. 160).

Gas plants

Candles and oil lamps were at first the only sources of artificial light in textile factories, but experiments at the end of the 18th and in the early 19th century demonstrated the commercial possibilities of coal gas, and factory demand was one of the factors which prompted the development of gas lighting.[60] Supplies of coal gas for mills came from two main sources, gas plants on mill sites, and the gas companies which established themselves in many towns — by 1826 few towns of more than 10,000 inhabitants were not served. It is of interest that H Lodge's mill in Sowerby Bridge, lit by gas in 1805, was the first textile mill in Britain to be so lit.[61] Many of the larger mills, among them Bean Ing Mills, Leeds (85), Marshall's Mill, Holbeck (57), Meltham Mills, Meltham (98), and Glasshouses Mill, High and Low Bishopside (55), built their own gas plants, as did a number of smaller and often rural mills such as Healey New Mill, Ossett (107), and Griffe Mill, Haworth (51). Many mills, particularly the rural ones, were unable to benefit from the supplies of the early gas companies, and those which did not have the capital and could not justify investment in a gas plant continued to use traditional methods of artificial lighting until alternatives became available.

Few gas plants on mill sites survived to be recorded, most having been demolished either when firms chose to buy their supplies more economically from a local gasworks, or when they adopted electric lighting in place of gas. At Marshall's Mill (57), for example, gas lighting was installed between 1810 and 1814, and gas houses and gasometers were erected on the site. The plant was rebuilt and extended later in the century, but by the time of the mill's sale in 1883 it had been demolished and the company relied on municipal supplies. No substantially complete gas plant was therefore recorded during this survey, but an indication of the buildings which formed them is provided by evidence from a number of sites, among the earliest of which is Bean Ing Mills (85), for which Boulton and Watt provided designs for gas installations in 1806 and 1810. This original gas plant was superseded, shortly before 1831, by a new gas house and a circular, iron-roofed gas holder house, 12.2 metres in diameter, which housed a tank about 9 metres in diameter and perhaps 7.6 metres high (Fig 108).[62] The gas plant at Glasshouses Mill (55), built in 1864, is known from a plan of *c*1900 (Fig 109) to have included a lime shed, retort house, purifying house, meter house and two circular gas holders, the larger built after 1883. Coal from which gas was produced, and which fired the retorts, came to the retort house directly from the coal depot on the site, and the gas was purified by being passed through lime in the purifying house. Meltham Mills had a long, single-storeyed gas retort house with a purifying room at one end, a chimney at the other, and a circular gas holder in front, all of late 19th-century date. An earlier gas plant at this mill had also supplied the nearby Bent Ley Mill, Meltham (97). The late 19th-century gas retort house at Woodlands Mill, Steeton with Eastburn (135), built to serve a single gas holder, is a tall rectangular building with a chimney at one corner.

Transport

Transport facilities were required for the carriage of such bulky items as raw materials, finished goods and fuel, and a number of mills were therefore sited to take advantage of water and rail installations. A few mills built next to canals, including the 1831 spinning mill at Woodhouse Mill, Langfield (83) (Fig 110), and the warehouse at Saltaire Mills, Shipley (116), built in 1850–3 (Fig 172), had tiers of taking-in doors from which barges could be loaded or unloaded. A warehouse of the late 1830s at Bank Mills, Leeds (84) (Fig 111), made similar use of the River Aire, which at that point formed part of the Aire and Calder Navigation. Coal may also have been delivered to some mills, including Belle Vue Mills, Skipton (119), and Waterloo Mills, Silsden (118), which stood next to canals. A number of mills also made direct use of railway facilities. A siding at Saltaire Mills (116) served a coal drop for its boiler house, and another was built at Glasshouses Mill, High and Low Bishopside (55), in 1862, the year the branch railway opened, to serve coal depots which were built to the specifications of the North Eastern Railway Company. Commercial mill traffic used the adjacent public railway station in Glasshouses, but the scale of manufacture of some mills justified the construction of sidings on

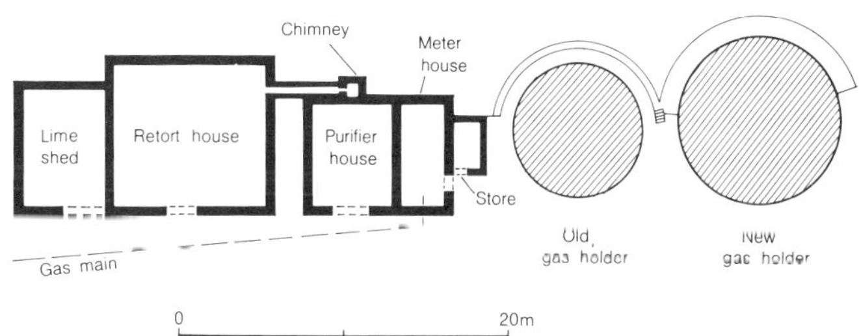

Fig 109 Gas plant at Glasshouses Mill, High and Low Bishopside (55), from plan of c1900.

Fig 108 Gas plant and gas holder house at Bean Ing Mills, Leeds (85).

Fig 110 Woodhouse Mill, Langfield (83), built in 1832 with taking-in doors to the Rochdale Canal.

Fig 111 Tow warehouse at Bank Mills, Leeds (84), built c1836–9 with taking-in doors to the Aire and Calder Navigation.

their sites. At Brookroyd Mills, Stainland (130), where they were run into the mill yard, they were probably opened in 1875, at the same time as the branch railway to Stainland which had been constructed largely through the influence of the mill's owner, Samuel Shaw. Sidings at Waterside Mill, Langfield (82), 'were run right into the warehouses, thus affording every facility for the direct receipt and despatch of large consignments'.[63]

Most textile businesses only used water or rail transport indirectly through the merchants and carriers who serviced their various needs. Until the introduction of the internal combustion engine, the horse and cart was the most convenient method of carriage, and self-sufficiency involved the provision of stables and cart sheds, sometimes combined in one building, sometimes in separate buildings. At Samuel Cooper's warehouse in Barnsley (14) (Fig 88), as well as at Cannon Mills, Horton (58) (Fig 112), the combined buildings are pedimented and recall the style of country-house stables, but it was more usual for these buildings to be utilitarian in style, like the range at Stoney Bank Mill, Wooldale (147) (Fig 113), or the smaller buildings on most other sites. Carts were sometimes housed in open-fronted sheds, and once petrol-driven vans and lorries were introduced, garages became a feature of mill sites, with hay lofts being superseded by petrol stores.

Fig 112 Stable block at Cannon Mills, Horton (58).

Fig 113 Cart shed at Stoney Bank Mill, Wooldale (147).

Structural aspects

The textile industry was in the vanguard of developments in building technology in the 18th and early 19th centuries, stimulating the construction of large multi-storeyed buildings and other specialised structures, and from the 1790s fostering the structural use of cast iron and the development of fire resistant and fireproof construction. From the 1840s, however, although mill design did not remain static, railway architecture and then the wider field of commercial and industrial buildings as a whole were greater influences on structural development. Since most structural components, especially columns, beams of different materials, roof trusses and the various types of fireproof construction, were used in more than one of the building types on mill sites, these are studied collectively below.

Structure

All the buildings constructed on textile mill sites in Yorkshire in the late 18th century had traditional internal structures with timber beams, joists and floorboards. Such buildings, in particular the multi-storeyed mills, were extremely susceptible to fire since combustible materials and floorboards saturated with lubricating oil could all too easily be ignited by candles, oil lamps or sparks from overheated bearings. Ponden Mill, Keighley (76), and Mill B at Marshall's Mill, Holbeck (57), for example, were among the textile mills in Yorkshire which were burnt down during the 1790s. The threat of fire, not only in mills but also in comparably large structures, prompted various investigations at this time into reducing the risk of total destruction or slowing the spread of fire. In 1782 the Navy Board was persuaded to sheath the wooden pillars and the underside of timber joists and floorboards with thin iron plates,[64] and James Watt, reacting to the fire in 1790 which destroyed Albion Mill, a steam-powered corn mill in London, proposed replacing floorboards with iron plates or covering exposed timber with a layer of plaster.[65] Iron plates were certainly used as a fire precaution in a number of early textile mills, including Boar's Head Mills at Darley Abbey in Derbyshire, and Lowerhouse Mill, Cheshire,[66] as well as in a few mills in Yorkshire. Benjamin Gott, having in 1804 discussed nailing them to the timber joists of mills, fixed them in 1807 to the roof timbers of part of Armley Mills, Armley (7),[67] as well as using them at another of his mills in Leeds, Bean Ing Mills (85), where an insurance policy of 1826 recorded the multi-storeyed mill as having 'floors covered with sheet iron'.[68]

Far more effective methods of reducing the risk of fire than just using sheet iron were developed during the 1790s. William Strutt, at two cotton mills and a warehouse built in Derbyshire between 1792 and 1795, retained the use of timber beams but supported them on cast-iron columns, and replaced the joists and floorboards with segmental brick arches. The arches sprang from skewbacks encased in sheet iron, and the exposed undersides of the beams were plastered to make them flame resistant.[69] A more radical departure from established building practice came shortly afterwards with Marshall, Benyon and Bage's Ditherington Mill at Shrewsbury, Shropshire,[70] which was built in 1796–7 to the design of Charles Bage and had cast-iron, not timber, beams supported by cast-iron columns and carrying segmental brick arches. Bage, in partnership with the Benyon brothers, repeated this basic iron-framed structure in Yorkshire's first fireproof textile mill, Benyons' Mill, Holbeck (56), which was built in 1802–3, and this type of construction, with changes particularly to the width and shape of the cast-iron beams, established itself as the principal type of fireproof structure among mill buildings in the county for much of the 19th century.[71] The cast-iron beams at Benyons' Mill (56), which had an inverted-T section with parallel flanges, became the established form in most fireproof mill buildings until the 1830s,[72] being used in buildings such as Armley Mills (7) of 1805–7 (Fig 114), the 1806 warehouse at Marshall's Mill (57) (Fig 92) and Old Lane Mill, Northowram (105) of 1825–8.

Fig 114 Fireproof interior of 1805–7 mill at Armley Mills, Armley (7).

Fig 115 The fireproof interior of Healey New Mill, Ossett (107), built in 1826–7, with cast-iron beams and joists supporting stone flags.

Experimentation was not stifled, however. At Marshall's Mill (57), the heated dryhouse or stove built between 1806 and 1817 had an unusual internal cast-iron frame which comprised a longitudinal vertical plate to which T-sectioned joists were bolted.[73] More significant was a small group of multi-storeyed mills built in the 1820s and early 1830s, including Healey New Mill, Ossett (107) (Fig 115), Carlinghow Mills, Batley (17) (Fig 121a), and other sites,[74] which had stone-flagged floors supported by a framework of cast-iron beams and joists, the whole carried on cast-iron columns. This system of construction saved the cost and weight of brick arches, but it was adopted neither widely nor by any large mill, and throughout the mid and much of the late 19th century the brick vault was customary in fireproof mill buildings. At Saltaire Mills, Shipley (116), an attempt was made to reduce the weight of the arches by using hollow bricks, but this practice was not widely followed and normal bricks were used in such mills as Britannia Mills, Lockwood (90), and Globe Mills, Slaithwaite (123), of 1887. There were, however, developments in the design of cast-iron beams, and the 1830s saw the introduction of beams with parabolic-shaped top and bottom flanges. William Fairbairn, the Manchester engineer, played a significant part in disseminating the new beam form,[75] using it at Orrell's Mill in Stockport in 1834–5 and in Yorkshire over the engine house at Robinwood Mill, Todmorden and Walsden (140), at Hunslet Mills, Hunslet (67) (Fig 116), where his involvement seems probable, and at Saltaire Mills (116). During the second half of the 19th century, however, as in the mills and warehouses built between 1859 and

1884 at Belle Vue Mills, Skipton (119), parabolic beam flanges were often abandoned in favour of a return to parallel sides.

Throughout the 19th and early 20th centuries, despite the development of fireproof construction, many multi-storeyed buildings, including large mills such as Robinwood Mill (140) and Knowle Mill, Keighley (73), were still built with timber beams and joists supported by one or more rows of cast-iron columns. In the second half of the 19th century a few mills, among them Zetland Mill, Bradford (27), and Lowertown Mill, Haworth (52), made use of flitched beams – timber beams bolted together through a central steel plate. The late 19th and early 20th centuries nevertheless saw considerable changes in building construction, most of them related to fireproof structures and involving the use of concrete, steel, iron and brick in various combinations. A number of advances were pioneered by Lancashire mill builders, whose architects sought to create the maximum span to house ever-larger cotton-spinning mules, but these were adopted in only a few new buildings in Yorkshire. The substitution of materials and alterations in form were features of this later period. At Manningham Mills, Manningham (93), the mill and warehouse of 1871–3 each had cast-iron columns and beams supporting segmental arches of concrete rather than of brick (Fig 117). There is little evidence that multiple brick-arched ceilings, the subject of a patent in 1871 by the Lancashire architect and engineer, A H Stott senior, but already in use as a system before 1865,[76] were much used in Yorkshire. A later patent of 1885 by A H Stott and Sons, with four shallow arches per bay, was used by the firm at Scarr Bottom Mill, Meltham (99), built in 1887 (Fig 118a), but it was soon refined to three arches per bay, as employed by them at Hare Mill, Stansfield (134), built in 1907–11[77] (Fig 118b). In both mills, cast-iron columns support pairs of longitudinal beams, perhaps of rolled iron at Scarr Bottom Mill (99), but of steel at Hare Mill (134), which in turn support the transverse beams carrying the brick arches.

Spa Mills, Slaithwaite (124), built in 1906–7, had stilted concrete arches supported on steel beams and cast-iron columns (Fig 118c), but flat concrete ceilings with intermediate joists were far more common, the concrete beams usually encasing a steel beam. These steel beams were sometimes supported by cast-iron columns, the arrangement at Victoria Mills, Elland cum Greetland (37), of 1893 and the New Mill of 1919 at Carlinghow Mills (17) (Fig 118d), but it was increasingly in character in the early 20th century for steel stanchions to be used. In Mill 3 at Blakeridge Mills, Batley (16), built in 1912–13 (Fig 118e), the stanchions are not part of a fully steel-framed building since the outer walls are load bearing. The Twist Mill at Meltham Mills, Meltham (98), of 1927–8, however, has a full steel frame, the uprights around the outside being hidden by brickwork. The first reinforced-concrete building in Britain, a flour mill in Swansea, had been built in 1897–8,[78] and this type of structure was adopted for the construction of some mills almost immediately: the multi-storeyed mill at Bridge Street Mills, Slaithwaite

Fig 116 The fireproof interior of Hunslet Mills, Hunslet (67), built in 1838–40, with cast-iron beams and brick arches.

Fig 117 Manningham Mills, Manningham (93), showing the fireproof concrete arches and elaborate cast-iron columns of the multi-storeyed mill built in 1871–3.

a

b

c

d

Fig 118 Fireproof construction of late 19th and early 20th-century date: a) Scarr Bottom Mill, Meltham (99), 1887; b) Hare Mill, Stansfield (134), 1907–11; c) Spa Mills, Slaithwaite (124), 1906–7; d) Carlinghow Mills, Batley (17), 1919; e) Blakeridge Mills, Batley (16), 1912–13; f) Brookroyd Mills, Stainland (130), c1920.

e

f

(122), was built in 1903, and subsequent structures included the New Mill at Brookroyd Mills, Stainland (130), of *c*1920 (Fig 118f) and Ardsley Mills, East Ardsley (35), of 1912.

Posts, columns and stanchions

The internal support required by the cross beams of many mill buildings was usually provided by cast-iron columns, although timber, steel and concrete were all used as alternatives at one time or another. No late 18th-century mill building in Yorkshire was wider than 9.45 metres, and timber beams were able to span these interiors without intermediate support. Timber posts were used in warehouses in the 18th century, as well as in a few textile mills, both to attain greater width and to counter excessive floor loading, but there is no evidence of their contemporary use in any Yorkshire textile mill.

Cast-iron columns had been used in a few non-industrial buildings in the late 18th century,[79] but their development and use on a wider scale came with the development and dissemination of the cast-iron frame during and after the 1790s. A variety of shapes of column evolved, some of them cast in a form capable of supporting transmission shafting. The earliest, which had been employed by both Strutt and Bage in the 1790s (see p64), was cruciform in section with a slight entasis or mid-height expansion (Fig 119a). This shape was designed to resist buckling under compression, and Bage used columns of this type in Benyons' Mill, Holbeck (56), in 1802–3. Cruciform-sectioned columns were used as late as the early 1830s, but there was some development in the shape of the cross section during this period. The columns initially had a straightforward cross-shaped section, but in Mill C at Marshall's Mill, Holbeck (57), built in 1815–16, an unusual quatrefoil shape was used (Fig 119b), and in the 1820s and early 1830s, on sites such as Cape Mills, Bramley (28), the section usually consisted of a cylindrical core braced by four ribs (Fig 119c).

An early alternative to the cruciform section was the hollow cylindrical cast-iron column which was first used in 1799 at Salford Twist Mill, Greater Manchester, perhaps because steam was to be passed through some columns to heat the building.[80] Its earliest use in a Yorkshire textile mill, probably for the same reason, was at Armley Mills, Armley (7), in 1805–7, where the columns had moulded capitals and bases (Figs 114, 119d). This basic cylindrical shape, usually hollow but occasionally solid, became the commonest type in use in textile mills in the 19th and early 20th centuries, and was used in both fireproof and traditionally built structures. The simple, elegant, classical shape represented by the Armley Mills (7) columns persisted as a type (Fig 119e, f), but variants were quickly developed. One of the earliest, which was never common and continued in use only until the early 1830s, had a tall, octagonal plinth and a commensurately short shaft (Fig 119g). These columns, which were frequently cast with a bracket or other type of bolting head to carry line shafting, were quite slender. As such they were evidently not strong enough to support fireproof buildings, and they were restricted to traditionally built mills. Their elaborate form was no doubt found both unnecessary and expensive, and they were superseded by cylindrical columns with D-sectioned bolting heads, which were developed and introduced during the 1820s (Fig 119h–j), and by the more versatile square-sectioned bolting head, capable of supporting a transmission bracket on two or even four faces, which was introduced in the 1840s (Fig 119k–m). All these principal types of cylindrical column remained in use into the early 20th century. As Figure 119 shows, capitals were sometimes reinforced by ribs, and different types of top-plate were developed to spread structural loads. Columns were almost always cast plain, but a few mills, including Saltaire Mills, Shipley (116), Manningham Mills, Manningham (93), and Globe Mills, Slaithwaite (123), went to the expense of building with columns with decorative foliage capitals (Fig 119n–p; see also Fig 117).

Column forms were occasionally specific to an individual building type. Several early weaving sheds built between the late 1830s and early 1850s, for example, had columns with open heads through which the line shafting passed (Fig 120; see also Fig 70). The size of columns was often specifically related to their place in a building: column diameters in multi-storeyed mills and warehouses reduced as upper floors were reached. In storeyed buildings constructed with timber beams, columns were not infrequently linked together, floor to floor. In some of these buildings, cast-iron plates of various shapes were set between the capitals and bases of columns in order to avoid compressing the wood in between (Fig 119e, f and m). In buildings with cast-iron or steel beams, the columns were always linked together between floors, usually by means of a socket. These junctions were complicated because beams also usually joined together over columns, and castings had to reflect this. Details from two mills dating from the 1830s (Fig 121) show how this aspect of construction was achieved, and the same principle, though with changes of form, continued in use into the 20th century.

Cast-iron columns supported beams variously of timber, cast iron and steel, but structural developments in the early 20th century led to changes. Multi-storeyed mills in particular were built either with steel frames in

Fig 119 Cast-iron columns: a) Marshall's Mill, Holbeck (57), 1806; b) Marshall's Mill, Holbeck (57), 1815–16; c) Cape Mills, Bramley (28), c1830; d) Armley Mills, Armley (7), 1805–7; e) Robinwood Mill, Todmorden and Walsden (140), mid to late 1830s; f) Kebroyd Mill, Soyland (129), 1905–6; g) Albion Mill, Batley (15), 1831; h) Marshall's Mill, Holbeck (57), 1826–7; i) Glasshouses Mill, High and Low Bishopside (55), 1837; j) Oats Royd Mills, Midgley (101), 1863; k) Folly Hall

Mills, Huddersfield (63), 1844; l) Syke Ing Mill, Soothill (126), 1883; m) Knowle Mill, Keighley (73), 1926; n) Saltaire Mills, Shipley (116), 1850–3; o) Manningham Mills, Manningham (93), 1880s; p) Globe Mills, Slaithwaite (123), 1887–8.

Fig 120 Cast-iron columns with open heads: a) Waterside Mill, Langfield (82), c1840; b) Armitage Bridge Mills, South Crosland (127), 1840s; c) Belle Vue Mills, Skipton (119), 1852–4.

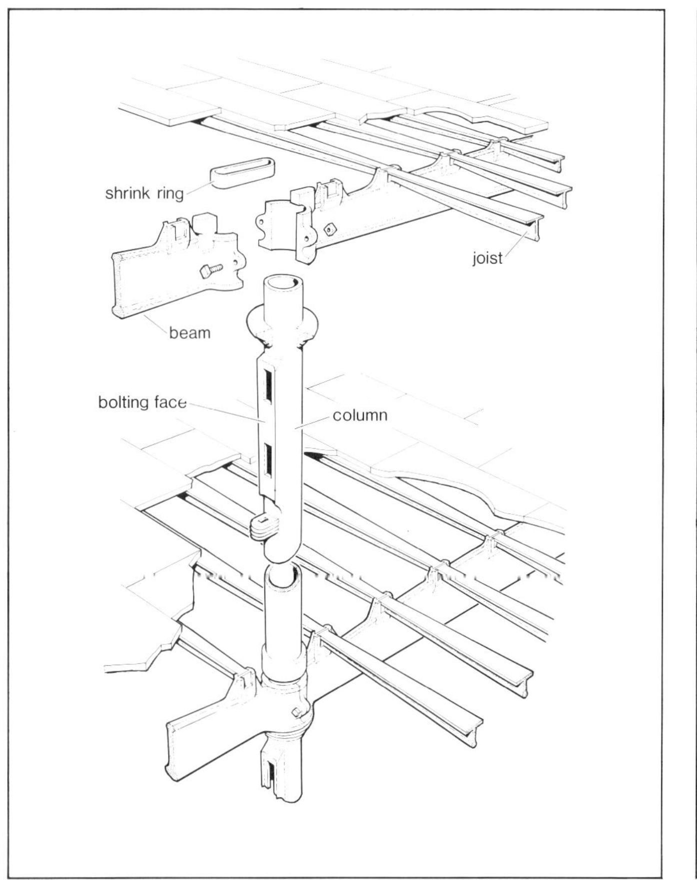

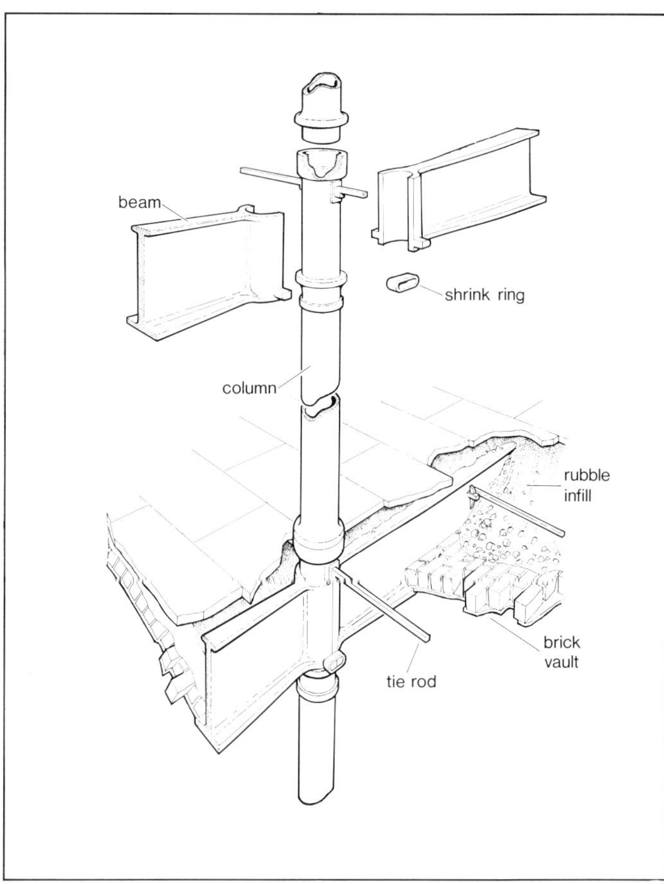

Fig 121 Diagrams showing the two main types of fireproof construction current during the early to mid 19th century, and the means of coupling cast-iron columns and beams: a) 1831 multi-storeyed mill at Carlinghow Mills, Batley (17); b) 1838–40 multi-storeyed mill at Hunslet Mills, Hunslet (67).

which steel stanchions replaced columns (Fig 118e), or with reinforced-concrete frames with an even more utilitarian appearance (Fig 118f).

Roofs

Conventional timber trusses were adequate for the first textile mill buildings, but as multi-storeyed mills and warehouses grew in size, and as new building types, particularly single-storeyed sheds, became ever more common, new types of truss, many incorporating iron, and later steel, components were developed. Existing types of truss continued in use where they were appropriate, sometimes adapted to span greater widths but new types were also created and employed.

King-post and queen-strut trusses were the two principal types of timber truss used to roof multi-storeyed mills in the late 18th century, and both continued in use in the 19th century for these mill buildings as well as for warehouses and other buildings. The king-post truss was the less commonly used of the two, since its central king post and struts rendered it unsatisfactory for any roof intended for storage. It was, therefore, used for roofs without this requirement, and was particularly favoured for multiple-span roofs, including those at Hunslet Mills, Hunslet (67) (Fig 122), and the 1895 mill at Cheapside Mills, Batley (18). The queen-strut truss was more versatile since the height of its collar could be raised and its posts set further away from the centre in order to create a more accessible and usable roof space. It was still used for some roofs which were not employed for storage, including a few multiple-span roofs, among them that at Oak Mills, West Ardsley (144), of 1906, but it was more frequently put to use to create good attic space (Fig 123).

Two main problems, the need to create fireproof trusses to complement the increasing number of fireproof mill structures, and the need to span ever wider buildings, faced roof designers in the 19th century. A number of solutions to these problems were tried, two of which involved the use either of cast iron or of a combination of cast and wrought iron, both at times in

Fig 122 Double-span roof at Hunslet Mills, Hunslet (67), built in 1838–40.

Fig 123 Queen-strut roof in 1863 warehouse at Whetley Mills, Manningham (95).

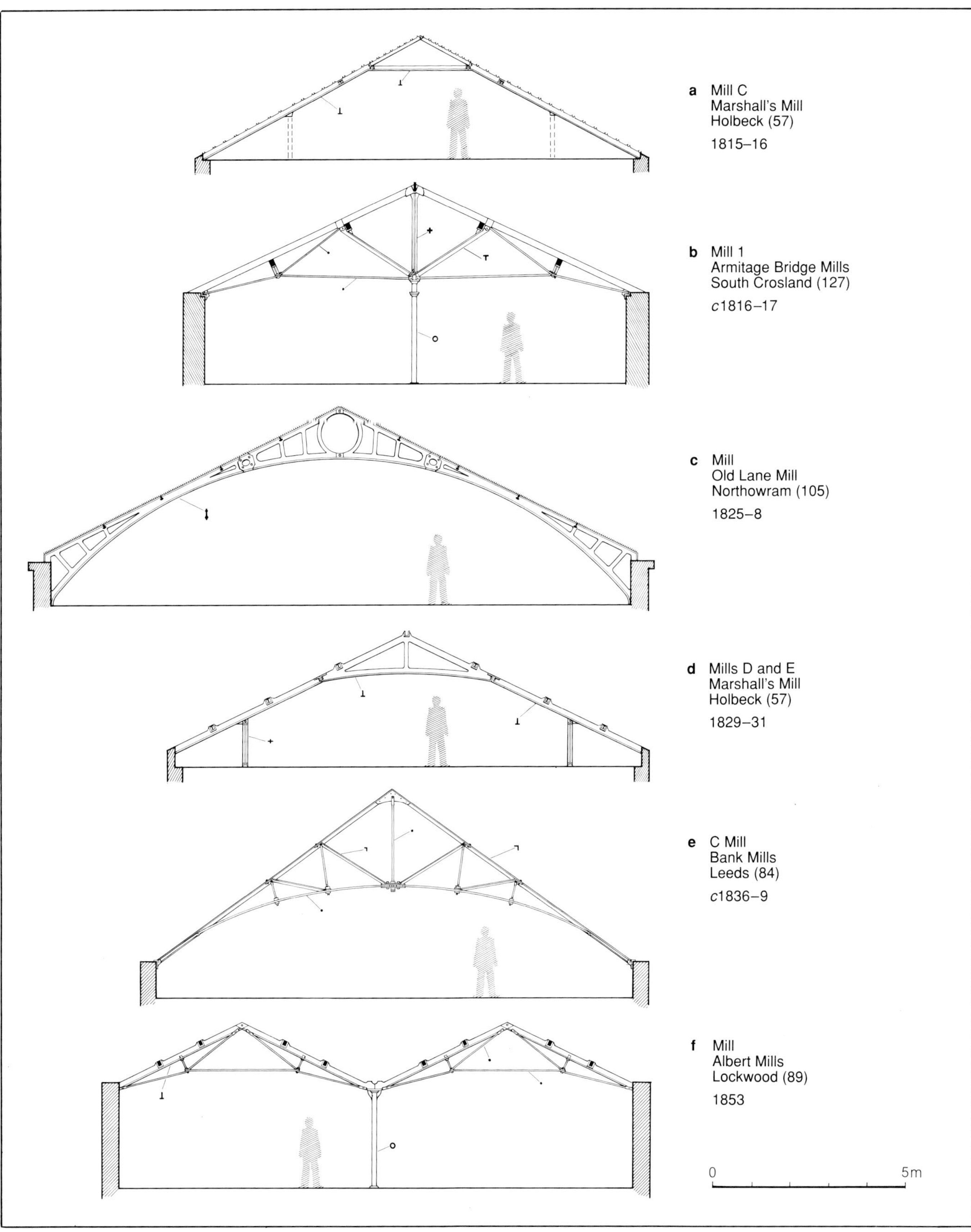
a Mill C
Marshall's Mill
Holbeck (57)
1815–16
b Mill 1
Armitage Bridge Mills
South Crosland (127)
c1816–17
c Mill
Old Lane Mill
Northowram (105)
1825–8
d Mills D and E
Marshall's Mill
Holbeck (57)
1829–31
e C Mill
Bank Mills
Leeds (84)
c1836–9
f Mill
Albert Mills
Lockwood (89)
1853
0
5m

conjunction with some timber members.[81] The shortest lived of these new roof types was the cast-iron roof, whose form was derived either from existing timber roofs or from the arched members of contemporary bridge building. The earliest surviving cast-iron mill roof in Yorkshire, that of 1815–16 on Mill C at Marshall's Mill, Holbeck (57) (Fig 124a), copies features of timber roofs in its diminished principals, collar and side posts, and the trusses of 1830–1 over Mills D and E on the same site (Fig 124d) seem to derive from a similar source although they also show some influence from arched trusses. Full, arched trusses were a more popular form of cast-iron roof: those over Old Lane Mill, Northowram (105), built in 1825–8, may be the earliest in Yorkshire (Fig 124c); others are known at Carlinghow Mills, Batley (17), of 1831–2, Folly Hall Mills, Huddersfield (63), of 1844, and Zetland Mill, Bradford (27), of 1850–1, as well as over a boiler house of 1863 at Oats Royd Mills, Midgley (101) (Fig 246). These trusses differ from each other in detail, although they were all cast in two or more parts which were bolted together through butt or lap joints.[82]

Cast-iron trusses, particularly the arched type, were heavy, expensive to construct, and suspect since they expanded when heated and thereby put stress on the walls of buildings. A more successful way of using cast iron was found to be in combination with wrought iron, the former material being used for members in compression, the latter for those in tension, with timber not infrequently used for principal rafters and purlins. The roof of the mechanics' shop at Marshall's Mill, built about 1817, was among the first to combine the two types of iron, using cast-iron principal rafters and wrought-iron tension rods,[83] as did Mill 1 at Armitage Bridge Mills, South Crosland (127), built *c*1816–17 with cast-iron struts, wrought-iron rods, and principal rafters and purlins of timber (Fig 124b). Both these trusses were triangulated in design, and although wrought and cast-iron members were combined in the arched trusses of C Mill at Bank Mills, Leeds (84), built *c*1836–9 (Fig 124e), it was the triangulated type which subsequently established itself as the norm, taking its lead from the roofs of railway station train sheds.[84] The roof at Saltaire Mills, Shipley (116) (Fig 125), built in 1850–3, has both wrought-iron rods and cast-iron struts, whereas at Albert Mills, Lockwood (89) (Fig 124f), the roof has just wrought-iron rods. Later mills, among them the New Mill at Dalton Mills, Keighley (71), of 1869, the 1871 warehouse and 1903 mill at Legrams Mill, Horton (60), and Cannon Mills, Horton (58), of 1880, had roofs similar to that at Saltaire Mills. Some of these composite trusses spanned the full width of mills, while others covered mills in two or three spans.

Fig 125 Roof over multi-storeyed mill at Saltaire Mills, Shipley (116), built 1850–3.

Fig 126 Extended queen-strut roof of 1850s at Cape Mills, Bramley (28).

Fig 127 Collar-truss roof dating from 1840s at Holmbridge Mill, Austonley (9).

Fig 124 Early and mid 19th-century iron roofs.

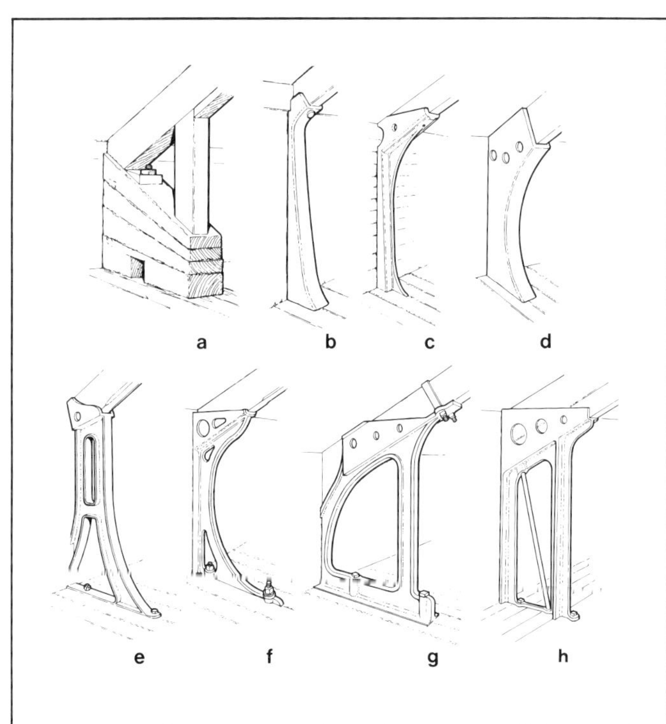

Fig 128 Roof trusses with raised feet: a) Washpit Mill, Wooldale (149), 1840; b) Oats Royd Mills, Midgley (101), 1855; c) Oats Royd Mills, Midgley (101), c1857; d) Oats Royd Mills, Midgley (101), 1863–4; e) Lower Providence Mill, Keighley (75), 1874–5; f) Ebor Mill, Haworth (50), 1870s; g) Oats Royd Mills, Midgley (101), 1870; h and photograph) Lower Providence Mill, Keighley (75), between 1884 and 1908.

Fig 129 Laminated timber-arched trusses of 1856 at Lumb Lane Mills, Manningham.

Iron was by no means the only way of spanning wider buildings. As noted earlier, timber roofs with king-post and queen-strut trusses continued in use into the 20th century, covering buildings either in a single span or in multiple spans. In some buildings, among them a multi-storeyed mill at Cape Mills, Bramley (28), the roof had extended queen-strut trusses (Fig 126). A few all-timber trusses with collars were used, including a roof of *c*1840 at Holmbridge Mill, Austonley (9) (Fig 127), but collars, sometimes supporting short king posts, far more frequently formed part of trusses which, to create more headroom, were raised up either on timber blocking pieces or on cast-iron brackets. Trusses with timber blocking pieces (Fig 128a) were first used in the 1820s or 1830s, but from the 1840s until the 1880s, after which the type was little used, cast-iron brackets were more common (Fig 128b–h). Clear working areas were also achieved in the mid 19th century by the use of roofs with laminated arched trusses (Fig 129).[85] In the early 20th century the Belfast roof, an elliptical truss with cross bracing, was occasionally used to create clear spans (Fig 130).

The single-storeyed shed was one of the building types for which a specialised roof structure was developed. A variety of types and shapes of north-light roof was tried until, from the mid 19th century onwards, the simple saw-tooth profile roof, called a 'shed roof', became more or less standard (see pp42–3). A few multi-storeyed mills and warehouses were built with similar roofs, and it is clear that their application to these buildings was considered at the same early date as to single-storeyed sheds. William Fairbairn, responsible for a new mill at Bean Ing Mills, Leeds (85), wrote to its builders in 1829: 'I shall immediately direct my attention to the roof and endeavour if possible to give you vertical lights with a northern aspect.'[86] Despite this correspondence, there is little evidence for the use of shed roofs on multi-storeyed mill buildings until the late 19th century. The multi-storeyed mill and warehouse built in 1871–3 at Manningham Mills, Manningham (93) (Fig 174), are among the earliest surviving examples. The shed-roof trusses in these multi-storeyed buildings were constructed with a variety of materials: timber at Lowertown Mill, Haworth (52), in 1895, angle iron at Becks Mill, Keighley (70), in 1907 (Fig 131), and reinforced concrete copying the form of timber trusses at the New Mill at Brookroyd Mills, Stainland (130), built *c*1920 (Fig 132).

Fig 130 Timber Belfast roof at Imperial Mills, Longwood (91), of c*1918–22.*

Fig 131 Angle-iron shed roof at Becks Mill, Keighley (70), of 1907.

Fig 132 Concrete shed roof of the New Mill at Brookroyd Mills, Stainland (130), built c*1920.*

3
The development of the textile mill complex

The Yorkshire textile mill – using the term to cover the complex as a whole – assumed a wide range of forms, some being no more than single buildings on small plots, others having many component buildings disposed over large areas. The number of different building types on a particular site corresponded generally to the range of operations undertaken there: the integrated woollen mill of *c*1860, for example, producing finished cloth from raw materials, often had a multi-storeyed mill, weaving sheds, warehouses, dyehouses, dryhouses and other buildings, while the cotton-spinning mill might have just a multi-storeyed mill and a warehouse. The mill complex thus reflects the way in which production was organised, and this chapter will examine the degree to which the different types of mill complex were associated with particular branches of the textile industry and the influences underlying change in this pattern.

Domestic production before 1770

By the mid 18th century, the Yorkshire textile industry, organised on a domestic basis, was both diverse and, in some areas, dominant in the local economy. Domestic production took two principal forms, known to historians as the domestic system and the putting-out system. Under the domestic system, small clothiers bought raw material, worked it into a finished product employing few people beyond their own families, and sold it in the market place. In the putting-out system the manufactur-

Fig 133 The woollen clothier taking his cloth to market (West Yorkshire Archive Service, Yorkshire Archaeological Society: MS 1000).

Fig 134 Eighteenth-century merchants' houses in Westgate, Wakefield. Behind them lay warehouses and finishing shops, replaced later by large mill buildings.

er had a co-ordinating role, buying raw material but sending it out to employees for preparatory processes, spinning and weaving. The family production of the domestic system can be contrasted, therefore, with the wage-labour method of the putting-out system.

There was a general correspondence between the two main branches of the Yorkshire industry – woollen and worsted – and the domestic and putting-out systems respectively. The typical figure in the woollen branch was the small clothier (Fig 133), that in the worsted branch the substantial stuff manufacturer. Both branches, however, showed great variety. Some woollen manufacturers were large employers of wage labour, with men like William Thomas of Wadsworth sending wool to Lancashire for spinning and, at his death in 1714, holding large stocks of finished woollen cloths.[1] In the worsted branch, wealthy manufacturers like Samuel Hill of Soyland, who in one period of three weeks in 1737 despatched nearly 1,000 cloths to various destinations in Europe, operated alongside a numerous body of independent weavers working only one or two looms.[2]

In both the woollen and worsted industries the finishing processes were largely treated as a separate business. The woollen clothier used public mills for fulling his cloth, and both woollen and worsted cloth was generally sold undyed and unfinished to a merchant. The merchant either sent it out for dyeing and dressing to specialist concerns, usually urban based, or undertook the work himself using wage labour in his own workshops.[3]

Flax and linen production was organised along different lines, dictated by the nature of the materials and processes. Initial retting and bleaching at both yarn and cloth stages involved an extremely long interval between first investment in raw materials and the sale of the finished article, and as a result only the largest operators could afford to follow the sequence through from beginning to end. There was, therefore, a common division between those who concentrated on preparing and spinning flax and those who undertook weaving and finishing linen. Both large and small-scale producers were engaged in the flax and linen industry, which was thus characterised by a mixture of the domestic and putting-out systems.[4]

Architectural evidence for the textile industry before 1770 reflects the way in which it was organised. Industrial premises – fulling and finishing mills for the woollen branch, dyeworks and finishing works for all branches – have not survived, later expansion having caused their demolition, but other buildings show a strong link with manufacturing and commerce. Manufacturers' and clothiers' houses, particularly those of the upper Calder valley, frequently incorporated a textile workshop at one end of the building.[5] Towns like Halifax, Wakefield and Leeds retain fine merchants' houses, mainly of 18th-century date, although the ranges of workshops and warehouses commonly sited at the rear of the dwellings have usually perished[6] (Fig 134). The supply of raw materials was conducted by

Fig 135 A wool warehouse in King Street, Wakefield, built in the early 19th century by a woolstapler.

woolstaplers who built large warehouses, similar perhaps to the slightly later examples surviving in Wakefield (Fig 135), and markets were held first in the open air but increasingly from the early 18th century in cloth halls (see pp168–9). The cloth halls provided a secure environment in which buyer could meet producer. Some halls had large trading areas, but others had numerous small rooms occupied by individual manufacturers. Most halls have been demolished, but the Halifax Piece Hall, built between 1775 and 1779, stands as a monument to 18th-century industry and commerce (Fig 136). The linen industry left no such evidence, Knaresborough having only an open market and Barnsley adopting a system of direct sales between manufacturer and merchant.[7]

The early phase of mill building, 1770–1825

The textile mill, by definition a building or complex employing mechanical power, had a limited role in the Yorkshire industry under the traditional system of domestic production. By the 1770s the woollen branch was served by over one hundred fulling mills and by frizing and raising mills involved in the finishing of woollen cloth, and in 1760 a silk-throwing mill was opened in Sheffield.[8] Otherwise production was home or workshop based, using hand power.

Mechanisation changed this picture dramatically. New machines for carding and spinning were rapidly

Fig 136 Halifax Piece Hall, opened in 1779.

applied to the Yorkshire industry after 1770. Hundreds of new mills, using animal, water and, later, steam power, were built to house the new machinery before the end of the century. Scribbling and carding engines were in use in the Yorkshire woollen industry in the mid 1770s; the first Yorkshire cotton mill, Low Mill, Keighley (74), was built in 1780; and 1787 saw both the opening of the first worsted-spinning mill, Low Mill, Addingham, and the patenting of flax-spinning machines which opened the way for the construction of new mills in this branch.[9] By 1800 the Yorkshire industry had grown in diversity, with the cotton branch in particular contributing an important new element, and had changed in nature through the expansion in mill working.

The builders of early mills came from a wide variety of backgrounds and had different motives for investment. Many woollen, worsted, and flax and linen mills were built by families already involved in the industry on a domestic basis. In the late 18th century some worsted manufacturers switched branches to build cotton mills, doubtless hoping for a share in the profits generated by the cotton boom of the period. Merchant capital was also important, especially in the woollen branch. Speculation was responsible for the construction of some mills, men like Richard Paley of Leeds seeing in industrial premises a good return on their capital.[10] Landowners too saw mills as a way of increasing the value of their estates, and men like the Earl of Dartmouth in the Colne valley and Morley, and Sir James Graham in Leeds built a number of woollen mills and installed tenants to run them. Partnerships were a further mechanism by which mills could be financed, and the skills of an experienced manufacturer were commonly combined with the capital of a speculator to provide the means to both build and run a new mill. In the woollen branch small clothiers formed joint-stock companies to finance the building of a 'company mill'. When capital was required for mill building, the growing banking system provided loans, as did family members, professional people and anyone with an eye for speculation. When John Marshall set up his new flax-spinning mill in Holbeck in 1791 he drew on relatives, neighbours and friends, and borrowed substantial sums from Beckett's Bank and a local merchant-manufacturer.[11]

The vast majority of early mills were built to provide mechanised working for the proprietor, tenant, partnership or company. In cases where mills were built or run by concerns already engaged in textiles, they comprised merely the mechanised aspect of businesses otherwise conducted by traditional hand-powered methods using a dispersed workforce. In the woollen branch, Mill House Mill, Sowerby (128), was built by the Rawsons, a manufacturing and merchanting family, to provide scribbling, carding and fulling services for their business, which employed weavers as far away as Rochdale, 13 miles distant. John Wrigley and Sons of Honley operated on a similar if less dispersed basis. Mechanised scribbling, carding, slubbing, milling and finishing were conducted at their Cocking Steps Mill, but, they stated to the 1834 Factories Inquiry Commission, 'we have all our spinning, weaving, burling and wool picking worked at our servants' own houses, in the neighbourhood . . . from 300 to 400 of them are in our employ'.[12]

Other mills were not part of wider concerns. Where branches had a strong base in domestic employment, there was some scope for specialised production to meet local demand. In Nidderdale, new flax-spinning mills were established to supply Knaresborough weaving firms, and some worsted-spinning mills had exactly the same function. Barkerend Mills, Bradford (26), for example, was built by the Garnett family to produce yarn for sale to local stuff manufacturers, and the family never became involved in weaving.

Yarn production could also be viable where a particular branch lacked a long-established local base. Flax and cotton-spinning mills were built in Leeds, for example, not to supply a deeply entrenched industry based in the immediate vicinity but as speculative ventures. In the absence of a well-developed local market for the yarn produced by these mills the expectation was doubtless that of selling to other areas initially and, potentially, of building up the supporting structure of weaving, dyeing and finishing that the better-established branches enjoyed. The Leeds cotton-spinning mills soon proved a failure, crucially not breaking into the Scottish market in the way that brought fortunes to some Manchester cotton spinners, but the flax mills found a strong demand for their yarn in Barnsley and further afield. Leeds and its hinterland never developed as a major weaving centre for either of these branches.[13]

All the mill types discussed so far were private mills, that is, they were built to process material owned by the proprietor or tenant. There was, however, one type of mill which was primarily intended to provide public services. This was the woollen scribbling, carding and fulling mill. The woollen industry had always depended on public fulling services and water-driven fulling mills had served the domestic clothier since the medieval period. When scribbling and carding were mechanised in the 1770s, the cost of building and equipping private mills to perform both these processes and fulling was beyond the means of most clothiers. Instead the system of public provision was continued and extended, and the public scribbling and fulling mill was the most common type of early woollen mill. Built by speculators, landlords, wealthy clothiers or companies, the mills were generally run by tenants who received raw wool from the clothiers for scribbling and carding and then fulled, scoured and tentered the cloth when it was returned to the mill.[14]

Just as the private mill was able to provide commission services at times, the public mill also developed a private role, for most of the men who ran the mills developed their own out-working businesses. Members of the Ramsden family of Ramsden Mills, Linthwaite (87), were variously described as clothiers, scribbling and fulling millers and woollen manufacturers, and it is clear that the mill was both open for public services and at the disposal of the family for use in its own manufacturing concerns. While the broad distinction between public and private mills remained valid, therefore, each type could in fact function differently.

Fig 138 Knox Mill, Hartwith cum Winsley (46), a water-powered flax-spinning mill built in the early 19th century.

The specialised mill complex

The vast majority of Yorkshire textile mills built in the period 1770–1825 specialised in just one or two stages in the production of finished cloth. The progress of mechanisation meant that the first cotton and flax mills were involved in carding and spinning, the first worsted mills in spinning, the first pure and waste-silk mills in throwing and spinning respectively, and the first woollen mills in scribbling, carding and fulling. These specialist functions are reflected in the simple form of most early mill complexes.

Fig 137 Gayle Mill, Hawes (47), a water-powered cotton-spinning mill built c1785.

Not all early mills were purpose built. There is documentary evidence for the conversion of existing buildings to new textile use, with corn mills in particular being subject to redevelopment, as at Glasshouses Mill, High and Low Bishopside (55). Fulling mills built before 1770, many of them on sites used for centuries, generally gained a wider function, scribbling and carding engines being sited in them to take advantage of the existing power system.[15] Where the new machinery could be worked by hand or animal power, the scale of building required was very small, and all sorts of property could be adapted for use.

Most mills built after 1770, however, required extensive new structures or were located on new sites. The similarity between the machines employed in the various textile branches encouraged the adoption of standard building types (see Chapter 2). Where the complex comprised just a multi-storeyed mill and perhaps attached or detached minor structures there was little difference between, say, a cotton-spinning mill like Gayle Mill, Hawes (47), a flax-spinning mill like Knox Mill, Hartwith cum Winsley (46), and a woollen scribbling, carding and fulling mill like Crank Mill, Morley (102) (Figs 137–9).

In other specialised mills, ancillary buildings were grouped around the main structure. Warehouses were sometimes modest in size, like that at Ellar Carr Mill,

Fig 139 Crank Mill, Morley (102), a steam-powered woollen mill built c1790 by Lord Dartmouth for scribbling, carding and fulling.

Bingley (21), built into the hillside and with a range of dwellings over (Fig 90), but others were large, especially those at urban spinning mills. At Marshall's Mill, Holbeck (57), John Marshall built a sizeable warehouse in 1806 to allow stockpiling of flax as an insurance against difficulties of supply (Fig 92). The warehouse range at Barkerend Mills, Bradford (26), a worsted-spinning mill built in 1815 and later, is set on the road frontage: the earliest stage may date from 1815, an originally five-storeyed addition is dated 1823, and further extensions were made later (Fig 140).

In the worsted and flax branches the preparatory stages of production – combing in the former, heckling and carding in the latter – were sometimes undertaken on mill sites. It was remarked in 1819 that worsted manufacturers 'who spin by machinery have wool combers at their mills, and they usually employ combing machines as well'.[16] No purpose-built combshop survives in recognisable form today, and the same is true of the hand-heckling shops which formed a part of some flax mills (see pp16–18).

In most branches of the textile industry, drying facilities were needed, for materials and cloth were processed with liquid and washed one or more times in the course of production. Traditional open-air methods of drying continued in use in the early mills. Joseph Rogerson, a Bramley scribbling and fulling miller, noted in his diary in March 1808 that he was 'flagging a place to dry wool on', and in February 1809 he was 'drying wool on our stones out of doors for the first time this year'.[17] Woollen cloth was traditionally stretched and dried on tenters in tenterfields, very commonly associated with early woollen mills (Fig 143). In some flax mills, wet yarn was dried in air drying houses using natural ventilation. Documentary references occur only for the largest mills, suggesting that it was only the major operators like Marshalls of Holbeck and the owners of West House Mill, Fewston (40), who could afford the capital investment required in their construction.

Fig 140 The warehouses at Barkerend Mills, Bradford (26), close the mill off from the public road. The arched entrance has a keystone with the date 1823.

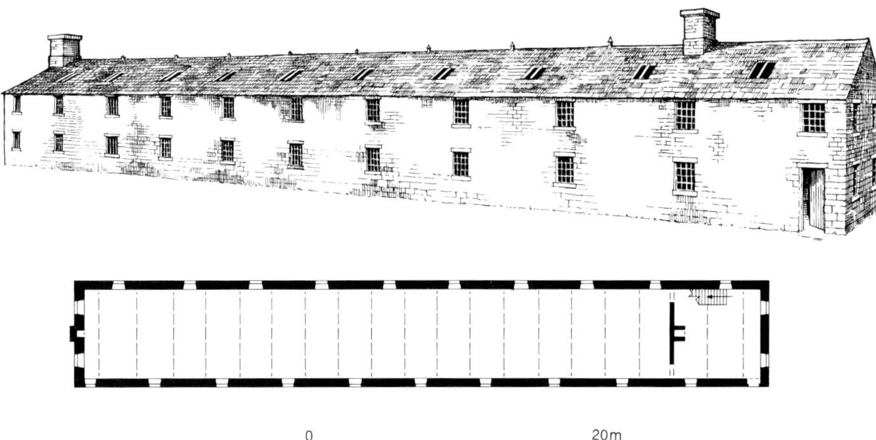

Fig 141 The early 19th-century heated cloth dryhouse at Cape Mills, Bramley (28), shows the typical small windows and long narrow plan of the building type. Heat here was probably provided by a furnace shared with a gas plant.

Improvements on natural methods of drying were made in Yorkshire in the early 19th century (see pp44–8). In some mills, raw material and yarn drying were conducted in rooms over a boiler utilising the rising warmth, and in some flax, woollen and silk mills there were specially constructed stoves or heated dry-houses. Drying in the finishing stage of production created the greatest problem in the woollen branch for, after fulling, the cloth had to be both dried and stretched, involving the full extension of the cloth. Heated cloth dryhouses were built in woollen mills from the early 19th century: that at Cape Mills, Bramley (28) (Fig 141), is a good example of average size and typical form. Open-air tentering continued in use in the woollen industry for a long time after the introduction of hot-air drying: blankets were tentered in the open at Dewsbury Mills even in the early 20th century.[18]

In the cotton and the flax and linen branches of the textile industry, cloth was generally finished by bleaching, sometimes followed by printing. These stages of production remained largely separate trades, and no specialised mill is known to have included them. In wool textiles, dyeing was the equivalent process, and here too this stage of production was generally treated as a separate trade, particularly in the worsted branch. Some woollen mills, however, had dyehouses: Rogerson's public scribbling and fulling mill in Bramley had one, for there are many references to it in his diary, and early insurance policies and other documents frequently list a dyehouse among the buildings of a woollen mill complex. In 1805, for example, Stone Bridge Mills, Wortley (151), had a dyehouse, and in 1821 a dyehouse with six dyeing pans formed part of Winker Green Mill, Armley (8). Their failure to survive implies that they were generally small buildings, replaced as the scale of production increased.

Early specialised mills varied, therefore, from single buildings to complexes of some size. Many early insurance policies record little other than the principal mill buildings on some sites: thus in 1792 Aireworth Mills, Keighley (69), comprised simply a 'cotton mill house, counting house and chambers communicating', with adjoining barn and stables, and at Holmbridge Mill, Austonley (9), only a 'water scribbling and fulling mill' is listed in a policy of 1800. At the other end of the scale were factories with many buildings, some with a general purpose or housing more than one operation, others designed specifically for a single process. The best examples of these complexes are the larger flax and woollen mills. By 1825 Marshall's Mill (57), for example, comprised three multi-storeyed mills, used mainly for spinning and heckling as well as two large warehouses, one incorporating an office, hand-heckling shops, a mechanics' shop, a dryhouse, a stove, and all the buildings associated with the generation of power (Fig 142). The public and private woollen mill, too, could present a wide range of structures, including the main mill for scribbling, carding and fulling, perhaps a small warehouse, a dyehouse and a cloth dryhouse, sometimes supplemented by a tenterfield. Such a complex is perfectly illustrated by an early view of Aspley Mills, Huddersfield (Fig 143). In an age of rapid technological and organisational change, long-term planning of mill complexes was always likely to be overtaken by innovation, and mills, especially the larger ones, tended to evolve in a piecemeal fashion as needs and space dictated. In 1843, for example, Marshall's Mill (57) was said to comprise 'an assemblage of structures of different sizes and ages, resembling a little town which has grown with the growth of its manufactures, not on any very symmetrical plan, but as convenience from time to time suggested'.[19]

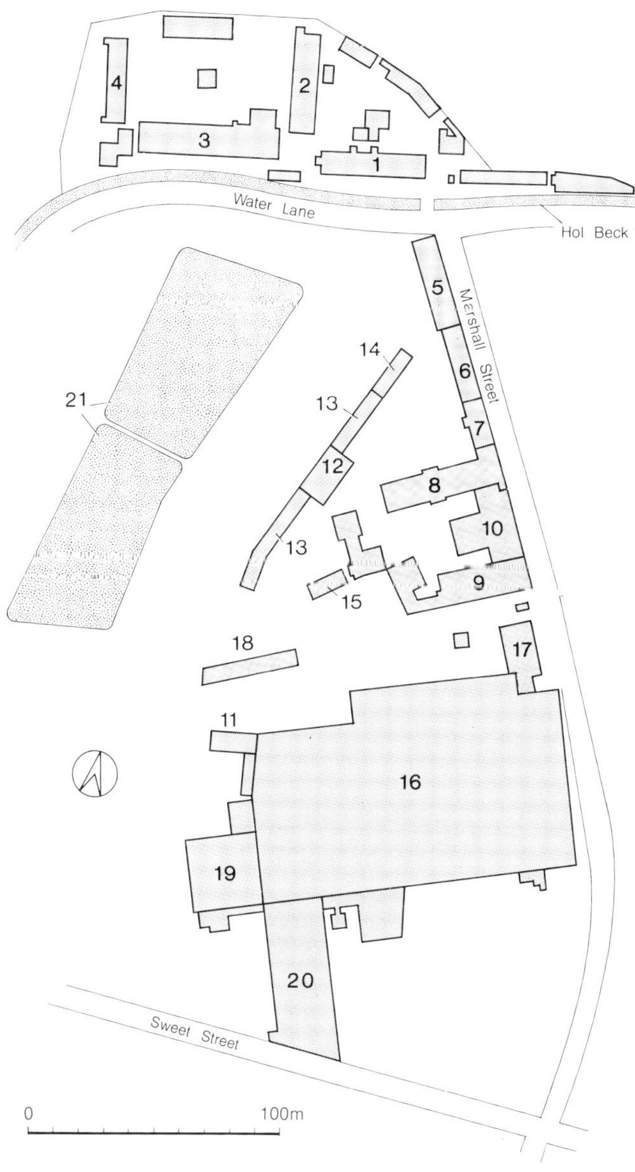

Fig 142 Marshall's Mill, Holbeck (57), showing the development of the complex. Pre-1825 buildings lie in the northern part of this extensive site.

- **1** Mill A 1791
- **2** Warehouse 1791
- **3** Mill B 1794–5, rebuilt 1796
- **4** Heckling shops 1796
- **5** Warehouse and office 1806
- **6;7** Stove; mechanics' shop, reeling room 1806–15
- **8** Mill C 1815–16
- **9** Mill D 1826–7
- **10** Mill E 1829–31
- **11** Infants' school 1832
- **12** Warehouse *c*1838
- **13** Wood sheds *c*1838
- **14** Smithy *c*1838
- **15** Joiners' shop *c*1838
- **16** Temple Mill 1838–41
- **17** Offices 1842–3
- **18** Stables
- **19** Steeping sheds after 1847
- **20** Reeling shed 1854–5
- **21** Reservoirs

Off-site working in the early textile industry

Mill working was complemented by a wide range of related activity outside the factory, organised either by millowners co-ordinating both aspects of production or by people performing specialist functions independently. The mechanisation of scribbling and carding in the 1770s put an early end to outworking in the preparatory stage of production in the cotton and woollen branches, but flax heckling and worsted combing continued after this date as hand-powered processes undertaken sometimes in mills but frequently by independent businesses in premises – warehouses in the case of flax dressing, combshops in worsted combing – of modest size (see pp16–18).

The fullest evidence for organisational change outside the mill relates to the weaving stage of production, traditionally undertaken on a domestic and family basis. The better-quality housing provided for textile workers from the late 18th century often included a loomshop (see pp19–20), showing the continued importance of family-based production, but loomshops housing a large number of looms were also built from the early 19th century. The size of these buildings demonstrates the adoption by employers of supervised wage-labour methods. Examples of non-factory loomshops are those in Chapel Street, Addingham (3) (Fig 144), built before 1817 by a cotton manufacturer, and in Ramsden Mill Lane, Golcar (43) (Fig 145), built *c*1840 and combining some domestic accommodation with two upper floors for weaving.

Certain specialist trades remained outside the mills. These principally concerned finishing, especially dyeing, bleaching, printing and calendering. It has been noted that some woollen mills had dyehouses, but in this and the other branches specialist dyeworks were common, located mainly in the towns which acted as the market centres of the industry. Leeds, in particular, had a large number of dyers, thirty-eight in 1822, forty-six in 1853.[20] The nature of dyeworks in this period is not known in detail. They probably comprised a grouping of single-storeyed buildings including dyehouses, a heating plant and offices. In 1833, slightly later than the period under review, the works of Thomas George of Leeds, dyer and finisher of worsted goods, included areas for crabbing (which prevented the wrinkling of the cloth), singeing, drying, rolling, scalding and 'quirking', as well as black, copperas and pattern dyehouses.[21]

Also important in the woollen branch were cloth finishers, again concentrated in towns like Leeds, where in 1822 there were sixty-one establishments engaged in the dressing of cloth.[22] Some of these cloth-dressing works were sizeable establishments. In 1841, Elmwood Mills, Leeds, had boiling and drawing places, a hand-raising place, a press shop, a dryhouse, a dry-beating place, a gig place, a brushing place and a cutting room, and in 1831 Joseph Armitage of Huddersfield, cloth finisher, had nine finishing machines, two raising gigs, three brushing mills, forty-three pairs of cropping shears and a 'woollen cloth drying stove, steam heated, cast iron pipes, iron tenters'.[23] Similar works served the industry before 1825. Bleachworks, needed for cotton and linen, were similar in form to dyeworks, with mainly single-storeyed buildings housing the vats, boiling pans and kettles and providing space for washing. In 1783, Craythorn Mill, used for bleaching, had bittering houses, a boilhouse and a sourhouse.[24] The need for large fields on which to lay out the material for bleaching meant that rural locations were favoured, although Leeds had extensive bleachfields just to the west of the built-up area in the mid 19th century, shown on the large-scale Ordnance Survey maps.

The integrated mill

Before 1825 the textile industry was dominated by organisational or geographical fragmentation: many mills and works were run by people with a limited range of interest in the industry – spinners, flax dressers, woolcombers, scribbling and fulling millers – or with a broad scope, divided between mill and non-mill working. There were, however, some experiments with the

Fig 143 Aspley Mills, Huddersfield. This letterhead view of the 1830s shows a typical early woollen mill complex, with multi-storeyed mill, heated dryhouse, tenterfield and a cluster of other buildings, some industrial, others apparently domestic (West Yorkshire Archive Service, Kirklees: KC57).

integration of all, or nearly all, processes on the same site, combining the newly mechanised processes and the hand-powered stages of production within the same mill complex. Most of these integrated mills were woollen mills, but a few of the largest flax and linen manufacturers also concentrated production within their mills.

The special association between integration and the woollen sector suggests a paradox. The woollen branch, generally characterised by small-scale operation and dominated by the domestic clothier, showed the tardiest mechanisation and had the most deeply entrenched domestic system. Nevertheless, it produced some of the most complex mills in the early period and was the first branch to achieve full factory production. Integrated woollen mills were in operation in the early 1790s, little more than a decade after the first use of the new scribbling and carding engines. Sowerby Bridge Mills, Warley (143), was insured as an integrated mill in 1792, and in the same year Benjamin Gott, a woollen merchant, began construction of Bean Ing Mills (85), in the west end of Leeds.

Lacking consistent documentary evidence, it is impossible to determine how many integrated woollen mills were working by 1825; they were certainly heavily outnumbered by specialised mills, but merely by their complex organisation they made a considerable impression on the industry. In 1806 fears were expressed that the traditional structure of the woollen branch would be eroded by 'the increasing habit of merchants concentrating in themselves the whole process of a manufactory',[25] and by 1819 it could be said that:

> the smaller manufacturers in Yorkshire were at first benefited by the introduction of machinery, but in a little time large capitalists began to engage in the woollen trade, and performing all the processes with their own machinery, they were enabled to work cheaper and undersell the smaller makers . . . Soon after 1800, the number of small manufacturers began rapidly to decrease, many of them being ruined by the change which had taken place, and compelled to become workmen in the factories of the large capitalists.[26]

Even if these reports exaggerated the immediate impact of the new integrated mills, they were correct in identifying them as the beginning of the end for the small clothier and the domestic system.

The new integrated mills were both private – that is, facilities were generally used exclusively by the proprietor – and, by the nature of their wide range of functions, large in scale. This scale is reflected in the valuations put upon integrated mills in insurance policies: Bean Ing Mills (85) (valued at over £15,000 in

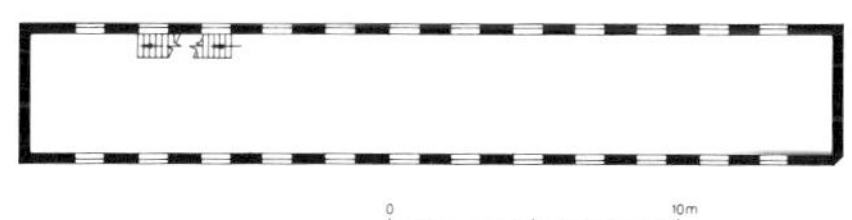

Fig 144 The loomshop in Chapel Street, Addingham (3), built shortly before 1817, accommodated sixty-two cotton handlooms in 1829. The plan shows the first floor as originally built (redrawn from plan in Thornes 1981, 20).

1800) and Sowerby Bridge Mills (143) (over £7,000 in 1797), for example, were, with a few Leeds cotton mills and a scatter of other establishments, among the most highly rated of contemporary factories.[27] It was, therefore, men of large capital, or men able to raise large sums through their creditworthiness, who alone could build integrated woollen mills. Evidence suggests that both merchant and manufacturing wealth financed the new mills; Gott, the builder of Bean Ing (85), was a merchant; the Greenup family of Sowerby Bridge Mills (143) were known as both manufacturers and merchants; and the Brookes of Armitage Bridge Mills, South Crosland (127), active in the textile industry since the 16th century, both co-ordinated manufacture and acted as merchants.

The motives for establishing integrated working varied according to the background of the builder. Benjamin Gott was a special case. With a purely mercantile career behind him, he probably saw the construction of Bean Ing Mills as the means of establishing a closer link between his merchanting activities and the way in which cloth was produced to satisfy his orders. Gott was never a manufacturer in the strict sense. Rather than becoming involved in the detailed running of his mill, he adopted an overall controlling role. The mill was run by five independent manufacturers, all tenants and all producing cloth to Gott's orders.

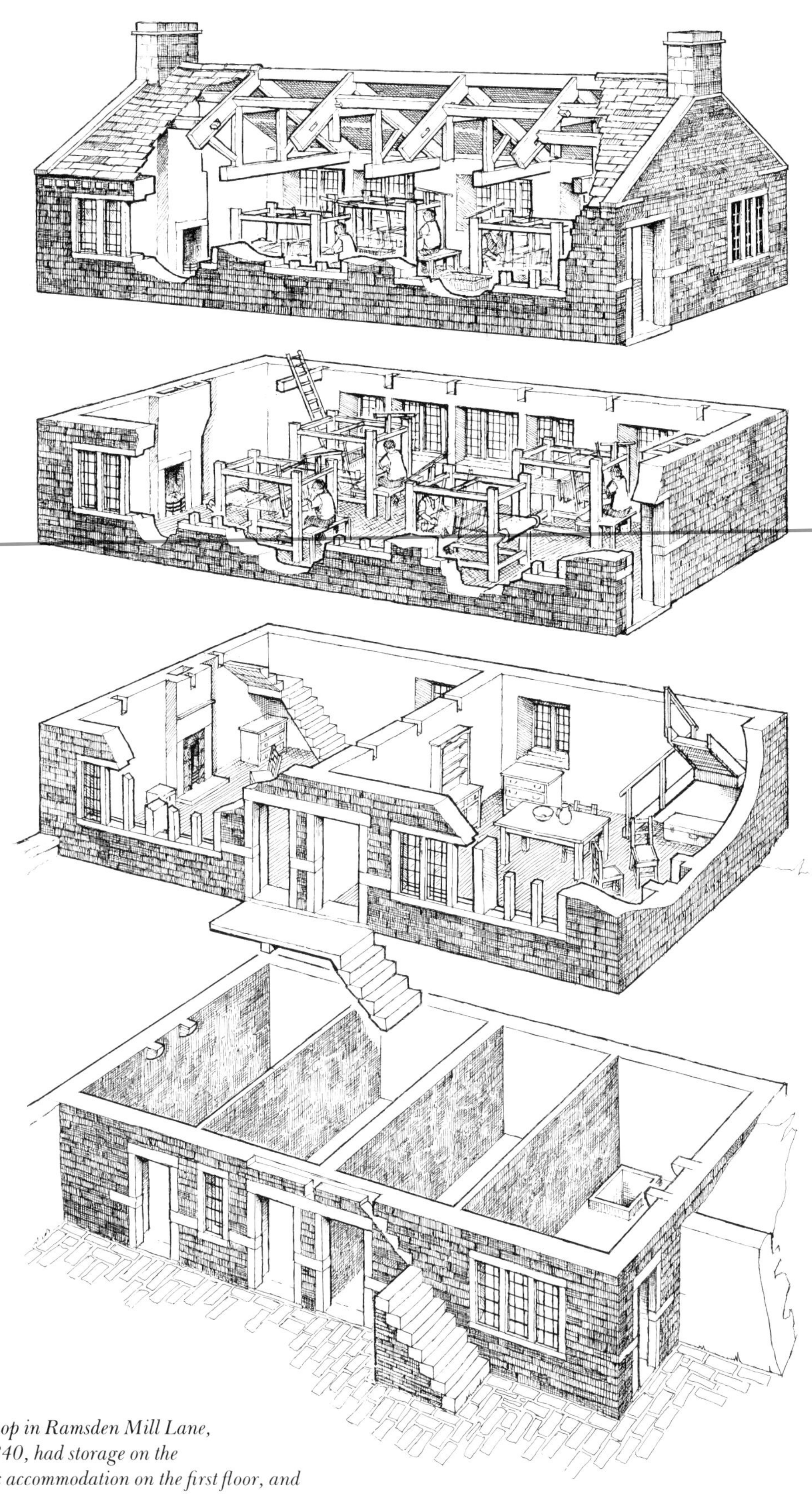

Fig 145 The loomshop in Ramsden Mill Lane, Golcar (43), built c1840, had storage on the ground floor, domestic accommodation on the first floor, and loomshops, with taking-in doors in the gable wall, on the two upper floors.

Gott remained a merchant first and foremost, and Bean Ing was probably envisaged as no more than the servant of his wider commercial interests.[28]

For others, direct control over manufacturing and the greater efficiency offered by integrated working were the reasons for the construction of a new mill. The Brooke family of Honley, with a centuries-old background in the woollen industry, had, by the early 19th century, a large manufacturing and merchanting business with cloth production divided between domestic employment on the putting-out system and cloth finishing at their mill in Honley. In the second decade of the century, however, the family completely restructured their business by purchasing a mill site at Armitage Bridge (127), about one mile from their old base, and concentrating there all the different aspects of production. Similarly, the Ellis family of Batley Carr, Dewsbury, outgrew the company mill in which they had been the dominant partners and built a new mill, Batley Carr Mills (29), next door to bring together a dispersed workforce. As early as 1795 it was suggested that integration would lead to increased productivity, and the savings in transport – a time-consuming and costly business when wool, yarn and cloth had to be carted from mill to cottage and back to the mill – were obvious.[29] The increasing use of more expensive foreign wool after 1770 made embezzlement more of a temptation to the domestic spinner and weaver and more of a loss for the manufacturer; a Huddersfield merchant and manufacturer stressed that he had established a weaving shop in his mills 'principally to prevent embezzlement, as we use Spanish wool. If we meet with men we can depend upon we prefer having them (the pieces) wove at their own houses.'[30] The clearest contemporary analysis of the benefits of integration is provided by Thomas Cook of Dewsbury Mills, who, considering the addition of a weaving shop to the mills, wrote in 1820 that 'it will be better and more independent of the workmen to have the weaving done here. It will also save the carrying out of the yarn and ensure the safety of property which is supposed to be a good deal purloined by sending it out to work.'[31]

In the context of the contemporary woollen industry, integrated woollen mills were big, diverse complexes, made up of many buildings and containing individual structures larger than any in the 'public' sector of the branch. Most of the buildings were used in a similar way to those in public mills, but the complex contained others which were not found in specialised mills. The layout of the integrated woollen mill was

Fig 146 Mill 1 at Armitage Bridge Mills, South Crosland (127), built c1816–17 as part of an integrated woollen mill, housed the powered processes of fulling on the ground floor and scribbling and carding on the upper floors. Waterwheels were housed in the low building in the foreground. Mill 2, of 1828–9, is in the background.

largely dictated by the functions of the different buildings and by the nature of the power involved. Whilst it is incorrect to think in terms of a consistent element of planning in these complexes, there is a clear clustering of those processes which required mechanical power and a loose grouping of other buildings housing the hand-powered or unpowered stages of production.

Figuratively, and often physically, at the heart of the integrated woollen mill was the main multi-storeyed mill building, almost invariably the largest single structure on the site. It contained all the processes which required power – scribbling, carding, fulling and, in some mills, finishing and dyewood grinding. There was a wide range of size in these buildings. The original mill at Batley Carr (29) was small and of comparable size to many public woollen mills. Others, however, were much bigger than this, the mills at Sowerby Bridge Mills (143) and Armitage Bridge Mills (127) being considerably larger than almost all public mills (Fig 146). The main structure at Bean Ing Mills (85) – twenty bays long and four and a half storeys high – was, as far as is known, the biggest structure in the woollen branch of the period. Associated with the main building was the power system, the mill either including space for, or being attached or adjacent to, an engine house or waterwheel chamber, as appropriate.

Grouped around the main mill were other buildings used for unpowered processes. Pre-1825 dyehouses have not survived, but in some mills they were clearly sizeable buildings. At Bean Ing (85), for example, there were two dyehouses covering an extensive area. Heated cloth dryhouses, similar to those in specialised woollen mills, were a common feature after their first recorded

Fig 147 The early 19th-century brick range at Stone Bridge Mills, Wortley (151), originally contained rooms for hand spinning.

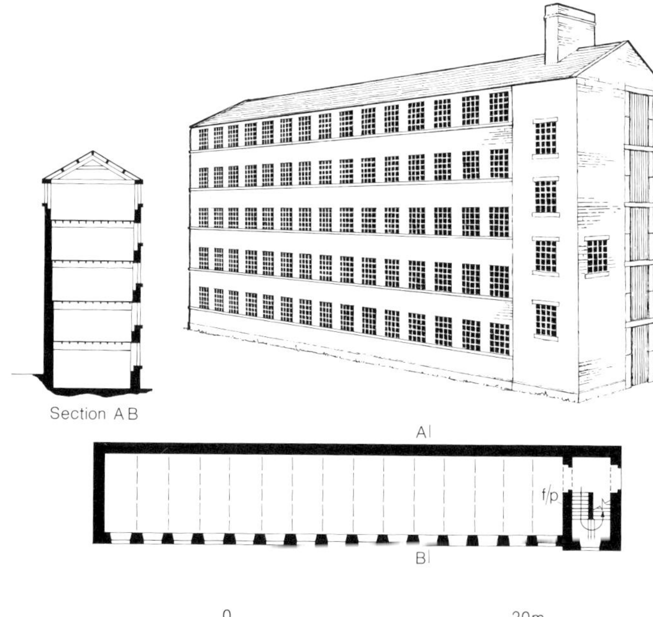

Fig 148 This loomshop at Armitage Bridge Mills, South Crosland (127), built c1830, gave five floors for handloom weaving; taking-in doors permitted easy movement of goods.

use at Bean Ing Mills (85) in 1814.[32] The size of cloth dryhouses varied, but few, perhaps, were as large as that at Bean Ing, three storeys high and of great length.

The inclusion of hand spinning and handloom weaving in integrated woollen mills represents the achievement of full factory production. Hand spinning on the jenny, in common use until the 1820s, required little in the way of special accommodation (see pp18–19). In some mills hand spinning was sited on the upper floors of the main mill building but spinning shops were also provided: at Sowerby Bridge Mills (143), a four-storeyed range may well have been built or mainly used for spinning, and a two-storeyed range at Stone Bridge Mills, Wortley (151), probably had the same function (Fig 147).

Handloom weaving, however, required special-purpose buildings. The design of factory loomshops is studied in Chapter 2, but considerations of space and site constriction influenced the form which they took within different complexes. On sites with no effective limit on space, loomshops were low but of great length; the larger of the two loomshops at Bean Ing (85) was over 100 metres long but of only two storeys. In other mills, however, space was limited, and shorter, taller loomshops were built; at Armitage Bridge Mills (127), for example, a five-storeyed loomshop was added *c*1830 (Fig 148). The date of this building illustrates the way in which handloom weaving persisted in the woollen branch.

Buildings housing the important finishing processes are not well represented in surviving structures. It has been noted that powered finishing could be located in the main mill building, but hand-powered machines were usually housed in separate ranges. At Bean Ing Mills (85), there were hot-pressing shops, glossing shops and a brushing mill in 1801. Other mills had raising and shearing rooms, often described just as 'cloth dressing rooms'. At Stone Bridge Mills (151) the press shop was a ground-floor room with a spinning floor over.

The integrated woollen mill commonly had a warehouse which provided the extensive storage capacity required by the larger manufacturers for both raw wool and finished cloth. At Armitage Bridge Mills (127) the warehouse, at the centre of the complex, was originally the largest building on the site (Fig 149). Benjamin Gott's storage requirements were large enough to demand the use of town-centre warehouses to supplement those within the Bean Ing Mills (85) complex. Some warehouses contained offices, but only Bean Ing is known to have had purpose-built offices; these had a near-circular plan and their siting in the main mill yard allowed a view over the principal buildings. In mills of all types and periods the siting of offices, which controlled access and provided security, was an important consideration in the planning of the complex. This is discussed in detail elsewhere (pp57–9).

The element of planning in integrated woollen mills is difficult to assess. As stated earlier, the main powered mill usually lay at the centre of the complex, with other buildings grouped around, but there is no evidence for the implementation of a widely recognised 'ideal' arrangement. Spinning and weaving shops were set together in some mills but apart in others; warehouses were linked with spinning shops and weaving shops in some mills but not in others; and large yards formed a conspicuous feature of some mills, especially Bean Ing, but not others (Figs 150, 151). The grouping of the first buildings around a yard at Bean Ing has been explained by the use of the enclosed space as a tenterfield, giving protection from theft.[33] A yard arrangement, whether approximately square as at Bean Ing (85) or elongated as at Sowerby Bridge Mills (143), had another advantage, however, for integration of processes involved a great deal of movement of goods from department to department. A generous space for the flow of traffic therefore eased congestion, even if the flow of processes was less than logically arranged.

The integrated woollen mill represented a new departure in terms of industrial organisation, certainly within the textile industry, for it dispensed entirely with the established system of outworking on the domestic or putting-out method. The development of integration has a significance on two counts. First, it was to provide

Fig 149 The warehouse of c1816–17 at Armitage Bridge Mills, South Crosland (127). At the extreme right of the photograph is part of the original range of hand-spinning and handloom-weaving shops.

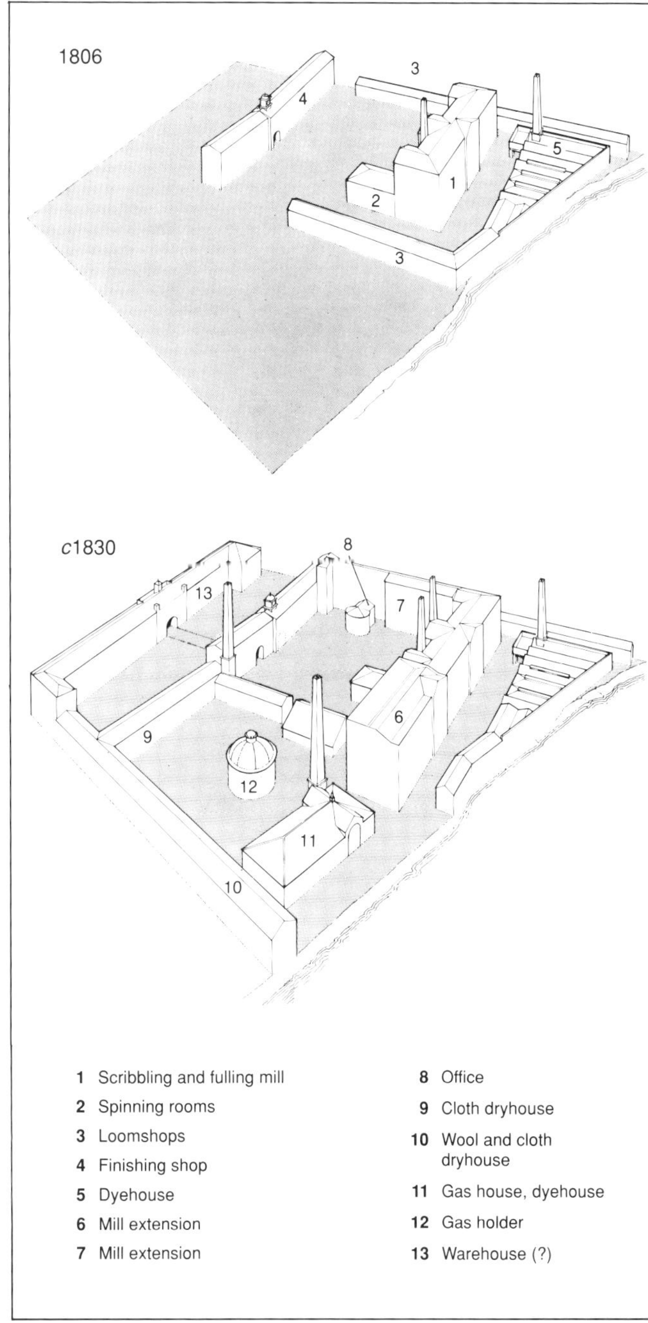

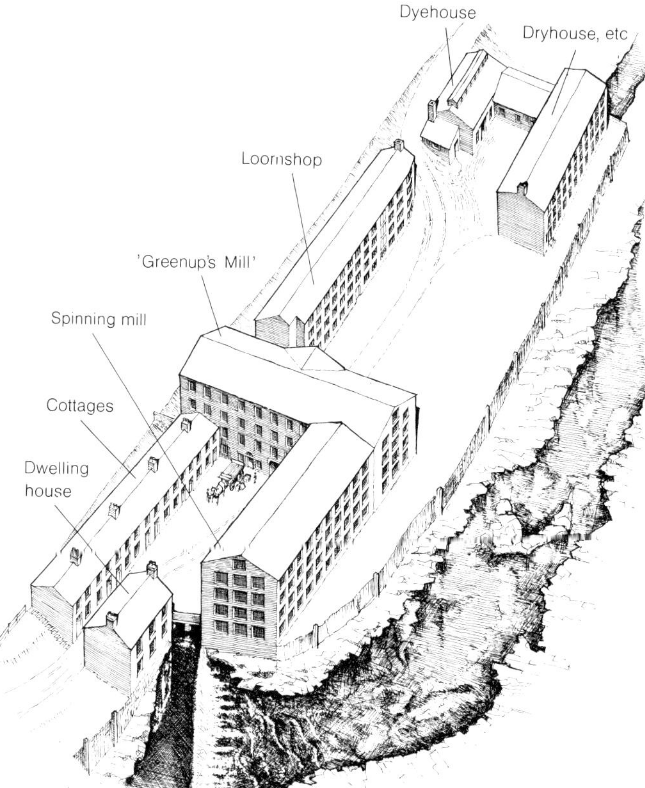

Fig 150 Bean Ing Mills, Leeds (85). In 1806 weaving shops, dyehouses and storage and finishing buildings were grouped around the main steam-powered multi-storeyed mill. By the mid 1830s the mill had been extended following the introduction of powered spinning and weaving, heated cloth dryhouses had been built, offices overlooked the main yard, a new gas plant provided light for the complex, and a large warehouse formed the frontage to the main road.

Fig 151 Reconstruction of the early 19th-century form of Sowerby Bridge Mills, Warley (143), perhaps the first integrated woollen mill in Yorkshire. Waterwheels in 'Greenup's Mill' provided power for scribbling, fulling and dyewood grinding. Hand-powered processes – spinning and weaving – were accommodated in adjacent buildings, and a dyehouse and dryhouse were sited at one end of the yard.

the model for the later development of the woollen industry, for by 1867 nearly half of operating woollen mills had concentrated production in the same way. Second, integration was developed not simply as a response to mechanisation, since both spinning and weaving remained hand-powered at this date, but instead arose out of the organisational requirements of the largest manufacturers of the day, who demanded better control and more direct supervision of production than domestic employment permitted.

Integrated mills were less common in the flax and linen branch than in the woollen sector, probably because processing was so much more protracted and because geographical specialisation, a feature of the traditional industry, was strengthened in the era of mill production. Small numbers of integrated mills were, however, built. As early as 1793 Marshall's Mill, Holbeck (57), had twenty-eight handlooms on site, although by 1800 loomshops had been established away from the mill complex. Marshall's former partners, Benjamin and

Thomas Benyon, arranged integration at their mill in Holbeck (56) in a way familiar to woollen manufacturers, for in *c*1804–5 they added loomshops to their newly built spinning mill. The layout of the site (Fig 152) suggests indeed that loomshops were envisaged from the beginning, for the narrow ranges form a 'U-plan' around the perimeter and enclose a large mill yard. West House Mill, Fewston (40), also had a brief existence as an integrated mill after Jacob Wilks, a Knaresborough linen manufacturer, became a partner in the mills in 1807. Wilks developed the site from one engaged in spinning to one where weaving was also carried on, in a 'Weaving Factory with looms, utensils and stock'. Like the weaving shops at Benyons' Mill (56), the 'weaving factory' was a long, narrow range, probably two or three storeys high.

The integrated flax and linen mill was every bit as complex as its counterpart in the woollen branch. Again, the main mill dominated the site, housing machine spinning and, after 1808, frequently also machine heckling. Air and heated dryhouses, dressing shops and other buildings were grouped around the main mill, as in simple flax-spinning mills, and loomshops provided the essential ingredient for integration. Bleaching was rarely undertaken on integrated mill sites. Marshalls, for example, owned a bleachworks at Wortley, a mile or so from their mills. The best description of a fully integrated flax and linen mill is given in an insurance policy of 1816 relating to West House Mill (40). The site comprised a flax and yarn warehouse, two flax mills with carding and breaking engines, engine and boiler houses, a workshop, a weaving factory, a counting house, thread shop and air drying room, and bleaching and drying houses for warps (Fig 153; see also Fig 272). Outside the mill there were houses, cottages and two apprentice houses.

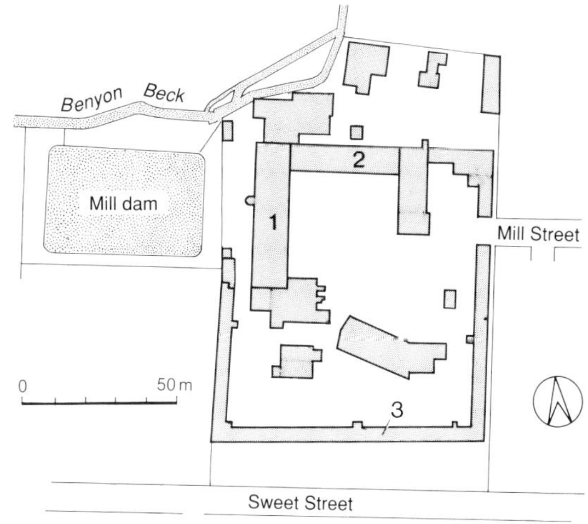

Fig 152 Benyons' Mill, Holbeck (56), became an integrated flax and linen mill c1804–5 with the addition of weaving shops to the earlier spinning mill. The resulting courtyard plan is similar to that of Bean Ing Mills.

The achievement of full factory working, 1825–1900

In the fifty years before 1825, the Yorkshire textile industry progressed dramatically. Mill numbers increased, together with employment at machines, and some mills were both large and complex in organisation. The links with the traditional method of production were, however, still strong. Domestic employment remained important, especially at the weaving stage, and non-factory workshops, for combing, weaving and other processes, still used hand power. Most mills, moreover, were very small, and even in 1834 the average workforce in a wool textiles (woollen and worsted) mill was less than fifty.[34] It would be wrong, therefore, to imagine that the Yorkshire industry was characterised by a thoroughgoing 'factory system' in this early period.

This picture altered radically after 1825. The most important development was the achievement of fully mechanised production in virtually all aspects of the industry. The principal innovation was the powerloom, largely unsuccessful before 1825, but applied to all branches, albeit at different rates, thereafter. The other major developments were the introduction of powered mule spinning in the woollen branch in the 1820s and of machine combing in the worsted industry in the mid 19th century. In all branches, less far-reaching but still significant advances were made. Technical innovations allowed a wider range of products to be made by machines which became larger, worked more quickly and were increasingly automatic and therefore labour saving.

A large increase in factory employment is clearly marked in this period. In the woollen branch the numbers of mills increased from 406 in 1835 to 998 in 1874, and employment from 23,600 to 76,800 over the same period. In the worsted branch there were 204 mills in 1835 but 520 in 1874, with 16,740 and 114,388 employees respectively.[35] Domestic employment declined in approximately inverse proportion as handloom weaving, hand combing and other domestic crafts were replaced by machine working in the mills. Only in the linen and woollen branches did off-site employment

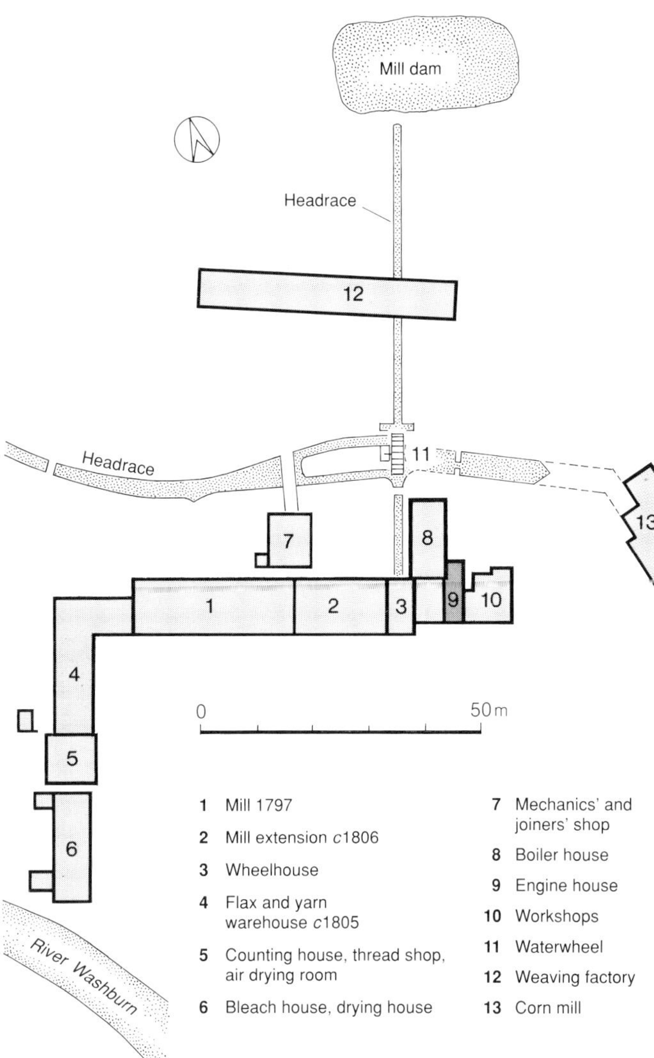

Fig 153 West House Mill, Fewston (40), became an integrated flax and linen mill in the early 19th century when a 'weaving factory' was added to the site. This plan, based on a sale plan of 1843, shows the probable uses of the different buildings in 1816, when the occupying firm went bankrupt.

maintain any importance after the middle of the 19th century. Outweavers remained numerous around Barnsley as late as the 1880s, and domestic handloom weaving of the intricately patterned fancy woollen cloths continued in the Huddersfield area until the late 19th century.[36]

The Yorkshire textile industry became more diverse after 1825. To the established woollen, worsted, cotton, and flax and linen branches were added the silk and recovered wool sectors. Both existed before 1825, silk since at least the mid 18th century and the recovered wool industry since *c*1809 when shoddy was first produced in Batley. They were, however, of negligible importance before 1825, and only really developed strongly after 1850. Silk became associated above all with Samuel Cunliffe Lister of Manningham Mills, Manningham (93), but the recovered wool branch was principally made up of many small shoddy and mungo manufacturers.

The diversity of the Yorkshire industry was reflected in its architecture. Some mill layouts were adopted by particular branches but not by others; one type – the shoddy and mungo mill – was unique to a single branch. The different mill forms will be studied in turn, and consideration will be given to their relationship with the branches of the industry. A recurring theme throughout the description will be the growth in scale of mills: the typical mill of 1875 was very much larger than its counterpart of 1825. Despite this, however, there was always room in the industry for a wide variation in mill size.

Mill types

The spinning mill

The specialised spinning mill was the most common type of textile factory in Yorkshire in 1825 and continued to be so until *c*1870, when the integrated mill took over its leading role. Certainly before 1850, and in many mills after that date, the specialised spinning mill was dominated, as it had been before 1825, by the multi-storeyed mill building. When first built, mills such as Castleton Mill, Wortley (150), and Sykes Mill, Haworth (53) (Figs 154, 155), comprised little more than the storeyed building for powered spinning, the engine and boiler houses and chimney, and minor attached or detached sheds and workshops. In a few mills a simple exterior disguised an interior with a number of different functions. At Robinwood Mill, Todmorden and Walsden (140), the main range of the U-shaped mill of *c*1835 was used for spinning, one wing for storage and the other wing in part for power generation (Fig 156).

Most spinning mills were, however, more complex in their layout, either because they evolved with no overall plan or because the requirements were too diverse to find accommodation within a single mill building. Probably the best example of both aspects in this period is Meltham Mills, Meltham (98), a cotton-spinning mill near Huddersfield. When a view of the factory was painted in 1868, the site comprised a long range of five linked but distinct mills (Little, Middle and Large Mills, in existence by 1834; Wing Mill and End Mill, added by *c*1845); a separate block giving two mills (Cotton Mill, *c*1848–51, and Cotton Mill Wing); large sheds for

Fig 154 Castleton Mill, Wortley (150), a fireproof steam-powered flax-spinning mill built in the early 1830s.

Fig 155 Sykes Mill, Haworth (53), a steam-powered worsted-spinning mill of c1847.

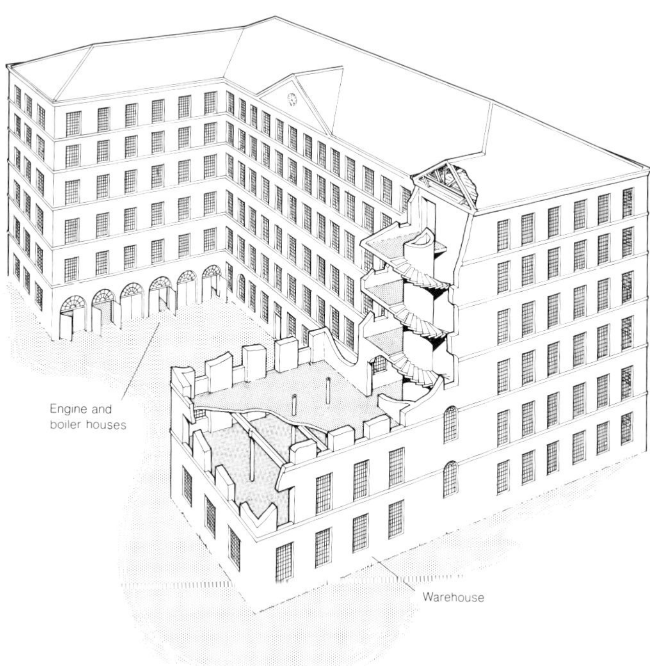

Fig 156 The U-shaped multi-storeyed mill at Robinwood Mill, Todmorden and Walsden (140), built in the mid to late 1830s, contained engine and boiler houses, warehouse and spinning capacity within a single building of compact form and impressive style.

warping, winding and dressing; and warehouses, counting houses, workshops, bleach houses, gasworks and a dining hall for the workers (Fig 157). The same progression is seen at mills in other branches, for example Barkerend Mills, Bradford (26), with its three spinning mills, sheds and warehouses (Fig 158). Planning was simply a matter of fitting expansion into the available space with, perhaps, some re-organisation of processes to make the working of the mill more convenient.

Where large spinning mills were planned and built either in one phase or over a short period, there is evidence for more coherent disposition of their component structures, particularly the mill, warehouse and power plant. This is especially the case with urban mills. Hunslet Mills, Hunslet (67), was built in the late 1830s as a flax-spinning mill, and its evolution before 1850 shows evidence for the deliberate creation of a courtyard plan. The first buildings – the massive spinning mill and the long warehouse – were built on the perimeter of the plot on two sides, and later warehouses further enclose the yard on a third side (Fig 159). The use of the yard is uncertain: it remained largely free of buildings for some years, but by 1869 it had been partly infilled with minor buildings. Smaller-scale urban planning is illustrated by Try Mills, Manningham (94), built in 1865 as a worsted-spinning mill. The restricted plot was developed first by the construction of a warehouse range along the main road frontage; a mill, and engine and boiler houses in a return range; and a second return range opposite the mill giving offices, dwelling, stables and coach house. The site was extended just a few months after the completion of the first phase. New buildings included an extension to the mill, added over the original boiler house, a stable and a warehouse. The site was then fully built up, with storeyed buildings grouped tightly around a narrow yard (Fig 160).

The introduction of machine combing after 1850 changed the form of the worsted-spinning mill. Some

Fig 157 Meltham Mills, Meltham (98), in 1868. A new village grew up around the mills during the 19th century (see *Chapter 5*).

Fig 158 Barkerend Mills, Bradford (26). This worsted-spinning mill has multi-storeyed mills of c1815, 1852 and c1870, with warehouses, sheds and other buildings added at different times.

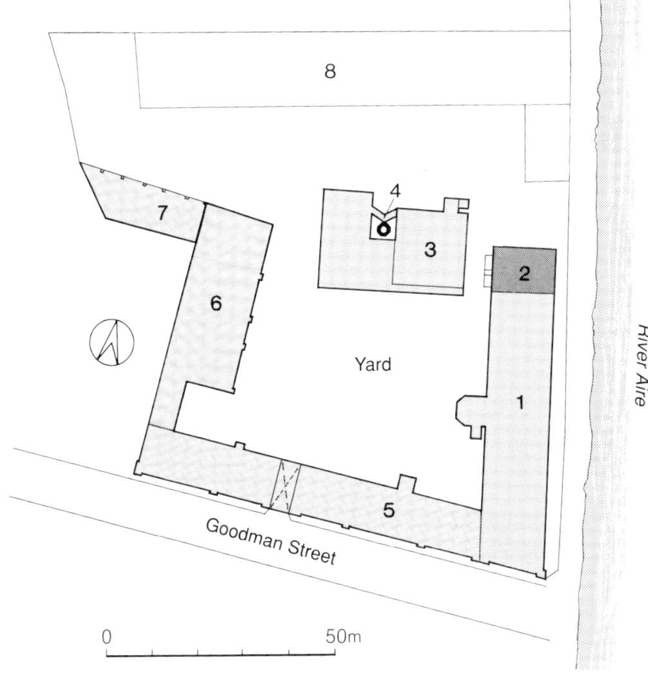

Fig 159 Hunslet Mills, Hunslet (67). By 1850 the mill had evolved to give a large courtyard plan, enclosed by a multi-storeyed mill, warehouses and a boiler house.

yarn spinners chose to have their wool processed by commission woolcombers, and thus the essential components of their mills remained simply the warehouse, mill and power plant. Other spinners, however, preferred to establish their own combing departments. In some mills, combing was accommodated on the ground floor of the main mill, but it became conventional to house the new machines in single-storeyed sheds. The addition of combing sheds to earlier mills is a common phenomenon in the worsted area; at Barkerend Mills (26), sheds were added in 1864, and five years later the same addition was made at Greengate Mills, Keighley.[37]

Perfect planning of the worsted combing and spinning mill was possible where new sites were developed, and the ideal arrangement is represented by Whetley Mills, Manningham (95), built to the designs of the Bradford architects Milnes and France in and after 1863 (Fig 161). The layout respects the sequence of production. On the main road frontage is a large warehouse for the storage and sorting of raw wool. Next to this is a shed used on the main floor for the different processes involved in combing – carding, backwashing, gilling and combing itself. A small basement below the shed was used in later years and probably originally for wool washing. The multi-storeyed mill housed the drawing, twisting and spinning machines which produced the finished yarn. Warehouses on the far side of the yard gave storage space for materials ready for despatch – yarn and wool waste, the latter probably the noils produced in combing, sold to the woollen industry. Offices and a foreman's house were set away from the processing area and the siting of the house next to the street was doubtless intended to give an added degree of security to the works. Because there were now two powered departments, the siting of the engine house was critical, and Whetley represents the optimum arrangement where a single engine was employed, sited at the junction of combing shed and main mill.

The association of spinning and the multi-storeyed mill was not invariable, for some mills were built providing only single-storeyed working space. At Bent Ley Mill, Meltham (97), silk throwing was accommodated in a shed of 1840, and in 1855–6 Hope Mill, Todmorden and Walsden (139), was built as a cotton-spinning mill in shed form (Fig 162). The reasons for these departures from the norm are not known, although the lower costs of a single-storeyed building may have been an influential consideration for entrepreneurs of modest means attempting to establish themselves in the industry.

The weaving mill

The introduction of powerloom weaving in the cotton and worsted branches in the 1820s, and in the linen, silk and woollen branches in the 1830s and later, made possible the building of specialised weaving mills, the successors to the off-site loomshops discussed above (see p21). While never as common as either spinning mills or integrated mills, weaving mills formed a significant proportion of Yorkshire textile establishments, especially after 1860, by which time the powerloom had ousted

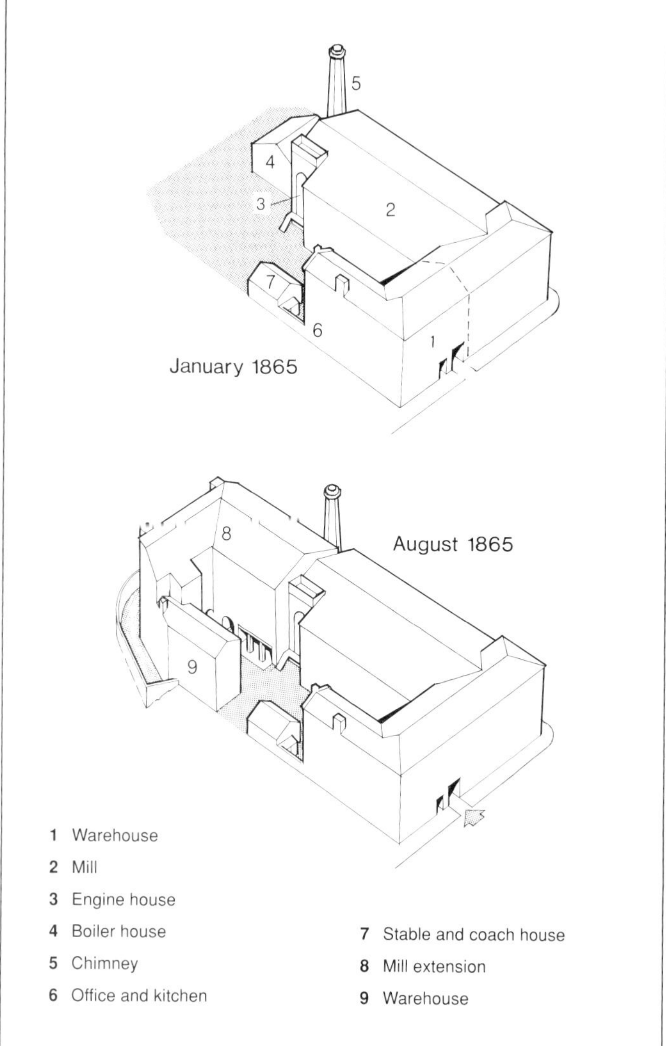

Fig 160 Try Mills, Manningham (94), was built in two phases in 1865, but the design of the first phase took account of likely expansion.

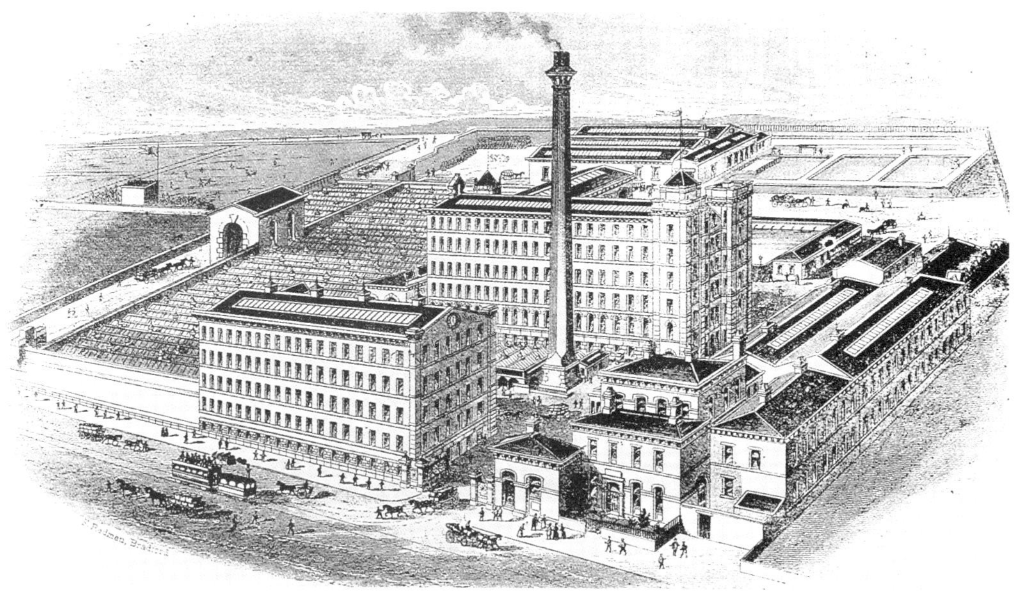

Fig 161 Whetley Mills, Manningham (95), in a late 19th-century view. The 1863 design for this worsted-spinning factory provided warehouses, combing sheds and a large multi-storeyed spinning mill (from Anon 1893, 65).

Fig 162 Hope Mill, Todmorden and Walsden (139), of 1855–6. Despite the single-storeyed form of the complex, the mill was originally used for spinning.

the handloom virtually everywhere. The woollen branch had few weaving mills, but in other textiles specialist weaving was important. In 1861, for example, it accounted for thirty-one per cent of both worsted and cotton mills and by 1889 this had risen in the worsted sector to thirty-eight per cent.[38] Weaving mills were cheap to establish, and room and power facilities (see pp107–10) were commonly available. The result was that weaving attracted the entrepreneur with limited capital, and firms were, on average, smaller than in other sectors.[39] In 1871, for example, the average workforce in Yorkshire weaving factories was seventy-seven, compared with ninety-eight in spinning mills and 158 in integrated mills.[40]

Specialist weaving firms were concentrated in different parts of Yorkshire. Barnsley became the centre of linen powerloom weaving, and Barnoldswick, Earby and to a lesser extent Skipton were the major specialist cotton-weaving towns, related, perhaps, more to Lancashire than to the Yorkshire textile industry. Worsted weaving was more dispersed; it was centred on Bradford, but extended also to Halifax, Keighley and the surrounding areas.

The processes involved in a weaving mill were less protracted than in other types of textile factory. Without underplaying the complexity of the operation itself, weaving was essentially the single major powered process. Yarns were often bought in almost ready for weaving, the warp on warp beams,the weft on bobbins. Warps were sized and some firms may have prepared their own patterns and therefore done their own warping, but few if any were involved in any finishing processes apart from checking the cloth for faults after it had left the loom.

The weaving mill, therefore, had a simple form. The requirements were storage for yarns, warp beams and cloth; an area for hand-powered processes such as sizing and checking; a manufacturing area for the looms; and a power installation. The principal components were simply a warehouse, a shed, engine and boiler houses, and a chimney. The earliest purpose-built weaving mill recorded in RCHME's survey was Lowertown Shed, Haworth (52), built for worsted weaving in 1856. This lacked a warehouse originally, but one was added a few years later. The perfect example of the type is Union Mills, Skipton (121), built in 1867 as a room and power mill for cotton weaving. Here all the components formed part of the original design, which in an extremely compact plan gave a single-storeyed shed with, along one side, a warehouse, an engine house, a boiler house and a chimney (Fig 163). A later example of the same layout is City Shed, Wyke (152), a silk-weaving mill built in 1899 (see Fig 338).

The integrated mill

Integrated mills were not common before 1825 and were apparently restricted to the woollen branch and in smaller measure to flax and linen (see pp84–91). After 1825, however, the possibilities for integrated working were increased considerably by the mechanisation of weaving. The powerloom, slowly in some branches,

Fig 163 Union Mills, Skipton (121), shows the typical weaving mill arrangement of a single-storeyed shed and attached warehouse and power plant. The 1867 phase lies in the foreground, with additions of 1871 beyond.

rapidly in others, made mill-based weaving a great advantage in most areas, and integration became much more common. By the 1870s integrated mills were the most numerous type in Yorkshire, with the woollen branch in particular being associated with this method of production.[41]

The majority of integrated mills achieved integration through the addition of processes to an earlier mill which had had a specialist use. In the woollen branch, powered spinning and weaving were added to existing scribbling, carding and fulling mills. The additions were commonly made in two stages, with first a spinning mill and later a weaving shed. Such is the evolution at Spinkwell Mills, Dewsbury (34), where the early scribbling and fulling mill was supplemented first by a larger mill, probably used partly for spinning, then by powerloom-weaving sheds, built *c*1850, then by a new spinning mill (*c*1862) and later by more weaving capacity (Fig 164). Woollen mills which had been integrated before 1825 changed their architectural character if not their function, for hand-spinning and handloom-weaving shops, suited to the earlier machines, were made redundant by the new mules and powerlooms. At Armitage Bridge Mills, South Crosland (127), this redundancy is expressed by the addition of a new spinning mill in the late 1820s and by weaving sheds in 1838 (Fig 165).

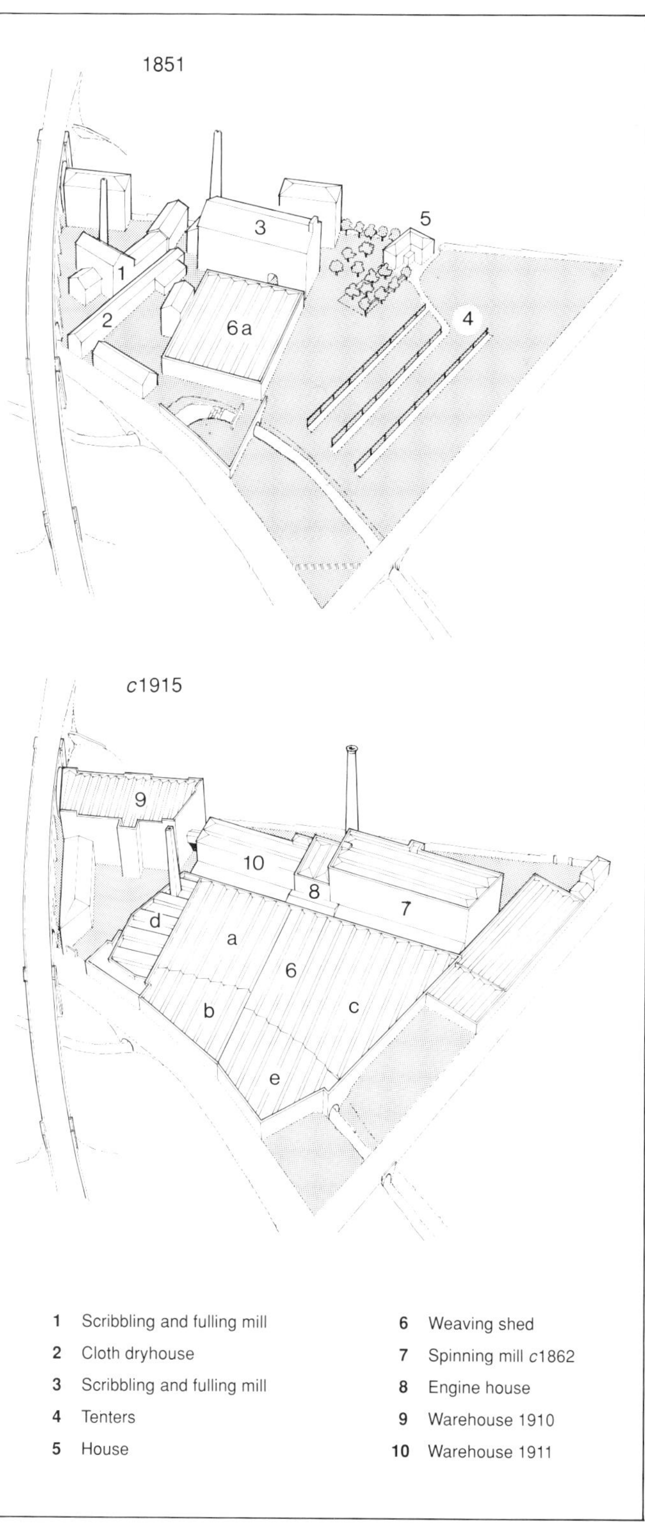

Fig 164 Spinkwell Mills, Dewsbury (34). By 1851 the original mill (1) had been supplemented by a second steam-powered mill (3) and by the first stage of the powerloom-weaving shed (6a). By 1915 the sheds had reached almost their full extent and a further mill (7) and new warehouses (9, 10) had been built.

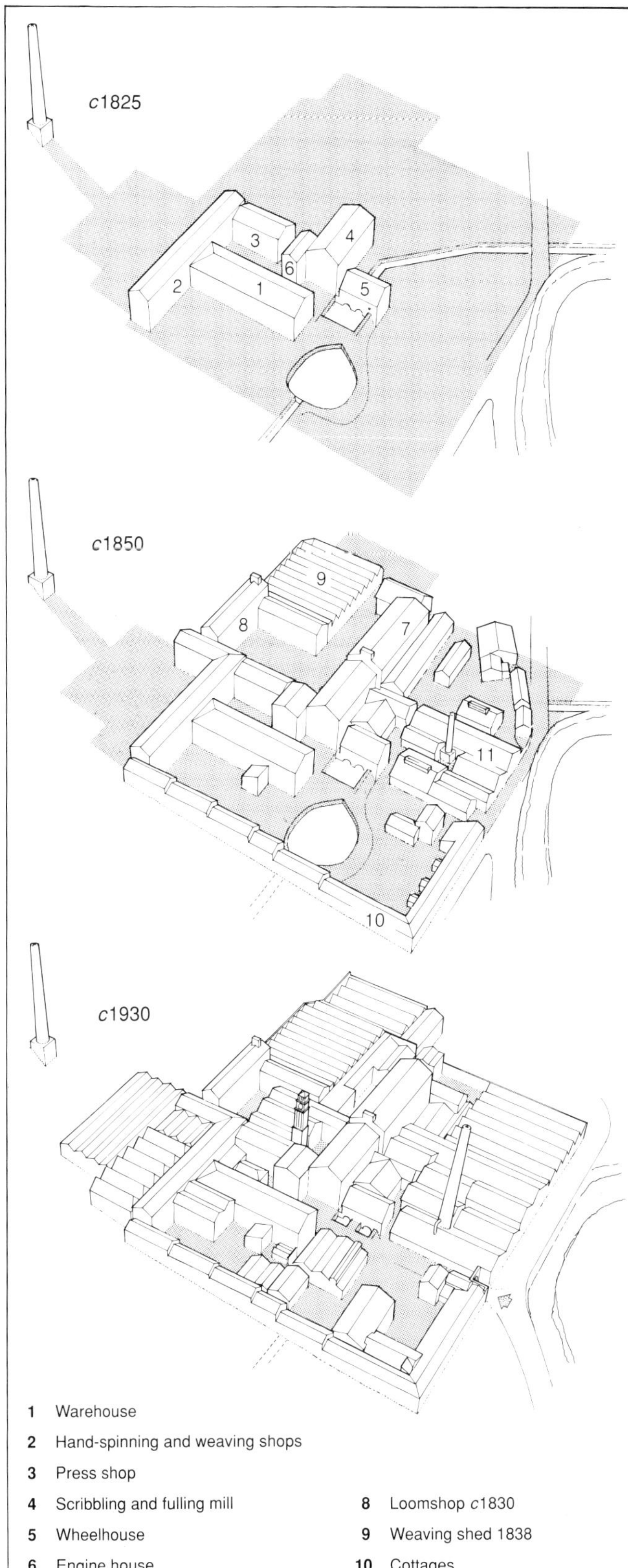

In the worsted branch, integration depended on the addition of powered weaving and combing to earlier spinning mills. At Oats Royd Mills, Midgley (101), the first building, dated 1847, was a spinning mill, but slowly new functions were added. John Murgatroyd, the owner, originally had powerlooms at a nearby mill and expanded output by commissioning weaving by a separate company. Expansion of the Oats Royd site, however, at first mainly taking the form of multi-storeyed mills, included provision for powerloom weaving. At various times, the ground or first floors of three mills were used for weaving, until in 1887 a large new shed was built. There was a similar evolution in the combing department, off-site hand combing being replaced by machine combing in 1858. The machines were sited on the ground floor of the first mill and in a small purpose-built shed adjoining. By 1885, these arrangements were inadequate and a new shed was constructed for combing (Fig 166).

In other branches, evolution was more straightforward. In cotton, the preparatory (scribbling and carding) and spinning stages were already mechanised before 1825 and had been successfully combined in mills of the early period (see p26). Since finishing remained a specialist concern, powered weaving was the single major requirement for integration, and a number of mills show the addition of a weaving shed. At Waterside Mill, Langfield (82), the Fieldens built sheds for 800 and 1,000 looms in 1829 and c1840 respectively, and at Langcliffe Mill, Langcliffe (81), a shed was built, probably c1840, to complement the spinning capacity (Fig 167). The unusual feature of this shed is its location, set half a mile from the parent mill to re-use the water for power.

In the flax and linen branch, weaving again was the major requirement for integration, and Castleton Mill, Wortley (150), built in the late 1830s as a flax-spinning mill, had by the 1850s become integrated following the addition of a weaving shed. The most unusual example of integration, or at least planned integration, was Marshall's Mill, Holbeck (57). The company had been largely a specialist flax-spinning concern despite early experiments with handloom weaving both on and off site, but in 1836, at a very early stage in the introduction

Fig 165 Armitage Bridge Mills, South Crosland (127). The first buildings of this integrated woollen mill included a warehouse (1), a building for hand spinning and handloom weaving (2), and a water-powered scribbling and fulling mill (4). By c1850 a new mill (7) had been added for powered spinning, weaving capacity had expanded with, first, a new loomshop (8) and then the addition of a shed for powerlooms (9); finishing buildings (11), including dyehouses, occupied the lower part of the site. By c1930 the mill had expanded further and the finishing area had been rebuilt.

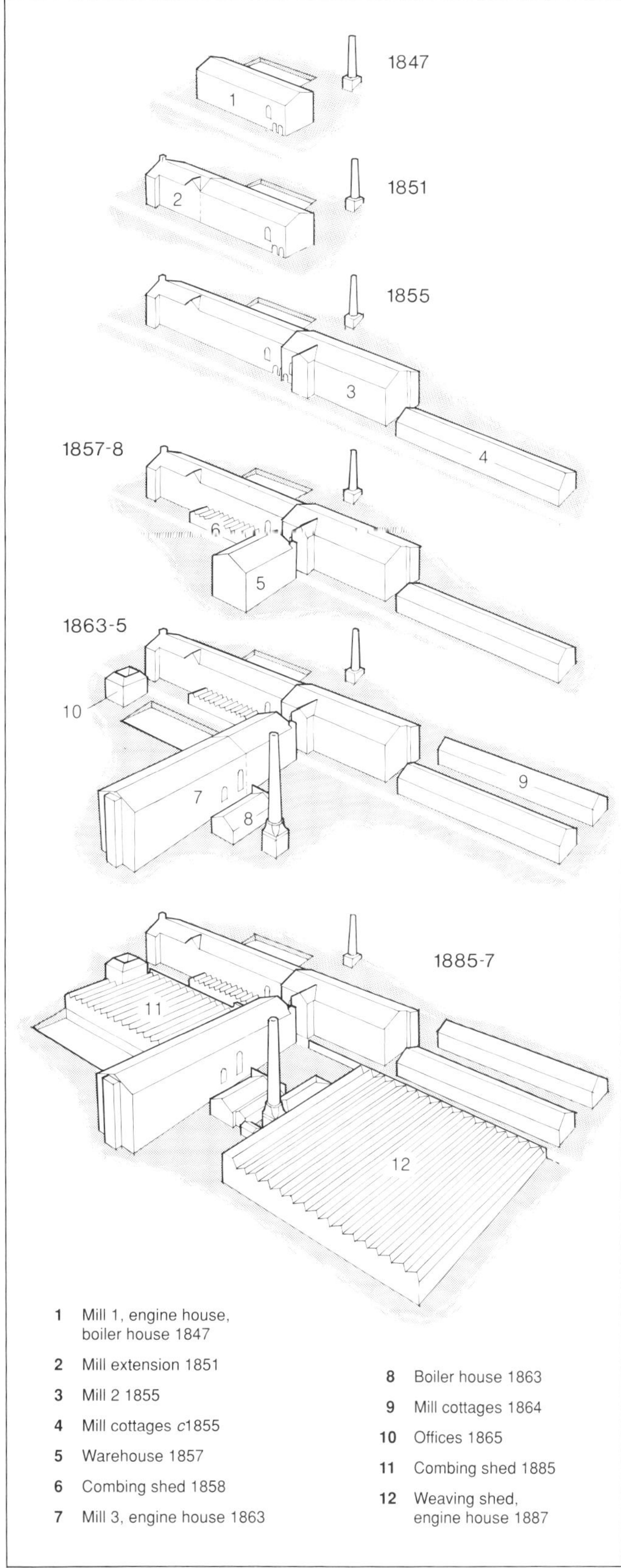

of powerloom weaving, a decision was taken both to expand its spinning capacity and to add weaving to the mill's range of functions. Instead of segregating these processes, however, they were brought together in a single building, the extraordinary Temple Mill, built between 1838 and 1841. The mill, in fact a large shed, is unique in its architectural character and, for its date, in its intended use, for it was designed to be used for preparing, spinning, twisting thread and weaving cloth (Fig 168). It was, therefore, by itself virtually an integrated mill on a single-storeyed layout.

Integration achieved by piecemeal addition could result in some sprawling mill plans. The split between spinning and weaving departments at Langcliffe Mill (81), noted above, cannot have been convenient. At some mills, expansion involved development of land beyond a public road, as at Oats Royd Mills (101), leading to problems of communication not entirely answered by subways and overhead walkways (Fig 169). At Manningham Mills, Manningham (93), the difficulty was partially overcome by moving the road to allow compact development of the large sheds. Site congestion could also be a problem. The success of Starkey Brothers at Longroyd Bridge, Huddersfield (65), made their island site, between the River Colne and the Huddersfield Canal, inadequate for normal working

Fig 167 Langcliffe Shed, Langcliffe (81), built as a water-powered weaving shed c1840, lay some distance from the parent Langcliffe Mill in order to re-use its water supply.

Fig 166 Oats Royd Mills, Midgley (101). The site evolved principally as a series of multi-storeyed mills before the 1880s, when sheds were built for combing and weaving.

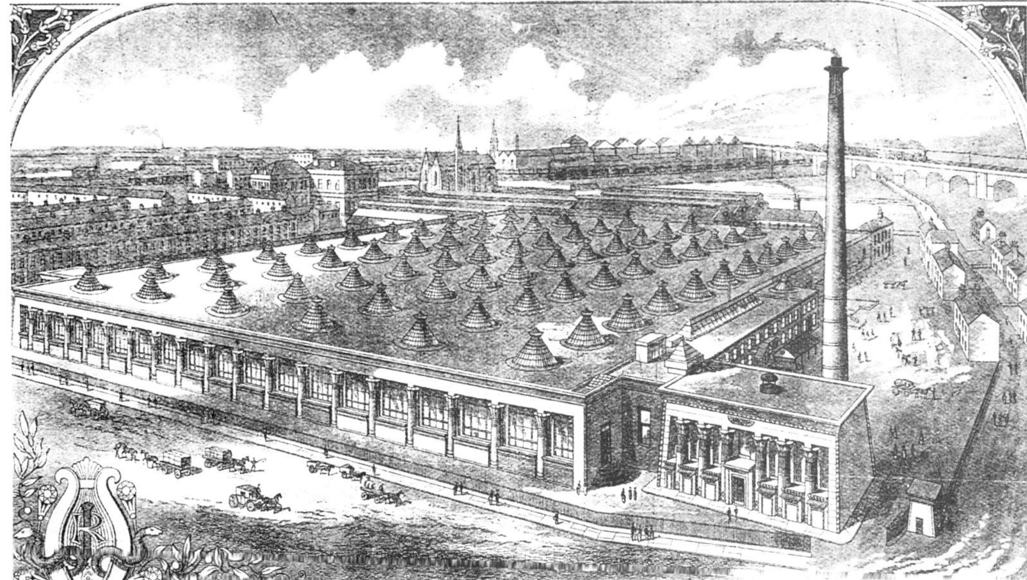

Fig 168 Temple Mill, part of Marshall's Mill, Holbeck (57), built 1838–41. The unusual method of top-lighting, the Egyptian decoration and the attached offices are shown in this view.

and encouraged intense exploitation of the available land, migration to neighbouring land and vertical as well as horizontal development. By 1835, there were four multi-storeyed mills within the factory, including some used for powerloom and handloom weaving, and other buildings included a press shop, a warehouse, dyehouses, gas house and drying stove. Later in the century further mills were erected on the opposite side of the canal and the site was as fully developed as convenience allowed (Fig 170).

The construction of new integrated mills allowed a closer approach to an ideal layout than was possible in mills where integration was achieved by piecemeal addition. The problems for the architect were those of using buildings of different forms, each appropriate to a particular process or sequence of processes; of disposing these so as to produce a logical flow between the stages in manufacturing; and of making the most efficient use of power. Few if any planned integrated mills were built in the flax and linen branch in this period, a fact which underlines its essentially fragmented nature and draws attention to the lack of new building after 1840 except in the field of specialist linen weaving. Examples from the four other primary branches, however, include the greatest mills of the era. Each branch had slightly different requirements and there is, therefore, some variety among integrated mills.

Cotton mills were probably simplest in layout, the requirements being a storeyed mill for carding and spinning and a shed for weaving, together with storage space, offices and other minor buildings. The best recorded example of an integrated cotton mill is Hollins Mill, Todmorden and Walsden (138), built between 1856 and 1858. The four-storeyed spinning mill contained 30,000 spindles, and the shed had 600 looms; both buildings were powered by an engine house attached at one side at their junction (Fig 171). A warehouse and office may have been part of the original plans, and a mechanics' shop was certainly built at the same time as the main part of the site. Late in the century, the owners and operators, Abraham Ormerod and Brothers, were described as involved in the 'whole process of manufacture from raw cotton to woven fabric ready for the finisher', exclusion of the finishing stages being typical of the cotton industry.

Fig 169 Oats Royd Mills, Midgley (101). The two parts of the site, divided by a public road, are linked by overhead walkways and by subways.

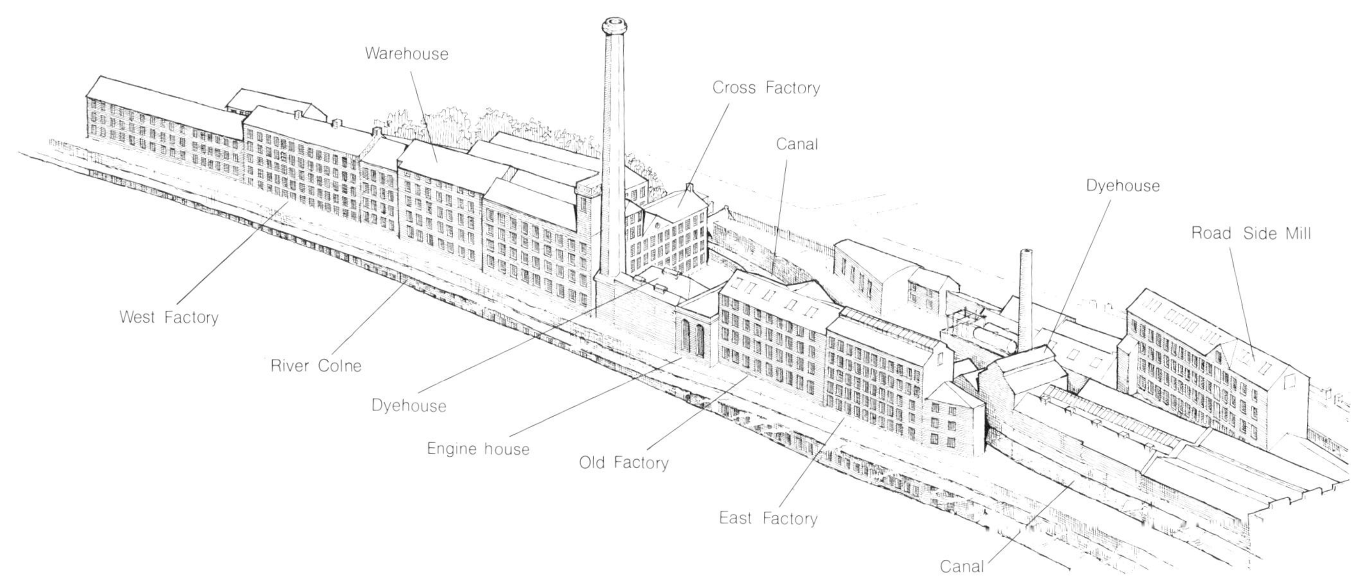

Fig 170 Starkeys' Mill, Longroyd Bridge, Huddersfield (65), an integrated woollen mill as it appeared in the mid 19th century. Powerlooms were housed in multi-storeyed buildings since there was no space for a shed.

Integrated mills in other branches were more complex. In worsted, full integration, incorporating powerloom weaving and machine combing, was delayed until the mid century, when Lister's combing machines became available. The greatest integrated worsted mill was Saltaire Mills, Shipley (116), built by Titus Salt between 1850 and 1853. It is the perfect illustration of planned integration, comprehending not only the processes within the complex but also the relationship between the mill and its surroundings. The new settlement of Saltaire was part of the original plan and the mill was situated to take advantage of the river for water and the canal and railway for transport. Salt employed the leading local architectural practice, Lockwood and Mawson, and the greatest engineer of the era, William Fairbairn, and the planning of the mill suggests an intimate knowledge of the workings of the worsted industry (Fig 172). The spine of the mill is a five-storeyed warehouse, with loading doors facing the canal. In the warehouse the wool and hair were sorted before being taken to one of the adjacent sheds for washing, drying and then combing. The mill, five storeys high with a basement, housed spinning, whilst warping and weaving were housed in the second large shed. A range of offices was set on one side of the complex. Power was supplied by ten boilers in a detached boiler house and by two pairs of beam engines, located to either side of the central arch in the spinning mill. Only dyeing was not included in the original plans, and this omission was repaired when dyeworks were built between the canal and the river before 1871 (see Fig 299). The planning allowed a smooth flow of processes and the minimum of handling within the complex. Saltaire illustrates how the integrated mill for worsted differed from its counterparts, for it required two blocks of sheds, one for combing, one for weaving, a duplication not necessary for other textiles.

Fig 171 Hollins Mill, Todmorden and Walsden (138), built as an integrated cotton mill between 1856 and 1858. The engine house, lit by two tall round-headed windows, is sited so as to transmit power efficiently to both spinning mill and weaving shed.

Saltaire was unrivalled among worsted mills for its planning and execution. Within twenty years of its building, the slump in the lustre cloth trade, caused by a sudden change in fashions to all-wool worsteds manufactured primarily by the French, and the growing

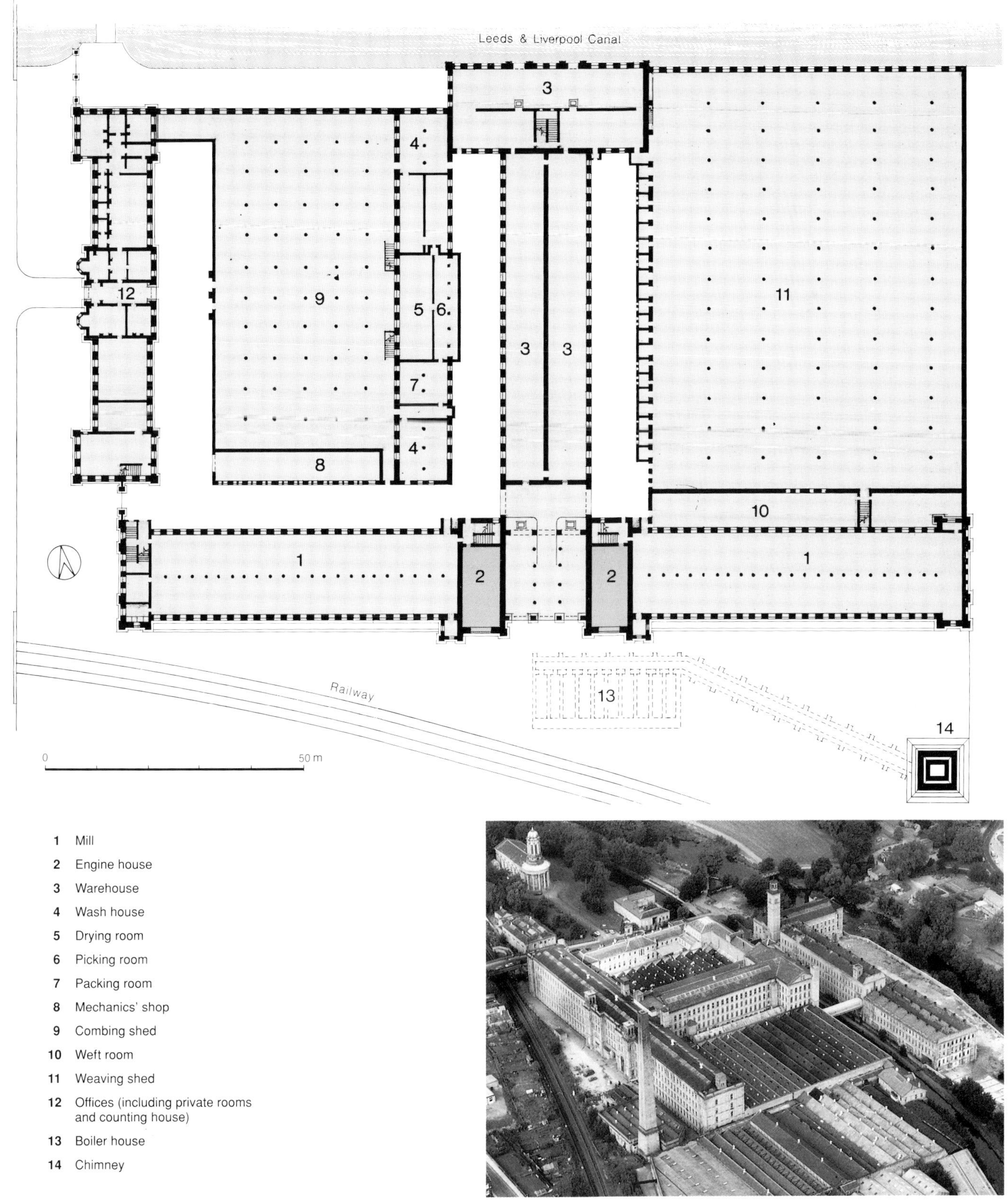

Fig 172 Saltaire Mills, Shipley (116), aerial view from the south-east and block plan showing the original layout of 1850–3 (redrawn from plan in Fairbairn 1854, pl 1).

importance of the yarn-exporting business, made integration less common.[42] Two Bradford mills, Legrams Mill, Horton (60), and Young Street Mills, Manningham (96), illustrate the changed conditions. Both were planned in the early 1870s as integrated mills, perhaps on the assumption that the boom conditions of the 1860s, when the Bradford worsted trade profited immensely from the difficulties of cotton supply, would continue. By the time construction began, however, the demand for Bradford worsteds was in decline and the mills were built only in part. The original design for Young Street included a storeyed mill for combing and spinning and a large weaving shed, but work on the former stopped at an early stage, leaving the site to function as a weaving mill from the shed. When the storeyed mill was eventually completed, probably in 1874–5, it housed a separate spinning company (Fig 173). At Legrams, the original plans by Lockwood and Mawson were very ambitious, and allowed for large combing and weaving sheds, a warehouse and a six-storeyed mill. The mill however remained unfinished and unused for thirty years, and the weaving shed was never built. Instead Legrams functioned only as a spinning mill, with the warehouse converted in part for spinning and with combing done in the attached shed.

Few Yorkshire silk mills were integrated, but the greatest among them, Manningham Mills (93), performed all operations from reception of raw silk through to the finished product. A large part of Manningham Mills burnt down in 1871, and Samuel Cunliffe Lister and his architects, Andrews and Pepper, were thus provided with an opportunity of building anew, taking limited account of remaining structures. The resulting site (Fig 174) is dominated visually by two large multi-storeyed blocks, one for spinning, the other intended mainly for warehousing, although including a wash house on the ground floor for boiling silk. To one side of the spinning mill were sheds for weaving, combing, doubling and carding. Dyehouses were incorporated from the surviving complex. The massive power plant comprised a boiler house with space for eighteen boilers, an engine of 1,800 horse power and the famous chimney. The engine was sited within one end of the spinning mill but adjacent to the sheds, at the nodal point, therefore, of the main working area in the complex.

Like integrated mills in other branches, the planned integrated woollen mill used storeyed buildings for preparatory and spinning operations and sheds for weaving. The best recorded example is Calder Bank Mills, Dewsbury (30), despite the loss by fire over a hundred years ago of its principal building, a mill of five storeys. Built first in 1861, the complex consisted of the main mill, used for scribbling, carding and spinning; attached engine and boiler houses; large sheds for weaving; a dyehouse; a cloth dryhouse; and other sheds containing a variety of processes (Fig 175). It was usual in many woollen mills to house the milling and scouring operations on the ground floor of the main mill, but at Calder Bank these processes were located in a range of sheds attached to the weaving department. These sheds also housed a willeying department, in which the raw wool was opened and blended, rag grinding, a common process in woollen mills in the Heavy Woollen area (see

Fig 173 Young Street Mills, Manningham (96), designed in 1871 as an integrated worsted mill, was built in stages and when complete housed separate spinning and weaving firms.

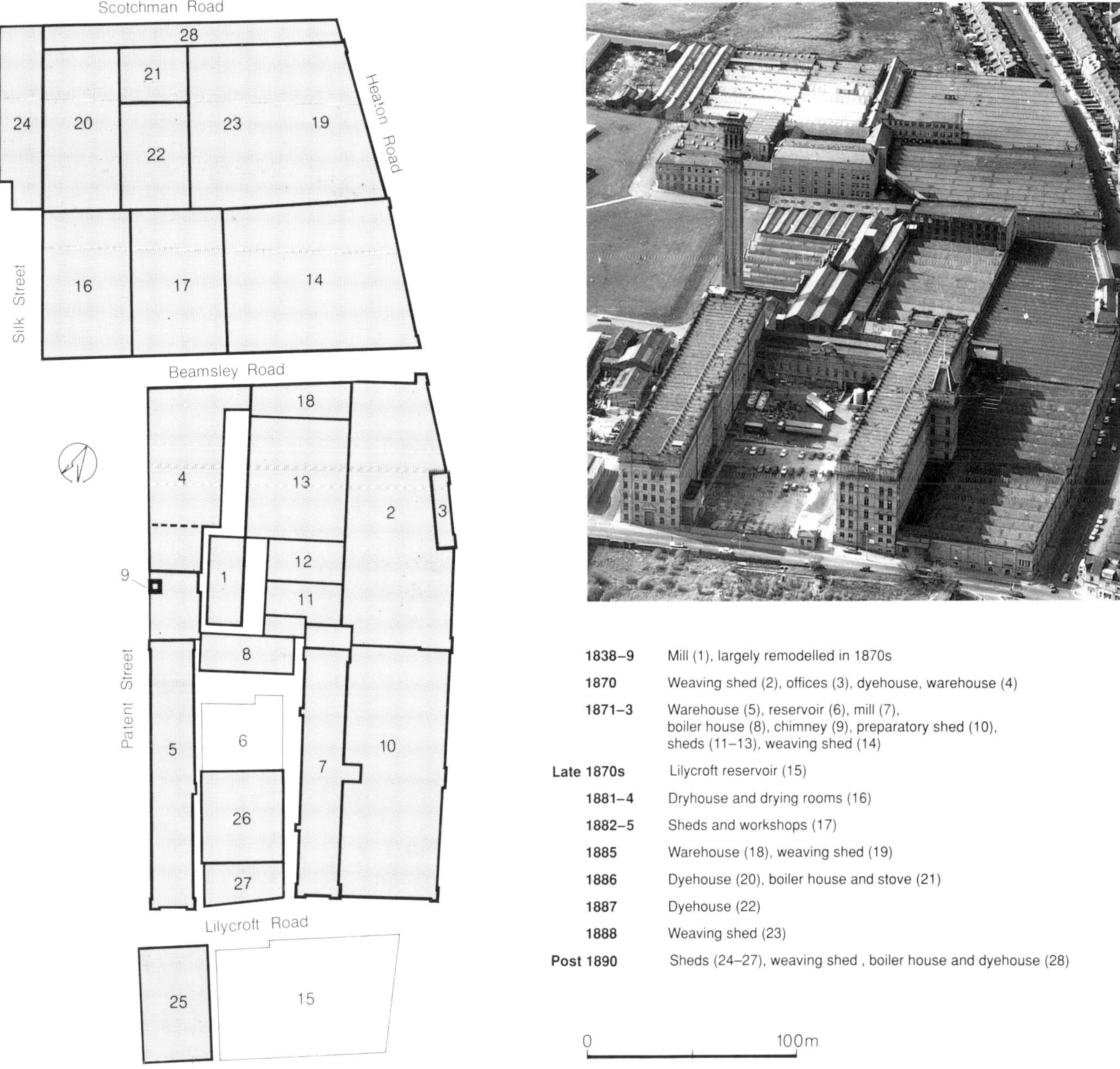

Fig 174 Manningham Mills, Manningham (93), largely rebuilt by Samuel Cunliffe Lister as an integrated silk mill in and after 1870. The aerial view is taken from the south east.

pp116–17), and a dyeware store, again common in woollen mills. Expansion at Calder Bank in the 1860s shows the large number of specialist areas in the integrated woollen mill, for a burling room, a teazel room, a tentering machine room, probably replacing wholly or in part the original cloth dryhouse, and a chemical shop were all added. A five-storeyed warehouse and further sheds, part used for weaving and part for finishing, were added later, as was a cooking place where the workforce could warm their meals.

Superficially similar but different in detail, integrated mills with both storeyed buildings and sheds were therefore common to most branches of the Yorkshire textile industry. There were, however, two other forms of integrated factory. One included all processes in a multi-storeyed mill, the other utilised a single-storeyed layout.

The combined use of a multi-storeyed mill for spinning and powerloom weaving was common in the early years of the introduction of the powerloom. Many

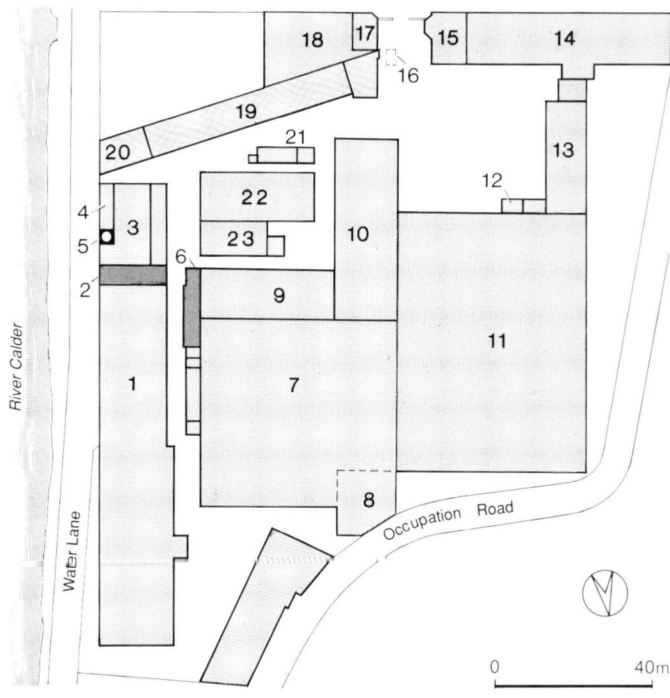

Fig 175 Calder Bank Mills, Dewsbury (30), aerial view from the north and block plan. Developed in the early 1860s as an integrated woollen mill, the first buildings included a multi-storeyed mill (burnt out in 1883), a power plant, weaving and finishing sheds, and a cloth dryhouse. Expansion westwards involved the addition of further sheds and a warehouse.

1 Main mill
2 Engine house
3 Boiler house, drying floors over
4 Economiser
5 Chimney
6 Engine house
7 Weaving shed
8 Beaming and warping place
9 Willey shed
10 Milling, scouring, rag-grinding shed and dyeware shed
11 Finishing and weaving sheds
12 Cooking place
13 Mechanics' and joiners' shop
14 Warehouse
15 Offices
16 Weighbridge
17 Watch house
18 Wool warehouse
19 Wool and waste store (former cloth dryhouse)
20 Cottage
21 Boiler house
22 Dyehouse
23 Tentering machine place

manufacturers removed machinery from parts of existing buildings to accommodate the new looms. In 1825, for example, 108 cotton powerlooms were installed in an existing spinning mill at Greenholme Mills, Burley,[43] and, in 1833, John Wood of Bradford, one of the largest worsted manufacturers of the area, housed powerlooms in the top storey of his five-storeyed Old Mill.[44] An early example of planned integration within a storeyed mill is Old Lane Mill, Northowram (105), built 1825–8 by James Akroyd, an innovative manufacturer who in 1822 had become the first to use worsted powerlooms successfully.[45] Akroyd planned on a monumental scale by the standards of the contemporary worsted industry, and the towering six-storeyed mill was designed to house spinning, weaving and warehousing (see Fig 56).

The advantages of using a storeyed mill for both spinning and weaving were particularly telling in urban locations, where plots were generally too small to permit the construction of sizeable sheds. A number of mills in Huddersfield, for example, built by woollen manufacturers in the period 1850–70, comprised either just a multi-storeyed mill with minor outbuildings, as at Firth Street Mills, Huddersfield (62), of 1865–6, or a mill and small sheds. Albert Mills, Lockwood (89), established in 1853, originally had a six-storeyed mill and a range of lesser buildings made up of a dyehouse, dyeware room, sizing room, stables and small shed. A second mill, a small shed and a warehouse were added *c*1866 (Fig 176). The shed is not of sufficient size to accommodate a weaving department able to complement the spinning capacity of the storeyed mills, and it is possible either that Berry and Turner, the owners, employed outweavers even at this late date, or that the storeyed buildings were used in part for powerloom weaving. By 1884 Albert Mills was in multi-occupation and two tenants used upper floors of the mills for powerloom weaving. It is not clear, however, whether such mills were used for integrated working by design or through expediency.

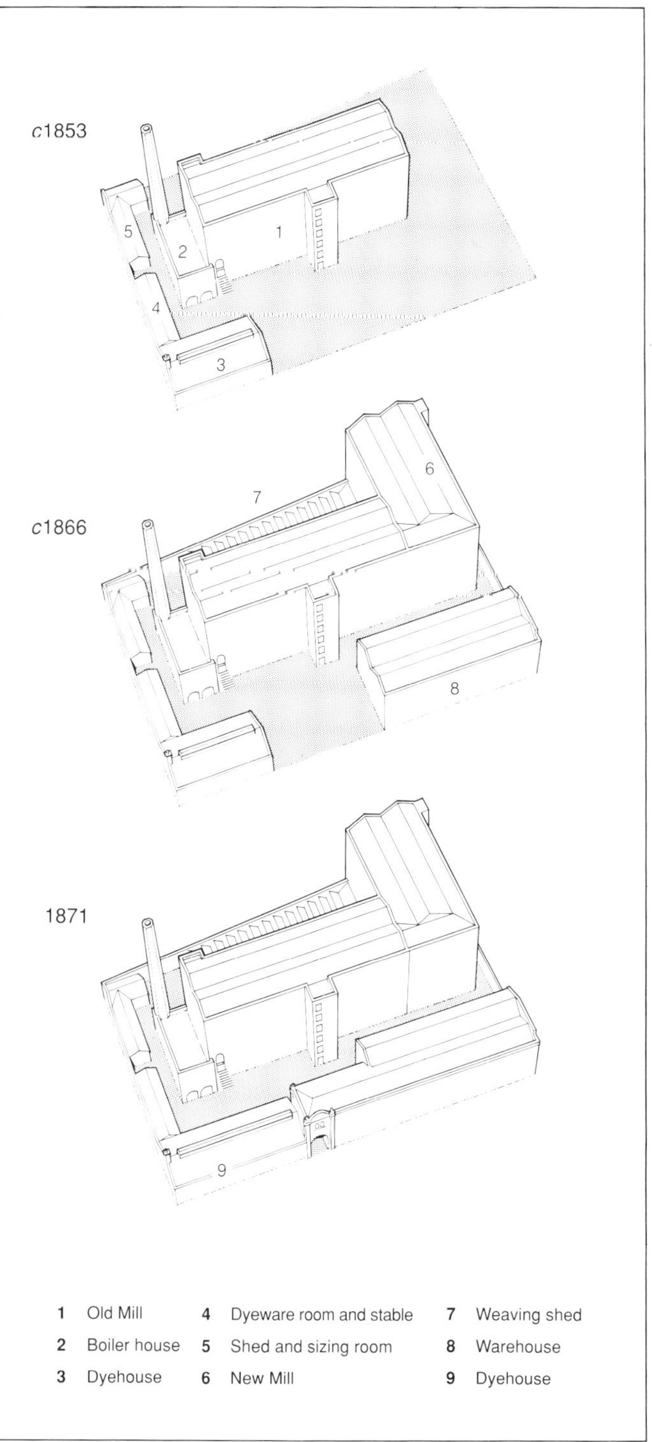

Fig 176 The evolution of Albert Mills, Lockwood (89), a steam-powered woollen mill.

The other alternative type of integrated mill had a single-storeyed layout. William Fairbairn designed and built several integrated cotton mills on this plan in India in the mid 19th century, and such an arrangement represented a radical re-thinking of the textile mill's design requirements, replacing the earlier division of function by a plan in which easy communication between linked departments was the paramount consideration.[46] The single-storeyed layout allowed materials to be moved about conveniently, and power could be transmitted efficiently within the working area. Moreover, construction was cheap and produced an environment with better lighting and ventilation. The need for a large site, however, restricted the number of single-storeyed mills, since only where land prices were low was such a design practicable. Only in the 20th century, after the great age of mill building, was the single-storeyed layout to become the standard industrial building form, adopted for clothing works, engineering works and a wide range of other factories.

Combined use of a shed for spinning and weaving was part of John Marshall's plan for Temple Mill, built in 1838–41 as part of Marshall's Mill (57), but this cannot be considered a true prototype since the bulk of the spinning continued to be conducted in early multi-storeyed mills on the site. The best examples of single-storeyed planning in Yorkshire are woollen mills: Alverthorpe Mills, Alverthorpe with Thornes (4), was built between 1870 and 1872 (Fig 177), and Westfield Mills, Yeadon (153), in 1888. Both mills either began with or quickly acquired a division between a main shed block and lesser detached sheds. At both sites raw material was stored either in the lesser sheds or in part of the main block. Processing began at Alverthorpe in a blending area and at Westfield in a willey house. The wool was then transferred to adjacent rooms for scribbling, carding and spinning, after which the yarn was taken to the weaving department in the next room. The woven cloth was milled (fulled) within the main sheds, and finishing processes (tentering, perching, raising and shearing) were either divided between the main block and the detached range (Alverthorpe), or undertaken in the main block (Westfield). In both mills, the cloth was dyed in the detached sheds, which also included a cloth warehouse for storing the finished product. All the main departments at both mills were grouped around an engine house, thus permitting a simple power transmission system, and the saw-tooth roofing gave good lighting throughout the main blocks of sheds.

Room and power mills

Most textile mills were owner-occupied. Others, constituting an unknown proportion, were designed for occupation by two or more tenants. The renting of rooms in a mill and multi-occupation were common in

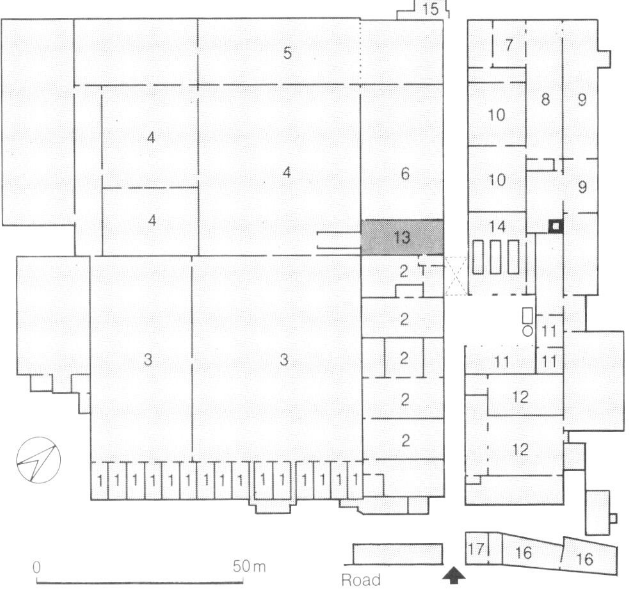

Fig 177 Alverthorpe Mills, Alverthorpe with Thornes (4), aerial view from the east and block plan. The mill was built in 1870–2 as an integrated woollen mill on a single-storeyed plan with different departments grouped around a central power source according to the sequence of production. The block plan shows recent uses of buildings, but these probably follow the original arrangements closely.

the earliest years of factory production, but were largely an opportunist arrangement. It was doubtless the clear demand for such arrangements which stimulated speculators to build mills specifically for the purpose. Room and power mills should be defined as factories built and maintained by a concern with the principal intention of providing rented workspace for a tenant or, more commonly, a number of tenants. The benefits for the builders included, obviously, a rental income from the tenants and the potential to take space themselves. For the tenants, the advantages of renting room and power lay principally in the low capital outlay; sometimes even machinery was available for hire. Men of very limited means could therefore participate in factory production, and room and power was extremely important in permitting the survival of small firms.

Room and power mills were being operated in Manchester from the late 18th century.[47] The origins of room and power working in Yorkshire are unknown, but rented accommodation was widely available by the early 19th century.[48] An observer of Huddersfield's development *c*1830 noted that several mills were in the course of construction on the west side of the town and that 'the man that built the largest of them, I was told, built it for the purpose of letting to the manufacturers to make cloth, on hire'.[49] The mill in question was probably Folly Hall Mills, Huddersfield (63), developed in 1825 and later by Joseph Kaye, a prominent local stonemason, builder and architect. Kaye built what turned into an industrial village, dominated by trades not only from the woollen industry but also including cotton spinners, engineers and ultimately many other occupations. The first mill was of six storeys; a second mill, built in 1835, had six storeys and an attic, and a third, smaller, mill existed by 1838. Grouped around these buildings were two stoves or cloth dryhouses, a gas plant, and a 'weaving factory', a long five-storeyed range. The result was a complex of great size (Fig 178). In 1861, twenty-eight separate businesses operated from the site (Table 1).

Cannon Mills, Horton (58), built in 1826 by Samuel Cannon, a worsted stuff merchant, was another early room and power mill. It provided John Foster, previously a manufacturer on the putting-out system, with his first factory premises when he took space there for spinning in 1834. The opportunities created by the availability of room and power are demonstrated by Foster's experiment, for just a year later he was able to move out of Cannon Mills to his own newly constructed spinning mill at Black Dyke, Northowram.[50] Black Dyke was doubtless built more out of long-term accumulated profits from his established stuff-manufacturing business than by the proceeds of a year's machine spinning,

TABLE 1 Folly Hall Mills, 1861 list of occupiers

Woollen textiles trades	Worsted trades	Cotton trades	Others
6 scribbling millers 3 woollen manufacturers 3 cloth finishers 3 rag grinders 1 fulling miller 1 woollen spinner 1 woollen spinner and scribbling miller 1 woollen and cotton dyer	1 worsted spinner	3 cotton spinners and doublers 1 cotton spinner 1 cotton warp manufacturer	1 machine maker 1 shuttle maker 1 steam saw mills

Source: Post Office *Directory of Yorkshire* (1861), 357

but nevertheless the availability of room and power was important in giving a start in mill working.

Room and power became more common, or perhaps just more formalised, after 1850. Large mills like Britannia Mills, Lockwood (90) (Fig 179), were built to let to tenants: in 1872, it housed nine different companies. Another Britannia Mills, this time in Huddersfield (61), was developed in and after 1860 as a speculation by a local engineer. The first buildings were two five-storeyed mills with an attached power plant, a warehouse and a small shed, and by 1880 the site was completed by the addition of further warehouses and an enlarged shed, grouped around a small central yard (Fig 180). As early as 1861, rooms were advertised to let, and in 1866 'three fireproof rooms' were vacant, their size (50 x 15 yards) showing that the rooms were in fact complete floors within one of the mills.[51] The diversity of Huddersfield's textile industry is illustrated by the range of occupiers in 1868, when a cotton spinner, two yarn spinners, two woollen spinners, two woollen manufacturers, a fancy woollen manufacturer, a cotton waste dealer, a wool cleaner and a woollen weaver all had

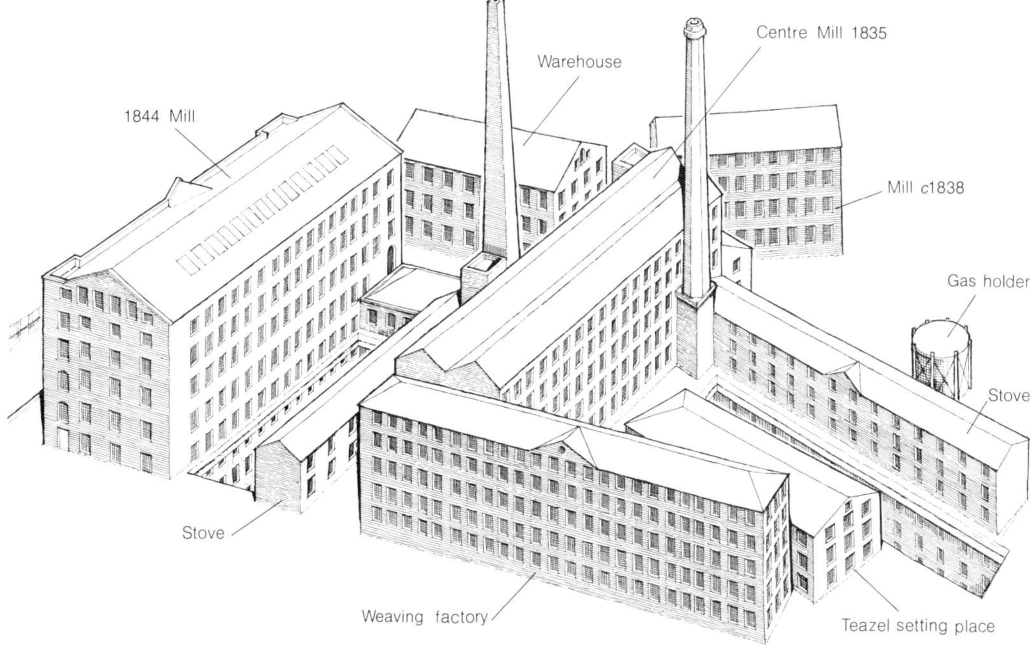

Fig 178 Folly Hall Mills, Huddersfield (63), in about 1850, showing the three powered multi-storeyed mills, the weaving factory, stoves and other buildings.

Fig 179 Britannia Mills, Lockwood (90). The builders, Firth and Sons, operated from the small mill in the foreground before the construction in 1861 of the large main mill.

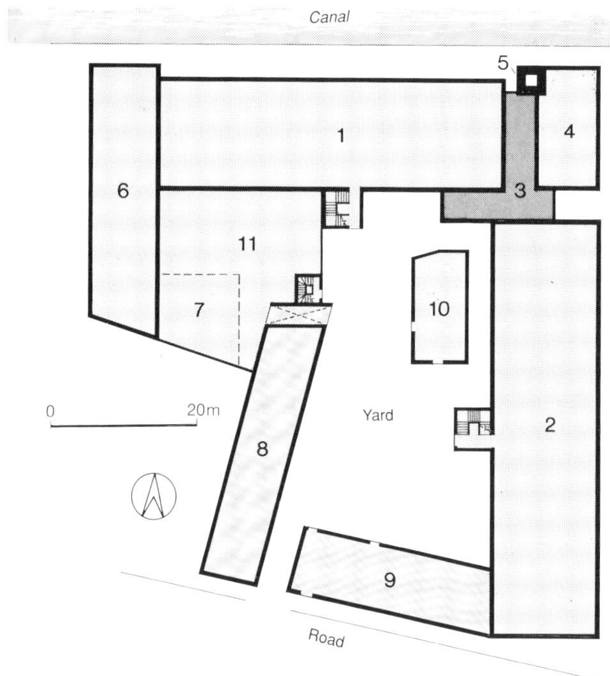

1	Mill 1860–2	5	Chimney	9	Warehouse
2	Mill 1860–2	6	Warehouse 1860–2	10	Warehouse 1876
3	Engine house	7	Shed 1860–2	11	Weaving shed 1879
4	Boiler house	8	Warehouse pre-1879		

Fig 180 Britannia Mills, Huddersfield (61), block plan. The site was developed after 1860 as a room and power mill.

space in the complex. In 1866 there had even been a waste-silk dealer in part of the complex.

Room and power became particularly important in specialist weaving areas. Weaving attracted men of limited capital, and the average size of weaving firms was smaller than that of spinning or integrated companies.[52] Room and power, therefore, was attractive to the manufacturer setting up in a small way. Pecket Well Shed, Wadsworth (141), built by the Pecket Well Weaving Shed Company Limited in 1858 (Fig 181), and Union Mills, Skipton (121), established in 1867 by the Skipton Land and Building Company, were both intended for letting to tenants. The shed at Union Mills was occupied in 1882 by four companies, and in 1920–1 by six, the largest running 372 looms, the smallest only fifty-two.

The special tenurial arrangements within room and power mills seem not to have been reflected in their design. In both weaving mills and mills of more general function, like Britannia Mills, Huddersfield (61), the principal design requirement was flexibility. Pecket Well Shed (141) was built to be let 'either altogether or as room and power, in small and large portions or sections, and either to one or more persons'. Changes in the numbers of tenants, caused by the success or failure of occupying firms, therefore made permanent subdivision a disadvantage. In multi-storeyed mills floors or parts of floors were let individually, and in sheds impermanent divisions were used to segregate companies: at one new mill in Todmorden in 1857–8 tenants began operations 'as fast as the shafting and sheet-iron division between sections could be fixed'.[53]

Specialist mill types

The mill types discussed hitherto were involved wholly or in part with one or both of the two central stages of production: spinning and weaving. Some, like the cotton-spinning mill, also took in preparatory processes, others, like the integrated woollen mill, were involved at the finishing stage as well. Throughout the period 1825–1900, however, there were many establishments which specialised in either the preparatory or the finishing stages of production.

COMBING AND TOPMAKING WORKS

Combing was the principal preparatory process in the worsted industry. Before the development of machines, the process was largely undertaken by specialist master combers working from small workshops (see p17). The sector's reaction to the introduction of machine combing in the mid 19th century was mixed. The major spinners and manufacturers – Salt in 1850–3, Fosters in 1854, Marriners in 1854 – could afford the high costs both of the new machines and of buildings to house them, but smaller businesses continued initially to rely on hand combing, either sending wool out to commission combers or employing their own labour force. The advantages of machine working, however, increasingly eroded the livelihood of the hand combers: one machine could do the work of one hundred manual workers.[54] Since the costs of setting up a combing department were so high, specialist commission combing works were established to satisfy the demand for mechanised services. Because Bradford was the commercial and supply centre of the worsted branch, these commission works became heavily concentrated in the town. In 1853, it was said that the very numerous hand combers were in a depressed state since their 'trade has lately been nearly annihilated by the substitution of machinery for manual labour', and four of the town's thirteen listed machine combers were stated to work on commission.[55] By 1893 there were sixty woolcombers in operation in the West Riding, mainly in and around Bradford but with smaller

Fig 181 Pecket Well Shed, Wadsworth (141), built in 1858 for letting to tenants, was doubled in size c1870. Attached to the first shed is a tall engine house, behind which is a four-storeyed building giving boiler house, sizing room, warehouse and office.

Fig 182 Cumberland Works, Manningham (92), a woolcombing works of 1875 and later.

numbers in the satellite towns and villages of the worsted area.[56]

The date of the first purpose-built combing works is not known. The largest Bradford establishment, Alston Works, was built by Isaac Holden in 1861, and this may be one of the earliest of the type. It developed into an enormous concern, occupying 15 acres and employing 1,000 people in 1885.[57] Cumberland Works, Manningham (92), begun in 1875 by James Burnley, illustrates the principal characteristics of the commission combing works. The main working areas were sheds, at Cumberland in two blocks, both of more than one phase and separated by a narrow yard (Fig 182). The slope of the land allowed a full basement under the main block, used for storing wool received from customers (Fig 183). The wool was taken up to the main floor for processing: after washing by machine and drying, it was carded, washed and dried again and then gilled (involving the straightening of fibres), combed and rolled into tops (Fig 184). At Alston, and probably at Cumberland, the sequence of production was arranged logically, with notional divisions in the shed between successive washing, carding, gilling and combing departments. A single floor, therefore, saw the transformation of raw wool into tops, ready for use in worsted spinning, and noils, sold to woollen manufacturers. A peculiarity of the power system at Cumberland, certainly at the planning stage although not in execution, was the proposed use not of a single engine to power the main shed but of multiple engines, presumably of small capacity, ranged along the side wall of the block. Such an arrangement was doubtless employed at Alston Works, where in 1885 there were nine engines.

Fig 183 Cumberland Works, Manningham (92). The fireproof basement floor provides storage space for wool awaiting processing.

Combing works required, or at least sometimes acquired, other buildings, associated with the washing of the wool. The grease removed from raw wool in the course of washing was potentially valuable; it was also a serious pollutant if released into the public water system. There was a double incentive, therefore, to recover it, and grease works were built in combing works and in mills which performed the washing operation. The works comprised a series of settling tanks in which the waste water could be treated with acid to separate the grease content from the water. The grease could be sold off, and different grades were used

Fig 184 Cumberland Works, Manningham (92). The main floor of the shed today houses modern scouring machines.

for paint making, ointments, lubricants and manure.[58] The vast increase in wool processing in the late 19th century, however, depressed the value of the recovered grease and it became increasingly uneconomic for companies to maintain their grease works. Whetley Mills, Manningham (95), had a grease works by 1877, expanded in 1883, and Cumberland Works (92) had one by 1885, again expanded in 1891. Neither survives.

The need for large quantities of soap for wool washing led some woolcombers, and some mills engaged in combing, to establish their own soap-making works. There was one at Black Dyke Mills in 1874, and by 1885 both Barkerend Mills, Bradford (26), and Cumberland Works (92) had one.[59] Again none has survived in recognisable form, but plans show that the main building at Cumberland Works (92) was single-storeyed, perhaps with a basement, and ventilated by a louvred central roof section.

In the late 19th century, commission combers added an important function to the range of their activities. The use of vastly increased amounts of imported wool, especially from Australia and New Zealand, in the post-1850 period weakened the position of the woolstapler as the supplier of the West Riding worsted industry. The woolstapler had acted as a co-ordinator of domestic wool supplies, but many manufacturers had bypassed them to make direct purchases from producers. Imported wool was even further beyond the stapler's control, and was bought by manufacturers at London auctions. Offering little but supply, the woolstapler declined in importance. There was, however, scope for an intermediary between sale room and producer, and commission combers increasingly filled this role. Acting as wool buyers and as combers, they could offer for sale a product, tops, which was used at the start of processing by spinners and manufacturers. The only loss to these interests was control over the important sorting stage, but the woolcomber was able to prove his skill in this department by offering a product suited to the customer's requirements. The woolcomber's role merged, therefore, into that of the topmaker, first recorded in 1874 but clearly then well established.[60] The position of the topmaker was further strengthened in the last decades of the 19th century, when growing quantities of tops were exported to the developing European worsted industry.[61] Today Woolcombers Ltd, based at Fairweather Green, Bradford, serves a world-wide market.

Fig 185 Cumberland Works, Manningham (92). These large warehouses date from 1887 and 1910.

The changed role of the woolcomber found prominent architectural expression. As the principal agency of wool supply to the West Riding industry, the topmaker had an enormous turnover of stocks and needed large storage capacity. In consequence, Bradford combing works developed by the addition of warehouses. Cumberland Works (92) was extended by the construction of two warehouses, the first built in 1887 and the second in 1910; the earlier building had a storage capacity of over 2,200 square metres, the later building one of over 3,000 square metres (Fig 185). The typical topmaking works, therefore, was dominated by two building forms, the multi-storeyed warehouse for the storage and sorting of raw wool, and the single-storeyed shed for washing and combing.

FINISHING WORKS

There were two principal types of specialist finishing works: bleachworks, important for cotton and linen, and dyeworks, common to all branches. The survival rate of both types has not been good, and their form is known largely from documentary evidence.

Bleachworks

The processes involved in bleaching – repeated washing, soaking in a mild acid solution and in caustic lye, and boiling – all used liquids, and bleaching was therefore almost exclusively carried out in single-storeyed buildings. Bleachworks were usually small in scale and comprised a close grouping of sheds for processing, warehouses for storage, and a power plant of engine house, boiler house and chimney. An 1895 plan of Swithen Bleach Works, Kexbrough (77), shows the component buildings (Fig 186). Walton and Co of Castle Mill, Scriven with Tentergate (114), used the nearby Crimple Mill as its bleachworks. Added to the early spinning mill were two bleaching sheds, warehouses, a yarn-drying stove, cloth-drying sheds, a counting house and watchman's house. The bleaching sheds housed liquor troughs, pans for boiling yarn and cloth, chlorine cisterns and sour tubs, as well as a wash house. The yarn-drying stove, 14.9 by 6.3 metres, had timber posts and rails and a stone flag floor; the cloth-drying sheds had just poles and drying must have been naturally by air.[62] The atmospheric bleaching of

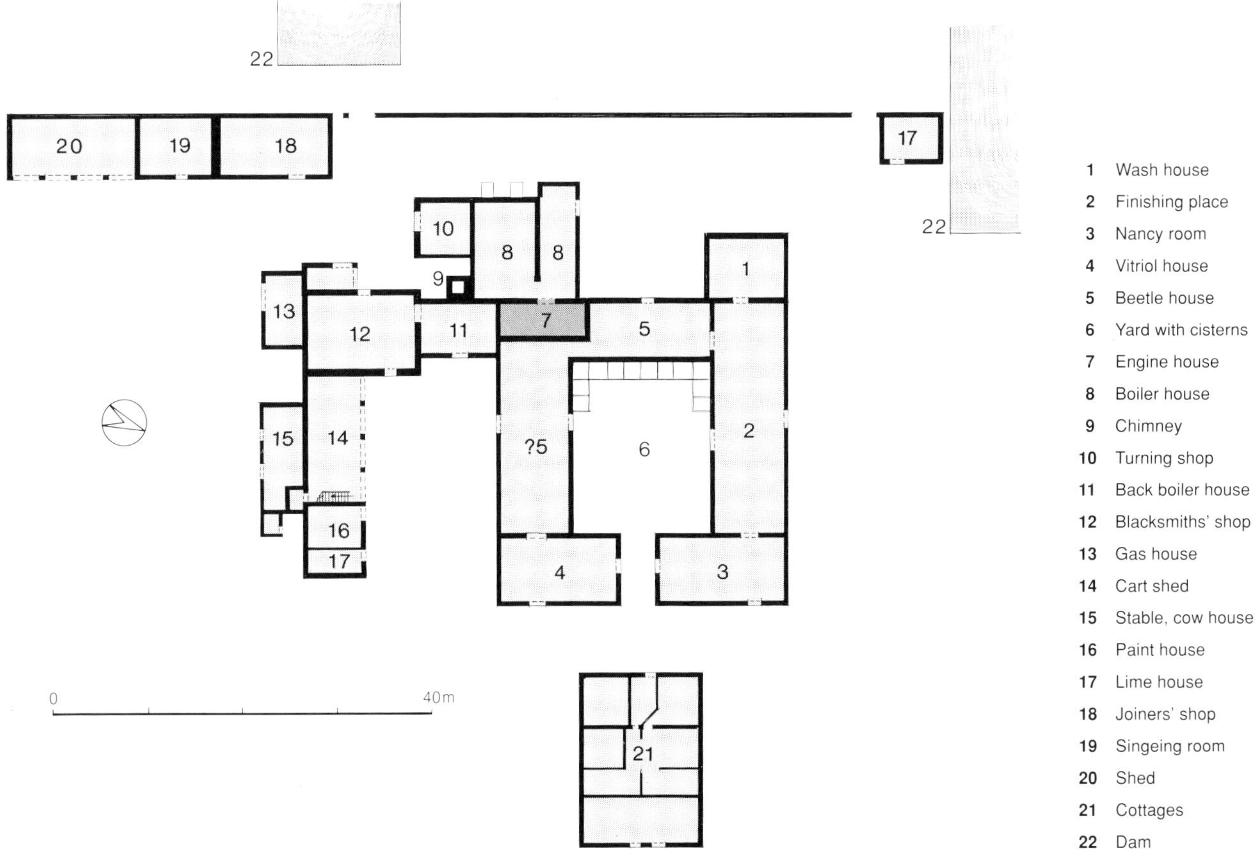

Fig 186 Swithen Bleachworks, Kexbrough (77). Plan of the complex, redrawn from a plan of 1895.

Fig 187 Crimple Mill, Scriven with Tentergate, showing the fields in the foreground used for open-air bleaching.

cloth involved both laying it out on the grass and hanging it on posts and rails (Fig 187).

Calendering, that is, the rolling of linen cloth between cylinders to give a smooth finish, was undertaken by some bleachworks, but specialist calendering units also served the industry. Little is known about the layout of such sites, although Hope Mill, Barnsley (12), which also became involved in printing linen, comprised storeyed buildings including a mill and warehouses.

Dyeworks

Specialist dyeworks had a long history in the Yorkshire textile industry. Leeds was the dominant dyeing and finishing centre before 1825, and after 1825 other towns, especially Bradford, developed a strong specialist involvement. The principal obstacle to progress in the dyeing industry was the difficulty of obtaining good results in mixed-fibre cloths: in a cotton-warp worsted cloth, for example, the cotton and wool content reacted differently to treatment.[63] Considerable advances were made, however, in both mixed-fibre and single-fibre cloth dyeing, but the increasingly scientific nature of the occupation encouraged manufacturers to use the services of commission dyers. Some dyeworks were small in scale. Jesse Street Dyeworks, Horton (59), for example, originated as warehouses before being adapted for use as a dyeworks at the end of the 19th century (Fig 188). At Bridge Royd Dyeworks, Stansfield (132) (Fig 189), cotton corduroy was processed; the material was first stored in a warehouse (14) and dried in a shed (15). The surface of the cloth was then raised in another shed (13) and the corduroy cut in another building (12). Scouring, in shed 3, and washing, in part of the dyehouse (2), removed the size from the cloth, which was then dried (4). Dyeing, or bleaching if needed, then took place in the dyehouse, and finally the cloth was dried in a tentering machine, inspected and packed (11).

Perhaps the largest dyeworks were located in Bradford, where the textile industry was served by cotton, worsted and mixed-cloth dyeing concerns. Oakwood Dyeworks developed after 1873 as a cotton dyeworks, first taking in yarn and later cloth. The complex comprised a number of single-storeyed sheds, some with saw-tooth roofs, some with equal-pitched roofs, with storeyed buildings for warehousing, offices and drying rooms (Fig 190). The greatest of the Bradford dyeworks, however, was the Bowling Dye Works of Edward Ripley and Sons (Fig 85). Now almost entirely demolished, this huge complex developed rapidly in the mid 19th century and at one stage was said to employ 1,500 workers and be capable of processing 25 million yards of cloth every year.[64] The site covered five acres and had four dyehouses (for black, blue and coloured dyeing) and departments for crabbing (to prevent later shrinkage), singeing and checking. Ripleys, like other dyeing concerns, were also finishers, and the site

Fig 188 Jesse Street Dyeworks, Horton (59), converted from warehouses in the late 19th century, was among the smallest dyeworks in Bradford.

Fig 189 Bridge Royd Dyeworks, Stansfield (132), aerial view from the west and block plan showing the flow of processes.

included rooms for tentering and pressing. The company had its own private railway siding for the delivery of coal and logwood, and the preparation of dyes was done in a dyeware mill, a dyestore and a chemical laboratory.[65]

The importance of water supply to finishing companies – whether bleachers or dyers – is obvious. In the early 1870s, Ripleys used 450 million gallons annually and even a small bleacher such as William Wood, employing thirty-two hands at Rawdon near Leeds, used 4 million gallons.[66] The need for water influenced location, and sites by rivers and becks were commonly employed. Subterranean reservoirs freed the industry to some extent of the influence of surface drainage and many Bradford dyeworks, and many mills too, sank wells and boreholes to draw on these supplies.

The shoddy and mungo mill

The successful development of machines for the grinding of soft, loosely woven rags *c*1809 and of hard rags *c*1834, giving shoddy and mungo respectively, gave rise to an important recovered wool industry.[67] Located chiefly in the Dewsbury–Ossett–Morley triangle, the centre of the Heavy Woollen area, it produced material which was re-used by local mills in low-grade woollen cloths, the recovered fibre being blended with new wool at the preparatory stage of production.

Detailed knowledge of the industry before 1850 is lacking, but evidence suggests that the main period of growth came after 1860, when the English industry developed better techniques and offered, therefore, a better product. Before 1860 most shoddy and mungo was produced by woollen manufacturers within their own mills, but the diversification of the industry in terms of the sources of supply and types of rag made possible the emergence of a strong specialist sector. In 1889 seventy-one firms were listed as mungo manufacturers, rag grinders or shoddy manufacturers, concentrated mainly in the Heavy Woollen area but with significant representation also in Leeds and Huddersfield.[68] The industry was volatile since it depended on the price of new wool: if this was high, shoddy and mungo were in demand, but declining prices removed the advantage of using recycled material and led directly to the failure of many of the small operators who made up the bulk of the sector.[69]

The larger part of the shoddy and mungo produced in Yorkshire was made in established woollen mills. In the Heavy Woollen area there were 'one, or at most two (rag-grinding) machines in each large woollen mill' in 1842, and in the mid 1860s the majority of Morley's woollen mills had between one and four rag-grinding

Fig 190 Oakwood Dyeworks, Bradford. This letterhead view of c1900 shows the large complex of buildings. The works specialised in cotton goods, taking in yarn and cloth.

machines.[70] Even in the early 20th century, rag-grinding capacity within woollen mills exceeded that of shoddy and mungo manufacturers.[71] Machines could simply be placed in the ground floor of multi-storeyed mills or in small detached sheds. At Albion Mill, Batley (15), a small shed for two machines was built near to the mill before 1850, and at Cheapside Mills, Batley (18), a three-bay shed, later extended by two bays, was built in the mill yard (Fig 191). At Oak Mills, West Ardsley (144), built in 1906, a rag-grinding bay was incorporated into a range including a milling department and engine and boiler houses (see Fig 203).

From the 1870s, purpose-built shoddy and mungo mills were constructed as specialist textile establishments working independently of woollen mills. The essential components of the type produced mills of unique character. The first requirement in a shoddy and mungo mill was for storage. The warehouse, therefore, occupied a prominent position although, because the overall size of the mill was usually small, it was customarily of modest dimensions and frequently lacked elaboration. At Perseverance Mill, Ossett (109) (Fig 192), the warehouse is of two storeys and includes heated offices on the ground floor, but at Gedham Mill, Ossett (106) (Fig 334), the large block of sheds was used as the main storage area. Carbonising and dyeing, where undertaken, appear to have been sited away from the main storage and processing buildings, probably because they were unpleasant processes. At Runtlings Mill, Ossett (110), these departments were located along two sides of the yard. Dyehouses were small, in keeping with the scale of the works, and carbonising plants, too, were limited in size. Wet carbonising involved soaking rags in an acid solution, so pits or vats were required, housed in a shed. Dry carbonising was carried out using a gas produced by heating acid in a retort. The gas was then introduced to a revolving cage filled with mixed-fibre rags, the cotton content of which was destroyed. Carbonising plants, therefore, comprised one or more of these cages with their retorts and furnaces, and

Fig 191 Rag-grinding sheds dating from c1870 in the mill yard at Cheapside Mills, Batley (18).

Fig 192 The warehouse and office block at Perseverance Mill, Ossett (109), a rag-grinding mill of 1873–4.

Fig 193 Carbonising machinery at Chickenley Mill, Ossett. The carbonising cage was contained within a brick chamber, and the remains of the retort are visible on the left.

evidence indicates that it was conventional to encase the carbonising drum with its furnace and retort in brick (Fig 193).

The main process in the mill was the grinding of the rags by rag-grinding machines or 'devils' to produce shoddy or mungo. There is documentary evidence for the use of these machines in upper storeys of buildings, but it became the practice to house them in single-storeyed sheds. The process was noisy, had a high fire risk, and was dangerous and a health hazard. As a result, machines were isolated one to a bay. The bays were generally arranged in a line producing a long, narrow range of sheds divided internally by brick walls. Machines in such a layout drew their power from a main drive-shaft, which extended from an attached engine house through the length of the building. At Runtlings Mill (110) there were at first six, later seven, bays for rag-grinding engines, and at Gedham Mill (106) there were six grinding bays and a double-width bay for scribbling (Fig 194). The sheds at Runtlings and Gedham appear to have been among the larger examples of the type: although some firms ran many more machines there is no evidence for single sheds of commensurate size. Runtlings Mill (110) shows the typical arrangement of sheds within the shoddy and mungo mill complex, isolated from other departments and drawing power from an attached engine house (Fig 195).

The supply of rags to shoddy and mungo manufacturers was an important aspect of the trade. The system of rag collection, extending throughout Britain and Europe, lay mainly outside the control of West Riding users of the materials. Inside the Heavy Woollen area, however, rag merchants, usually of small capital, found a role in the supply system. Their function was to hold stocks of rags and in some cases to sort them according to colour and grade. The rag merchants, employing a few sorters and packers, operated from warehouses, concentrated in the Bradford Road area of Dewsbury, close to the railway stations. Machells' Warehouse, Dewsbury (32), a good example, was built in 1863, and comprised offices and a four-storeyed storage, sorting and packing area (Fig 196). Ossett also developed a large rag merchant group, specialising in mungo supplies, and Spedding Oddy's rag warehouse, Ossett (111), built in 1864–5, combines a modest dwelling at the front with a working area at the rear (Figs 197, 198). Some merchants became involved in the supply not only of rags but also of the finished product, shoddy and mungo, selling direct to local woollen manufacturers. These supplies, however, were largely imported, mainly from Germany, and a colony of German merchants controlled the trade. Many became established in Dewsbury and Batley, the names – Reuss, Stross, Lindemann and Galaup – standing out in directories and other sources from the local Thackrahs and Howroyds. Their warehouses could be impressive both in design, shown by Klein and Steigerwald's 1876 expansion of their Dewsbury premises, and in size, S Stross and Sons' Scout Hill base having a very large storage capacity (Figs 199, 200).

Fig 194 Gedham Mill, Ossett (106), built in 1897–8 as a mungo mill, has a shed block which contained six rag-grinding machines and a scribbling engine.

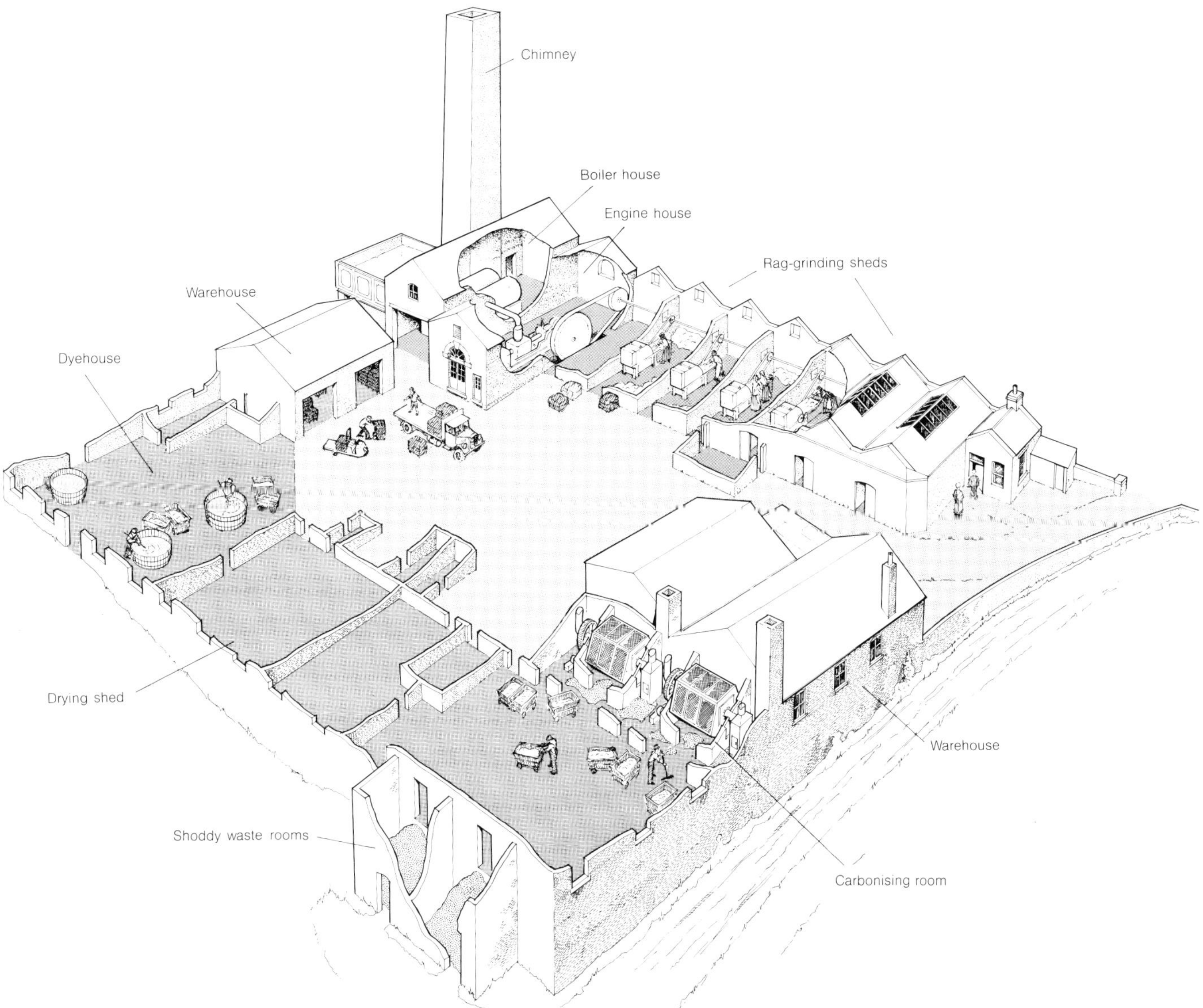

Fig 195 Runtlings Mill, Ossett (110), built c1907, shows the typical form of the shoddy and mungo mill, with a range of sheds for rag grinding, attached engine and boiler houses, dyehouses, sorting areas, carbonising department and warehouse.

Mills in the early 20th century

The history of the Yorkshire textile industry in the 20th century ultimately shows a picture of decline in overall output, employment and numbers of mills in operation. The start of the decline is not obvious, however, and the process was far from even. The different branches of the industry show varying experiences. The flax and linen sector was already in terminal decline before 1900, and not even a shift away from linens to low-grade articles like canvas and rope proved successful.[72] The Yorkshire cotton industry had performed well in the late 19th century but its fate was ultimately dependent on the fortunes of the Lancashire industry and on those of the Yorkshire wool textiles sector, both of which it supplied.[73] Silk mills continued in production in small numbers; one, at Low Bentham, closed only in 1970.[74]

In the wool textiles sector the late 19th century had witnessed declining sales to Europe and the USA in the face of competition from home-based manufacturers and of prohibitive tariffs. This loss was, however, off-set by the exploitation of new markets in South America, the Far East and, especially, the Empire. Home demand, too, was always important, particularly in wartime. The wool textiles sector reached record production levels before the First World War, and the war itself brought massive government orders.[75]

Fig 196 Machells' Warehouse, Bradford Road, Dewsbury (32), built in 1863 by rag and wool merchants.

Fig 197 Spedding Oddy's rag warehouse, Ossett (111), built in 1864–5, was in use for rag sorting until recent years.

Building activity between 1900 and 1930 had two aspects. Many long-established mills either expanded with the addition of new sheds or mills, or replaced existing buildings by new ones. Entirely new mills were also built, however, frequently by existing companies. Some, like Becks Mill, Keighley (70), were constructed as 'daughter' mills to a main works elsewhere. Others, like Oak Mills, West Ardsley (144), and Park View Mills, North Bierley (103), were built by companies relocating from rented or room and power premises. Relocation was also the reason for the construction of Ardsley Mills, East Ardsley (35), built by Thomas Ambler and Sons, but in this case the move, from a long-established base in Bradford, was justified by the availability of cheap coal supplies and female labour at the new site. One new mill – Hare Mill, Stansfield (134), later renamed Mons Mill – was erected by the newly formed Hare Spinning Company for cotton spinning. Four of the directors were, however, already involved in the cotton industry in the Manchester area.

Most new mills were specialised in function, concentrating on either spinning, weaving, or shoddy and mungo production. Spinning mills were usually of medium or large size, reflecting the fact that the builders were frequently already well established in the business. In the spinning mills the impression is one of simplicity, with a single main building and its associated power plant dominating the site (Fig 201). The mill building was now all but synonymous with the factory. At Knowle Mill, Keighley (73), there was a small shed at the rear of the site, at Ardsley Mills (35) there was a detached office block, and at Becks Mill (70) there was a

Fig 198 The top floor of Spedding Oddy's warehouse, showing rags in the process of being sorted.

Fig 199 Klein and Steigerwald's mungo warehouse, Dewsbury, proposed extension, 1876 (West Yorkshire Archive Service, Kirklees: Dewsbury Building Plans, no. 2971).

Fig 200 Scout Hill Mills, Dewsbury, used by S Stross and Sons for rag sorting.

low structure attached to one corner, but warehouses for raw material and yarn, common in earlier spinning mills, were absent. Site planning at three mills – Mons (134), Becks (70) and Knowle (73) – was affected by plans for further expansion in 'double-mill' form, the first mill being positioned to allow room for later additions, but only at Knowle were plans realised.

Simplicity was also the dominant characteristic of the specialist weaving mills of the early 20th century. The requirements of the weaving mill were established by the 1850s, and no great changes followed. Twentieth-century weaving mills were generally small and comprised a warehouse and a weaving shed (Fig 202). The warehouse was usually storeyed and gave space for offices, storage, minor powered processes such as winding and warping, and unpowered operations such as checking and mending. At Devonshire Mills, Keighley (72), the warehouse was used for yarn storage in the basement, for offices and storage on the ground floor, for storage on the first floor, and for mending on the top-lit second floor. At Park View Mills (103), the storage and other functions of the warehouse were contained in a single-storey unit along one side of the shed, with further storage in the basement. New Close

Fig 201 Ardsley Mills, East Ardsley (35), built in 1912 for worsted spinning. The engine house projecting from the centre of the mill provided rope drive. Company housing and a detached office block stand in the vicinity.

Fig 202 Stadium Mills, North Bierley (104), built in 1912 as a worsted-weaving mill, has a simple layout with shed and attached warehouse.

Shed, Silsden (117), lacked a warehouse of any description in its first phase. Weaving was housed in the shed attached to the warehouse. At Park View Mills (103), the shed had two levels, basement and main floor, but in the other mills there was just a single level. The nature of the power systems used in these mills – gas engines at Stadium Mills, North Bierley (104), and New Close Shed (117), electricity at Devonshire Mills (72) and Park View Mills (103) – assisted in the compact design and contrasts with the large steam installations required in some contemporary spinning mills. At Stadium Mills (104) the engine was housed in a small room at the corner of the shed, and at Devonshire (72) and Park View Mills (103) electricity was purchased from a public company. The small size of the firms which built these weaving mills is evident from the number of looms which they ran: it is known that there were 140 looms at Devonshire Mills (72), 130 at New Close Shed (117) and only 54 at Stadium Mills. The average number of looms in a Bradford worsted manufacturing business in 1919–20 was a little short of 200.[76]

New integrated mills were also built in the early 20th century. Oak Mills (144), an integrated woollen mill of 1906, is typical of its area in date and range of functions (Fig 203). Its design, however, is unusual, for it originally combined spinning and weaving in the main mill, with powerlooms on the ground floor and preparatory and spinning stages on the upper floors. A detached range provided engine and boiler houses, and sheds for milling, willeying and rag grinding. This modest beginning proved successful, and in 1929, at the very end of the period covered by this volume, a weaving shed was built in a planned expansion. Thereafter Oak Mills corresponded to the conventional pattern of woollen mills, in which the functions of spinning and weaving were segregated, one contained in a storeyed building, the other in a shed.

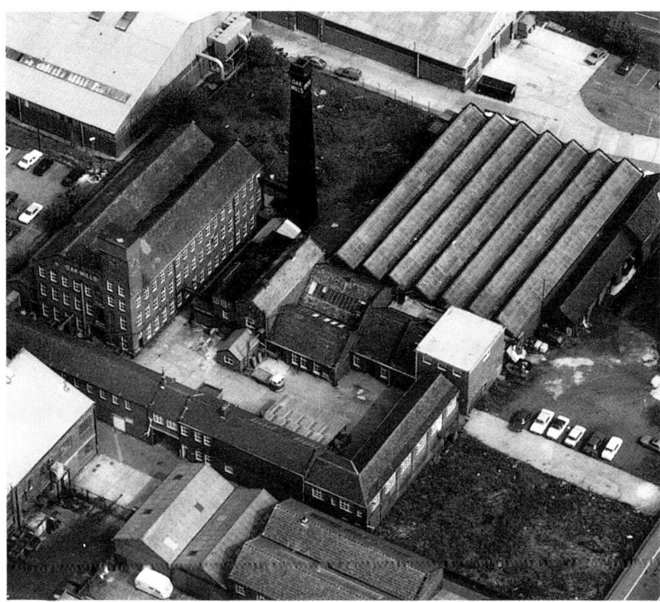

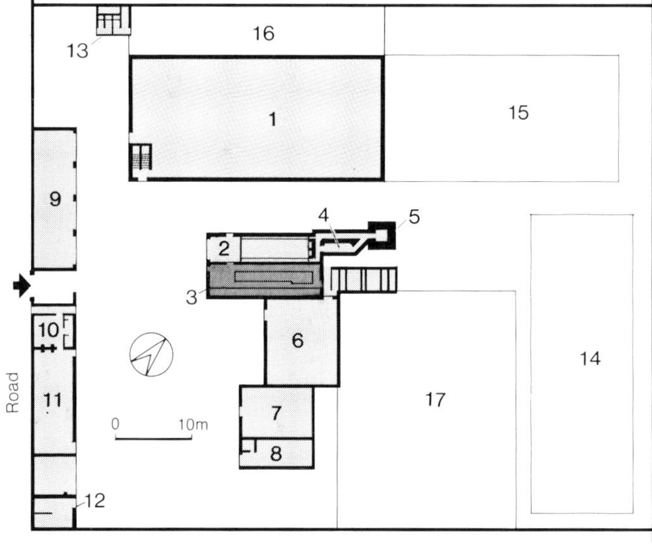

1	Mill	7	Willey place	13	Privies
2	Boiler house	8	Rag-grinding place	14	Reservoir
3	Engine house	9	Mungo shed	15	Future extension of mill
4	Economiser	10	Office		
5	Chimney	11	Warehouse	16	Future shed
6	Milling Place	12	Stable	17	Future weaving shed

Fig 203 Oak Mills, West Ardsley (144), aerial view from the south and block plan showing the layout of this integrated woollen mill in 1910. The plan includes provision for expansion of the mill (not executed) and for the construction of a weaving shed, built in 1929 (plan redrawn from 1910 architects' plans).

4
Power and power transmission

The application of mechanical power to manual crafts and trades was the key element in the process by which Britain emerged as an industrial economy in the 18th and 19th centuries. It is no longer accepted that steam power was the mother of invention in the textile industry, for it has been shown that many of the early mechanical improvements were designed with muscle power in mind. Nevertheless the link between the adoption of mechanical power, generated first mainly by water and later mainly by steam, and the very rapid expansion of the textile industry from the 1770s is universally acknowledged.

The use of mechanical power distinguishes the textile mill from the workshop, and thus the arrangements made to provide and transmit power are of special interest in the study of the evolution of the mill. This chapter will examine the different forms of power adopted in textile mills between the late 18th century and the early 20th century; will show what architectural provision was made for the generation of power; and, finally, will study the different methods by which power was transmitted within the mill.

The subject of power generation, transmission and use concerns machines, broadly defined. In William Fairbairn's words:

> the machinery of mills . . . may be generally divided into three classes:– the *prime movers*, from which the power is derived for keeping the machinery of the mill in motion: the *transmissive* machinery or *millwork* (shafting, gearing etc.) by which the power obtained through the prime mover is distributed over the different parts of the mill . . . and lastly, the *machines*, technically so called, by which the special operations of the mill in the preparation of its manufactures are carried out.[1]

The vital importance of an economical and efficient power system in textile mills caused, if not constant change, then at least intermittent alterations to or, more rarely, wholesale replacement of existing installations. The result is that Yorkshire mills rarely retain substantial elements of their original power systems. Few waterwheels and no beam or vertical engines remain *in situ*; only a handful of horizontal engines survives; and early transmission systems were almost universally replaced in this century by electrical drive. The buildings of the textile mill, however, show the siting of prime movers, and the form of wheelhouse and engine house indicates the general nature of the machines they housed. Furthermore, in most mills the type of transmission system adopted originally is usually evident, and it is frequently possible to chart the major changes with some precision. Despite the fact, therefore, that a mill today may represent a shell with no contents, architectural evidence can usually indicate the broad outline of the means of generating power and of transmitting it to the principal working areas.

Animal and hand power

All branches of the textile industry, apart from shoddy and mungo, originated in the era of hand power. Before the late 18th century, fulling, raising, beetling and silk throwing were the only mechanised processes, and for the rest the industry was dependent on the spinning wheel, the handloom and other small hand-operated machines. The key inventions of the 1760s and 1770s were originally designed to use animal or manual power. Arkwright's spinning frame was envisaged as a horse-driven machine; Cartwright's abortive experiment with a powerloom used a bull for power; donkeys were used by Paul and Wyatt to drive their roller frames; and Hargreaves' jenny and Crompton's mule were built first for manual operation.[2] The advantages of using mechanical power, which allowed machines to grow in size and production to increase, soon became obvious, but the contribution of hand and animal power in the earliest years of mill working should not be overlooked.

Evidence for the use of animal power in Yorkshire mills is derived exclusively from documents. Insurance policies, newspaper advertisements and other sources reveal that a number of woollen scribbling and carding mills used horses in the late 18th century.[3] In Otley there was a horse-driven cotton mill and there was a two-horse mill at Skipton in 1793.[4] While the nature of the power made it particularly appropriate in the smallest mills, it is known that in some Lancashire and Nottinghamshire mills as many as ten or a dozen horses could be used, generating a power equal to that of many waterwheels and early steam engines.[5] The technology of the horse wheel was fully developed by the late 18th century and the employment of horses freed manufacturers from the locational constraints imposed by the use of water power. The only requirements were the animals, a horse wheel and a building to contain them. Horse power was thus cheap to set up, but running costs were high owing to the need for shifts of horses to ensure continuous working. It is not known how long animal power persisted. Steam engines replaced horses in some Lancashire and Nottinghamshire mills as early as the 1780s and 1790s,[6] and as steam engines became more reliable in the early 19th century the same change doubtless took place in the few Yorkshire mills which depended on horses. Of the Yorkshire textile firms making returns to the 1834 inquiry into child employment, only one used animal power, Thomas Taylor of Barnsley having 'one horse . . . employed for winding yarn upon bobbins from the hanks, in a large chamber over the warehouse'.[7] The common replacement of horses by other forms of power is illustrated by the progress of a Mirfield woollen mill, established *c*1779, where 'the first power employed was a horse: afterwards water, from a small brook, at present steam'.[8]

Hand power had a longer currency. In the late 18th century hand power was used in some woollen scribbling mills; it was used, as noted above, for early mules, and jennies were hand operated in the woollen industry until the 1820s.[9] Even in the mid 19th century hand power remained important, in the worsted branch until machine combing was widely adopted and in the woollen branch, especially in the fancy cloth trade, for weaving. So indispensable was hand power that special-purpose buildings, in particular loomshops (see pp19–22), were erected to house the processes dependent on it. The absence of evidence in some mills for the original use of power on some upper floors of multi-storeyed buildings may be further evidence that provision was being made for hand-powered working. At Winker Green Mill, Armley (8), for example, a woollen mill, the upper floors in the 1833 mill appear to have been unpowered originally. The importance of manual operation has, in fact, never been threatened in some stages of production, for wool sorting, the checking of the cloth for faults (perching) and mending remain to this day skilled hand operations. These processes demanded good light, either from large windows in the side walls or by top-lighting in sheds and on the top floors of some storeyed buildings (Fig 204).

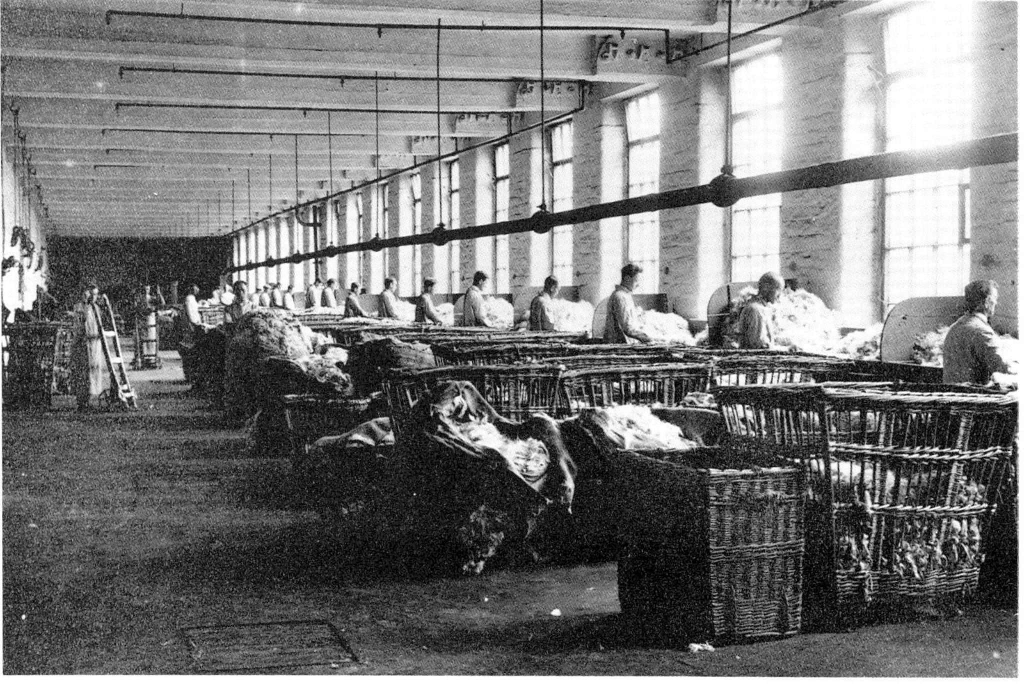

Fig 204 Wool sorting in the warehouse at Saltaire Mills, Shipley (116).

Water power

The waterwheel was the major source of power in pre-industrial England. Wherever there was a need for more than human or animal muscle the demand was most often met by water – in mining, metallurgy, corn grinding and cloth fulling.[10] In the West Riding of Yorkshire fulling mills are recorded as early as the 12th century and by the middle decades of the 18th century over one hundred were in operation, all of them probably water-powered.[11]

Scientific study, particularly in the 18th and early 19th centuries, improved the efficiency of water-power technology. Before 1700 wheels rarely gave more than ten horse power, but advances by John Smeaton, John Rennie, Thomas Hewes and others allowed better control of water flow and an increase in the output of wheels. These improvements concerned the construction of the wheel, with iron replacing wooden parts and with the development of the suspension wheel; the design of features on the wheel such as the buckets and gearing mechanisms; and the control of water flow through sluices.[12] By the early 19th century some waterwheels could generate one hundred horse power or more; Fairbairn's two Catrine (Scotland) wheels of 1824 were each capable of producing 120 horse power, far more than contemporary steam engines.[13] More commonly, however, wheels were of much lower power: the average output of water-powered installations recorded in Yorkshire mills in 1834 was rather less than twenty horse power, quite adequate for many early factories.[14] Where water supply permitted, output could be increased by adding another wheel. At Armitage Bridge Mills, South Crosland (127), for example, there were by 1834 three wheels, of thirty, thirty and sixty horse power, and there are numerous examples of mills with two or more wheels.

The dependence of the textile industry on water power before the 1790s is reflected in the distribution of mill sites, located where the capacity of rivers and becks permitted.[15] Even after the introduction of steam power, water remained an important source of power, dominant before 1800 and maintaining an important role well into the 19th century. The amount of water power available in Yorkshire mills increased steadily until the 1860s, even though it declined in proportion to that generated by steam.[16] A large new wheel was installed at Rishworth Mills, near Sowerby Bridge, in 1864, and as late as 1882 Marriners of Greengate Mills in Keighley considered the installation of a new wheel to be a better option than complete reliance on steam power.[17] In remote upland areas such as upper Wharfedale and Nidderdale's tributary valleys, away from railway lines and therefore cheap coal, water power remained the dominant source throughout the 19th century and wheels continued to turn machines into the 20th century on some sites.[18] The development of efficient water turbines in the mid 19th century gave water power a new lease of life,[19] and in many mills wheels were replaced by turbines.

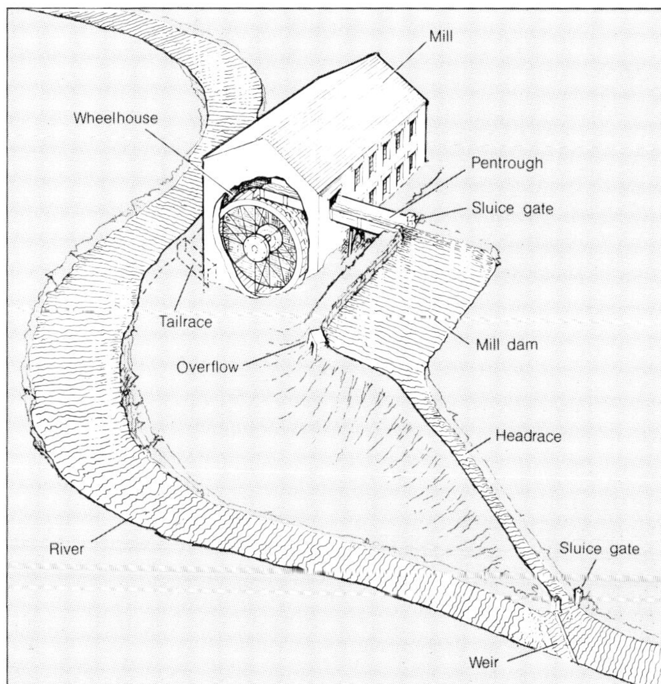

Fig 205 The components of a typical water-powered system.

Water power was not, of course, free. There were obvious costs such as those of the waterwheel itself and the construction of a system of water supply and disposal. There were sometimes hidden costs as well, like rental charges on the favoured sites, or loss of working time in periods when the waterwheel could not function owing to irregular water supplies.[20] Waterwheels varied in price according to size and method of construction. A wheel of modest size could be purchased for £350 in the late 18th century, but large iron wheels, such as that installed at Dewsbury Mills in 1827–8, could cost as much as £3,000 or more.[21] Once working, however, a water-powered system was cheap to maintain and gave a smooth, easy motion advantageous in the operation of textile machinery.

Water continued to be an important source of power within the industry for a number of reasons. To some extent the early dependence of the textile industry on water power bound the two together longer than otherwise might have been the case. The early difficulties in the operation of steam engines and, as we shall see, the high cost of their purchase and running in some locations, made water power competitive. Water power, too, was efficient and, especially in the early decades of mill building, gave greater output than the first steam engines. The continuing appreciation by millowners of the advantages of water power is clear when it is considered that the combined effect of the spread of the railways, the fall in the price of coal and the vastly superior steam engines of the mid 19th century could not persuade many of them to scrap an existing water-power system.

A water-power installation had a number of components. Rotative motion was produced by a prime mover, either a waterwheel or a water turbine, usually contained within a wheelhouse or turbine house. Water supply was maintained by the use of a weir across a river or beck; a leat, channel, goit or headrace, often requiring earthworks and some masonry work, taking water from the main flow to or towards the mill; a mill dam, a term used here to denote both the necessary embankments and the water itself; a pentrough taking water from the headrace or mill dam on to the wheel; and a tailrace leading water back to the main flow (Fig 205).

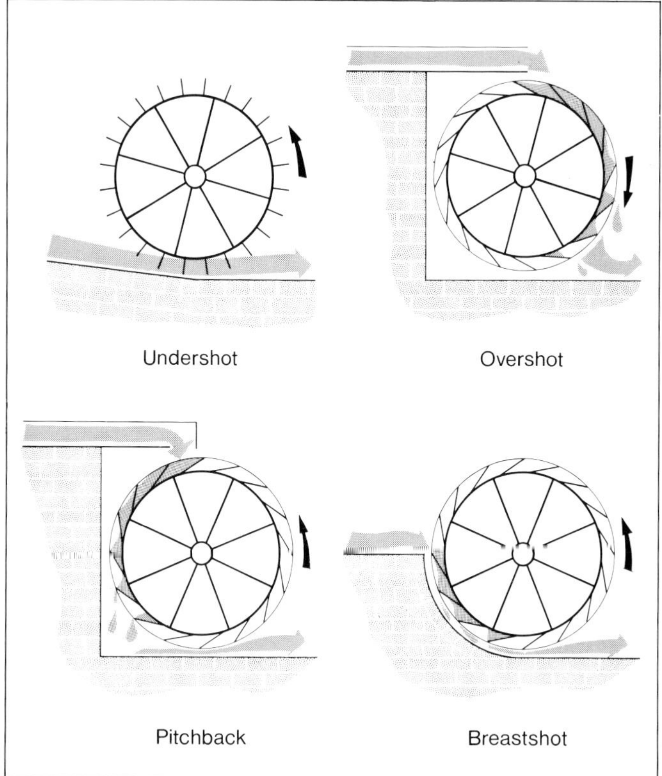

Fig 206 Waterwheel types.

The waterwheel and the wheelhouse

The waterwheel produces rotative motion by the action of water falling on to or pushing it. Power output depends in part on the volume of water available and in part on the height of the fall from the point at which the water is released to the level of the tailrace taking it back to the main stream. There were four types of waterwheel in use in Yorkshire mills, each suited to a different location (Fig 206). At Glasshouses Mill, High and Low Bishopside (55), one of the wheels was undershot, a type suited to a strong waterflow with a low fall. This type was not common in Yorkshire, where generally mill sites provided a good fall. The three other types of wheel – overshot, breastshot, and pitchback or high breastshot – all utilise the fall, and choice depended largely on terrain and rates of water flow. Wheel sizes varied widely in both diameter and breadth. Where the fall of water was only moderate but where supply was sufficient a wheel of small diameter but of generous breadth was used. Thus at Ramsden Mills, Linthwaite (87), the wheel was almost as wide (3.66 metres) as it was high (3.96 metres). The larger and broader the wheel, of course, the greater the energy, and one of the wheels at Armitage Bridge Mills, South Crosland (127), 7.6 metres in diameter and 4.58 metres wide, produced sixty horse power in 1834. Design improvements permitted greater power to be taken from later wheels, and Fairbairn's 1851 breastshot wheel at Glasshouses Mill (55), 7.6 metres high and 6.41 metres broad, could produce 120 horse power. Probably the largest wheel in a Yorkshire mill was the high breastshot wheel at Dale End Mill, Lothersdale, 13.74 metres high and 1.52 metres wide: installed in 1861 and still *in situ*, it could produce nearly forty horse power. Other surviving wheels either in Yorkshire mills or built for them are the timber-spoked overshot wheel at Fringill Mill, Menwith with Darley (100); the pitchback suspension wheel at Lumb Mill, Warley (142), dating probably from *c*1860; and the great iron breastshot suspension wheel built by Fairbairn for Glasshouses Mill (55) and now reconstructed at Quarry Bank Mill, Styal, Cheshire (Figs 207, 208).

Waterwheels were usually located either against or within the buildings they were designed to power (Fig 209). Wheels lying outside the main body of the mill were most commonly sited against the gable wall, either enclosed in the wheelhouse as at Lumb Mill (142) or exposed to the elements as at Folly Gill Flax Mill, Thornthwaite with Padside (Fig 210). Some mills had a waterwheel sited against the long side wall, as at Armley Mills, Armley (7), after 1805, and at Glasshouses Mill (55), Fairbairn's wheel was housed in a wheelhouse built against the side wall of one wing. Other external locations were the corner siting of the wheelhouse at Armitage Bridge Mills (127) and the end-on location at

Fig 207 The pitchback waterwheel at Lumb Mill, Warley (142).

Fig 208 Fairbairn's 1851 waterwheel at Glasshouses Mill, High and Low Bishopside (55).

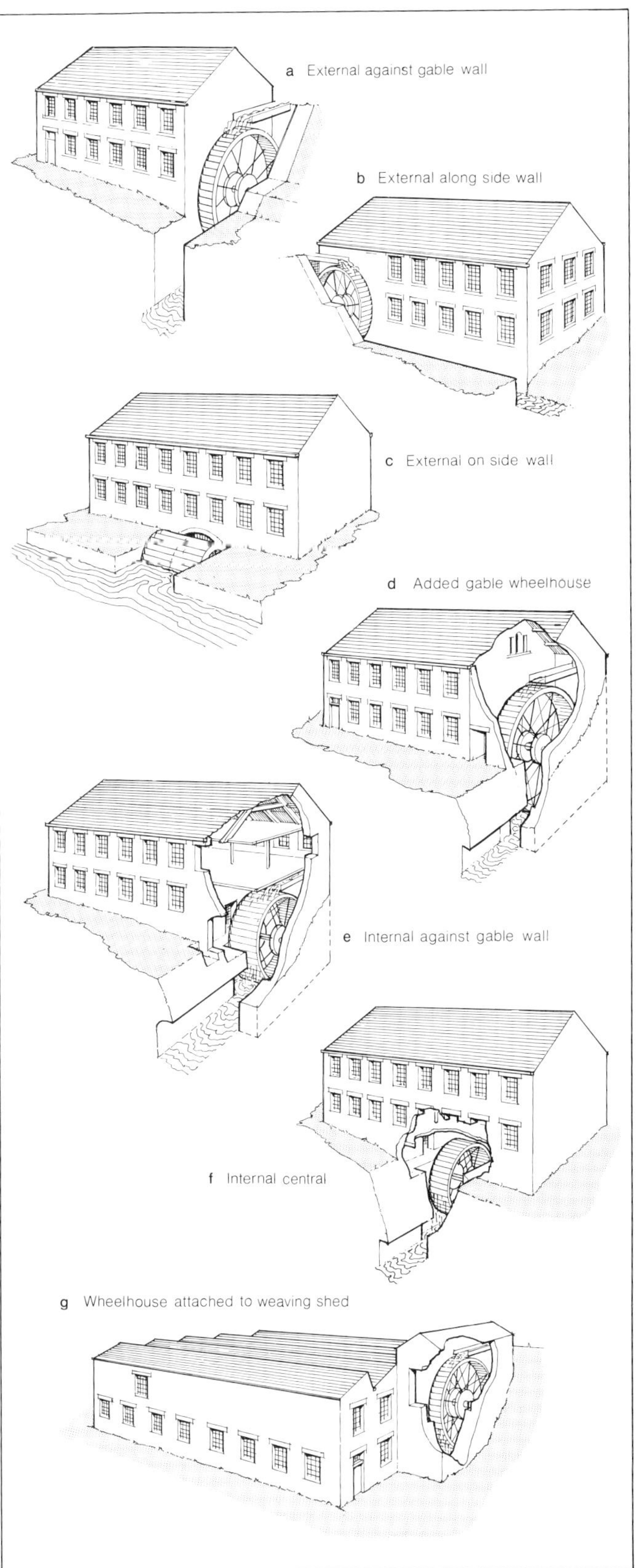

Fig 209 Waterwheel sitings in Yorkshire mills.

Fig 210 At Folly Gill Flax Mill, Thornthwaite with Padside, the wheel was exposed to the elements.

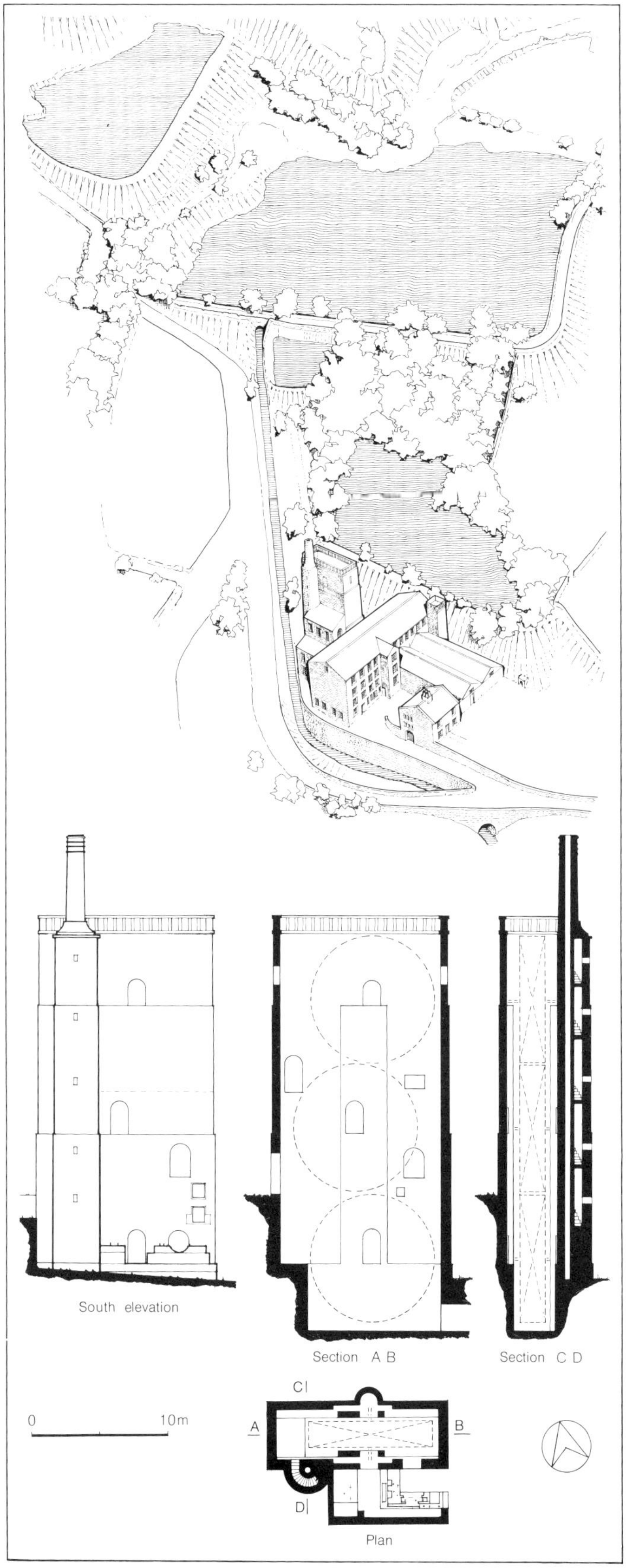

Fig 211 At Lumbutts Mill, Langfield, three dams supplied water to a unique tower housing three waterwheels.

South elevation
Section A B
Section C D
0 10m
Plan

High Mill, Addingham (1). Internal wheels were often sited inside the gable wall, usually with the upper floors of the mill running over the chamber as at Aireworth Mills, Keighley (69). At Woodlands Mill, Steeton with Eastburn (135), there were two internal end wheel-houses, the main one at the upper end of the mill, the other at the opposite end, re-using water flowing from the main wheel. Central or off-centre wheels were used at some mills: again the upper floors of the mill usually ran over the wheelchamber, as at Fringill Mill (100), where the terrain allowed the use of a basement and thus freed the ground floor for machine working. Some mills had more than one central or off-centre wheel, Sowerby Bridge Mills, Warley (143), for example, having two wheels. Wheels were not always associated with storeyed mills, for where sheds were either the dominant building or required their own power source they might have an attached wheelhouse, as at Langcliffe Shed, Langcliffe (81), and Eastwood Shed, Stansfield (133). At West House Mill, Fewston (40), the main wheel was located conventionally, within a wheelhouse at the end of the storeyed mill building, but a second wheel was detached from all buildings, set over the main wheel's headrace and apparently fed by a separate reservoir (Fig 153).

The most unusual wheelhouse is that at Lumbutts Mill, Langfield, near Todmorden, built probably *c*1830. Used to power a cotton-spinning mill, the wheelhouse took the form of a tall tower, about 30 metres high, with three overshot wheels, each 9.1 by 1.52 metres, arranged vertically inside (Fig 211). A system of dams above the mill supplied the wheels, but the precise means by which water was conducted to the different levels is not clear: a piped inverted-syphon system is the most likely arrangement. Within the tower the water was re-used from wheel to wheel, and at maximum flow the wheels could together produce over fifty horse power.[22]

In contrast to the engine house, which often received architectural embellishment, the wheelhouse was treated in a largely functional way. A Venetian window lit the wheels at Sowerby Bridge Mills (143), but in most other mills the wheelhouse is discernible externally only by the breakdown in the regular fenestration of the mill building and by arched openings allowing water to flow to and from the wheel (Fig 212). Internally the wheelhouse was a large open area varying in height and breadth according to the size of the wheel employed. The axle of the wheel demanded heavy ashlar mountings, often set within arched recesses in the side walls. Where breastshot and pitchback wheels were used the pit sometimes followed the curvature of the wheel, this work being carried out in well-engineered masonry (Fig 213).

Water supply

Difficulty with the supply of water was the major disadvantage of water-power installations. These difficulties could assume a number of different forms, illustrated by the returns to the 1834 Factories Inquiry Commission. Drought was probably the most common problem, and in dry seasons mills might have either to restrict their working hours or to stop entirely. At Robert Crossley's mill in Halifax it was reported that the 'stream of water is irregular, being in some parts of the year so scarce that it would not turn the machinery more than four hours per day' and at Hewenden Mill, Wilsden, 'deficiency of water' caused the loss of between seven and thirteen and a half hours on 118 days in the

Fig 212 Gayle Mill, Hawes (47), a water-powered cotton mill of the 1780s, showing the arched opening for the tailrace.

Fig 213 The wheelpit at Aireworth Mills, Keighley (69), showing the curved masonry of the pit.

summer of 1831 and the spring of 1832. Furthermore, 'besides this deficiency in hours, the mill ran at under-speed, and parts of the machinery standing'.[23] Floods, too, disrupted work, for excess water was dangerous and hindered the waterwheel's free movement by raising the level in the tailrace. The mills on major rivers were, perhaps, the most seriously affected by flood; on the River Calder, for example, Dewsbury Mills was 'subject to stoppages by flood-waters to the extent of from fifteen to twenty days a year', and drought too caused loss of time on this site.[24] In winter, frost and ice occasionally prevented work; this affected Mill House Mill, Sowerby (128), on the River Ryburn, and probably represented a more serious problem on minor becks with a slow flow of water.

Even when natural conditions were favourable, the flow of water to and from a mill could be affected by other users, especially on congested stretches of a watercourse. Millowners higher up a river might store water for later use and disrupt supply: this problem affected Mill House Mill (128), where 'the water . . . depends much on the dams of the mills on the stream above . . . we use the water when it comes down to us. We cannot work frequently in summer before ten or eleven o'clock A.M., and must work in the evening as long as the supply of water lasts.'[25] Storage of water by a lower mill could also prevent working by raising water levels in the tailrace. Joseph Rishworth's mill at Elland, on the River Calder, was affected by this problem and 'stood sixty hours in back-water' over one winter.[26]

Loss of time meant loss of profit to the millowner, and therefore there was a considerable incentive to invest in providing a supply system which would minimise disruption and permit regular working routines. The complexity of such systems varied considerably according to power demand and location. Jennifer Tann's classification of types provides a framework for describing the Yorkshire evidence.[27] Tann identified three main types of system – mainstream, leated and combined – and all three are represented in Yorkshire.

In many of Tann's 'mainstream' sites, the waterwheel was located in the watercourse itself, but no recorded Yorkshire mill is of this type. Instead there are examples of a variant form, in which supply was provided by damming the river or beck above the mill.

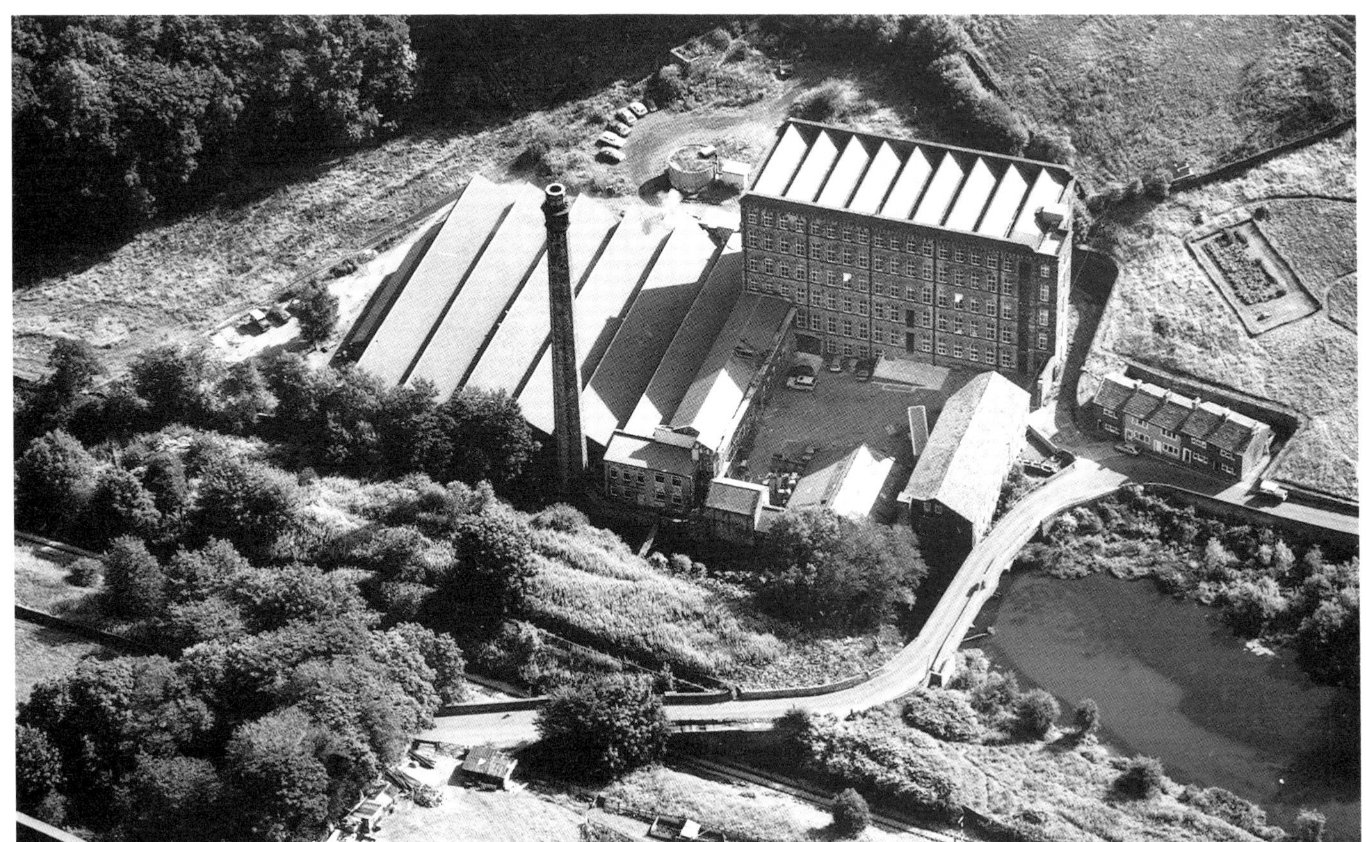

Fig 214 At Ebor Mill, Haworth (50), the stream was dammed to create a reservoir supplying a waterwheel in the small mill next to the road.

Fig 215 At High Mill, Addingham (1), a long weir across the River Wharfe raises the head of water for the mill.

This was practicable only on minor watercourses and was not a common solution to problems of supply. At Bowers Mills, Barkisland (11), the Black Brook was dammed to form a reservoir, with water flowing out into the natural course from one corner and into the mill from another. The system was used at Ebor Mill, Haworth (50), where the Bridge House Beck was dammed (Fig 214).

By far the most common arrangement was the leated system, in which a leat or headrace took water from the river or beck and led it some distance to the mill, the length of the headrace depending on the fall of the ground and the power requirements. On some sites the headrace led directly from a weir to the mill with no intervening dam. This was generally possible only on the major rivers. At High Mill, Addingham (1), and at Castle Mill, Scriven with Tentergate (114), a weir across the river (Wharfe and Nidd respectively) raised the level and thereby created a good fall of water, and the siting of the mill on the river bank necessitated only a short headrace (Fig 215).

Even major rivers proved deficient at times, and where mills were entirely dependent on water power a method of water storage was required to give some insurance against short-term difficulties. This was provided in the form of a mill dam, sited sometimes near the mill, sometimes a good distance away. At Aireworth Mills, Keighley (69), the original supply by a headrace was replaced in the 1840s by the creation of a large mill dam between river and mill (Fig 216). A similar alteration took place at Glasshouses Mill, High and Low Bishopside (55) in 1850, where the original simple leated system was abandoned on the creation of a 6-acre dam designed to ensure continuous working of Fairbairn's new suspension wheel. Most mills were probably built with a dam, producing a system such as that at Dunkirk Mill, Haworth (49) (Fig 217). Multiple dams were provided where terrain and local conditions demanded. At High Mill, Bishop Thornton (23), two small dams provided water for the mill wheel, and at West House Mill, Fewston (40), expansion in the early 19th century involved the creation of a second dam to power a new wheel.[28] At New York Mills, near Pateley Bridge, expansion took a rather different form; here the addition of a new wheel resulted in two independent systems, the original simple headrace leading to the old wheel and a second headrace to a new mill dam, from which water was piped over the River Nidd to turn a second wheel.[29]

The third major supply system – the combination of mainstream and leated arrangements – was adopted at a few Yorkshire mills. At Gayle Mill, Hawes (47), a shallow

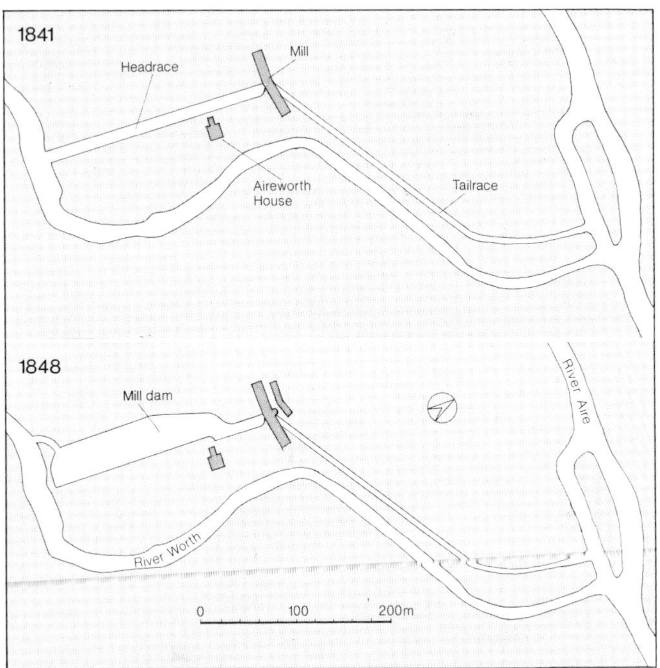

Fig 216 The evolution of the water supply at Aireworth Mills, Keighley (69).

channel took water out of the Gayle Beck for storage in a dam. This water was held in reserve until river levels were low; it was then released back into the beck and was taken off at a weir to flow along a headrace to the mill. A more substantial system was provided at Ellar Carr Mill, Bingley (21), where the mainstream – the Ellar Carr Beck – was restrained to form a large reservoir, out of which flowed two channels, one being the continuation of the beck itself, the other being a headrace nearly 100 metres long taking the water to the mill wheel. Above Fringill Mill, Menwith with Darley (100), three dams were created on the small Hick Gill, but it is no longer clear whether the wheel was turned by a headrace or by the continuation of the gill's course.

Despite the provision of dams on most mill sites, the water supply in even the major valleys came under great pressure as new mills multiplied after 1770. The solution to the problem was the provision of large reservoirs supplying a number of mills together. Schemes for the construction of these reservoirs were financed either by such landowners as Lord Dartmouth, motivated by the need to enhance the value of their tenanted mills, or by co-operative effort on the part of millowners.[30] In the Luddenden valley, a tributary valley of the Calder to the west of Halifax, the millowners formed the Cold Edge Dam Company in the early 19th century, and by the 1830s the company maintained three large reservoirs high on the moors.[31] The reservoirs supplied up to ten mills, mostly in textile use but including a corn mill and a paper mill (Fig 218). Significantly, the water-powered mills remained small in scale, but the one wholly steam-powered mill in the valley, Oats Royd Mills, Midgley (101), sited high on the valley sides and founded in the era of cheap coal, expanded hugely in the middle decades of the century until it became one of the largest worsted mills of the county. The relationship between mill size and the nature of the power supply, not evident in the pre-1850 period when the industry was still not fully mechanised, is clearly demonstrated in the contrasting fortunes of these mills after 1850.

The water turbine

The development of the water turbine in the mid 19th century provided a variant form of water power. Early turbines were not very efficient, demanding the great flow of large rivers or great falls of water, but by the 1860s improvements had given the turbine an efficiency similar to that of all but the best waterwheels.[32] Turbines were more compact than a waterwheel and had the advantages of operating efficiently in times of full and partial water supply and with low falls of water.[33] Many mills installed a turbine either in place of or as a supplement to their waterwheel in the second half of the 19th century and later. At Gayle Mill, Hawes (47), the wheel was replaced by a turbine of 1879, and at Glasshouses Mill, High and Low Bishopside (55), a turbine was installed in the 1890s to replace one of 1871 and to work alongside earlier waterwheels and a steam engine (Fig 219). Water supply to a turbine differed from the system used to feed water on to a wheel, for flow to the turbine was most efficiently contrived by the use of pipes rather than by a simple fall from a

Fig 217 At Dunkirk Mill, Haworth (49), the mill dam lies behind the main building.

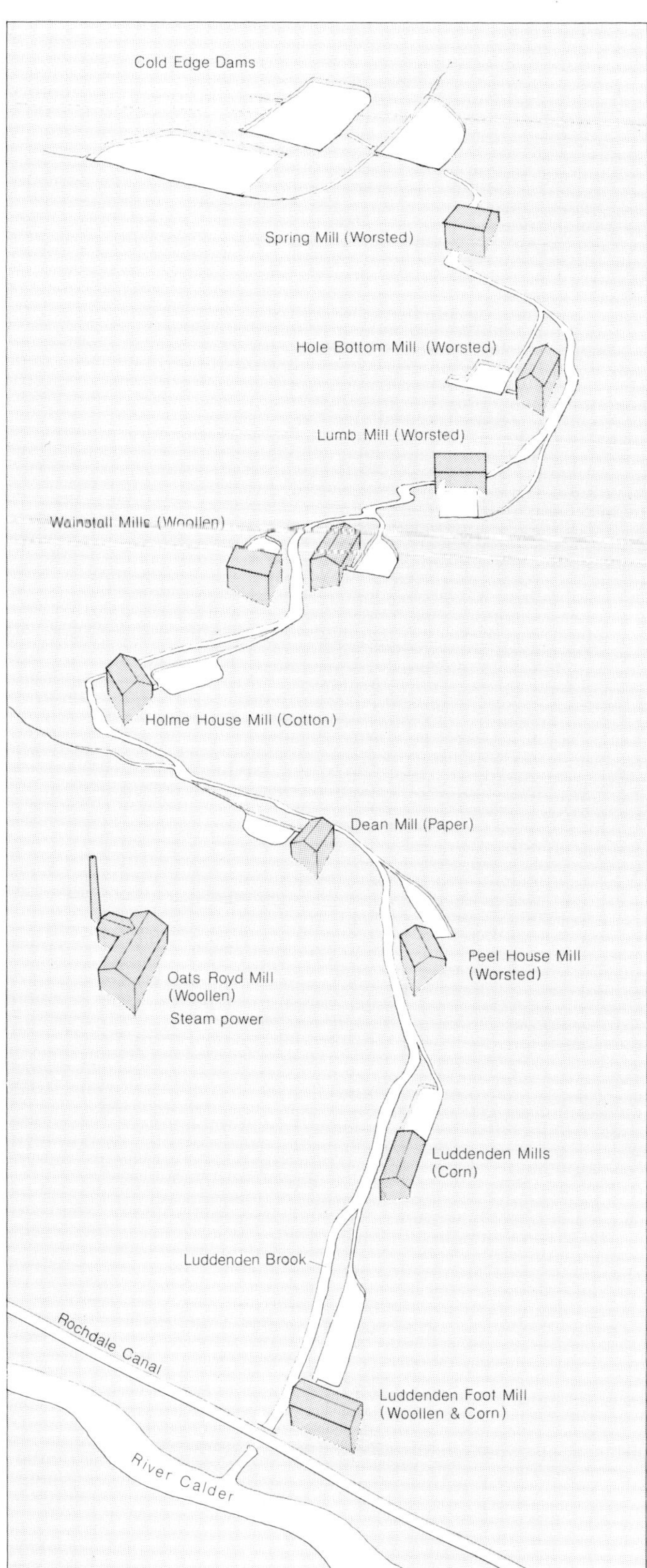

Fig 218 Water power in the Luddenden valley in the mid 19th century.

pentrough (Fig 220). A pipe increased the pressure of water and a good fall was ensured by setting the turbine low within the mill.

Steam power

Steam power was used in Yorkshire textile mills from the 1770s through to the mid 20th century. Three principal stages in the development of steam power may be identified, each overlapping widely with the next. In the first stage, steam engines were pumping engines used in conjunction with waterwheels; in the second stage, rotative engines able to power mills directly were introduced; and in the third stage the steam turbine, used to generate electricity, was developed. The second stage had the longest currency and the greatest variety; there were, for example, many types of rotative engine and, equally important, boiler design improved immensely over the period. The architectural and documentary evidence relating to Yorkshire mills illustrates the changing provision made for the steam power plant.

The pumping engine in Yorkshire textile mills

In the early 18th century Thomas Newcomen developed a reliable steam pumping engine. Improved later by, among others, John Smeaton, these simple engines came to be widely used in mines to pump out surplus water by the action of an oscillating beam.[34] They could also be employed to pump water from the tailrace of a mill back into the dam for re-use, and at many water-powered textile mills in Yorkshire such auxiliary engines were installed to ensure a continuous supply where and when water was not plentiful. The engine in this system was not capable of working textile machinery directly and was intended purely as a means of gaining maximum use of a waterwheel. At least thirty-five industrial sites in Yorkshire, most of them textile mills, had Savery or Newcomen type engines in operation before 1800, and this number included some of the most prominent mills of the period: Low Mill, Keighley (74), the first Yorkshire cotton mill, built in 1780, and John Marshall's first mill in Water Lane, Holbeck (57), built in 1791, both employed a steam engine as an auxiliary to water power.[35] As rotative steam engines improved in efficiency, the advantages of installing a pumping engine to assist a waterwheel diminished, however, and it is probable that few if any such engines were installed in Yorkshire mills after 1825.

Fig 219 The water turbine at Glasshouses Mill, High and Low Bishopside (55), dating probably from the 1890s, was installed in a turbine house of 1871.

Because the use of auxiliary steam engines was a relatively short-lived phenomenon, there is a lack of architectural evidence for the character of the power installation. An engine house of tall proportions, housing perhaps a small boiler and cylinder and sheltering half of the working beam, was required, sited so as to allow the action of the beam to draw water from the tailrace back up above the mill.[36] No such installation has been recognised in recorded Yorkshire mills, and it is likely that the early obsolescence of the pumping engine led to the destruction of its associated buildings.

The development of the rotative engine

Rotative motion from a beam engine was developed first by James Pickard, who in 1780 patented the crank method of making the action of the engine's working beam turn a wheel. In the last two decades of the 18th century a number of engine makers began producing rotative engines, but dominating the market, in reputation if not in terms of numbers of engines supplied, was the Birmingham firm of Boulton and Watt. James Watt was responsible for increasing the efficiency of the steam engine; his separate condenser allowed the engine to work more economically, and his parallel-motion apparatus allowed the piston rod and working beam to maintain the correct relationship to each other, thus improving the efficiency of power transfer.[37]

Early rotative steam engines were of small capacity. Before 1790 an output of ten horse power or less was common, and by 1800 Boulton and Watt engines rarely exceeded twenty horse power.[38] This was, however, perfectly adequate for the small mills of the period, although it can be argued that the limited output of the engine may have had a direct influence on mill size. By the 1830s engine capacity had increased. The average steam installation recorded in Yorkshire mills had risen to thirty horse power, significantly more than those of most water-powered mills.[39] In the middle decades of the 19th century a number of improvements were made to boilers, allowing them to work at higher steam pressures and thus to give greater power to the engine, and in the use of steam within the beam engine itself, involving the use of high and low-pressure cylinders to re-use the exhaust steam. This latter innovation, known as compounding or 'McNaughting' and patented in 1845, was incorporated in new engines and added to existing ones: in Yorkshire the first known instance of McNaughting was at Black Dyke Mills in 1848.[40] When such improvements were combined with the use of paired beam engines, an enormous power output became possible: at Saltaire Mills, Shipley (116), for example, the two pairs of beam engines working together were considered capable of producing 1,250 horse power. By the mid 19th century, therefore, steam power was able to answer the vastly increased demand for power which followed the virtually complete mechanisation of the textile industry.

The period 1860–90 was one of transition in the field of steam power technology. The beam engine had been made reliable but it had reached virtually its full potential, and major advances in power generation concerned instead the development of horizontal engines of different types. Horizontal engines had been in use for many decades, with small versions, called 'thrutchers', used to assist beam engines where additional power was required, and larger types had been chosen in preference to beam engines on the grounds of their economy, compactness and lower price. Before 1860 the problems associated or thought to be associated with uneven wear in the cylinder hindered their adoption, and William Fairbairn for one turned first to the beam engine in new installations.[41] Improvements to the horizontal engine, however, allowed it to work at high speeds while maintaining smooth and economical running, and after 1860 it began to supplant the beam engine.[42] In Yorkshire, Murgatroyds of Oats Royd Mills, Midgley (101), considered installing a horizontal engine in a new mill in 1862 but rejected the option in favour of a vertical engine, and the first use of a horizontal engine in a recorded Yorkshire mill dates from *c*1864–5 when Whetley Mills, Manningham (95), opened with two pairs of horizontal engines.[43] Other early installations include those of 1870 at Dean Clough Mills, Northowram, and Belle Vue Mills, Skipton (119). There ensued a period of two decades during which beam and horizontal engines were both used in new installations, but the latest known instance of the starting of a new beam engine dates from 1889, when a double-beam engine was installed at Waterside Mill, Langfield (82). After that date the horizontal engine virtually monopolised the field until the close of the era of steam power (Fig 221). By the early 20th century it had reached a state of maturity and was capable of efficient, smooth running with a high power output: the 1907 engine at Hare Mill, Stansfield (134), for example, generated 3,000 horse power. In some special circumstances other engine types might be preferred to the horizontal. At Waterloo Mills, Silsden (118), for example, considerations of space probably influenced the choice of an inverted vertical engine.

Fig 220 The water turbine in Dunkirk Mill, Haworth (49), is supplied by a large pipe leading from the reservoir behind the mill.

The use of steam power in the Yorkshire textile industry

The first recorded use of a rotative steam engine in a textile mill was in 1785–6, when Boulton and Watt supplied engines to two Nottinghamshire millowners.[44] A Watt engine was first ordered for a Yorkshire mill in 1792 and by 1800 fourteen engines were or had been in operation.[45] In addition, local engine makers such as Fenton, Murray and Wood of Leeds and the Low Moor Iron Company of Bowling were supplying Yorkshire mills. In the wool textile branches alone eighty-one steam engines were in use in or before 1800, and although many of them were probably pumping engines there were undoubtedly many mills, like Crank Mill, Morley (102), which were powered by rotative engines built by firms other than Boulton and Watt.[46] After 1800 steam power became more common. In 1824 the Leeds area had ninety steam engines in eighty-one mills and dyeworks; some engines were very small, one in a flax mill having a capacity of only two horse power, but the majority produced between ten and forty horse power: the largest was the seventy horse power engine at Marshall's Mill, Holbeck (57).[47] By the mid 1830s steam power was the dominant generating force in Yorkshire mills, with more capacity in total and with a higher average output than water power.[48]

The advantages of steam power over water power were not absolute, for we have seen that waterwheels were retained where water supply was available and sufficient to answer local needs. The steam engine, however, largely freed the textile industry from the constraint imposed by the availability of water. New mills could be built virtually anywhere: for example, Bradford, before 1800 mainly an exchange centre, developed in the early 19th century as a major manufacturing base with steam-powered worsted mills dominating the local industrial scene. By the early decades of the 19th century steam engines could provide a power output equal to or exceeding all but the largest waterwheels. The progress of Marshall's Mill (57) illustrates the superiority of steam: first built in 1791 with a steam-assisted waterwheel, the mills grew until by 1821 there were six steam engines at work, each added at a different stage of the mills' evolution; together the engines gave 234 horse power.[49] Such expansion was impossible at most sites dependent on water power. Costs of a steam engine and a steam-raising plant could be high, especially in Boulton and Watt installations. This is reflected in the status of the millowners who purchased early Watt engines, for among their number were John Marshall, Benjamin Gott and other prominent manufacturers. Running costs involved the purchase of coal and constant maintenance, and in the early years there were certainly some problems with the standard of engine manufacture and with shortages of skilled operators.[50] For the millowner, however, the prospect of continuous running independent of weather conditions and geographical restrictions, together with its flexibility, made steam power attractive. The triumph of steam is evident in the returns to the Rivers Pollution Commission of 1871. Nearly 400 Yorkshire millowners made returns to the Commission, and of this number eighty-four per cent used steam power alone, twelve per cent used steam and water combined, and only three per cent relied entirely on water power. Saltaire Mills (116), with a capacity of 2,000 horse power, had more power available than the total of all the water installations in the textile district.[51]

a

b

Fig 221 Horizontal engines in Yorkshire mills: a) 'Rhoda', a Marsden single-tandem engine of 1908 in Runtlings Mill, Ossett (110); b) 'Agnes', a Pollit and Wigzell engine of 1909 in Washpit Mill, Wooldale (149).

The steam power plant

A steam power plant comprised two main elements – the engine itself and the boiler or boilers. The buildings required were an engine house, a boiler house and a chimney. From the mid 19th century a new component, the economiser, was commonly included; this used the heat from the exhaust gases to warm water for the boilers, and was sited in an economiser house.

The engine house

The design of the engine house was dictated by the form of steam engine which it contained. For virtually the first century of the use of rotative steam power, the engine was dependent on the engine house not just for shelter but also for the support of its superstructure, and it was only with the advent of the horizontal engine that the building and the machine could be treated as separate components. The beam engine, the dominant engine type before 1870, required support principally for its working beam which had to be kept in a consistent relationship to piston rod and connecting rod. Support for the beam at its pivotal point was contrived in a number of ways, most of which utilised the walls of the engine house. In the late 18th century support was

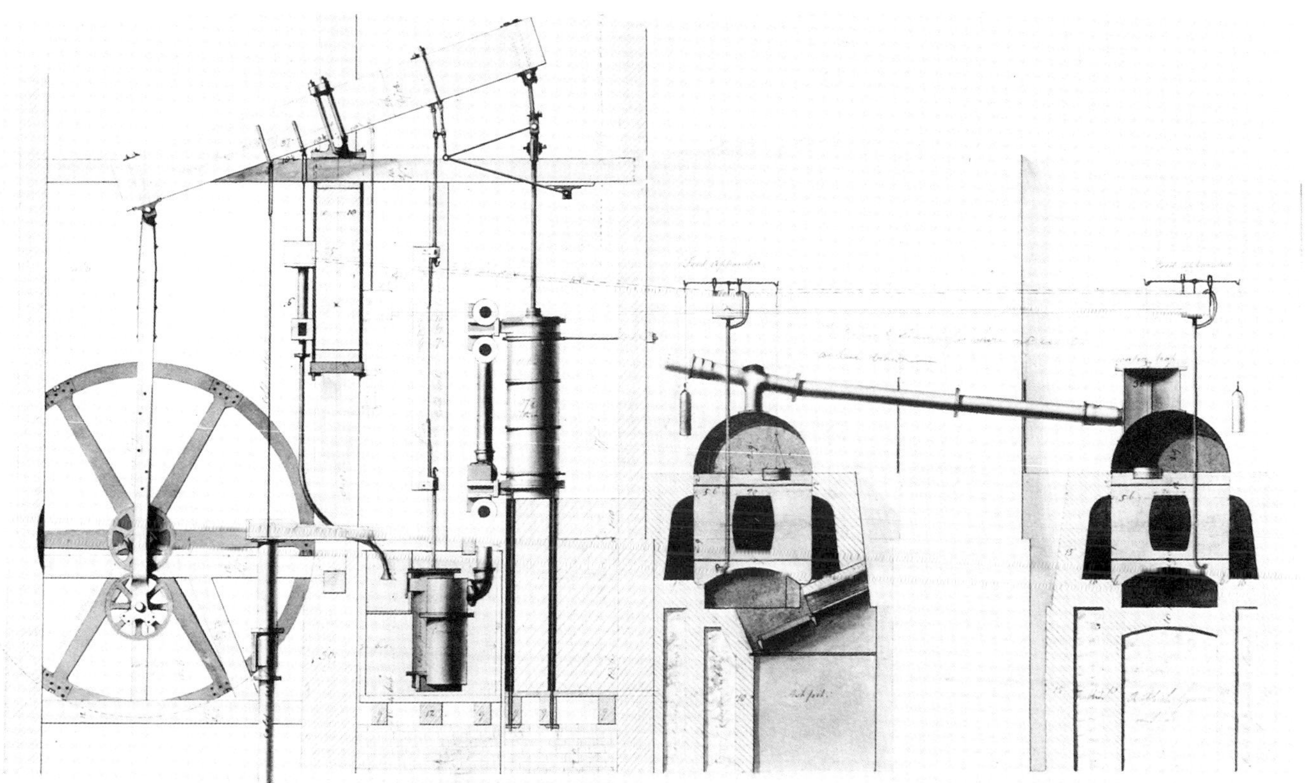

Fig 222 The Boulton and Watt beam engine of 1794 at Marshall's Mill, Holbeck (57). The drawing shows a lever wall in the engine house, a wooden trestle supporting the flywheel, sun and planet drive for the flywheel, wooden working beam, and wagon boilers (Boulton and Watt Collection, Portfolio 110, Birmingham Library Services).

Fig 223 Crank Mill, Morley (102), built in the early 1790s. This mid 19th-century view shows the exposed connecting rod, crank and flywheel of the steam engine. The cylinder was contained in the structure attached to the end wall of the mill (Smith 1866, opposite p52).

achieved either by the use of a heavy masonry wall, termed a lever wall, which had the effect of dividing the engine house into two compartments, one for the cylinder, one for the flywheel, or by a massive timber trestle, secured by a grid of wooden beams let into the side and end walls of the engine house.[52] Timber was commonly used also for the working beam itself and for a trestle to support the flywheel. Marshall's Mill, Holbeck (57), had such a system, built to receive a Boulton and Watt engine in 1794 (Fig 222). Obsolescence caused the eventual replacement of these early installations, however, and architectural evidence for them no longer survives. At Crank Mill, Morley (102), the unusual engine house, sheltering only the cylinder, provided masonry support for the working beam, but here the lever wall is in fact the external wall (Fig 223).

From the early 19th century, iron and stone began to replace timber in the engine and as its method of support. In most new engines a working beam of cast iron was held in place by an entablature beam supported on columns, and a grid of lesser beams gave a 'beam floor' permitting maintenance of the upper parts of the engine. All components of the supporting system were of cast iron. The different parts of the engine were bolted to a massive engine bed made up of deep courses of ashlar masonry. The engine was still house-built to the extent that the cast-iron grid forming the beam floor was embedded in the walls of the compartment, but the removal of the lever wall was a major step in making the engine independent of the building.

The beam-engine house was usually a tall room, the height permitting free movement of the overhead working beam and of the flywheel, which was secured to the high masonry engine bed. When set within a main mill building, the engine house might rise through as many as three storeys, as at Albert Mills, Lockwood (89). Where a single engine was used, the room was narrow, usually occupying perhaps two bays within a mill building. By about 1835 the demand for greater power created by the vastly increased use of mechanically powered machines was met in part by the introduction

Fig 224 The decorative surround to the engine house window in Old Lane Mill, Northowram (105) (1825–8). The window lit a tall engine house fitted with a single-beam engine.

Fig 225 The engine houses in the main mill at Saltaire Mills, Shipley (116) (1850–3), have decorative glazing and contained double-beam engines.

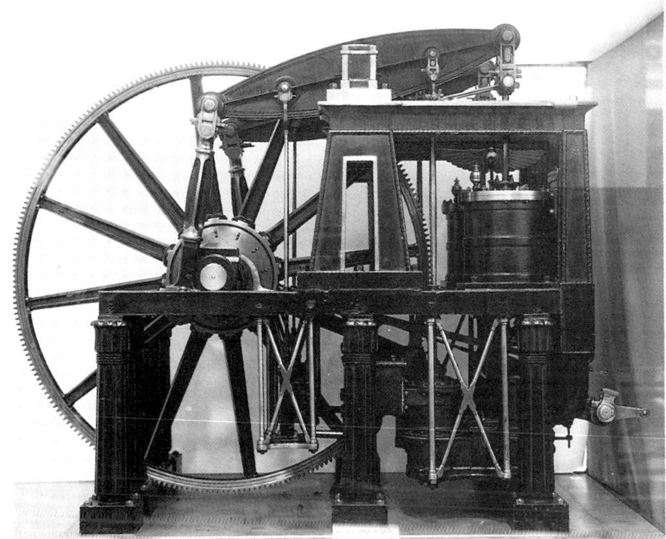

Fig 226 A model of the beam engine powering Temple Mill (1838–41) in Marshall's Mill, Holbeck (57), showing the Egyptian-style ironwork. The toothed flywheel drove a pinion wheel powering shafts below the shed floor (Science Museum, Neg 80/57).

of paired beam engines working a single flywheel. Where paired engines were used, the engine house was broader, taking up three bays within a mill: Hunslet Mills, Hunslet (67), of 1838–40 is an early example of the type, and Saltaire Mills, Shipley (116), of 1850–3 had two such engine houses each with a pair of engines in three-bay engine houses (Fig 225).

The architectural treatment of the beam-engine house changed over the period under review. Few pre-1825 engine houses survive in substantial form, but the evidence suggests that distinctive external features were restricted to large windows, usually arched and with a plain surround. After 1825, however, greater architectural emphasis was given to the engine house, reflecting the new confidence in steam technology. The large windows commonly received some modest ornamental treatment, as at Old Lane Mill, Northowram (105), and decorative glazing within the windows was also used, as at Saltaire Mills (116) (Figs 224, 225). One window was sufficient in small engine houses, but where paired engines were used two windows usually lit the

a

b

Fig 227 Beam-engine houses: a) an early view of the engine house of c1830 at Cape Mills, Bramley (28), showing the fluted columns, beam floor, entablature beam, connecting rod, and the flywheel set in a recess in the wall; b) the empty engine house of 1832 at Woodhouse Mill, Langfield (83): this doubtless had a similar engine and fittings to that at Cape Mills but shows the type of evidence remaining once the engine has been removed. In the foreground is an ashlar pier which acted as a seating for columns supporting the entablature beam.

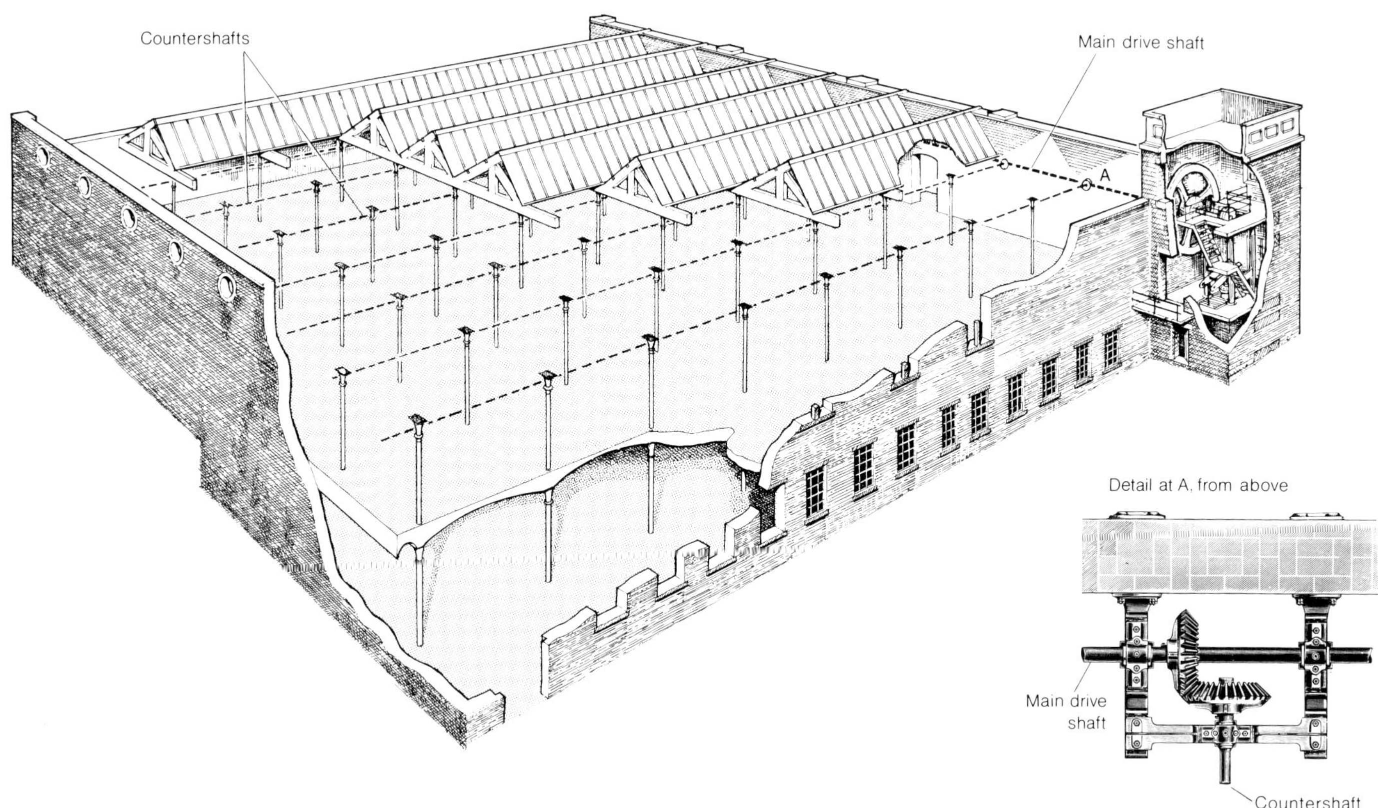

Fig 228 The weaving shed of c1875 at Brackendale Mills, Idle (68), was powered by a vertical engine in an engine house at the corner of the building. The inset shows the transfer of power by bevel wheels from the main shaft to the countershafts.

wider chamber. In some mills, for example Healey New Mill, Ossett (107), and Hunslet Mills (67), the opportunity to mark out the engine house externally was rejected in favour of uniform fenestration across the whole mill façade. At Healey New Mill (107) only the irregular spacing of the windows suggests the site of the engine house, and at Hunslet Mills (67) even this indication is absent.

The interior of a beam-engine house had a number of special features apart from its proportions. Decoration was often applied, frequently to the engine itself and its method of support, sometimes to the engine house as well. At Marshall's Mill (57), the beam engine powering Temple Mill continued the building's Egyptian theme in its design (Fig 226), and at many other mills the engine had decorative ironwork in the form of fluted columns, moulded beams and shaped beam floors with decorative railings (Fig 227a). At Old Lane Mill (105), the engine house had an ornamental plaster ceiling and a cornice, and a cornice was used in some other engine houses. Even when the engine, its method of support and any decoration have been wholly or partially removed, the beam-engine house still displays evidence of its fittings. Beam floors survived the removal of engines in some mills, and their form, with either one or two openings, reveals whether single or paired engines had been in use. Where the beam floor has been removed, ashlar blocks in the side walls indicate the position of the entablature beam on which the working beam pivoted. In some engine houses one side wall incorporated a large arched recess for the flywheel, and many engine houses retain substantial parts of the engine bed, with a masonry pier or piers for cylinders, a central support for columns and a heavy anchorage for the flywheel (Fig 227b). Where paired engines were used, the engine bed was arranged to leave space for a central flywheel. Boltholes in the bed reveal the position of the main engine components. Hoist rings in the ceiling, embedded in heavy cross-beams, assisted in the lifting of engine parts during repair and maintenance.

In some mills space was so limited that there was no room for a beam engine. In these circumstances a vertical engine could be used, for by setting the flywheel directly over the cylinder only a small floor area was required. A vertical-engine house, therefore, could fit compactly into the corner of a mill, as in the 1863 mill at Oats Royd Mills, Midgley (101). Vertical engines were also used where there was no restriction on space, as in the shed at Brackendale Mills, Idle (68) (Fig 228). The engines were house-built, since the flywheel support was built into the walls of the compartment. At Brackendale, the three outer walls of the engine house have heavy ashlar blocks designed to stabilise the superstructure of the engine.[53]

After 1870 the horizontal engine became the most common type in new installations in Yorkshire mills. The form of the engine house varied widely according to the nature of the engine. The simplest engines were of single-cylinder type and smaller versions required a narrow room of no great length. Where the single-cylinder engine was large, however, long rooms were required: at Whetley Mills, Manningham (95), the 1879 building for a Hick Hargreaves engine was 26 metres long (Fig 229). Where high and low-pressure cylinders were used together they could be arranged either one behind the other, in a tandem-compound style, or one on each side of the flywheel, in cross-compound style. The tandem-compound engine tended, therefore, to require a long room, and the cross-compound engine a broad room. At Runtlings Mill, Ossett (110), for example, the 1906 tandem-compound engine was housed in a long narrow room, but the 1913 cross-compound engine at Ardsley Mills, East Ardsley (35), was set within a much wider engine house. The need for length in horizontal-engine houses is illustrated by alterations to some mills when beam engines were replaced; at Meltham Mills, Meltham (98), Oats Royd Mills (101) and Syke Ing Mill, Soothill (126), the beam-engine house was extended to give the extra length required for the insertion of the new engine (Fig 230).

Fig 230 At Syke Ing Mill, Soothill (126), the original beam-engine house of c1840 was extended in 1897 to receive a horizontal engine. The multi-storeyed mill was rebuilt in 1883.

The height of the horizontal-engine house varied considerably. Some, including the 1870 engine house at

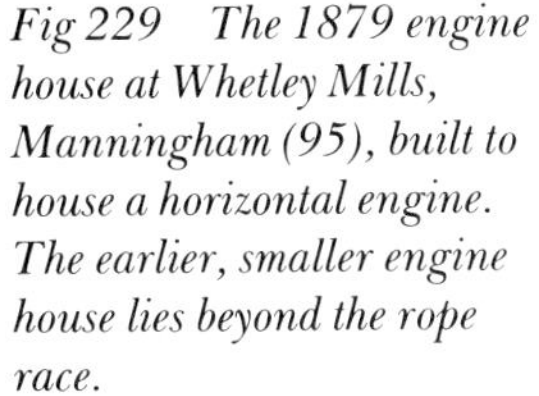

Fig 229 The 1879 engine house at Whetley Mills, Manningham (95), built to house a horizontal engine. The earlier, smaller engine house lies beyond the rope race.

Fig 231 Belle Vue Mills, Skipton (119). The 1870 multi-storeyed mill had a horizontal engine in a low internal end engine house.

Belle Vue Mills, Skipton (119), were low, since great headroom was not a strict necessity (Fig 231), but in others, such as Hare Mill, Stansfield (134), the engine was set within a very lofty chamber. In these rooms the engine was a much less dominating presence than in a beam-engine house, and the simple layout was assisted by the fact that the horizontal engine was not house-built. The engine base was bolted to an ashlar or concrete bed, and there was no need for additional support in the side walls of the engine house. Travelling cranes, used for maintenance, were frequently installed high in the engine house.

Perhaps because the horizontal engine itself lacked great potential for display, its engine house sometimes received ornamental treatment. As in beam-engine houses, windows were usually large and often arched: single or double windows in the end walls can suggest whether tandem or cross-compound engines were installed originally. Internally wood-boarded walls were common, and at Spinkwell Mills, Dewsbury (34), this was taken further to give a complete panelled room enlivened with pilasters and elaborate carved friezes (Fig 232). From the late 19th century, decorative tiles were in vogue for floors and walls: the engine house at Hare Mill (134) was one of the best Yorkshire examples, having green and yellow glazed wall tiles and chequer-pattern flooring (Fig 233).

One of the alternatives to the horizontal engine in the late 19th and early 20th centuries was the inverted-vertical or marine engine. Like the vertical engine, this was compact in terms of ground-floor plan, but it demanded an engine house of great height. At West Vale Mills, Elland cum Greetland (39), the 1902 engine house rises above the earlier engine house which it replaced (Fig 234), and at Waterloo Mills, Silsden (118), the 1916 engine house rises to the same height as the earlier beam-engine house, converted to act as a rope race (Figs 235, 236).

The siting of the engine house

Yorkshire textile mills show a wide variety of engine house sites (Fig 237). The most important factor in the choice of position was the need for efficient power transmission from engines of different types, and there is a general distinction between the sites associated with the shaft method of transmission and those used in association with rope drive.

Where power transmission was contrived through shafts leading from the engine to individual buildings or floors within buildings, the most direct connection between engine and main buildings was desirable. In storeyed mills, therefore, a position within or against one end of the building was generally favoured, allowing a direct link between the engine flywheel and the transmission system. Such sites were usually associated with beam engines and vertical engines, the major types employed with shaft transmission. The internal end engine house was the most common type before 1850 and continued in use for some time after that. Examples are C Mill at Marshall's Mill, Holbeck (57) (1815–17) and Waterloo Mills, Silsden (118) (*c*1870). After 1850 the attached end engine house became common (Fig 238) and was especially favoured where engine houses were added to existing water-powered mills, as at Armley Mills, Armley (7), and at Little Hebble Mill, Ovenden (112) (Fig 33). Central beam-engine houses were also used. In large mills, such as Zetland Mill,

Bradford (27), the problem of transmitting power over great distances may have encouraged a central rather than an end position (Fig 51), but in some smaller mills the central engine house marked a functional division between working areas. At Healey New Mill, Ossett (107), for example, built in 1826–7, the engine house divided a main working area from a warehouse. Unusual positions for a beam engine include the detached

Fig 232 The engine house at Spinkwell Mills, Dewsbury (34), was decorated in the late 19th century with woodwork, including fluted pilasters and richly carved panels.

site at Woodhouse Mill, Langfield (83), and the siting at Winker Green Mill, Armley (8), where in 1836 a second beam-engine house was attached to the side wall of the earlier mill. Corner engine houses were particularly suitable for vertical engines, for they allowed direct connection with the main transmission system. Where beam engines or vertical engines were attached to sheds and linked through a shaft method of transmission, an internal or attached corner location was usually chosen.

The introduction of rope drive encouraged the use of slightly different engine house positions. The principal requirement where multi-storeyed buildings were concerned was not the closest possible communication between the engine flywheel and the transmission system but instead a slight removal of the components to allow the optimum angle for connection between the flywheel or rope drum and each of the floors within the building. Thus external sites were favoured, using prominently projecting engine houses at either the corner or the centre of a mill, as at Lowertown Mill, Haworth (52), of 1895, and Ardsley Mills, East Ardsley (35), of 1912 (Figs 330, 201). Internal positions were also adopted, but only where existing buildings or consideration of space dictated. At Globe Mills, Slaithwaite (123), for example, the narrow plot necessitated an internal central engine house with a very steep angle between the rope drum and the pulley wheels on the upper floors. In sheds, rope drive could be contrived through the use of a corner engine house, as at Young Street Mills, Manningham (96), of *c*1871, but a more efficient siting was in the centre of a side wall, allowing power to radiate out from a mid-point: this position was adopted in the 1887 shed at Oats Royd Mills, Midgley (101) (Fig 266). The peculiar requirements of the rag-pulling industry and the unusual type of shed adopted made the siting of the engine house at one end of a single-storeyed range the preferred option, seen most perfectly at Runtlings Mill, Ossett (110), of 1907 (Fig 195).

The piecemeal and unpredictable evolution of many mill sites, together with the limited output of early steam engines, created power systems which were a response to the needs of the hour rather than installations planned with a longer view. Probably the first mill to experience the problems attendant on expansion was Marshall's Mill (57), which had six steam engines in 1821 and expanded further thereafter. Oats Royd Mills (101) had four dispersed engines at one point and Manningham Mills, Manningham (93), had seven. Where expansion was more limited, an existing power source could sometimes answer the extra demand. At Brookroyd Mills, Stainland (130), the addition of a new mill in 1866 to one of 1860 required no additional power, probably

Fig 233 The engine house at Hare Mill, Stansfield (134), of 1907–11, showing the horizontal cross-compound engines, the decorative walls and floor, and the rope drive feeding into the rope race.

because spare capacity had been built into the engine of the first mill, and at Cape Mills, Bramley (28), the post-1860 construction of a new spinning mill and of weaving sheds appears to have required no addition to the existing power system, a beam engine sited within the mill of *c*1830.

The multi-phase progress of some mill sites before 1850 resulted from the difficulties of planning for the future in an era of rapid technological and organisational change. By the middle decades of the century, however, a combination of circumstances – the achievement of virtually full mechanisation in the textile industry and the production of engines of great power – permitted more rational planning, an important consideration in a period marked by increased integration in the woollen, worsted and cotton branches. In wholly new mills a single power plant could be designed to serve the complete site, and where storeyed buildings and sheds required power, as in an integrated mill or in a worsted-spinning mill with its own combing shed, it was conventional to site the engine house between the two elements, allowing direct communication with both. At Hollins Mill, Todmorden and Walsden (138), the large engine house was attached to the shed block but overlapped with the storeyed mill sufficiently to allow the transmission of drive to that building (Fig 171), and a similar arrangement was used at Whetley Mills, Manningham (95). One of the largest mill complexes to be designed as a unity in the mid 19th century was Saltaire Mills, Shipley (116), and here the power system incorporated two engine houses, both sited within the main mill and each powering half the mill itself and one of the large sheds for combing and weaving. The increased power of engines also encouraged the rationalisation of pow[illegible] stems in mills which had evolved over a long p[illegible] some mills the multiple engines needed in a[illegible] pid change and expansion were either repla[illegible] gle engine serving the whole site or reduced [illegible] At Spinkwell Mills, Dewsbury (34), differ[illegible] or two mills and a weaving shed were scrap[illegible] r of a single power source in *c*1890, and [illegible] Oats Royd Mills (101) two beam engines we[illegible] in 1889 by a single horizontal engine.

Boiler house, economiser house, chimney and reservoir

Just as a mill depended on an engine for its power, the engine required steam raised in a boiler or boilers. The vital role of the boilers did not, however, confer on the boiler house the prestige manifest in the architectural treatment of the engine house. The building's simple function – that of sheltering one or more boilers and providing a firing place from which the furnaces could be stoked and the ashes cleared – is generally reflected in its utilitarian style.

The earliest boilers used in textile mills were of 'haystack' or 'wagon' design (Fig 239).[54] The haystack boiler was an iron or copper cylinder with a domed top, raised up to allow space for a fire below. It was contained within a simple brick casing rather than within a boiler house proper and lacked a roof.[55] Such installations, operating at low steam pressures, eventually became redundant and none now survives. The circular plan of this type of boiler is shown on some Boulton and Watt plans, and some haystack boilers continued in use up to the mid 19th century to be recorded on large-scale Ordnance Survey town plans.

The wagon boiler, often associated with James Watt, had a similar sectional form to the haystack boiler but was instead either rectangular in plan with square ends or of similar length but with egg-shaped ends. An internal flue increased the heating surface in some designs and the wagon boiler was able to work at greater steam pressure than the more primitive haystack model. Boulton and Watt drawings indicate that wagon boilers were typically between 3.66 and 4.5 metres long, and varied in number according to the power required. Some mills had a single boiler, most had two, and John

Fig 234 West Vale Mills, Elland cum Greetland (39). At the end of the multi-storeyed main mill of c1860 is the original engine house, lit by two round-arched windows and possibly designed for a double-beam engine. Beyond this is the plainer 1902 engine house built to take an inverted vertical engine.

Fig 235 The internal end engine house at Waterloo Mills, Silsden (118), was lit by the round-headed window visible over the boiler house roof. The later engine house attached to the corner of the multi-storeyed mill was built in 1916 for an inverted vertical engine.

Fig 236 The inverted vertical engine of 1905 at Waterloo Mills, Silsden (118).

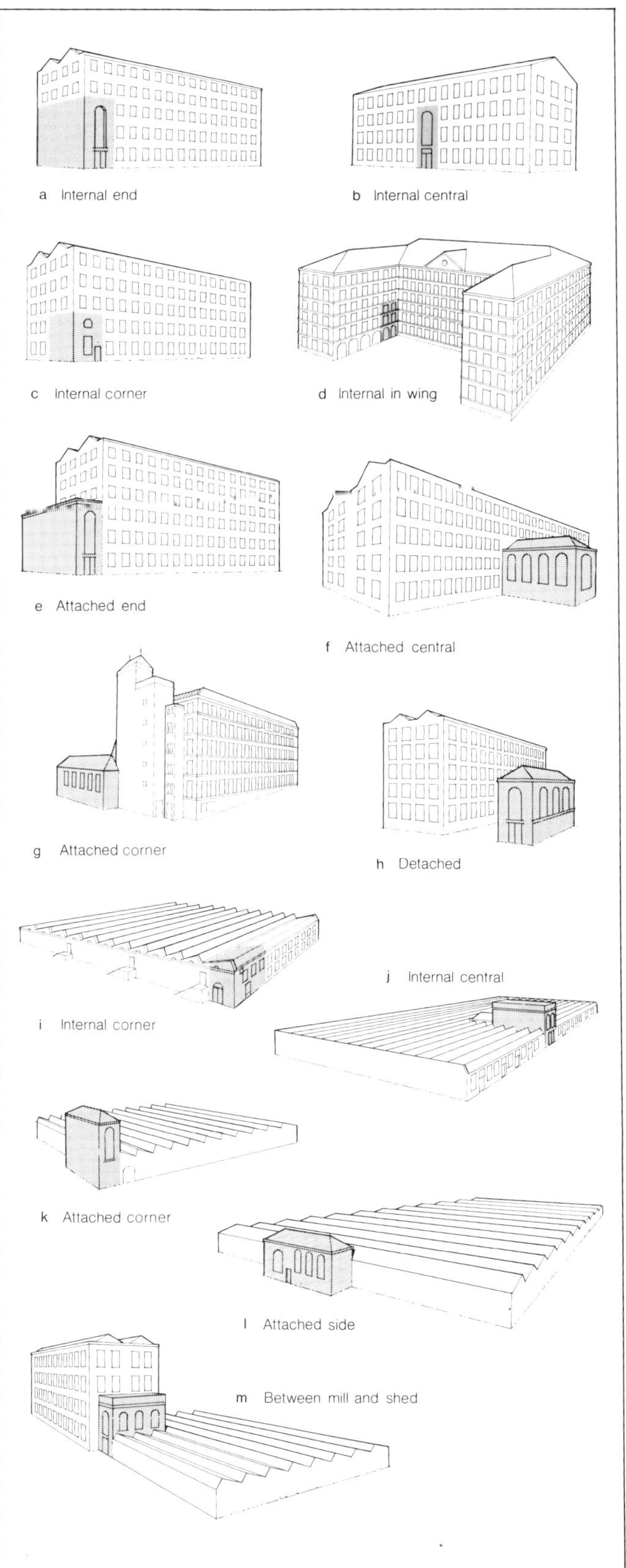

Fig 237 Common engine house positions in Yorkshire textile mills.

Wood's factory in Bradford had five in 1825.[56] Wagon boilers were generally enclosed within a boiler house, and early drawings suggest that these were simple buildings with brick casings for the boilers, a firing place inside the main doors and a pitched roof. As with the haystack design, the wagon boiler became redundant once working steam pressures increased, but at Stone Bridge Mills, Wortley (151), the early boiler was successfully re-used in inverted form as a water tank (Fig 240).

The need for economy in fuel consumption and for higher steam pressures led to the development of the Cornish, Lancashire and Yorkshire boilers, all taking the form of a long cylinder. The Lancashire boiler, patented by Fairbairn and Hetherington in 1844, was probably the most common in mills: this design had two internal flues, each with its own furnace. Because they were generally longer than early wagon boilers, greater depth was required in the boiler house, but otherwise no special features were required. Some mills could work with just a single boiler, but where greater power was needed two or more could be grouped within the boiler house: at Saltaire Mills, Shipley (116), the original boiler

Fig 238 The steam-powered multi-storeyed mill of c1860 at Ramsden Mills, Linthwaite (87), was powered by an attached end engine house. In the foreground is the boiler house, which incorporates drying floors over the boiler room.

house of the early 1850s contained ten boilers of special design[57] (Fig 241), and in 1889 Manningham Mills, Manningham (93), had thirty-two boilers in different locations to provide power for the vast complex.

The boiler house, whether containing wagon or Lancashire boilers, could be a detached structure, a building attached to a mill or engine house, or contained within the main mill structure. The question of position took account of conflicting considerations, for while proximity to the engine minimised the loss of steam heat, a detached siting reduced the risks to the more valuable buildings – the mill and engine house – from fire or explosion in the boiler house. The boiler house was most commonly attached to the engine house, which usually acted as a buffer between the boilers and the mill itself. An early example, known from Boulton and Watt drawings, is Bean Ing Mills, Leeds (85) (1792); an example from the mid 19th century is Ramsden Mills, Linthwaite (87); and Hare Mill, Stansfield (134) (1907), provides a late and slightly modified version of the plan. Detached positions became common after *c*1825. In

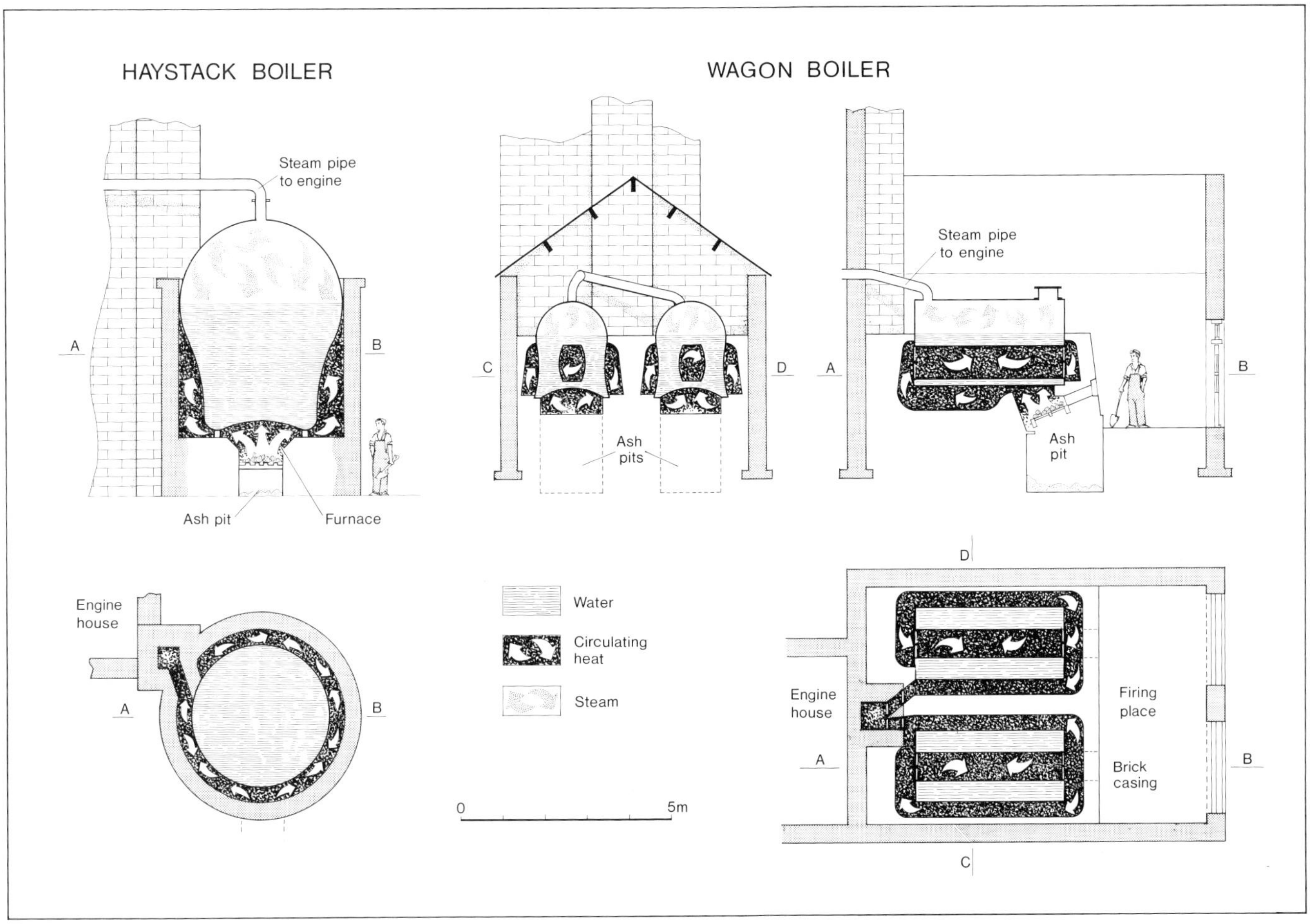

Fig 239 Haystack and wagon boilers.

Fig 240 The early 19th-century wagon boiler at Stone Bridge Mills, Wortley (151), inverted to serve as a water tank.

some mills a detached siting was used to take advantage of transport facilities; at Saltaire Mills (116), for example, the boiler house was set in front of the main mill but at a subterranean level to allow coal to be dropped from an overhead railway siding, and at Belle Vue Mills, Skipton (119), the boiler house was located next to the canal, permitting the easy transfer of coal. Some mills used the canals for a supply of boiler feed water. The boiler house located within a storeyed mill or warehouse was never common, but examples are known from different dates. At both Winker Green Mill, Armley (8), and Try Mills, Manningham (94), the first mill, of 1833 and 1865 respectively, had a boiler house attached in a linear extension, but the addition of a second mill in line enveloped the boiler house and made it effectively an internal room. At Oats Royd Mills, Midgley (101), the 1847 mill had an engine house dividing a main working area on each floor from three bays at one end of the building, the ground floor occupied by boilers and the upper floors probably giving storage space. Late in the period, the rebuilding of Frostholme Mill, Todmorden and Walsden (137), in 1896, provided a storeyed warehouse block containing a large boiler house at one end.

The boiler house had a number of different forms. Detached boiler houses were usually single-storeyed, as at Oats Royd Mills (101) (Fig 242), although at Balm Road Mills, Hunslet (66), the boilers occupy the ground floor of a four-storeyed building (Fig 243). Attached or internal boiler houses were also sometimes of just a single storey, but where the heat of the boilers could be utilised for the purposes of drying either raw material or yarn, rooms were set over the boiler house and warmed by air rising through floors of perforated cast iron (Fig 79). Albert Mills, Lockwood (89), Calder Bank Mills, Dewsbury (30), and Winker Green Mill (8) all had one or more drying floors over the boilers (Fig 252). Utilisation of heat for drying was common in woollen, flax and silk mills but not, apparently, in mills in other branches. Many worsted mills, for example Cannon Mills, Horton (58), have single-storeyed boiler houses, and in some cotton mills boiler houses within storeyed buildings were sealed by fireproof vaults, indicating that the principal consideration was the need to minimise the risk of fire rather than to borrow heat. Hollins Mill (138) and Frostholme Mill (137), both in Todmorden and Walsden, have brick arches over the boilers (Fig 244).

Boiler houses of all types had certain standard features. The front wall incorporated large openings – usually round-arched but square in some buildings – which allowed the installation of prefabricated boilers and facilitated the movement of coal. The number of openings corresponded to the number of boilers actually or potentially housed within. The openings were usually the focus of any decorative treatment given to the boiler house: at Oats Royd Mills (101), for example, they have a rusticated ashlar surround (Fig 242). On rare occasions the boiler house was incorporated into an overall scheme of decoration: the outstanding example is Manningham Mills (93) (Fig 245). In some mills, such as Calder Bank Mills (30), water tanks were set on the roof of the boiler house to provide feed water. Internally the boilers were arranged in a row, set back from the front wall to give a firing place from which their furnaces could be stoked manually or fed automatically by a hopper, and from which ashes could be removed. Brick casing was used to retain the heat and to provide

Fig 241 The Lancashire boilers at Saltaire Mills, Shipley (116), with an automatic hopper feed system.

flues for the circulation of gases around the boilers and then to the chimney. In single-storeyed boiler houses, and even in some with a floor over the boilers, the roof was often of iron, which would not warp or split in the hot, dry conditions and which would be some insurance against the spread of fire (Fig 246). The size of the boiler house reflected the demand for power within the mill, although there is evidence that provision was sometimes made for future expansion. At Greengate Mills, Keighley, for example, Marriners received advice in 1836 that they should 'have 2 boilers of 20 Horse Power each and have the Boiler House built to hold 3 Boilers and you might put the third in at some future period'.[58]

The development of the economiser in the 1840s allowed savings to be made by utilising the exhaust gases from the boiler furnace to heat boiler feed water, thus reducing the energy required to produce steam. The production of economisers was dominated by Edward Green of Wakefield, who supplied his first products to

Fig 242 The 1863 boiler house at Oats Royd Mills, Midgley (101), extended by a bay probably in 1887.

Fig 243 At Balm Road Mills, Hunslet (66), the boilers occupy the lower part of a substantial warehouse built in the 1880s.

Yorkshire mills in 1846 and improved the workings of the device thereafter.[59] The economiser became a standard fitting in steam installations and comprised stacks of metal pipes arranged in the flues leading from the boiler to the chimney (Fig 247). Water was pumped through the pipes to be heated by the exhaust gases and a scraper mechanism was commonly employed to prevent soot building up on the outside of the pipes. The economiser house, therefore, was simply a shelter for this installation and was most conveniently sited directly between the boiler and the chimney (Fig 248). At City Shed, Wyke (152), it was sited internally in a neat linear arrangement (see Fig 338), and at Waterloo Mills, Silsden (118), it was a detached building straddling the flue to the chimney.

The mill chimney became a symbol of industrialisation, and many early views over towns emphasised the canopies of smoke pouring from factory chimney stacks. The chimney had a two-fold function: it was intended both to carry off exhaust fumes from the boiler furnaces and to create a draught to assist in the workings of those furnaces. Both functions were affected by the height of the chimney, greater powers of dispersal and draught being derived from tall chimneys than from small. The design of chimneys varied, therefore, according to the amount of power required in a mill. Further variety followed from the choice of shaft section and building material and from the degree to which the chimney was treated as a decorative feature rather than a purely functional structure.

The obsolescence of the first generation of steam

Fig 244 The 1896 boiler house at Frostholme Mill, Todmorden and Walsden (137).

Fig 245 The boiler house at Manningham Mills, Manningham (93), built in 1871–3.

plants caused the replacement of many early chimneys by later, larger structures, but surviving architectural evidence combined with documents demonstrates that the most common type of chimney in the pre-1830 period was of square section, with a gradual but marked taper towards the top. The small capacity of the steam plant in this era demanded a chimney of only modest height, as at Healey New Mill, Ossett (107) (Fig 249a). Stone and brick proved equally suited to the square section, choice probably being dependent on local availability.

After 1825, and particularly towards the middle of the century, chimneys became higher in response to the demand for power. Square chimneys continued to be built and some rank among the most ornamental of the period. The chimneys at Saltaire Mills (116) (1850–3), Manningham Mills (93) (1870–1) and Dalton Mills, Keighley (71) (*c*1866), were all treated in a decorative way (Fig 249b), linking with the ornamental treatment of the mills themselves, but others, such as that at Lowertown Mill, Haworth (52) (Fig 330), were simple, plain structures. The most common chimney type in Yorkshire mills was the octagonal stone chimney, used for example at Winker Green Mill (8) (1836), and at Globe Mills, Slaithwaite (123) (1887). Circular stacks were also built, an early example being that at Old Lane Mill, Northowram (105) (1825–7), a later one that at Lower Providence Mill, Keighley (75) (*c*1875). Octagonal and circular chimneys offered less resistance to the wind than square stacks and were preferred for tall stacks where little or no decoration was applied. Ornament was usually restricted to the cap, the oversailing courses of which both prevented downward movement of the exhaust gases and offered some potential for elaboration, and to the lower part, where a massive base, often square in section, might support heavy moulded ashlar work at the bottom of the chimney shaft itself or a decorative cresting, as at Meltham Mills, Meltham (98) (Fig 249c).

After 1900 the square chimney enjoyed a revival. Some, like those at Oak Mills, West Ardsley (144) (Fig 249d), and Runtlings Mill, Ossett (110), were not tall, but others, like those at Becks Mill (70) and Knowle Mill (73), both in Keighley, were substantial. The circular

Fig 246 The interior of the 1863 boiler house at Oats Royd Mills, Midgley (101).

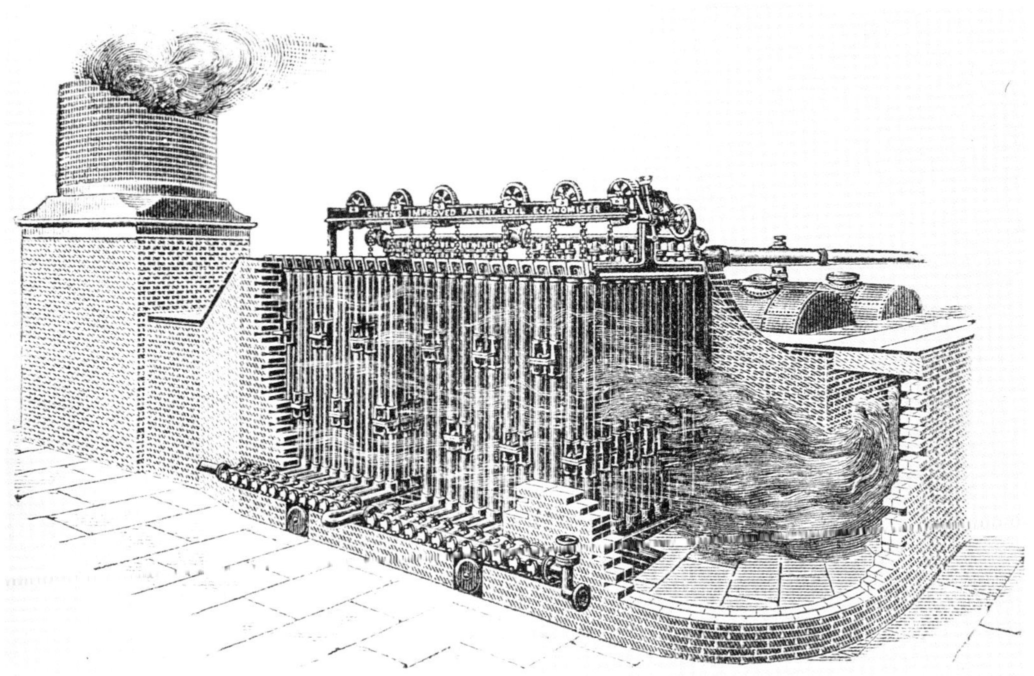

Fig 247 Green's Economiser (Nasmith and Nasmith 1909, fig 114).

Fig 248 The arrangement of buildings at Ebor Mill, Haworth (50), has a logical flow, with exhaust gases travelling from the boiler house (lit by the round window), through the economiser house (the gabled building beyond) towards the chimney.

brick chimney, similar to the contemporary Lancashire type developed by architects such as Stott, replaced some earlier stacks in this period, as at Belle Vue Mills (119) (Fig 249e) and Armitage Bridge Mills, South Crosland (127), and was also used in new sites like Hare Mill (134). Some post-1900 chimneys, of both square and circular section, had the name of the mill picked out in white brickwork, as at Oak Mills (144).

Chimneys were generally sited as close to the boiler house as practicable. In early mills they frequently rose from within the boiler house or against or even within the mill, as at C Mill at Marshall's Mill, Holbeck (57). Later they were usually sited close to, but detached from, the boiler house unless considerations of terrain dictated or encouraged an alternative siting. At Armitage Bridge Mills (127), for example, the chimney was built on the hillside with a flue connecting with the distant boiler house and contributing to the draught.

The final element in the power-generating complex was the reservoir. Steam installations required a large water supply, and while many mills were deliberately sited by rivers to guarantee this and while others sunk boreholes to tap subterranean supplies, some factories required reservoirs. The reservoirs were used both to supply the boilers and to receive the hot water condensate from the steam engine. Reservoirs could occupy a large area: the two dams at Marshall's Mill (57) were each an acre in extent, and Whetley Mills, Manningham (95), had three reservoirs, used, incidentally, for an annual factory swimming gala.

a

d

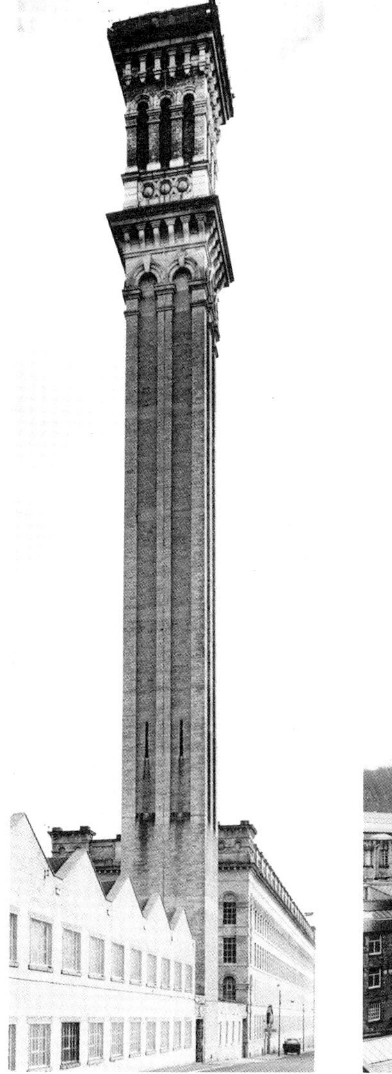

b

c

e

Fig 249 Yorkshire mill chimneys: a) Healey New Mill, Ossett (107), a tapering square chimney of 1825–7; b) Manningham Mills, Manningham (93), the Italianate chimney of 1870–1; c) Meltham Mills, Meltham (98), chimney of 1845 with a typical mid 19th-century octagonal section; d) Oak Mills, West Ardsley (144), 1906, with engine house (the gabled building with the round window) detached from the mill; e) Belle Vue Mills, Skipton (119), chimney of 1901–2 by Stott and Sons.

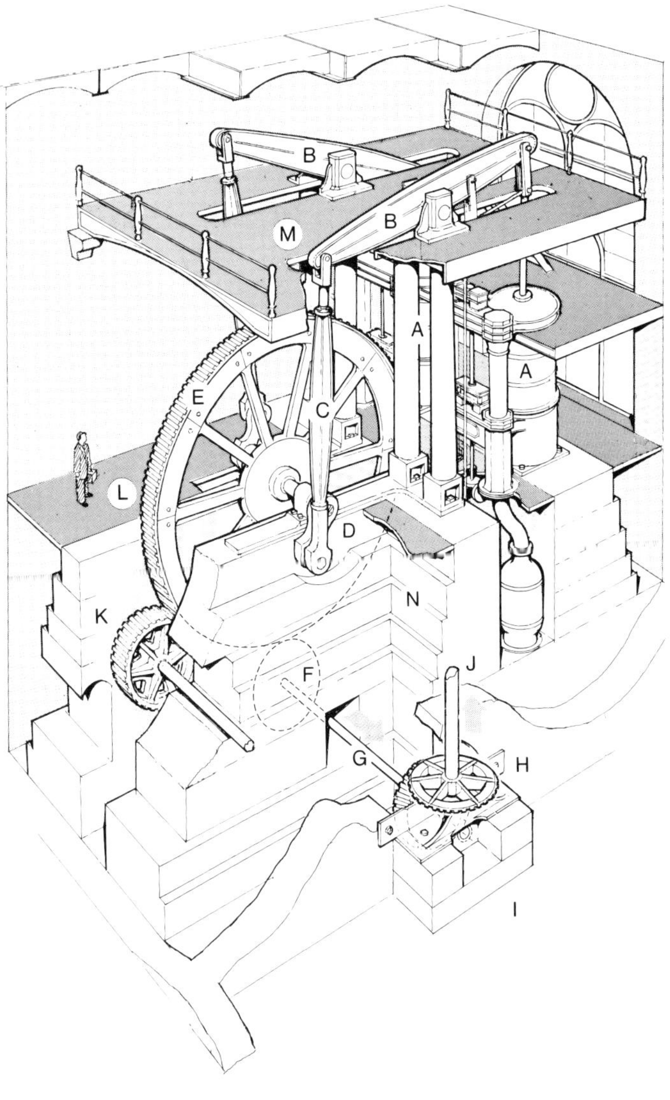

A Cylinders	**F** Pinion wheel	**K** Pinion wheel for drive to shed
B Working beam	**G** First motion shaft	**L** Engine house floor
C Connecting rod	**H** Bevel wheels	**M** Beam floor
D Crank and crank shaft	**I** Footstep bearing	**N** Ashlar engine bed
E Flywheel	**J** Upright shaft	

Fig 250 Power transmission using an upright shaft (reconstruction based on Saltaire Mills, Shipley (116), from Fairbairn 1863, 103–4).

Fig 251 The iron wall box on the top floor of the main multi-storeyed mill at Spinkwell Mills, Dewsbury (34), held the top of the upright shaft, the bevel gears attached to it and the end of the line shaft.

Power transmission

Every textile factory required a means of transmitting the rotative motion produced by the prime mover – waterwheel, turbine or steam engine – to the machines on the floors of mill and shed. It was part of the job of the millwright, later the mill engineer, to devise and maintain the system of power transmission. Good site planning reduced the complexity of the task, but since few mills remained unchanged there was a constant need to amend arrangements to meet new requirements. Despite some standard features, each mill's system was or became unique in detail.

Transmission systems may be divided for study into primary and secondary stages. The primary stage may be defined as the means of linking the prime mover with the different floors or buildings in the mill complex, while the secondary stage distributed drive within those areas, leading it to the point of use, the working machinery. Primary transmission was contrived first by the use of a series of interconnecting shafts and later by rope drive.

The shaft method of power transmission

Throughout the period under review the multi-storeyed mill was the dominant building on the large majority of textile mill sites. Before the construction of the first powerloom-weaving sheds in the 1820s, it was frequently the only structure designed to house mechanically driven machines, and the close association between it and the prime mover has already been noted. In many mills, therefore, the problems of power transmission centred around the means of connecting the different floors of a mill to the prime mover.

Before *c*1880 the upright shaft rising through all or part of a mill was almost invariably the principal component in a primary system of power transmission which comprised at least two shafts connected by toothed wheels. Water-powered corn mills provided a model for imitation in the late 18th century,[60] and timber was at first used for the main shaft. Rennie's Albion Mills, London, of 1784–5, however, demonstrated the supremacy of cast iron for the shafts and wheels, and textile mills rapidly followed this example.[61] The upright shaft was turned by indirect connection to the prime mover. In the first decades of mill building, waterwheels and the flywheels of steam engines commonly had a toothed spur wheel on the same axle, and a pinion wheel meshing with this wheel turned a 'first motion shaft' connected by bevel wheel to the upright

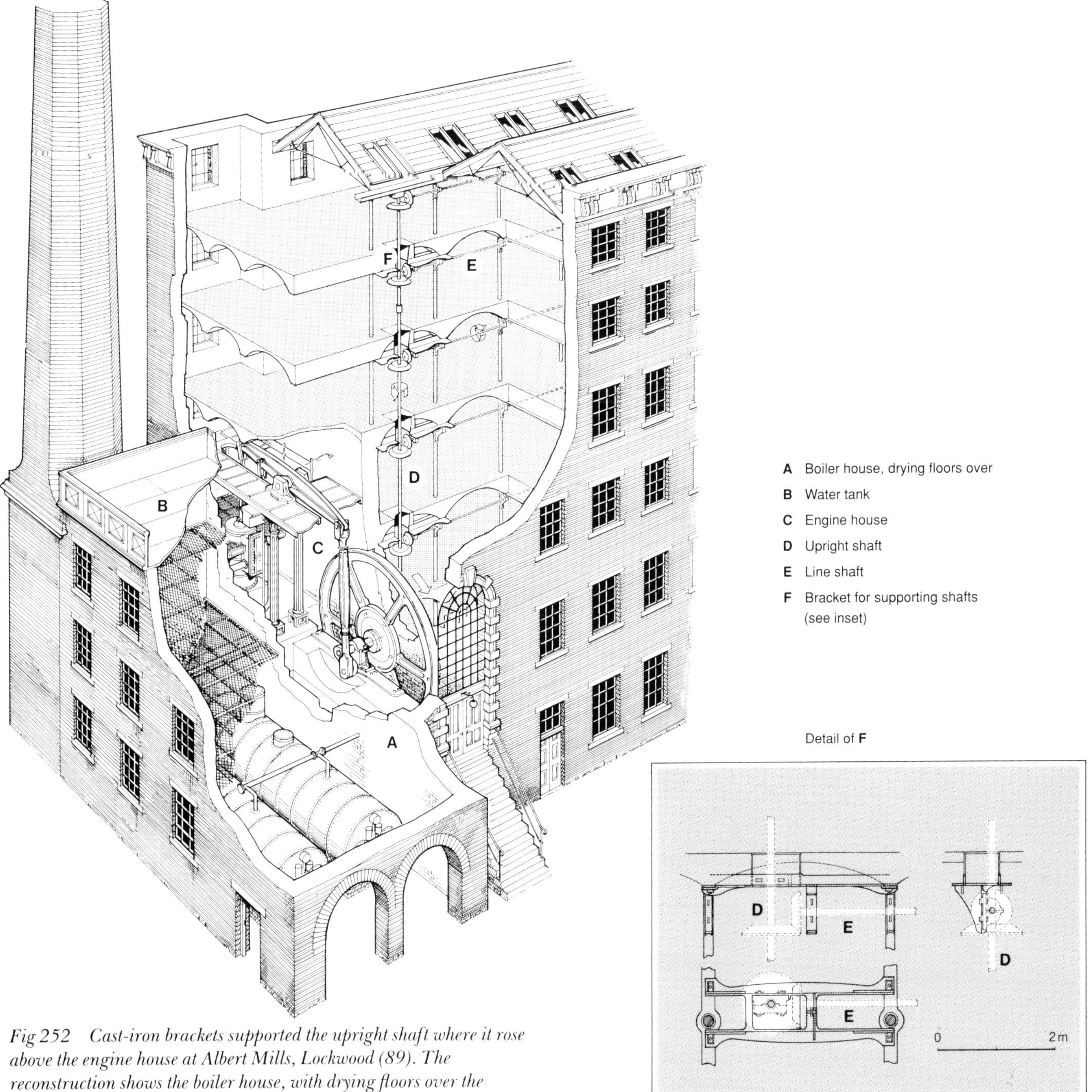

Fig 252 Cast-iron brackets supported the upright shaft where it rose above the engine house at Albert Mills, Lockwood (89). The reconstruction shows the boiler house, with drying floors over the boilers, the beam-engine house, and part of the fireproof mill of c1853.

shaft. This system was commonly replaced by a more direct one in which the waterwheel or flywheel was given a toothed rim connecting with a small pinion wheel on the first motion shaft.[62] The ponderous speed of the prime mover was translated into higher speeds in the shafts by means of gearing, a single revolution of the large waterwheel or flywheel producing a number of revolutions in the much smaller pinion wheel (Fig 250).

A massive system of support was required for the upright shaft and first motion shaft, together with their connecting wheels. The base of the upright shaft was commonly held in place in a footstep bearing of iron and brass, set on an ashlar foundation. The shaft was generally sited against either the end wall of a mill or an internal dividing wall to permit support at each floor level. Cast-iron plates bolted to the wall and iron boxes and brackets embedded in the wall supported the junction of upright and line shafts (Fig 251). Wall boxes were usually set in recesses framed with ashlar blocks to give firm anchorage for the bolts holding the plates and brackets. Where the upright shaft was unsupported by a wall, usually where it rose above an engine house, it could be held by cast-iron brackets slung beneath beams (Fig 252). Traps in the floors, contrived by simple trimmer joists in wooden-floored buildings but by iron castings in fireproof structures, allowed the shaft to rise through the mill. The upright shaft was most often sited in the central area of a mill's span, but at Woodhouse Mill, Langfield (83), it rises in one corner of the working area, and at Glasshouses Mill, High and Low Bishopside (55), an upright shaft, linked to either an added engine house or a turbine, is sited against the side wall of the mill (Fig 253). In the main mill at Hunslet Mills, Hunslet (67), there were two upright shafts, one serving the lower floors and the other the upper floors. A late development was the siting of the upright shaft in a tower on the end wall of the mill. This removed the shaft from the working areas, making conditions safer and quieter. Used first in the 1860s and never becoming common, shaft towers usually projected externally, as at Whetley Mills, Manningham (95), and Dalton Mills,

Fig 253 One of the upright shafts at Glasshouses Mill, High and Low Bishopside (55), retains its toothed bevel wheel; this transmitted drive to a line shaft.

Fig 254 The internal shaft tower in Dene Mill (1870) at Kebroyd Mills, Soyland (129).

Fig 255 The ashlar band at Brackendale Mills, Idle (68), shows the boltholes used to secure the brackets supporting the main drive shaft.

Keighley (71), but in Dene Mill at Kebroyd Mills, Soyland (129), an internal tower was used (Fig 254).

When applied to single-storeyed buildings, the shaft method of transmission could be simplified. In sheds with an attached or internal engine house the first motion shaft connecting with the prime mover formed the main drive shaft and generally ran the length of the building, usually supported by brackets on a side or internal dividing wall (Fig 228). The brackets were securely bolted through substantial ashlar blocks, sometimes forming a continuous band, in the wall (Fig 255). Alternative methods of supporting the main drive shaft included the use of ashlar blocks projecting from the inner face of the wall and of heavy cast-iron columns (Figs 256, 257). A few sheds used underground transmission, with the main shaft in a tunnel below the shed floor. This was used in Temple Mill at Marshall's Mill, Holbeck (57) (1838–41), and later by Fairbairn in the weaving shed at Saltaire Mills, Shipley (116) (1850–3) (Fig 258).

Upright and main drive shafts – the primary stage of transmission – connected with the secondary stage within each working area. The secondary stage comprised a line shaft or shafts on each floor of most multi-storeyed buildings and countershafts within a shed. The junction between the two systems was usually effected by bevel wheels, sometimes geared to raise the

Fig 256 Stone corbel blocks supported the main drive shaft in the 1867 weaving shed at Union Mills, Skipton (121).

Fig 257 This heavy column supported the main drive shaft in Lily Shed (1871–3) in Manningham Mills, Manningham (93), and is shaped to enable drive to be transferred to a line shaft.

Fig 258 Below the weaving shed of 1850–3 at Saltaire Mills, Shipley (116), is a tunnel for a main drive shaft, with further tunnels at right angles for countershafts. Electric motors such as the one in the foreground replaced this system.

Fig 259 Holes in the brick vaults over some floors of the main multi-storeyed mill at Saltaire Mills, Shipley (116), permitted belts to power machines on the floor above.

speed of the secondary shafts. Storeyed buildings most commonly had a central line shaft running the length of each floor. In some mills power was transferred from the central shaft to parallel line shafts, and in others cross-shafts, bevel-geared to the line shaft, were used to lead power at right angles where required. A variation in the system of transmission was used at Saltaire Mills (116) and in the 1860 mill at Brookroyd Mills, Stainland (130): instead of a line shaft connecting with the upright shaft on each floor, belt drive through slots in the fireproof vaults allowed power to be transferred from some floors to the one immediately above, thus reducing the number of heavy bevel wheels on the upright shaft (Fig 259). In sheds, countershafts – often one in each bay – connected with the main drive shaft by bevel wheels. At Brackendale Mills, Idle (68), for example, seven countershafts were driven from the main shaft (see Fig 228). In sheds where the main drive shaft was underground, countershafts ran in tunnels below the shed floor (see Fig 258).

Line shafts and countershafts were supported in a number of ways. Line shafts could be slung beneath beams on cast-iron hangers. Where the beams were wooden, the hangers were bolted to their soffit or side, but in fireproof mills the hangers clasped the beam flange. In some fireproof mills of pre-1830 date the cast-iron beams incorporate plates for the fixing of hangers (Fig 260). Columns supporting the beams were also used for securing shafting. A number of different column types were tried in an experimental period, but by the mid 19th century columns with D-shaped or square tops became fairly standard (Fig 261a–d). These

Fig 260 Mill D in Marshall's Mill, Holbeck (57), built in 1826–7, has cast-iron beams with plates for the attachment of hangers supporting line shafts.

Fig 261 Cast-iron columns in Yorkshire textile mills: a) a shaped column top in the mill of c1800 at Stone Bridge Mills, Wortley (151); b) a column with an open top in the same mill; c) a hanger in the 1863 mill at Whetley Mills, Manningham (95); d) line shafting supported on columns with D-shaped heads in Carlton Mill (c1865–70) in Sowerby Bridge Mills, Warley (143); e) in Genappe Mill (1868) at Dalton Mills, Keighley (71), the line shaft was held on a transom between columns.

Fig 262 Hangers slung from the valley gutter supported shafting in the 1867 shed at Union Mills, Skipton (121).

columns gave one or more flat bolting faces for the attachment of a hanger or plummer block. At Dalton Mills (71), the use of paired columns and a transom to support the line shaft allowed an unusual degree of ornament (Fig 261e). In sheds there is similar evidence of experiment with the form of the columns used to support countershafts. In Yorkshire's earliest surviving weaving sheds, those of the late 1830s at Armitage Bridge Mills, South Crosland (127), and Waterside Mill, Langfield (82), columns with an open circle at the top were employed (see Fig 120b for an example from the 1840s weaving shed at Armitage Bridge Mills), but columns with a flat bolting face became standard later. In some sheds countershafts were supported not on the columns but by hangers suspended from tie beams or valley gutters (Fig 262).

The final stage of transmission involved the transfer of power from line shaft or countershaft to individual machines. A belt system was most commonly employed, with drums spaced at intervals on the shafts and connecting with a corresponding drum on the machines by endless leather belts (Fig 263). The method was efficient, since friction loss was low, and adaptable, for clutch wheels allowed disengagement when a machine was not in use.

Rope drive

In the last quarter of the 19th century, rope, belt and cable drive replaced shafting as the most common form of primary power transmission in new installations.[63] Rope drive was the most common method used in Yorkshire mills. Made possible by the development of a durable cotton rope, probably in the mid 1870s, it was introduced to Yorkshire a few years later. At Whetley

Fig 263 A spinning room at Legrams Mill, Horton (60), showing the system of line shafting, pulley wheels and belt drive.

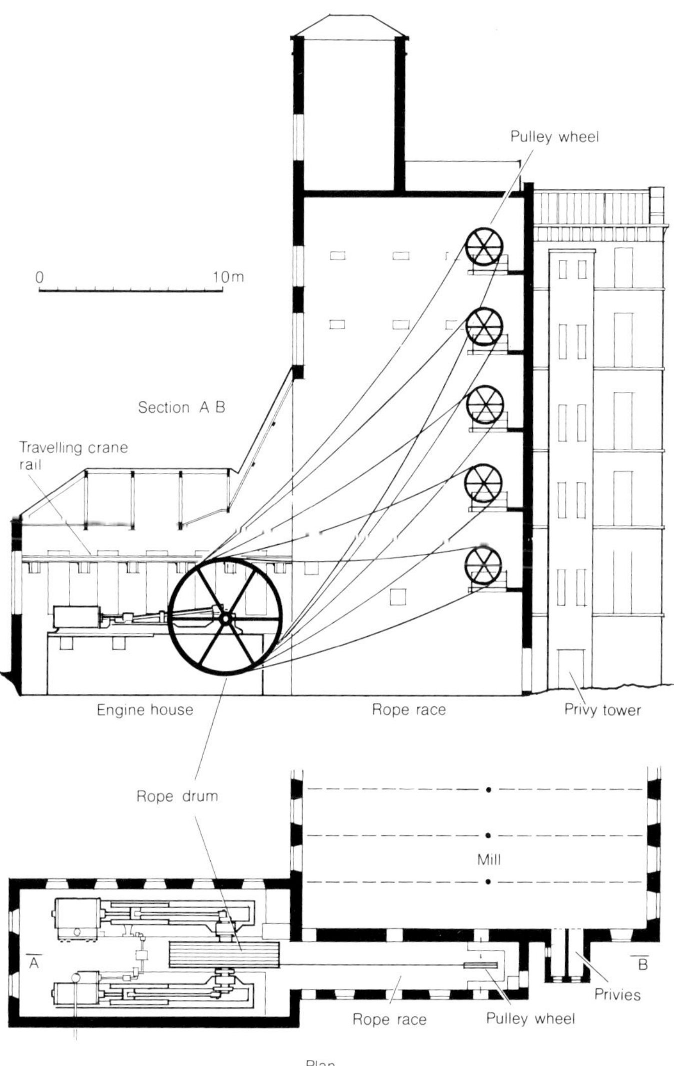

Fig 264 The rope drive in the 1895 multi-storeyed mill at Lowertown Mill, Haworth (52).

Fig 265 The rope race added to the mill of c1870 at Barkerend Mills, Bradford (26).

Mills, Manningham (95), alterations of 1879 involved the installation of a new horizontal engine powering spinning mill and combing shed by rope, and this dual change – new engine, usually of horizontal type replacing an earlier beam engine, and new transmission system – was repeated in many other mills in the next decades. Most new mills were built with rope drive, and Lowertown Mill, Haworth (52), of 1895, is typical of this generation of rope-driven factories (Fig 264). A few mills, notably Woodvale Mills, Hipperholme cum Brighouse, built in 1880, used the same principle of power transmission but substituted steel or leather bands for the ropes.[64]

Rope drive worked by connecting the engine flywheel with the pulley wheels on the ends of line shafts in storeyed buildings and of countershafts in sheds. The engine flywheel or rope drum was grooved to take a large number of ropes, sometimes as many as sixty but more commonly in the region of thirty, and these ropes were grouped to lead to grooved pulley wheels at different levels within a mill and in sheds. Gearing was supplied by the difference between the size of the rope drum and that of the pulley wheels. The system had many advantages over shafting. It was simpler in operation since there was less to go wrong and because the failure of a single rope did not cause the disruption which followed the breaking of a main shaft or bevel wheel. It was also more efficient, for it was not subject to the loss of power involved in the use of complex and weighty shafts and wheels. It was, furthermore, quieter and safer in operation, for it was commonly segregated from the working areas.

In storeyed mills the engine's rope drum was sited to connect with a rope race, a bay or part-bay usually open

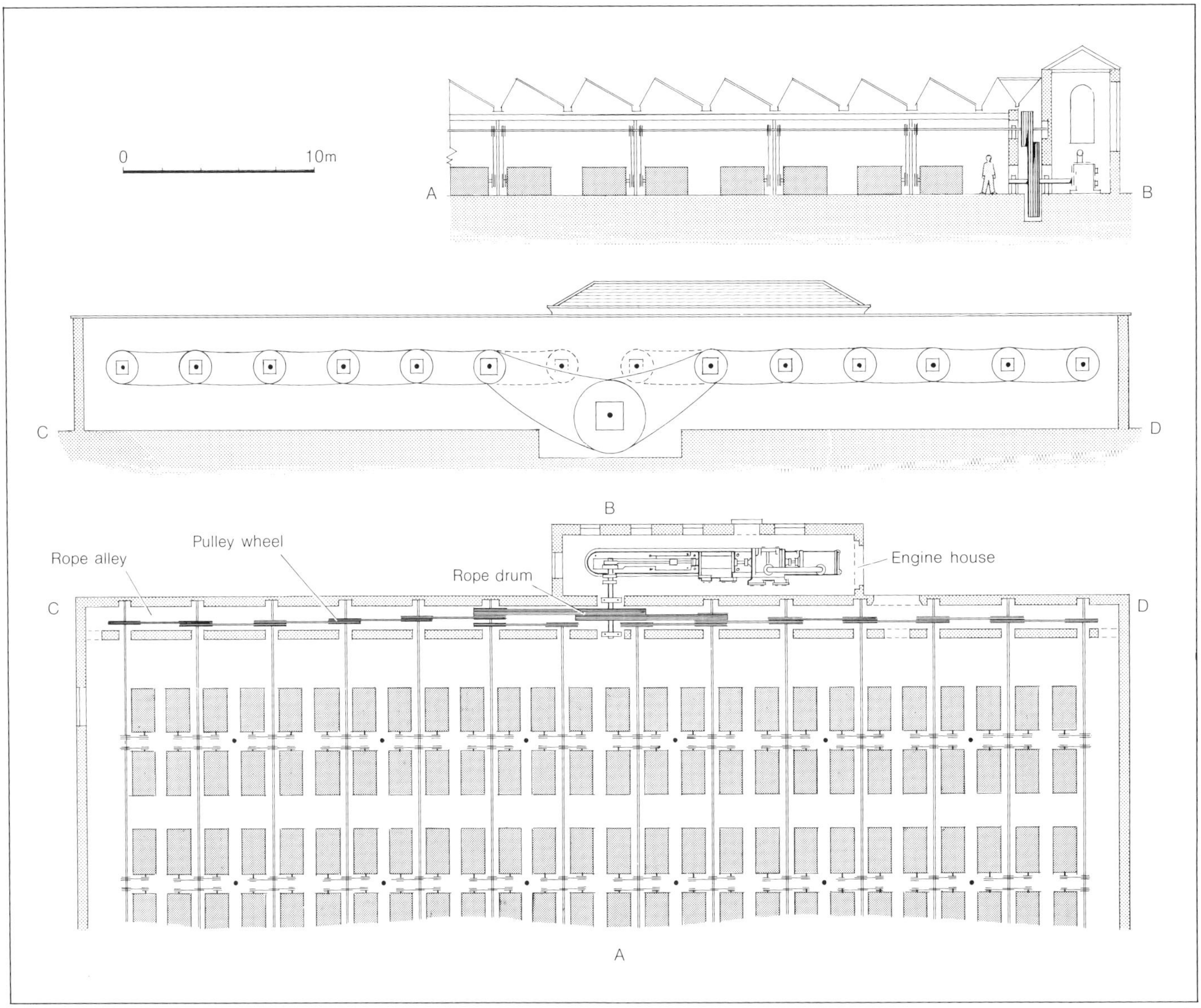

0 10m
A B
C D
B
Pulley wheel
Rope alley
Rope drum
Engine house
C D
A
a

the full height of the mill. The rope race was occupied only by pulley wheels, each on the end of a line shaft, at different floor levels, and by steps and platforms permitting access to the wheels for maintenance purposes. The rope race was generally contained within the end bay of a mill or in a central bay. In some mills the rope race was attached to the end or side wall, and such installations are recognisable externally by the sloping roof rising above the engine house (Fig 265).

Rope drive worked most efficiently when the angle between the rope drum and the highest pulley wheel did not exceed 45 degrees. It was common, therefore, to set the rope drum at a sufficient distance from the pulley wheels to permit the best working angles, and in consequence the projecting engine house was preferred

b

Fig 266 The rope alley in the 1887 weaving shed at Oats Royd Mills, Midgley (101): a) plan and sections; b) view showing the pulley wheel in the centre of the rope alley.

where circumstances permitted. A few mills, however, had an internal engine house, which required a steeper angle between the rope drum and the pulley wheels. At Globe Mills, Slaithwaite (123), for example, the angle between the rope drum and the highest pulley wheel was 52 degrees. Even vertical drives could be arranged successfully.[65]

Rope drive was contrived differently in sheds. The rope drum and the pulley wheels were sited in a rope alley, the equivalent to the rope race of a storeyed building and usually occupying a narrow bay along the full length of the shed. Within the rope alley the rope drum, most efficiently sited somewhere in the centre, connected with adjacent pulley wheels which both turned the countershafts on which they were mounted and passed on drive by rope to the pulley wheel in the next bay (Fig 266) By passing drive from one pulley wheel to the next, a long series of shafts could be turned, but inevitably there was some loss of power in this indirect system. Partial rope drive was introduced to some existing sheds by connecting a rope drum, often turned by a new horizontal engine, to the main drive shaft, which continued to turn countershafts by bevel wheels.

Steam turbines, electric power and the elimination of power transmission

From the mid 19th century various alternatives to steam power were explored. A gas engine was developed in 1859 and refined thereafter to make it competitive,[66] and some small Yorkshire mills – Stadium Mills, North Bierley (104), of 1912 and New Close Shed, Silsden (117), of 1913 – were powered by a gas engine originally. Oil engines, too, were successfully developed, although there is no evidence for mills being entirely powered by them. The major development, however, was the introduction of electric power, permitted by the production of a successful steam turbine and of a linked electric generator, both patented by Charles Parsons in 1884.[67] This allowed electricity to be applied for the purposes of powering textile mills, but application of the new inventions was slow in Britain. In the United States of America, mills were being run entirely on electricity as early as the 1890s,[68] but in Yorkshire the earliest known example of a mill powered by electricity is Becks Mill, Keighley (70), built in 1907. After that date mills converted to electricity in increasing numbers, although steam engines were still installed in textile factories for a few more years. At Ardsley Mills, East Ardsley (35), for example, built in 1912, power was provided by a steam engine of 900 horse power. By the end of the First World War, electricity was in common use, with thousands of electric motors in textile factories across the country producing about 2 million horse power in 1919.[69]

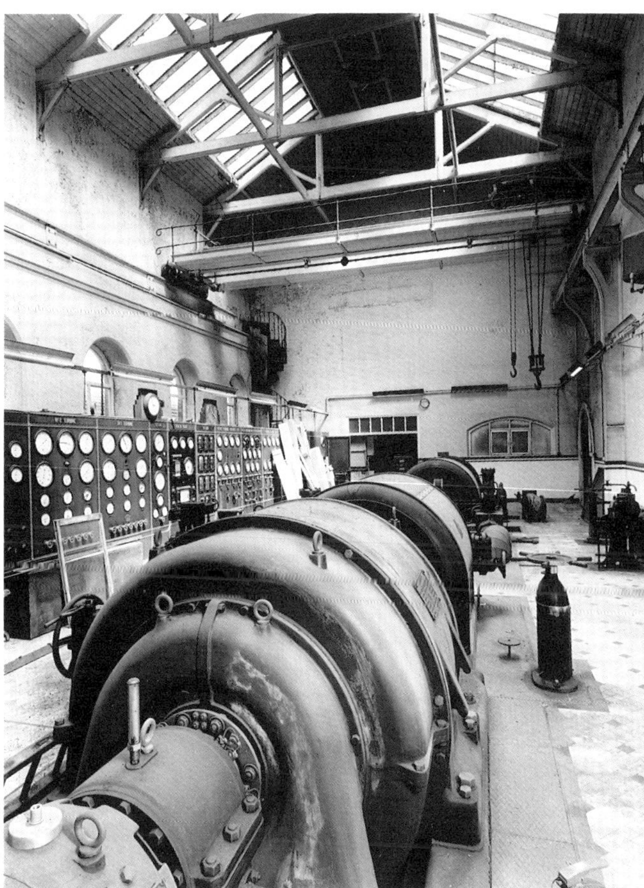

Fig 267 The 1930s turbine and switch room at Manningham Mills, Manningham (93).

The new source of power could be produced on site or bought in from a public company. It offered great advantages to the millowner, for it competed well with steam power in terms of price and was highly efficient in its application. Buildings designed for electric power could be more cheaply constructed, since transmission problems were virtually eliminated, and the option of buying power from an electricity company removed the need for a large capital outlay on plant.[70]

Where a millowner decided to generate his own power, the plant required included boilers, a steam turbine and an electric generator. Turbine and generator houses had few special architectural needs apart from a heavy concrete bed. At Manningham Mills, Manningham (93), the turbines were installed in the engine house designed for a 2,000 horse power steam engine (Fig 267), and at Cheapside Mills, Batley (18), the

Fig 268 The 1914 transformer house at Robinwood Mill, Todmorden and Walsden (140).

Fig 269 A group-drive electric motor in Saltaire Mills, Shipley (116).

new turbine house of 1934–5 was a large lofty chamber, lined internally with white glazed bricks. The alternative to providing private supplies was to purchase from a public company, and the absence of generating rooms at both Devonshire Mills, Keighley (72) (1909–10), and Park View Mills, North Bierley (103) (1924–5), indicate that this option was chosen. A transformer house was the principal building required where electricity was purchased, and at Robinwood Mill, Todmorden and Walsden (140), it is a small structure added in 1914 to the perimeter of the site (Fig 268).

Electricity effected a revolution in the method of power transmission, for it eventually eliminated shafts, pulley wheels and belts. In early electrical installations, large motors were placed one to a floor or where demand required (Fig 269). These motors, capable of producing up to 200 horse power, turned a main shaft serving a complete floor or area within a mill, the shaft either transferring drive to lesser shafts or powering machines directly by belt.[71] This method of transmission was called group drive, because a single motor was used to power a large number of machines. It enjoyed great advantages over earlier power transmission systems: no power was lost in turning either massive cast-iron upright or main drive shafts or the pulley wheels of a rope installation; and noise and danger levels were reduced considerably. Examples of Yorkshire mills

Fig 270 When Robinwood Mill, Todmorden and Walsden (140), was converted to electric drive in the early 20th century, a motor tower housing an electric motor for each floor was added to the multi-storeyed mill. The scar left by the now-demolished tower can be seen in this view.

Fig 271 Individual electric motors on machines in a spinning room at Legrams Mill, Horton (60), created a much less cluttered environment than the belt-drive system shown in Figure 263.

which adopted the group-drive system are Becks Mill (70), built in 1907 with motors in one corner of each floor, and Robinwood Mill (140), which by the early 20th century was powered by electric motors in a 'motor tower' built against the side wall of the mill (Fig 270).

The group-drive system retained some of the inefficiencies of the earlier method of transmission: power was not always used most economically, since a motor might have to run to drive just a single machine, and belt drive was seen as wasteful and detrimental to the working environment, obstructing light and being noisy and dangerous. The introduction of electric motors attached to each machine removed these inefficiencies. Small motors, of as little as one and a half horse power, allowed complete flexibility, working only when the individual machine was in operation. This represented a substantial saving compared with the earlier system, in which the whole expense of running a steam engine was required whether the whole factory or just a few machines were at work. The elimination of belt drive and of shafting produced a quieter, healthier and lighter environment (Fig 271), and new buildings could be less substantially constructed since they no longer carried a weighty transmission system. The contrast between the power transmission systems in early and late mills is symbolised by the changing role of the mill engineer. In the early period, the engineer or millwright was concerned with upright shafts, bevel wheels, belts and heavy cast-iron installations, but by the early 20th century the work principally involved wiring and motor maintenance. The modern working environment is, therefore, in large measure the result of the application of electric power to the factory.

5

The impact of the textile industry on the landscape

Textile manufacture was for long one of Yorkshire's most important industries, but it was only during the post-medieval period that it came to have national importance and in its growth made a permanent impression on the landscape of the county. As early as the beginning of the 18th century, Daniel Defoe drew attention to the 'vast clothing trade' which had so markedly raised the wealth and opulence most particularly of the West Riding. He remarked especially on the concentration of housing in the bottoms and on the sides of valleys, observing, on a journey across the moors from Rochdale to Halifax, 'look which way we would, high to the tops, and low to the bottoms, it was all the same; innumerable houses and tenters, and a white piece (of cloth) upon every tenter'.[1]

The visual impact which the industry made was even more marked in the era of the textile mill when mill buildings, especially those rising to three or more storeys, dominated their immediate landscape. The impact was strong even in the early period when mills were mainly rural (Fig 272), seeking water power in the streams and rivers of the dales, where their neighbours, the houses of villages and farmsteads, were rarely more than one or two storeys high. This first main phase of mill development, in the decades after 1770, also had a major influence on domestic settlement patterns as villages and hamlets grew up around individual mills. In Nidderdale, for example, Glasshouses (see pp173–5), Smelthouses, New York and Shaw Mills all grew up around and were sustained by textile mills.

Textile mills became more numerous during the era of steam power when, freed from the restrictions imposed by the need for a site on a stream or river, they were more frequently sited in existing villages and towns. During the 19th century, quite large agglomerations of mills developed in and around the towns of Leeds, Bradford, Keighley, Dewsbury, Huddersfield and Halifax, with smaller numbers in such centres as Wakefield, Barnsley, Elland, Brighouse, Bingley, Batley, Cleckheaton and Shipley (Fig 1). The mills were often concentrated in areas on the edge of town centres, as in Leeds where between 1790 and 1840 a series of mills,

Fig 272 West House Mill, Fewston (40), a large, integrated flax and linen mill built between 1797 and 1816 in a remote part of the Washburn valley, shown on a mid 19th century letterhead.

mainly for woollen and flax production, was built on the south-western and south-eastern edges of the town. These multi-storeyed buildings, now also highlighted by tall chimneys, added a new dimension to a skyline which was previously broken only by the towers and spires of the city churches (Fig 273). The distribution of mills around Leeds was matched by that around Huddersfield where a series of mills, among them Folly Hall Mills (63) (Fig 48), was built in the first half of the 19th century to the immediate south of the town. The freeing of land further east during the third quarter of the 19th century led to the creation of a heavily built-up industrial quarter, largely composed of textile mills, which had a highly distinctive character (Fig 274).

The changed appearances of Leeds and Huddersfield typify the impact which the textile industry made on most West Riding towns in the 19th century, but the mills themselves were only one of a far wider range of buildings which were erected to serve either the industry or its workforce. Commercial buildings of a number of types, housing developments, and a variety of community buildings, together contributed to the rich townscapes of the county.

Commercial buildings and townscapes

Textiles were only one of Yorkshire's industries, but they stimulated the construction of a series of commercial buildings which included cloth halls and different types of warehouse as well as exchange centres and the buildings of the regulatory agencies. These buildings, most of them large and imposing, all contributed to the appearance of the county's towns.

Domestic textile production in Yorkshire developed to such a scale during the 17th and 18th centuries that

Fig 273 Charles Fowler's Western Panoramic View of Leeds, published in 1832, shows the impact of textile mills and their chimneys on the appearance of the town.

Fig 274 Aerial view of the river and canal area south of Huddersfield town centre which developed as a predominantly textile manufacturing suburb in the mid 19th century. Folly Hall Mills (63) lie in the middle of the photograph, Firth Street Mills (62) and Larchfield Mills (64) at the top.

even before the growth of an extensive mill-based industry a number of cloth halls or piece halls in which clothiers and manufacturers sold their cloth were built. The first cloth hall in Yorkshire had been built in Heptonstall in 1545–58, and another was built in Halifax later in the century, but all the others, in Wakefield, Leeds, Penistone, Huddersfield and Bradford, were built or rebuilt in the 18th century.[2] Cloth halls varied in size, according to the number of clothiers whom they were intended to serve. Some, including the Bradford Piece Hall and Wakefield Cloth Hall, were simple rectangular buildings, but others, among them the various Mixed and White Cloth Halls in Leeds, and the Halifax Piece Hall (Fig 136), were built around courtyards. As large buildings these cloth halls were physically dominant in towns, but architecturally they were not always particularly impressive. The cloth halls built to courtyard plans, for example, usually had blind outer walls for security and other practical reasons, although important elevations were sometimes relieved by blank arcading. The detail was always classical, and entrance to the courtyards was generally through a pedimented gateway which was sometimes surmounted by a cupola. Internally these buildings had either streets of trestles on which cloth was displayed or individual shops.

Cloth halls continued in use into the mid 19th century, but by then both their function and contribution to urban architecture had been largely taken over by the different types of warehouse built by both

Fig 275 Shop and warehouse at 97 Main Street, Addingham.

manufacturers and merchants. Early warehouses, especially those built in Barnsley and Knaresborough by the linen manufacturers who put yarn out for domestic weaving, were generally unexceptional buildings. They were distinctive in size, being several storeys high and many bays long (Fig 88), but since they were generally utilitarian in appearance they differed little from most contemporary mill buildings. There were occasional exceptions, however, among them the shop and warehouse built in Addingham in the early 19th century by the Cockshotts, a local family who had been grocers and calico manufacturers since the late 18th century and who in the early 19th century built loomshops there at The Rookery (2) (Fig 29) and in Chapel Street (3) (Fig 144). This building, which presented a Doric, pedimented, ashlar façade to the street (Fig 275), had a ground-floor shop where cloth could have been displayed for sale, and a first-floor warehouse, served by a taking-in door in a side wall, in which the finished pieces of cloth would have been stored.[3]

All the major towns of the West Riding of Yorkshire developed commercial centres during the 19th century, and in many towns, especially those in which the wool textile industry was significant, warehouses were built in substantial numbers, often concentrated in particular parts of towns. The major woollen manufacturers all had warehouses in town centres or at local railheads, and this was most conspicuous in Batley and Dewsbury. Station Road in Batley, which led from the railway station shared by the two railway companies which served the town, was lined by many impressive warehouses built during the third quarter of the 19th century (Fig 89).[4] These buildings were the public face of the manufacturers, and their elaborate decoration was in strong contrast to the utilitarian style of the mills they served. In Dewsbury a number of imposing warehouses were built on or near Wellington Road (Fig 276), directly opposite the London and North Western Railway Company's station.

Fig 276 Warehouses in Wellington Road, Dewsbury, opposite one of the town's railway stations.

Fig 277 Priestley's Warehouse at 66 Vicar Lane, Bradford, built in the Little Germany area of the town in 1867.

The worsted industry, which was centred on Bradford, developed a different system of sales from the woollen industry, and instead of direct selling to a domestic market, its mainly export-based trade was handled largely by merchants, many of whom built substantial and architecturally impressive warehouses. These warehouses, built in the mid to late 19th century, were mainly grouped along and behind Hall Ings and Leeds Road, not far from Bradford's two railway stations. Demolition has reduced this concentration, but the area known as Little Germany, immediately north of Leeds Road, has survived largely untouched. Little Germany, so-called because German merchants were particularly important in the commercial structure of the worsted industry, has streets lined with large warehouses.[5] The majority of Little Germany's warehouses were built in the great boom period of the worsted industry, between 1860 and 1874, most of them in the then fashionable Italianate style (Fig 277).

Warehouses were only one of a number of town-centre buildings associated with the textile industry, and Dewsbury well illustrates the wider contribution which the whole range of commercial and industrial buildings could make to the form and appearance of a town. In

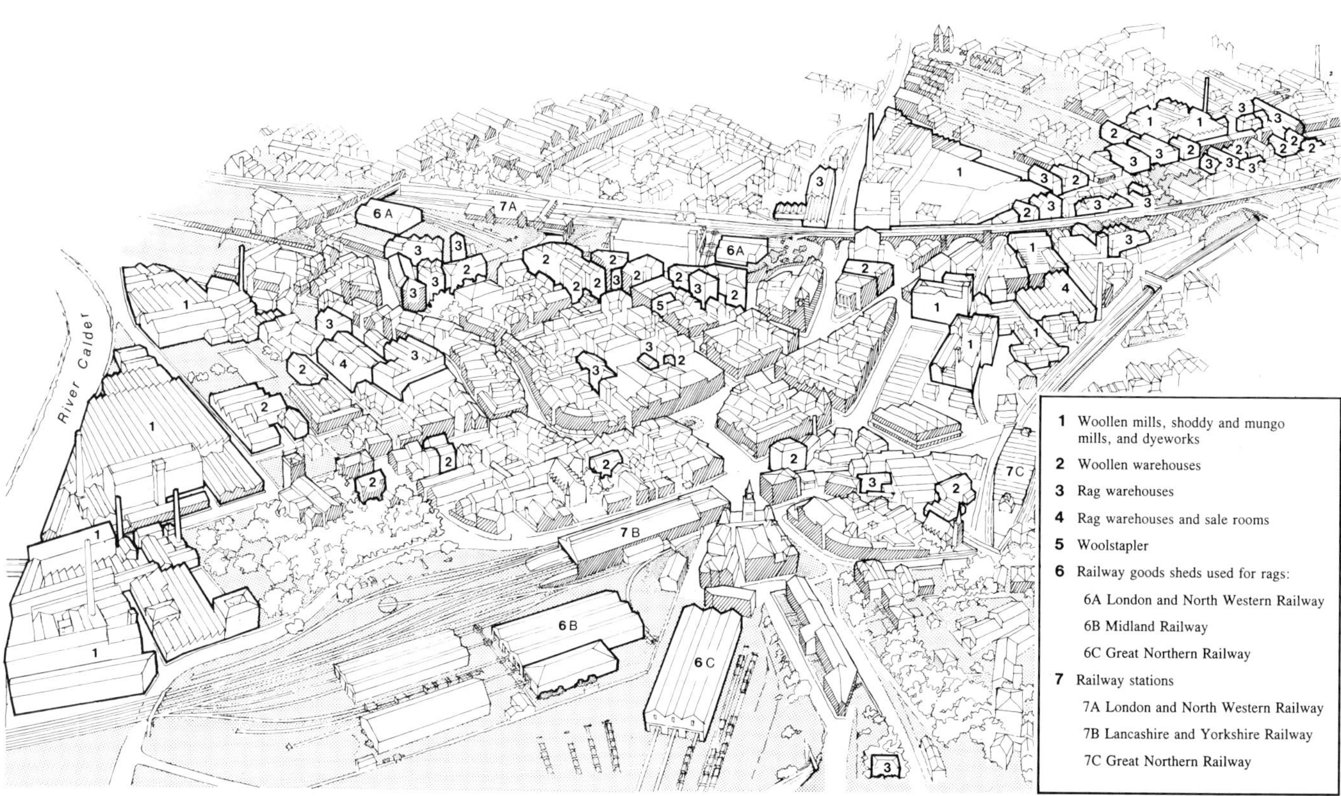

Fig 278 Dewsbury town centre showing the buildings associated with the town's wool textile industry in the early 20th century.

Fig 279 A consignment of rags at Batley Carr Goods Station.

Fig 280 Thornton's Rag Warehouse and Auction Rooms in Savile Road, Dewsbury.

1893 Dewsbury, sited in the heart of the woollen district, was described as having 'risen from comparative insignificance to the position of a populous and thriving manufacturing town' with 'mills of great power, many first-class warehouses, and . . . suburbs containing a large number of villa residences'.[6] These suburbs, of course, also contained the housing required by the bulk of the textile industry's workforce, as well as the shops, schools, churches and chapels which also made up the community. In the early 20th century, the centre of Dewsbury (Fig 278) had woollen mills, rag and shoddy mills, warehouses of various types, including rag warehouses, and auction rooms for rags, all of them the product of a flourishing textile industry.

Dewsbury, together with the neighbouring towns of Batley, Morley and Ossett, concentrated on the production of blankets and heavy woollens which made use of wool recovered mainly from rags. These towns, unlike others in the county, were therefore characterised by large numbers of rag warehouses (Figs 196–9), used either purely for storage or also for sorting, and built both by merchants and by the railway companies which transported large quantities of rags from far afield. The sight of great masses of rags awaiting collection or sale in and around the railway stations of the area became familiar. A visitor arriving at Batley Station in 1858 remarked on the 'great packets or bales piled up in stacks or laden on trucks, every bale branded *Anvers* . . . here were rags shipped at Antwerp from all parts of northern Europe . . . from pediculous Poland, from the gipseys (sic) of Hungary, from the beggars and scarecrows of Germany, from the frowsy peasants of Muscovy'.[7] The scene changed little over the decades, and a 20th-century view of Batley Carr Station shows just such a picture (Fig 279). Regular rag and shoddy auctions were held in Batley and Dewsbury from the mid 19th century, and auction rooms were built by a number of companies for the sale of rags. Most have been demolished, but Robert Thornton and Son's premises in Savile Town, Dewsbury, completed in 1915, survives (Fig 280).

Cloth halls and the various types of warehouse reflected, as much as the mills themselves, the growth of the Yorkshire textile industry and changes in its organisation. In Bradford this growth was reflected in many ways, among them the construction, between 1864 and 1867, of a new Wool Exchange.[8] Designed by Lockwood and Mawson, one of the principal architectural practices in the town, the building (Fig 281) has a central hall surrounded by an ambulatory, with a news room to one side and offices on the first and second floors. It was used for the local distribution of wool, although many worsted manufacturers and topmakers obtained their supplies directly, often from auctions in London or, later, Australia. A later building, the Conditioning House in Canal Road, was built by Bradford Corporation in 1900–2 to provide laboratories for checking that worsted cloth was of the correct weight and length, and in good condition (Fig 282).

The mill community

The primary industrial buildings of the textile industry, the mills themselves and their associated commercial buildings, were only part of a wider range of buildings constructed as a result of the growth of a mechanised textile industry. The construction of textile mills led to the expansion of many existing settlements as well as to the growth of new ones, including a series of industrial communities and model villages. The principal result of all this growth, in building terms, was the construction of a substantial amount of workers' housing as well as of more superior manufacturers' houses, together with a range of community buildings which included schools, churches and chapels, institutes and libraries, hospitals and almshouses as well as other buildings associated with public administration and life. These may be

Fig 281 The Wool Exchange, Bradford.

studied both in relation to communities, and as individual buildings.

Industrial communities and model villages

The end of the 18th century and the early 19th century saw the construction of a number of industrial communities in Britain which offered housing and other facilities. Most were built for the early cotton industry, and they included Dale and Owen's New Lanark, Arkwright's Cromford, the Evans' Darley Abbey and the Gregs' Styal.[9] No equivalent communities were, however, built in Yorkshire at this time, largely because of the structure of the county's textile industry. Its early cotton industry, as well as the contemporary flax and linen industry, had a lower individual level of capital investment than elsewhere, and a commensurably smaller size of workforce. The long-established, domestically based wool textile industry of the county, whose woollen branch was not mechanised until a comparatively late date, also worked against the early foundation of the large mills which fostered such industrial communities.

The first half of the 19th century, however, saw the industrialisation and attendant urbanisation of Yorkshire create appalling living conditions with all their attendant social, political and moral problems. One of the consequences of this was the creation of a small number of industrial communities and model villages during the years around and following 1850. These communities, which were intended to provide a well-disciplined environment where the middle-class virtues of thrift, sobriety and self-improvement could be more effectively inculcated,[10] varied in size, form and situation. An indication of the range of buildings and facilities which they provided is given by case studies of three of them, Glasshouses, which grew up around Glasshouses Mill, High and Low Bishopside (55), Meltham Mills, which grew up around Meltham Mills, Meltham (98), and Saltaire, established next to Saltaire Mills, Shipley (116).

Fig 282 The Conditioning House, Canal Road, Bradford.

Glasshouses, situated in a remote part of Nidderdale, developed over a period into a loosely planned village which was not unlike Joseph Hirst's Wilshaw, set high in the hills above Meltham. Hirst, who owned Wilshaw Mill and Royd Edge Mill, and rented Manor Mill, all of them in Meltham township, created the village of Wilshaw during the twenty-five years leading up to his death in 1874, from what had been disparate groups of cottages. The architects John Kirk and Sons designed housing as well as a school, church and some almshouses (Figs 318, 320, 323). Meltham Mills (98) was also a remote settlement, but the size of its principal mill, the scale of that mill's production and its profitability far exceeded those of Glasshouses Mill (55), and its buildings, though similarly dispersed, were more numerous as well as grander, and also reflect a fuller range of patronage. Saltaire (116) was one of the earliest of the handful of model villages built by Yorkshire millowners, and over a period of twenty-five years it was provided with a range of public buildings and facilities as adequate as those of many towns. Its planned form was like that of Edward Akroyd's Copley and Akroydon, Sir Henry Ripley's Ripleyville, and the Crossleys' West Hill Park, Halifax, but it overshadowed them all by its size and completeness. Akroyd's Copley, which he built from the late 1840s for the workers at Copley Mill, Skircoat, was principally a development of houses which a school and a series of social initiatives transformed into a community. Akroydon, closer to Akroyd's main mill at Haley Hill, Northowram, was more ambitious in its buildings, layout and style than Copley. Designed in 1859 by Gilbert Scott, who had built the church of All Souls, Haley Hill, for the family in 1856–7, its original plan envisaged 350 houses around a large square (Fig 283). Only ninety-two houses were eventually built, but a range of other community facilities was provided. Ripleyville, built in the third quarter of the 19th century, was described in Sir Henry Ripley's obituary as a thickly populated suburb of Bradford built almost solely by him. It housed the workforce of Bowling Dyeworks in Bowling, and he erected or provided land there for a school, church and almshouses to serve them. The Crossleys, whose wealth came from carpet production at Dean Clough Mills, Northowram, built the West Hill Park estate in Halifax between 1863 and 1868. The family had previously built an orphanage and almshouses in the area, as well as creating the People's Park, building their own mansions, and contributing to some grandiose rebuilding in the centre of Halifax.[11]

Glasshouses

The village of Glasshouses, some 2km from Pateley Bridge, developed around Glasshouses Mill, High and Low Bishopside (55), a flax-spinning mill built in 1812 on a site next to the River Nidd. The mill was taken over by the Metcalfe family in 1828, but it was not until after they had purchased it in 1835 that it was significantly enlarged, two rear wings being added in the late 1830s and a warehouse and office in 1844. Despite an increase

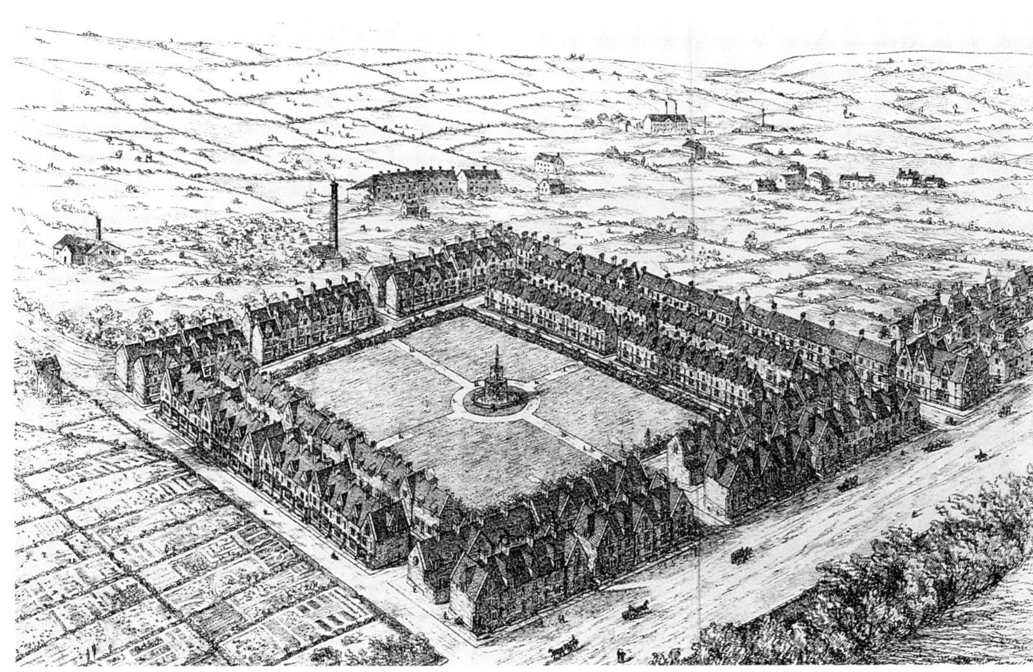

Fig 283 An artist's impression of the original plans for Akroydon proposed by George Gilbert Scott (Hole 1886, frontispiece).

in the workforce from seventy-eight in 1833 to 264 in 1851, there was still no community around the mill in 1850, although over the next twenty-five years the Metcalfes created one, building a considerable amount of housing, a school and a chapel, and supporting other ventures.[12] Their architect at this time was usually William Reid Corson, who from the late 1840s was in practice in Leeds with his brother, George Corson, but from 1861 worked from Manchester with William Aitken.[13]

The Metcalfes' land holding at Glasshouses extended from the valley bottom up a steep valley side, and the community which they fostered was consequently somewhat dispersed, although there was some concentration in the immediate neighbourhood of the mill (Fig 284). The Metcalfes acquired some existing houses when they purchased their estate, and a number of these, including Valley View and West Riding Terrace, show signs of subdivision into multiple occupation under the pressure of a growing mill workforce. However, much of the Metcalfes' purpose-built housing took the form of terraces of workers' cottages. Guisecliff View (Fig 285a) designed and built in 1858, Albert Terrace (Fig 285b) of 1869 and Fir Grove Terrace (Fig 285c) of 1873 were terraces of six, twelve and nine cottages respectively, and they reveal a progressive improvement in house design. All were single-fronted, but while those in Guisecliff View were just one room deep with a rear service wing, those in Albert Terrace and Fir Grove Terrace were all two rooms deep, the houses in the latter also each having a rear service wing. These advances appear to reflect the Metcalfes' interest in housing standards, for among the family papers is a pamphlet published in 1864 by the Society for the Erection of Improved Buildings, as well as a design for a pair of cottages published by the Central Cottage Improvement Society.

The status of the head of the household, together with family size and the ability to pay the rent, are all likely to have influenced the allocation of mill cottages. Guisecliff View came to be favoured as a residential site by overlookers in the late 19th century, perhaps because it enjoyed the advantage of extensive views across the valley. A pair of cottages (Fig 286) overlooking the back of the mill, perhaps by Perkin and Backhouse of Leeds who designed two terraces of houses with similar

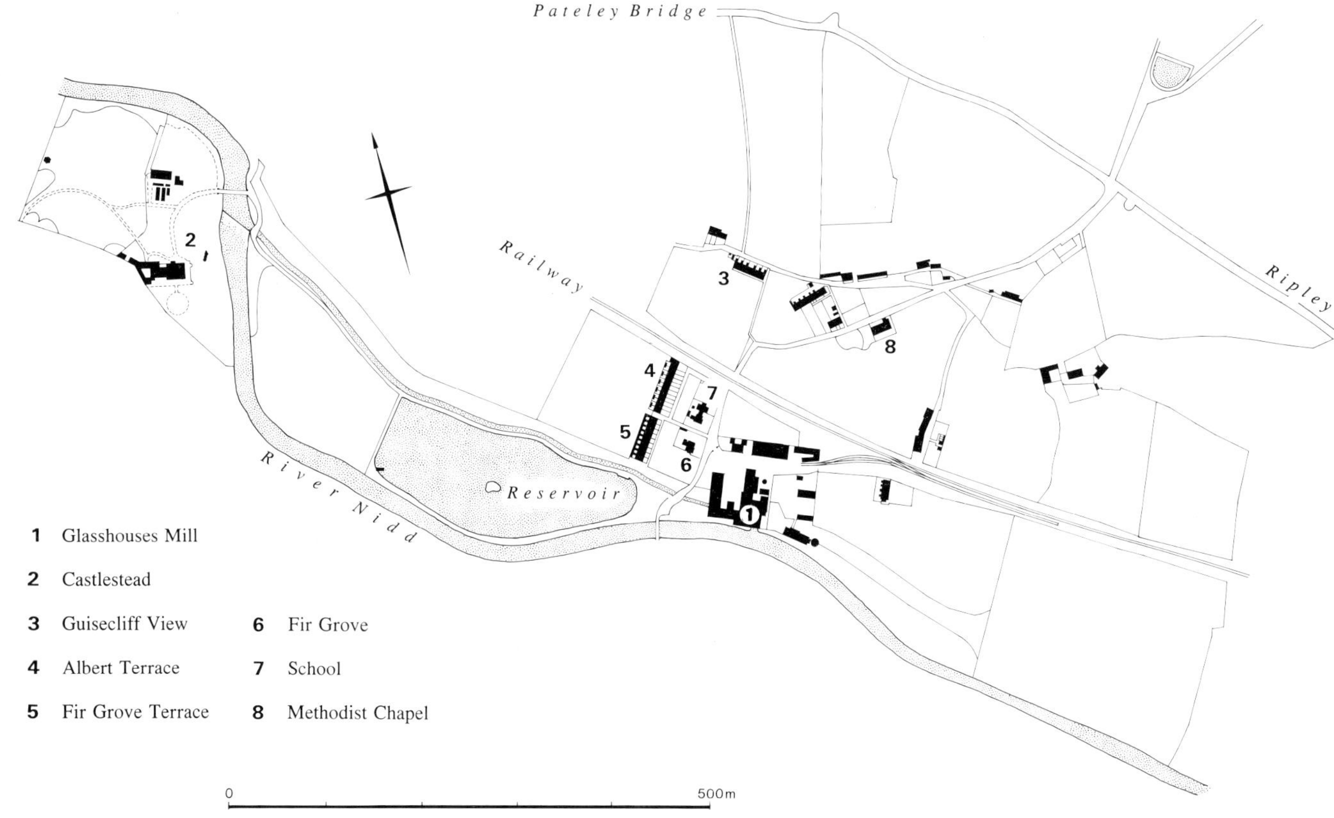

Fig 284 Plan of George Metcalfe's Glasshouse Mill Estate, based on a survey of March 1883.

a

b

c

Fig 285 Workers' housing at Glasshouses: a) Guisecliff View, built in 1858; b) Albert Terrace, built in 1869; c) Fir Grove Terrace, built in 1873.

detailing for the brewing and quarrying branch of the family in Pateley Bridge in 1853, are better detailed than the main terraces and may have been for overlookers too. Fir Grove (Fig 287), opposite the mill entrance, was built by the Metcalfes for their mill manager in 1869–70, from 1881 serving as the residence of the Wesleyan Methodist minister in the village. The house, more finely detailed than others in the village, has interior fittings of good quality, and a parlour, dining room, kitchen and pantry on the ground floor. The grandest piece of domestic architecture in Glasshouses, sited upstream from the village on a terrace overlooking

Fig 286 Cottages at the head of the yard to Glasshouses Mill, High and Low Bishopside (55).

the river, is Castlestead, built by George Metcalfe junior in 1861–2, and gradually extended by him over the next sixteen years. The house (Fig 288) is Gothic in style, and Metcalfe calculated that its construction and furnishing cost £16,000. The 1883 map (Fig 284) shows it in ornamental grounds which included croquet lawns and a vinery.

The Metcalfes' concern extended beyond merely housing their workforce. The combined warehouse and office added to the end of the west wing of the mill in 1844 reportedly included an upper room which was used as a schoolroom until, in 1859–60, the family built a Gothic-style school and schoolhouse close to the mill (Fig 289). Designs for a Lecture Hall in the village were made in 1863 (Fig 319) and although the building was never erected, George Metcalfe proved his commitment to encouraging knowledge by providing the Glasshouses Mechanics' Institute, newly founded under his patronage, with rent-free accommodation in West Riding Terrace. The Metcalfes, pillars of the Wesleyan Methodist Connexion, taught at a Sunday School in the village school and in 1866 George Metcalfe junior paid for the construction of a Methodist Chapel (Fig 290) as a memorial to his father, George, who had died in 1861, and his uncle, John, who had died in 1865. Further work, including provision of a minister's vestry, a classroom under the chapel, a gallery and the construction of the flèche, was paid for in 1875. The Broadbelt Hall, next to the chapel, was built as a Sunday School in 1931 on land given by Frederick Atkinson, who had taken over Glasshouses Mill (55) in 1912. It was designed by A Brocklehurst of Manchester, and when opened had a large schoolroom and four other classrooms, with a kitchen and other facilities in the basement.

Fig 287 Fir Grove, Glasshouses, built in 1869–70 for the mill manager to designs by Corson and Aitken of Manchester.

Fig 288 The millowner's mansion of Castlestead, built a short distance upstream from Glasshouses Mill in 1861–2.

Meltham Mills

The small hamlet of Meltham Mills, just outside Meltham and near Huddersfield, contained a few small textile mills at the beginning of the 19th century, but one of these mills, which took the name of the settlement, grew under the direction of the Brook family into a major textiles complex. In the second half of the 19th century and in the early 20th century, the Brooks' Meltham Mills (98) and the Dewhursts' Belle Vue Mills in Skipton (119) were the two greatest cotton thread producers in Yorkshire.

The settlement of Meltham Mills stands in the bottom of the valley of the Thick Hollins Dike, and the Brooks' cotton-spinning mill there already comprised three multi-storeyed mills in 1833, and a further three were built before 1850. Subsequent expansion was mainly of ancillary buildings. The range of associated buildings which the Brooks erected or contributed to was extensive, ranging from workers' housing, mansions, churches and schools to a Convalescent Home and other public buildings (Fig 291).[14] Some of these buildings were close to the mill, while others were further afield (Figs 157, 291).

The scale of the Brooks' textile business was considerable: in 1833 they had 623 employees, and by the end of the 19th century, almost 2,000. Such numbers were never all accommodated in the immediate neighbourhood, but the Brooks, both of necessity and for

Fig 289 Glasshouses School, Glasshouses, built in 1859–60. The left-hand wing housed the schoolhouse.

philanthropic reasons, built a significant amount of workers' housing. By 1850 they had built about forty-six cottages in four, two-storeyed terraces on the mill site itself, and during the next ten years they erected a further terrace of thirteen cottages there. The expansion of the textile mill buildings in the mid 19th century meant that the subsequent workers' housing which they built had all to be constructed off the mill site. Few precise details are available about when they built houses away from the mill, but by 1872 they owned a series of terraces of cottages along the valley side south-west of the mill. These included Upper and Lower Mount, Spring Place and Manor Buildings, as well as the most monumental, Bank Buildings, a terrace with thirty-four under-dwellings and over-dwellings of various sizes built in about 1860 (Fig 292). The dwellings in Bank Buildings came with allotments and hanging grounds for washing, and the adjacent valley bottom, running up to the mill, was made into a landscaped park known as The People's Pleasure Grounds. Joshua Major of Leeds, the most important landscape gardener resident in Yorkshire in the 19th century,[15] created paths and arbours, bridges over the stream, a cascade opposite the centre of Bank Buildings, and planted selected trees and shrubs. More extensive but less grand housing was subsequently built immediately west of Bank Buildings at Calmlands where, by the end of the 19th century, seven terraces provided forty-one two-storeyed two and three-bedroomed houses. Built on slightly rising ground, a terrace of eleven houses built before 1872 overlooked three later pairs of terraces each of five houses, all with front gardens and rear yards. The terraces (Fig 293) are simply detailed with central, gabled projections, shaped window heads and

Fig 290 Methodist Chapel and Broadbelt Hall, Glasshouses.

Fig 291 Map showing property owned or built by Jonas Brook and Bros Ltd of Meltham Mills, Meltham (98).

simple door hoods; further terraces, built after 1914, were altogether plainer.

The Brooks built housing only for a proportion, albeit a significant proportion, of their workforce, and while some lived in housing in Meltham Mills and nearby Meltham, others travelled by special trains from Huddersfield on the purpose-built Meltham Mills branch line which was begun in 1864 and opened for passenger traffic in 1869. A station at Meltham Mills Halt was erected solely for the employees of the Brooks in return for the sale of land for building the railway, and tickets were issued at the mill office until the station closed in 1934.

The Brooks became men of substance as their business flourished. Initially they all lived in or around Meltham or Huddersfield in houses of increasing grandeur, one of which was Meltham Hall, built in 1841 by William Lee Brook. The house (Fig 294), subsequently enlarged, is classical in style and was set in landscaped grounds. Charles Brook junior, who died in 1872, was the first member of the family to follow the steps of other *nouveaux riches* manufacturers and become a landowner, purchasing the Enderby Hall estate in Leicestershire in 1864.

The Brooks spent a great deal of money in building, extending and restoring churches, as well as in building schools, in the neighbourhood of Meltham Mills. The family were Anglicans, and their first expenditure, in 1835, was on the addition of a west tower, designed by J P Pritchett, to St Bartholomew's Church in Meltham, a church which came to contain a number of their family monuments. Subsequent expenditure was principally at Meltham Mills itself where the Brooks added to the small, established community. In 1838, 'fully sensible of

Fig 292 Bank Buildings, Meltham Mills.

Fig 294 Meltham Hall, Meltham Mills.

the increased responsibility attached to increasing wealth', James Brook erected a 'neat and commodious Gothic edifice . . . designed to serve the double purpose of a church and school' which also included residences for a clergyman and a schoolmaster.[16] The building was again designed by J P Pritchett, but the church, which had seating for a congregation of 250 people, was soon found inadequate and in 1844 Pritchett drew up plans for new and separate buildings. St James' Church, Meltham Mills (Fig 295), consecrated in 1845, was designed to seat nearly 400 adults and about 250 children; the cost of the nearby school (Fig 296) was borne jointly by the Brooks and the National Society and the Committee of the Council of Education. In about 1860 the Brooks built a vicarage next to the church (Fig 295).

Charles Brook junior, despite his family's construction of schools, was less inclined to encourage the self-education of his adult employees. He only grudgingly allowed the new Meltham Mechanics' Institute to use rooms in his mill in 1849, although by contrast J W Carlile, his successor as head of the firm, was not only president of the Institute but in 1890, at his own expense, donated the Carlile Institute to Meltham as a library and premises for community functions and adult education (Fig 297). The adjacent Meltham Town Hall (Fig 325; see pp196–7), built in 1898, was paid for by another member of the board of directors, Edward Brook.

In a further expression of philanthropy, Charles Brook junior built a Convalescent Home in 1868–71 on land diagonally opposite Bank Buildings. Stone-built, Gothic in style, with a central service and administrative block linked to symmetrical wings (Fig 298), it cost £40,000 to build and endow, and could hold sixty patients who were admitted either on the recommendation of the Huddersfield Infirmary or on that of its trustees.[17]

Fig 293 Housing at Calmlands, Meltham Mills.

Fig 295 St James' Church and Vicarage, Meltham Mills.

Fig 296 St James' School, Meltham Mills.

Saltaire

Saltaire was one of the most complete model villages to be built in the 19th century.[18] Titus Salt, its builder, had made a fortune largely through exploiting the use of alpaca and mohair in worsted manufacture, and by 1850, the year in which he served as its lord mayor, he was Bradford's biggest employer of labour, running six mills in the city. It was also the year in which Salt approached the Bradford architects, Lockwood and Mawson, for the design of a mill he intended building on a new site on the southern slopes of the Aire valley, three miles north of Bradford. This mill, Saltaire Mills, Shipley (116), which opened in 1853, was intended to carry out all the principal processes of worsted manufacture, and it was planned to ensure as smooth a flow of work as possible (Fig 172). Its massing and use of the Italianate style was intentionally impressive (Fig 49), contrasting, in the words of Salt's biographer, Balgarnie, with the 'decided lack of architectural taste' of earlier manufactories.[19]

Salt constructed his new mill first, but an accompanying settlement was also envisaged, of necessity, as a philanthropic gesture following on from Salt's personal commitment, itself derived from his experience of working-class deprivation and alienation in industrial Bradford, and as a means of providing a well-disciplined environment and imposing an approved lifestyle. A report in 1852 noted that Saltaire, its name compounded from that of its builder and the adjacent River Aire, was to have 700 cottages and other dwellings, wide streets, spacious squares, gardens, ground for recreation, a large dining hall and kitchens, baths and wash houses, a covered market, schools and a church.[20] In 1854, Henry F Lockwood wrote of a plan which provided for a population of from 9,000 to 10,000, and also included sites for other buildings, namely a Mechanics' Institute, hotels, almshouses, an abattoir and a Music Room.[21] Some revisions were made to these schemes during the period of Saltaire's construction: more houses were built than envisaged, although they housed fewer people, but more or less all the public buildings were erected.

The plan of Saltaire and the design of its buildings were, like the mill, the responsibility of Lockwood and Mawson, and construction began immediately after the official opening of the mill on 20 September 1853, continuing until 1876. The village (Figs 299 and 300) was built on a grid-iron plan, its roads named after the queen, Victoria, and her consort, Albert, after the Salt family, including Titus and his wife, Caroline, their eleven children (excluding Titus junior) and a number of grandchildren, and the two architects, Lockwood and Mawson. Almost all the public and community buildings, the grandest buildings in Saltaire, were built on Victoria Road, the road which led to the mill and to the west of which most of the housing was erected. The houses, which were all built for rent, were intended for the various grades of the mill workforce, and although this was reflected in their style, size and situation, tenancies indicate that the division was not rigid and that separation by social distinction was less marked than might be supposed.[22]

The first phase of housing, completed in 1854, was bounded on the north and south by Albert Street and Caroline Street. A row of shops, with dwellings over, fronted Victoria Road (Fig 303e); William Henry Street (Fig 301a) and George Street had terraces of overlookers' houses with taller boarding-houses built at each end, as too did Amelia Street; and the four streets from Amelia Street to Herbert Street, including Edward Street (Fig 301b), all had identical terraces of workmen's houses. The overlookers' houses were the best appointed, having wider frontages than the workmen's

Fig 297 Carlile Institute, Meltham.

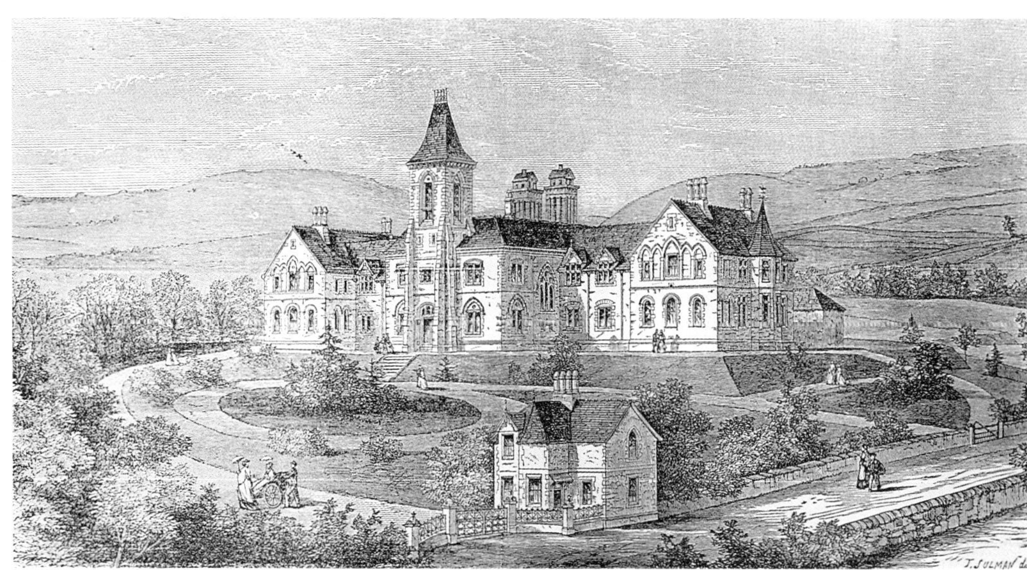

Fig 298 *Meltham Mills Convalescent Home, Meltham.*

houses, front gardens, and round-arched ground-floor openings with dressed stone heads. Internally they had a sitting room, kitchen, scullery, cellar and three bedrooms, the taller, middle houses having four to six bedrooms for larger families. The boarding-houses, rarely used as such and instead let out in multiple occupancy, have architectural detailing identical to that of the adjacent houses, as have the square pavilions on the ends of the terraces of workmen's houses which are themselves plain but for paired gutter brackets. These last houses, which open directly on to the street, had a living room, small kitchen, small cellar and two bedrooms. The second phase of housing, bounded on the north and south by Caroline Street and Titus Street, and running from Whitlam Street to George Street, was completed in 1857 as five streets of workmen's houses. The end houses were delineated as before, but those in between were entirely plain.

The first two phases of domestic building created blocks of terraced houses which ran up the slope, but subsequent developments of workmen's housing at Saltaire generally ran along the contours, and the individual houses were also larger and more generously detailed than before. Round-arched, Italianate-style openings were employed on the improved terraces in Constance Street (Fig 301c) and Shirley Street, which were completed in 1861. Terminated by gabled pavilions with triple, round-headed first-floor windows, these houses each had a living room, kitchen, half cellar and three bedrooms. Later terraces in Katherine Street, Jane Street and Dove Street, as well as Higher and Lower School Street, Lockwood Street and Mawson Street, all of them complete in 1868, were similar in style and had either two or three bedrooms. A further terrace of overlookers' houses was completed in 1868 in Albert Road, a street which, facing west across open countryside, was otherwise occupied by twenty-two large, well-appointed houses (Fig 302) whose tenants included senior executives of the firm. Smaller groups of houses for overlookers and minor executives were built along the Leeds-Bramley turnpike road, and along Gordon Terrace, the Bradford-Keighley turnpike road, where there were also more shops.

The growth in the size and population of Saltaire, with 163 houses and boarding-houses and about 1,000 people in 1854, 447 occupied houses and 2,510 people in 1861, and 824 houses and 4,300 people in 1871, was reflected in the gradual provision of public and community buildings. Initially some buildings served several purposes, particularly the Dining Room (Fig 303a), built in 1854 opposite the factory to provide cheap meals for workers travelling some distance, which was also used at first for religious services and as a schoolroom and public meeting hall. A Congregational Church (Fig 303b), one of the finest buildings in Saltaire, was built opposite the main entrance to the mill offices in 1856–9, and in 1866 Salt gave the Wesleyan Methodists the site for a new chapel, which was built largely by public subscription between Titus Street and the Bramley turnpike. A new school (Fig 303c), opened in 1868, provided elementary education for about 700 children, the boys' and girls' schoolrooms set in opposing wings with the infants in the centre. The Congregational Sunday School, now demolished but shown on Figs 299 and 300, was built in 1875–6 and had as its principal accommodation ten classrooms on two floors opening off a main assembly hall. Adult education in Saltaire was initially catered for by the Saltaire Literary Society and

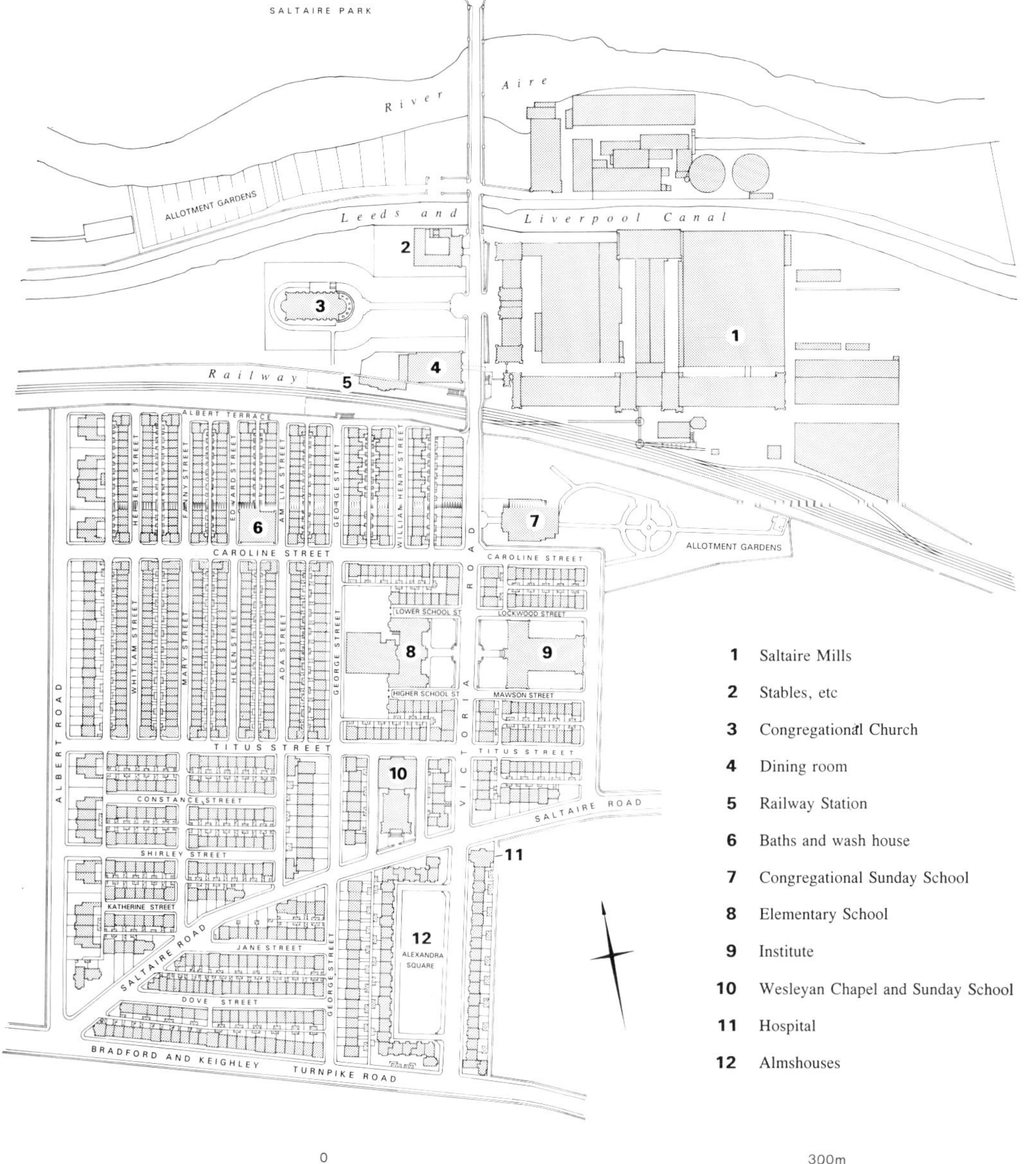

Fig 299 Plan of Saltaire and Saltaire Mills, Shipley (116) (redrawn from Plan showing the Town and Works of Saltaire, surveyed in 1881 by W and R Mawson; Bradford Libraries and Information Service, SAL 1881 MAW).

Institute, which was formed in 1855 and met for a time in one of the boarding-houses in Albert Terrace, where it housed its newspapers and library. In 1869, Titus Salt built an Institute (Fig 303d), multi-purpose in its functions, which included a reading room, library, games rooms, lecture halls for 800 and 200 people, a school of art, a drill-room, gymnasium and armoury.

Other more practical needs of daily life were supplied. Fourteen shops were ready for occupation in Victoria Road in 1854 (Fig 303e shows one block), and by 1871 the overall number in Saltaire had risen to forty. A baths and wash house was built in 1863 on Caroline Street: twenty-four baths were provided, twelve on either side of the building, for men and women respectively, and a Turkish bath in between. The wash house had six washing machines, wringing machines and a heated drying closet. Like the Dining Room, neither the baths nor the wash house was well patronised since the inhabitants preferred their own domestic arrangements. In 1868, forty-five almshouses for sixty pensioners were opened at the southern end of Victoria Road (Fig 303f). They were set around a square, and at the north-east corner was a small hospital and dispensary (Fig 303g) which grew out of the dispensary and casualty ward needed at the mill and was eventually enlarged to a three ward hospital.

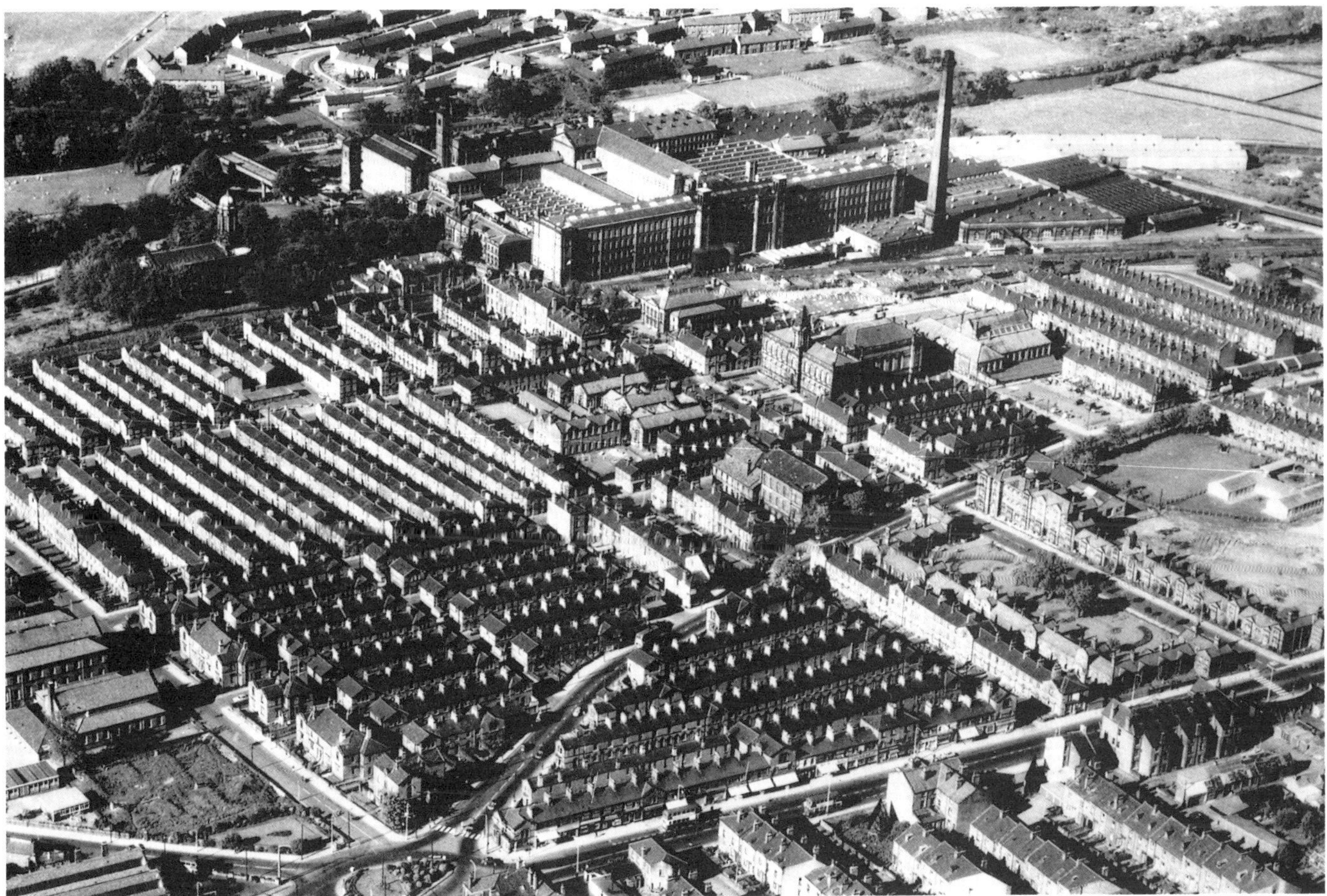

Fig 300 Aerial view of Saltaire and Saltaire Mills, Shipley (116), from the south west.

'Ground for recreation' was promised in 1852 (see note 20), and this was provided in 1870 with Salt's purchase of land north of the River Aire and the creation of Saltaire Park. The park was landscaped, provided with walks, and facilities were offered for organised cricket, tennis, bowls, rowing, fishing and archery.

Saltaire had a wide range of housing by the time of its completion, but none of it was home for members of the Salt family. In 1867 Titus Salt bought Crow Nest at Lightcliffe, a late 18th-century mansion[23] which he had leased from 1844 to 1858. Its distance from his mill at Saltaire was compensated for by the inclusion of a private suite of rooms within the office block there (Fig 100c). Salt's son, Titus, redressed the balance by building an extensive house, Milner Field, close to the mill in about 1873.[24]

Apprentice houses

Acquiring an adequate labour force, as well as housing it, was a problem faced by a number of textile mill-owners. The need for water power in early textile mills meant that many were built in remote and often poorly populated locations, but since most of these mills were also small in size, they were generally able to find sufficient adult and child labour within their neighbourhoods. The importance of children as a source of unskilled labour in early mills must not be ignored. Robert Heaton, who had built Ponden Mill in 1791–2, made an agreement in December 1792 with John Taylor of Stanbury, the nearest village to the mill, that Taylor's two children, Henry and Martha, should 'work in the Cotton Mill . . . Daily in any Place or work they are Sett to work at . . . .'[25] For some mills, however, particularly the larger rural mills, local supplies of labour were inadequate and parish apprentices had to be sought. Parish poorhouses were certainly keen to despatch inmates at this time: the churchwardens and overseers of Grantham in Lincolnshire advertised in 1804: 'To manufacturers. Several stout healthy boys and girls are ready to be put out as parish apprentices. For further particulars enquire . . . .'[26]

West House Mill, Fewston (40), a large flax-spinning

a

b

c

Fig 301 Housing at Saltaire: a) overlookers' houses and taller boarding-houses in William Henry Street; b, c) workers' houses in Edward Street and Constance Street.

mill in a remote position at the head of the Washburn valley, was one of the early Yorkshire mills which employed apprentices. Founded in 1797, and doubled in size within a few years (Figs 153, 272), its early 19th-century owners toured the workhouses and charitable institutions of London and other large towns for children to take as apprentices, and by 1816, when the firm went into bankruptcy, two apprentice houses, High Apprentice House and Low Apprentice House, had been built. Both buildings seem to have originated as cottages, unlike purpose-built apprentice houses with communal dormitories such as that built by Samuel Greg at Styal shortly before 1790.[27] High Apprentice House (Fig 304) originated as a stone-built three-storeyed terrace of three cottages which were probably built in or shortly after 1797 as part of the millowners' wider building programme to provide workers' housing. Their early conversion to an apprentice house is indicated by a one-bay, two-storeyed addition with undivided rooms on each floor which was reached only from within the building. The ground-floor room was evidently a communal kitchen and dining room, with a dormitory over. Low Apprentice House was smaller, originating as a two-room, two-storeyed, single-fronted cottage which was subsequently doubled in size. Insurance policies of 1816 relating to these two apprentice houses included household goods and wearing apparel, confirming that the employers not only housed and fed the children but also provided their basic clothing.

Accommodation for apprentices was sometimes provided on mill sites. No evidence has been uncovered in Yorkshire for the arrangement found in No. 4 Mill at New Lanark in Scotland, which was completed by 1793 and included dormitories which in 1796 accommodated 396 boys and girls in six sleeping apartments.[28] Greenholme Mills at Burley-in-Wharfedale, however, included a building near the mill which in 1797 was occupied 'as a House and Schoolroom with Chambers over as lodgings for the children employed in the Factory'.[29] The mill, a large cotton mill founded in 1792, was reported in 1833 to have once had several hundred apprentices from London. Members of the Poor Rate Board of Leeds, on a visit in 1805 to inspect the situation and management of the nine apprentices bound to the mill by their township, also met some children from London, and their report noted the existence of apartments, a dining room and kitchen at the mill, as well as favourably describing their food, clothing and other aspects of their life.[30]

The employment of pauper apprentices declined in the early decades of the 19th century. Fewer parish children became available, Factory Acts discouraged juvenile labour, and the increasing use of steam rather

Fig 302 Housing at Saltaire: senior executives' houses in Albert Road.

than water power enabled mills to be built 'in the midst of populous towns and instead of parish apprentices being sought after, the children of the surrounding poor were preferred'.[31] Certainly John Marshall and the Benyon brothers, who built Marshall's Mill (57) and Benyons' Mill (56) in Holbeck, on the edge of Leeds, and built apprentice houses at their Shrewsbury flax mills,[32] found it unnecessary to build any on the sites of their Yorkshire mills.

Workers' housing

Only a minority of millowners, whether in Yorkshire or elsewhere, ever provided housing for pauper apprentices, but more provided housing for whole families. Outside Yorkshire, a number of early industrialists created communities with a range of facilities (see p172), while others, among them the Strutts at Belper and Milford,[33] the Evans at Darley Abbey[34] and the Gregs at Lowerhouse,[35] at least initially restricted themselves to housing. Within Yorkshire, as the textile industry became a major employer of labour, so was additional housing increasingly built by speculators, by self-help and by other means.[36] Low Mill at Keighley (74), built in 1780, was the first cotton-spinning mill constructed in Yorkshire, and in 1783–4 the same firm of Claytons and Walshman built an almost identical mill, Langcliffe Mill at Langcliffe (81), immediately north of Settle. The contrast between the situations of the two mills, the first in a market town, the second in the countryside, albeit not far from the village of Langcliffe and market town of Settle, was sufficiently marked for it to be reflected in the problems of obtaining and housing the workforce required by Langcliffe Mill (81). In 1784 and 1785, immediately after the mill opened, workers had to be brought over from Keighley to undertake the sorting process of cotton picking, and some night spinning. The cotton pickers were children, and rather than build an apprentice house, Claytons and Walshman lodged them with families in the nearby village of Langcliffe,[37] as well as building workers' houses close to their mill. They advertised in 1787 that they were 'now erecting a number of convenient cottages at Langcliffe Place, which will be ready to enter at Monday next. Any people with large families that are desirous to have them employed, and can come well recommended, may be assured of meeting with every reasonable encouragement.'[38]

Remoteness, as well as the need to attract and retain a larger workforce than could otherwise be guaranteed, was the principal reason why, not just in the early stages of industrialisation but throughout the 19th and even into the early 20th centuries, millowners built workers' housing. The type and quantity of housing which was built varied with individual needs and circumstances, and the example of Langcliffe Mill (81), at which

a

c

b

d

e

Fig 303 Public buildings and amenities at Saltaire, all in Victoria Road: a) Dining Room; b) Congregational Church; c) Elementary School; d) the Institute; e) shops; f) almshouses; g) Sir Titus Salt's Hospital.

f

g

cottages were built close to the mill, was quite frequently followed. On a number of remote or isolated sites, the mill and its associated housing together created small settlements, albeit generally with few other facilities. High Mill (23) (Fig 41), a flax-spinning mill built in about 1804–5 a short distance from the village of Shaw Mills, Bishop Thornton, stimulated the construction of a variety of housing in its immediate vicinity (Fig 305). Among the earliest housing was a row of five, one-room deep, three-storeyed cottages built beside the mill, while shortly after 1850 a terrace of six, more spacious, two-room deep, two-storeyed cottages was built in front of it. At Armitage Bridge Mills, South Crosland (127) (Fig 165), an L-shaped range of cottages was built in the corner of the site in the early 19th century, and about a century later Thomas Ambler and Sons, who in 1912 built Ardsley Mills (35) on a site some distance from East Ardsley, constructed a number of terraces of workers' housing in its vicinity, including some in Common Lane (Fig 306). Company plans show that these were part of a more extensive scheme which was never completed.

Mills within or close to existing settlements frequently contributed to their growth as well as benefiting from their facilities. Merryweather and Whitaker, who in 1792 had built Greenholme Mills on the edge of Burley-in-Wharfedale, also owned a total of thirty-three cottages in 1796, and by 1848 this number had increased to sixty-eight, some of which, including Pleasant Row and New Road, were part of the enlarged village. The cottages in Prospect Street at Thornton (Fig 307) had a similar relationship with their locality: their occupants in 1841 and 1851 were mainly in the textile trade, and in 1851 they included two overseers and a watchman who probably worked in the nearby, newly opened, Prospect Mill, Thornton (136). The cottages pre-date the mill, although they were almost certainly built by its owner to house the worsted weavers to whom he had formerly put out yarn.

The various purpose-built industrial communities and model villages which the Yorkshire textile industry spawned varied considerably in size, but their workers' housing was generally of a higher standard than most contemporary housing, as well as being architecturally more distinctive. Back-to-back housing, subject to a national ban in 1909 but long before that also banned by some local by-laws, was rare in these communities. The earliest of Edward Akroyd's housing at Copley, of the late 1840s, comprised such houses, but his subsequent development of Akroydon, as well as the latest terraces at Copley, were all of houses with rear entrances. The successively better housing provided at Glasshouses has already been noted (p174), and it is further exemplified at Wilshaw where in the 1860s Joseph Hirst remodelled and extended the existing buildings at Lower Greave (Fig 308a) for his workforce, whereas at Upper Greave he demolished the farmhouses and cottages which he purchased in 1871 and in their place in 1873 built St Mary's Court (Fig 308b), a range of twelve houses around three sides of a courtyard closed by gardens and a space for hanging washing.[39]

The different standards of workers' housing frequently reflected the status of their occupants. Saltaire probably reveals this in its most complete form (see pp180–3), but it can also be observed elsewhere. Bent Ley Mill, Meltham (97), overlooks a range of houses (Fig 309) which originated as a row of three cottages against which a more imposing double-fronted house was added; they were once occupied by 'overlookers and some of the skilled workmen connected with the establishment'.[40] The quality and position of Brookroyd Terrace, a row of four double-fronted cottages built

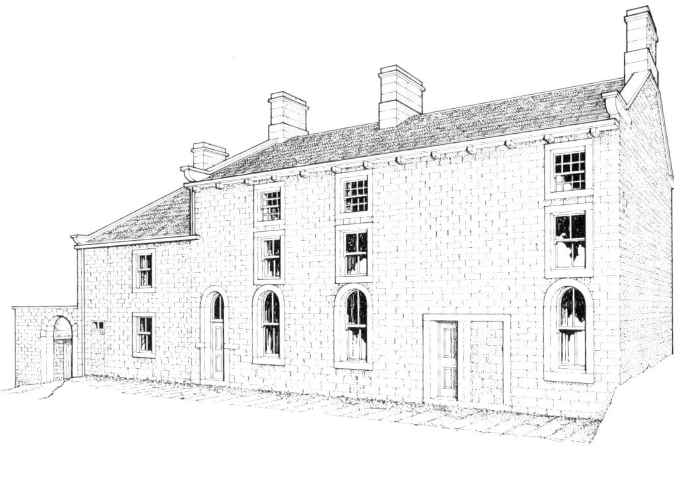

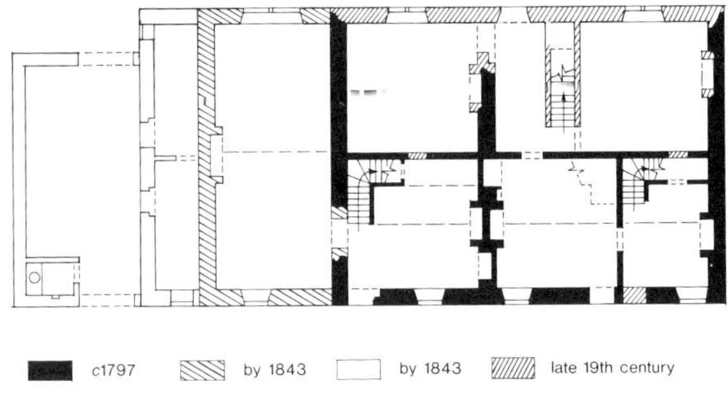

Fig 304 High Apprentice House, associated with West House Mill, Fewston (40).

Fig 305 The settlement around High Mill at Shaw Mills, Bishop Thornton (23), in Nidderdale.

*c*1860 on the edge of the curtilage of Brookroyd Mills, Stainland (130) (Fig 310), suggest that they too may have been occupied by overlookers at the mill. A number of better-quality houses in the industrial community of Glasshouses near Pateley Bridge were probably for overlookers (see p174), and Fir Grove (Fig 287) was built specifically for the mill manager.

Manufacturers' houses

The style and comfort of the few houses built for important members of a mill's workforce were as nothing compared with the houses which some mill-owners built for themselves. Over 2,000 textile mills were built in Yorkshire between 1770 and 1930, and although only a minority operated on a scale which produced profits large enough to finance the purchase of estates and the acquisition, extension or construction of great houses, a significant number generated a large enough living to enable the first or a later generation of owners to build houses of architectural distinction. The reasons for building were varied, but for many it was a statement of the social position which they felt they had attained, which was reflected in their local benefactions and interests, and which for some was ultimately confirmed by grants of baronetcies and peerages.

The style and scale of manufacturers' houses varied with time and the wealth of individual manufacturers. A few early entrepreneurs had sufficient capital to invest both in mills and in their own houses. In 1784 the Clayton family of Low Mill, Keighley (74), and of Langcliffe Mill, Langcliffe (81), built Langcliffe Place, a three-storeyed, five-bay house with classical detailing adjacent to the latter mill.[41] They were not alone in

Fig 306 Housing in Common Lane, built by Thomas Ambler and Sons of Ardsley Mills, East Ardsley (35).

Fig 307 Prospect Street, formerly Nicholas Street, adjacent to Prospect Mill, Thornton (136).

Fig 309 Housing on Huddersfield Road, Meltham Mills, next to Bent Ley Mill, Meltham (97).

building a house close to their mill. One of the original partners in West House Mill, Fewston (40), for example, built a modest house, enlarged by subsequent owners, in this position (Fig 272), and the fine house next to Barkerend Mills in Bradford (26), evidently built by the mill's founder, James Garnett, is one of many other examples (Fig 140). The relationship was slightly less close at Ebor Mill, Haworth (50), for both the original and later millowners' houses. Ebor House (Fig 311a) was built on a site overlooking the mill by Hiram Craven, who had established it in about 1819. The house is modest in scale and design, and it became the residence of Edwin Merrall, one of the partners of Merrall Brothers who took over the mill in about 1850. The Merralls were an established textile manufacturing family who already owned several other mills, including the nearby Lees Mill, Bingley (22), when they acquired Ebor Mill (50). The firm, which also acquired and developed Lowertown Shed and Mill, Haworth (52), became one of the largest worsted-spinning and manufacturing companies in Yorkshire, and with their wealth, built imposing houses in the vicinity of Ebor Mill (50) and Lees Mill (22). George Merrall built Law House, and Edwin Merrall's mansion, Longlands (Fig 311b), was built in an Elizabethan style in the early 1880s not much further from Ebor Mill (50) than was Ebor House.

a

b

Fig 308 Housing at Wilshaw: a) Lower Greave; b) St Mary's Court.

The Murgatroyds of Oats Royd Mills, Midgley (101), had even deeper roots in the textile industry than the Merralls, having been involved in domestic textile production since at least the 17th century. The family had built Oats Royd, a large house in the local vernacular style, in 1645, and John Murgatroyd, who founded Oats Royd Mills (101) on adjoining land in 1847, bought the house in 1846 and rapidly updated it by adding a front range, one room deep, with an Italianate façade (Fig 312a). In 1877 Murgatroyd's son, another John, rebuilt Broadfold as a substantial, Italianate-style mansion on a site some distance from the mill (Fig 312b).

The distancing of owners from their mills was a frequent consequence of business success. Benjamin Gott, who had established Bean Ing Mills, Leeds (85), in

Fig 310 Brookroyd Terrace, Brookroyd Mills, Stainland (130).

1792 and subsequently acquired other mills, bought Armley House and its estate in 1803. His mansion overlooked the Aire valley, the site of his mills, and he employed Robert Smirke to remodel the house and Humphry Repton to landscape the grounds. Inside, where Gott entertained important visitors to his mills, the house was enhanced by neo-classical sculptures and his collection of paintings.[42] John Marshall, the founder of Marshall's Mill, Holbeck (57), a near neighbour of Gott's Bean Ing Mills (85), initially lived in Meadow Lane, in a sparsely built suburb close to his mill. By 1805, with personal wealth of over £70,000, and now also with a family of six children, he moved to a more becoming residence, New Grange at Headingley, a large house where he employed more than a dozen servants. Within a few years he had bought a summer residence, Hallsteads, beside Ullswater in the Lake District, and in 1832 he purchased a London town house.[43] Marshall indulged his sons, in 1824 giving Patterdale Hall near Ullswater to his eldest son, William, and in 1829 building Headingley Lodge, Leeds, for another son, John, who bought an estate next to Derwentwater in 1832. Despite all his expenditure, John Marshall nevertheless retained an interest in his flax mill, as to differing extents did successive generations, although each one was successively more remote, lacking the founder's ingenuity, and frequently having a greater interest in country or public life than in business.[44]

The Fielden family of Todmorden, founders of what became the largest cotton-spinning and weaving business in Yorkshire, with its base at Waterside Mill, Langfield (82), were the builders of a series of fine

a

b

Fig 311 Manufacturers' houses associated with Ebor Mill, Haworth (50): a) Ebor House, built overlooking Ebor Mill, itself established about 1819; b) Longlands, whose staircase window is dated 1884.

a

b

Fig 312 Manufacturers' houses associated with Oats Royd Mills, Midgley (101): a) Oats Royd House, a house of 1645 with a mid 19th-century extension; b) Broadfold, built in 1877.

houses,[45] the most notable of which was Dobroyd Castle, built for John Fielden to designs by John Gibson in 1866–9. In contrast to Stansfield Hall and Centre Vale, houses which John Gibson extended and rebuilt for John Fielden's brothers Joshua and Samuel in 1862 and 1871, Dobroyd Castle was built on an exposed site with a castellated silhouette appropriate to its situation (Fig 313). The house, constructed with the most expensive materials and incorporating the latest technology, has an impressive central hall and staircase with carved details of the highest quality (Fig 314).

The scale on which manufacturers such as Gott, the Marshalls and the Fieldens could buy and build was equalled by others, among them the Akroyds and Samuel Cunliffe Lister, later Lord Masham, but it did not obscure the fact that most of the houses financed by textiles were more modest in size. North Dean House, Ebor House and Ashfield House (Figs 107, 311a, 315), and some of the large detached and semi-detached villas built for the growing middle class in the suburbs of Leeds, Bradford, Huddersfield and other towns,[46] were numerically more typical and contributed elegant and stylistically varied buildings to the county.

Public and community buildings

Housing was the millowners' commonest contribution to the built environment, but a range of public and community buildings, including some for educational, religious and welfare purposes, was also built. The most comprehensive series of buildings was found in some of the industrial communities and model villages which

Fig 313 Dobroyd Castle, built in 1866–9 for John Fielden of Waterside Mill, Langfield (82).

Fig 314 Entrance hall at Dobroyd Castle.

were erected in the course of the 19th century, but a number of philanthropic millowners also funded individual buildings close to their mills.

Buildings for education

Until the passing of W E Forster's Elementary Education Act in 1870, which enabled School Boards to be established throughout the country to supervise the provision of primary education for all children, education was almost entirely the responsibility of religious bodies and a variety of private benefactors.[47] A number of millowners in Yorkshire involved themselves with the provision of education, although their levels of commitment varied. John Marshall, the builder of Marshall's Mill, Holbeck (57), was long connected with a range of educational ventures in Leeds,[48] including the founding of a Lancasterian School, a Mechanics' Institute, and a Literary and Philosophical Society. He also subscribed to the Leeds Library, helped re-establish the *Leeds Mercury*, and in 1826 proposed the establishment of a university in the town. On a more local level, in 1822 Marshall persuaded the owners of other firms around Water Lane to join him in managing and paying for a school in Holbeck. The school ran at a loss, but although Marshall's associates soon withdrew, he continued his involvement. Attendance was erratic, a few children attending on a Saturday, more after work every Monday, but nearly 2,000 children, a high proportion of those employed, had attended before 1832 when Marshall built an Infants' School. This school, a two-storeyed, five-bay brick building (Fig 316), stood isolated to the south of the mills when first built, but it was later engulfed by Temple Mill. In 1842, Marshall built a Junior School in Sweet Street West and within the mill he established a mill library and reading rooms.

Marshall's example in providing education was followed by other Leeds flax spinners, among them the builders of Benyons' Mill, Holbeck (56), Bank Mills, Leeds (84), and Hunslet Mills, Hunslet (67). Elsewhere, Greenholme Mills at Burley-in-Wharfedale included a building which in 1797 was 'occupied as a House and Schoolroom with Chambers over as lodgings for the children employed in the Factory',[49] the Fieldens provided a factory school at Waterside Mill, Langfield (82), and at Glasshouses Mill, High and Low Bishopside (55), a combined warehouse and office built in 1844 also included a schoolroom, which was superseded when a school was built nearby in 1859–60 (Fig 289).

The schools which millowners erected were generally architecturally distinguished, usually Gothic in style, and they acted as visible signs of their philanthropy. Such was the case with the schools built by the Brooks at Meltham Mills (Fig 296), as well as at Centre Vale School, Todmorden (Fig 317), which was rebuilt *c*1871 by Samuel Fielden whose wife devoted many years to

Fig 315 Ashfield House, built c1860 for Joshua Craven of Prospect Mill, Thornton (136).

Fig 316 Infants' School, Marshall's Mill, Holbeck (57).

Fig 317 Centre Vale School, Todmorden.

the study of educational methods for younger children and engaged in educational work there.[50] Less extensive, but no less impressive, school buildings were erected at Glasshouses (Fig 289) and Wilshaw (Fig 318), both including schoolrooms as well as a schoolhouse.

The extent of John Marshall's interest in education was matched by a number of other millowners. Aspects of the Fieldens' involvement have already been noted, but Mrs Samuel Fielden was also a member of the first School Board for Todmorden, which was elected in 1874, as well as a benefactor to the University of Manchester, where she founded the Fielden Chair of Education.[51] Sir Titus Salt built a school and Institute at Saltaire (see pp181–2 and Fig 303c, d), whilst at Copley and Akroydon, Akroyd built schools, established a Lending Library, set up a Working Men's College, and was instrumental in founding a Literary and Scientific Society and a Working Men's Club.[52] Sir Henry Ripley had similarly wide interests, building a large and handsome school at Ripleyville, as well as being a founder of the Borough West School and member of the first School Board for Bradford. He supported the Bradford Church Institute, and the Philosophical Society, and headed the list of subscriptions to the building fund of the new Mechanics' Institute, which opened in 1871.[53]

In the wider community, Mechanics' Institutes, which by 1825 existed in the major towns of West Yorkshire, fulfilled some of the educative roles which Salt and Akroyd sought to foster in their Institutes and societies. Ripley's support for Bradford's Mechanics' Institute has been noted, and in other towns financial support also came from local industrialists. In Keighley, the first Mechanics' Institute had been established in 1825 by four members of the working class, although it prospered only with support and gifts from the town's wealthier employers. These industrialists also paid for the new and larger Mechanics' Institute which was built in 1868–70.[54] In smaller communities, individual millowners frequently played an important role. The Metcalfes and the Brooks each supported local Mechanics' Institutes (pp175, 179), and while the Metcalfes had plans for a Lecture Hall in Glasshouses prepared (Fig 319), but never carried out, the Brooks built the Carlile Institute in Meltham (Fig 297).

Churches and chapels

Anglican and nonconformist, but rarely Roman Catholic, millowners contributed to the construction, rebuilding, extension and repair of many local places of worship as the expanding suburbs of the towns, the growing villages and the new settlements created around textile mills between them stimulated a major wave of church and chapel construction. The financial commitment of some millowners was quite large. James Ickringill, whose mills were in Keighley, not only gave £1,400 to build Oakworth Road Mission Hall close to his

Fig 318 St Mary's School, Wilshaw.

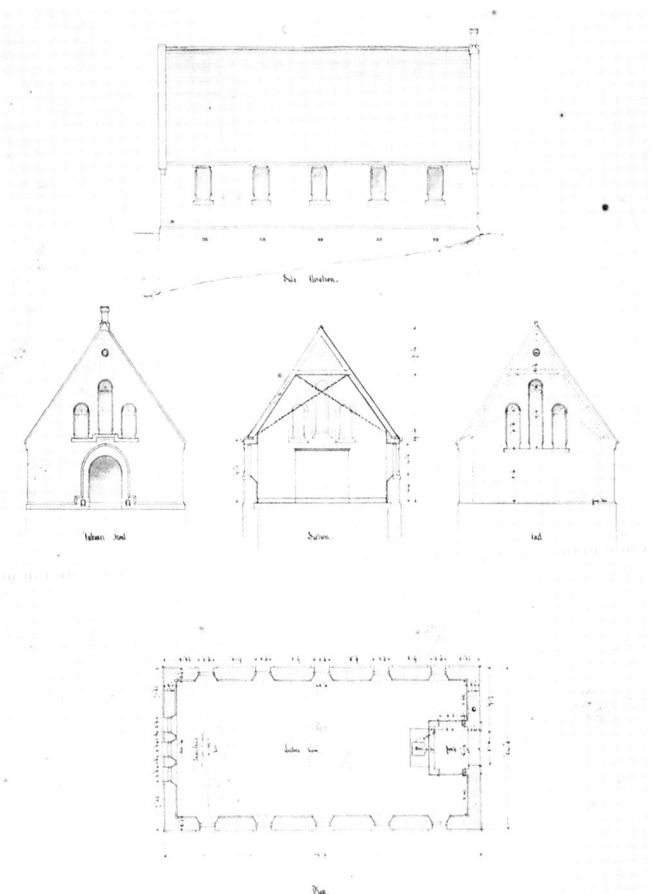

Fig 319 Design by W R Corson, dated 17 April 1863, for a Lecture Hall at Glasshouses.

Fig 320 St Mary's Church, Wilshaw.

home, and defrayed all its expenses for sixteen years, but every week received requests from all parts of the Primitive Methodist Connexion for financial aid in the erection of chapels, or the removing of debts, to most of which he gladly responded.[55] Sir Titus Salt was similarly generous (p181), and Sir Henry Ripley gave substantially to Horton Lane Chapel when he was a member of the Congregationalist body, and then to the Anglican Church after his conversion.[56]

Anglican churches built by millowners included St Paul's Church at Armitage Bridge, built in 1846–7 to the design of R D Chantrell, together with its parsonage house, 'a handsome Elizabethan mansion',[57] both paid for by the Brookes of nearby Armitage Bridge Mills, South Crosland (127). In Holbeck, James and Henry Marshall of Marshall's Mill, Holbeck (57), commissioned Gilbert Scott to design St John the Evangelist, built between 1847 and 1850; Scott later designed All Souls at Haley Hill, Halifax, for Edward Akroyd.[58] The Brooks of Meltham Mills, Meltham (98), also made notable contributions (see pp178–9 and Fig 295), as did Joseph Hirst of Wilshaw Mill, Meltham, who built St Mary's Church, Wilshaw, in 1863. This church (Fig 320), designed in a Romanesque style by John Kirk and Sons, was unusual in that its central porch and bell tower divided the church to its east from the Sunday School and vicar's house to the west.

Chapel building sometimes matched the scale and grandeur of the Anglican churches. Salt's Congregational Church at Saltaire, designed by Lockwood and Mawson and built in 1858–9 (Fig 303b), together with the Unitarian Church at Todmorden, designed by John Gibson and built in 1865–9 as a monument to John Fielden by his sons (Fig 321), are among the most notable buildings of their type. The simpler Methodist Chapel in Glasshouses (Fig 290), together with others in settlements such as New York which grew up around another Nidderdale flax mill,[59] balance the exuberance, and indeed extravagance, of the other buildings.

Some millowners also left other architectural legacies. Undercliffe Cemetery in Bradford, which was opened in 1854, includes some impressive sepulchral monuments to the men and families who contributed to the town's prosperity. Among the memorials are a number to members of the Illingworth and Holden families (Fig 322). The Illingworths had a long ancestry in the textile industry, and one of the tombs bears the names of Daniel Illingworth, builder of Providence Mills, Bradford, and of his son, Henry, who in partnership with his brother, Alfred, founded Whetley Mills in Manningham (95). Henry's marriage to Mary, daughter of Isaac Holden, baronet, created a link between two of Bradford's leading families of industrialists which the group of tombs in the cemetery confirms.

Hospitals and almshouses

The reliance on private benefaction for education before the late 19th century was also typical of the provision of care needed in sickness and old age. Although many millowners are likely to have subscribed to the construction and endowment of new hospitals, as did many of Keighley's millowners for the Cottage Hospital built in 1876,[60] few actually went as far as building them. Sir Titus Salt was, however, one who did both, building a hospital in Saltaire in 1868 (see p182 and Fig 303g), and subscribing to the Fever Hospital in Bradford which was opened in 1872.[61] Several millowners built convalescent homes. One of the last gifts of Charles Brook junior of Meltham Mills was of a Convalescent Home, built in 1868–71 to the south of the main textile mill (Fig 298). Woodlands Convalescent Home at Rawdon, opened in 1877 and intended for 120 inmates, was paid for solely by Sir Henry Ripley,[62] and James Ickringill, in a further philanthropic gesture, opened up his Morecambe home as a Convalescent Home for sick ministers.[63]

Fig 321 Unitarian Church, Todmorden.

Almshouses were often a better proposition for millowners, since like workers' housing they could, if required, provide a return on investment in the form of rents. They were most commonly built as part of model communities, as at Saltaire, Ripleyville and Wilshaw. The Saltaire almshouses, set around a square, were the most elaborate and the largest (see p182 and Fig 303f), while those in Ripleyville, originally built in 1857 but rebuilt and enlarged on a new site in 1881, were in a terrace and were Gothic in style.[64] The almshouses at Wilshaw, built by Joseph and Eleanor Hirst in 1870–1, took the form of three small Italianate villas set below the mill and overlooking St Mary's Church, each a semi-detached building containing two residences (Fig 323). They provided houses for between twelve and eighteen people, who were chiefly either retired Hirst employees or their widows, or were people from the immediate neighbourhood. The almshouses were let at Eleanor Hirst's discretion, and she required that the almspeople 'be persons of good moral character, professing religious principle' who should attend church or chapel on a Sunday.[65]

Fig 322 Memorials to the Illingworth and Holden families in Undercliffe Cemetery, Bradford.

Fig 323 St Mary's Almshouses, Wilshaw.

As with hospitals, chapels and other public buildings, some almshouses were built by combined voluntary effort. Among these were the Bradford Tradesmen's Homes, close to Manningham Mills, Manningham (93), which were built to designs by Milnes and France in 1867 and 1878, and were subscribed to by Sir Titus Salt, Samuel Cunliffe Lister and Sir Isaac Holden, three of Bradford's principal millowners and industrialists.

Civic buildings and amenities

Business success enabled millowners to express their wealth with philanthropic gestures, but some also obtained greater recognition from involvement in public life. John Marshall, the founder of Marshall's Mill in Holbeck (57), finding it difficult to enter the society of Leeds and Yorkshire in the early 19th century because of his family's background as drapers and his own beliefs as a dissenter and Whig, instead gave his attention to Cumberland, a county almost bereft of old and powerful landed families. He purchased estates in Cumberland, built Hallsteads on the edge of Ullswater, became Deputy Lieutenant and then, in 1821, High Sheriff. He eventually retired to Hallsteads, but for a few more years maintained his interests in Yorkshire, in 1826 being elected to Parliament as a member for the county, thereby becoming the first millowner to represent the commercial interests of the West Riding there.[66] John Fielden, W E Forster, Henry Ripley, Edward Akroyd and Titus Salt were among other millowners elected to Parliament. Some also became involved with local government in an elected capacity: Henry Ripley was a member of Bradford Council and an alderman, Titus Salt became Lord Mayor of Bradford, and Richard Edmondson, founder of Knowle Mill in Keighley (73), was a councillor, mayor and then alderman of the town. A few millowners also paid for public buildings. The Town Hall at Todmorden (Fig 324), built in 1870–5, was another of the buildings contributed to the town by the Fielden family and designed by John Gibson. Like the nearby Unitarian Church (Fig 321), it represented patronage on a grand scale. It was oversize for the town, but it well reflected the status of the Fieldens, and it housed the borough offices, magistrates' court and a public hall.[67] The Town

Fig 324 Town Hall, Todmorden.

Fig 325 Town Hall, Meltham.

Hall at Meltham (Fig 325) was not built on the scale, still less in the style, of that at Todmorden, but it was an equivalent gesture since it was built at the expense of Edward Brook of Meltham Mills in 1898, the year in which Meltham acquired its own Urban District Council.

Public parks were one of the amenities provided in towns during the 19th century. Titus Salt established one in 1870–1 across the river from his mill and model village at Saltaire, while at Akroydon, Edward Akroyd was instrumental in providing the nearby Shroggs Park, persuading the Savile Estate to lease the land to Halifax Corporation, landscaping it and then donating it to them.[68] In Keighley, textile manufacturers and other industrialists all gave generously to the purchase of Eastwood House and part of its grounds by the Corporation in 1891, prior to its opening as Victoria Park in 1892.[69] Ironically the house had been built in 1819 by William Sugden, one of Keighley's most successful worsted manufacturers,[70] while in nearby Steeton the Cloughs of Woodlands Mill, Steeton with Eastburn (135), provided the village with a Memorial Park, a children's playground and a public bowling green among other provisions.[71] A notable initiative on a smaller scale was undertaken at Meltham Mills, where 'The People's Pleasure Grounds' were created in the valley bottom south of the mills when Bank Buildings was constructed (see p177).

Fig 326 Cartwright Hall, Lister Park, Bradford.

Fig 327 Corner shops on Union Road, Vine Street and other streets built by the Tetleys of Cannon Mills, Horton (58).

Bradford provides a final example of combined public and private money. Samuel Cunliffe Lister of Manningham Mills, Manningham (93), sold his residence, Manningham Hall, and its estate, to Bradford Corporation in 1870 at a price well below market value. Renamed Lister Park as a token of gratitude, a statue of Lister, paid for by public subscription, was unveiled there in 1875. In 1898 Lister, by then Lord Masham, offered the Corporation £40,000 to replace his old family home with a new building which also commemorated Edmund Cartwright, who devised a woolcombing machine and a powerloom. Cartwright Hall (Fig 326), intended as an art gallery and museum, and combined with a suite of official entertaining rooms, was designed by Simpson and Allen of London and built in 1900–4.[72]

Shops

Schools, churches and chapels were among the most distinctive public buildings, but shops were just as vital, if not usually so dramatic architecturally. In most towns and villages, little incentive was required to build these, but they formed part of some mill developments, especially in model villages such as Copley, Akroydon and Saltaire. Copley and Akroydon each had Co-operative shops, that at Akroydon, built in 1861, being a substantial building in the Gothic style typical of the village.[73] The shops in Saltaire, on Victoria Road (see p182), were less ostentatious in appearance (Fig 303e), although they were grander than the corner shops set at the upper ends of the rows of workers' housing built by G G Tetley beside Cannon Mills, Horton (58), in the 1860s (Fig 327).

Postscript

The heyday of the Yorkshire textile industry was during the 19th century when it was both a major employer of labour and a force which influenced the form and appearance of the county's towns and countryside. Although decline set in, in some branches, in the 19th century, it was mainly during the 20th century that the industry shrank to a smaller, though not insignificant, size. Many of its buildings consequently changed use or ownership, while others were demolished. Lower Providence Mill, Keighley (75) (Fig 328), reduced from a cluster of buildings to an isolated chimney, reflects the fate of so many mills for which no alternative use was found. This mill was in many ways typical in its combination of different building types, its essentially utilitarian appearance, and its contribution to the appearance of its locality. Its loss reduced both the local and wider landscape, removing from it evidence of the industry which contributed so much to its economy. Sufficient buildings remain for it still to be possible to appreciate the architectural contribution which the textile industry made to Yorkshire, but each demolition reduces the impact and dominance which that industry once had.

Fig 328 Lower Providence Mill, Keighley (75), demolished but for its chimney in 1984, symbolises the impact which textile mills made on the landscape, and the gap which their demolition can leave.

Selective inventory

This selective inventory gives brief summaries of the buildings which were recorded in detail during the Royal Commission's survey of Yorkshire textile mills. It is arranged alphabetically by township, the name of the civil parish or parishes being given in brackets after the township where the two differ. Each entry is prefaced by the following information: a number which is also used in the main text to assist cross-referencing to the inventory; mill name(s); national grid reference; and the National Monuments Record file number. The historical and architectural evidence for the summary statements made are contained in the reports compiled for each site, which may be consulted at the places noted in the introduction to the Gazetteer.

ADDINGHAM, West Yorkshire

(1) *High Mill* (SE 0821 5021) (62271).
Water-powered cotton-spinning mill built in late 1780s, converted to worsted spinning before 1822 and to silk spinning in 1869 (Fig 215). Original three-storeyed six-bay mill incorporated wheelhouse of earlier corn mill. Warehouse remodelled and mill extended by four bays in early to mid 19th century. Partly demolished.

(2) *Loomshops, The Rookery* (SE 0785 4984) (34366).
Pair of small first-floor loomshops (one now demolished) set across ends of two terraces of cottages (Fig 29), all built by John Cockshott in or shortly after 1805. Cockshott, a local grocer and cotton manufacturer, had previously put out yarn to domestic weavers, and the loomshop represents a stage in controlling production which culminated in construction of Chapel Street loomshop (3).

(3) *Loomshop, Chapel Street, Addingham* (SE 0756 4986) (62331).
Three-storeyed twelve-bay loomshop built shortly before 1817 by John Cockshott (Fig 144). Represents culmination of Cockshott's textile business as cotton manufacturer (see 2) in era before cotton weaving joined spinning as a powered and factory-based enterprise.

ALVERTHORPE WITH THORNES (Wakefield), West Yorkshire

(4) *Alverthorpe Mills* (SE 3090 2140) (63624).
Built in 1870–2 as an integrated woollen mill. Rare example of single-storeyed layout with sequence of processes arranged logically within a main shed around central power source (Fig 177). Detached sheds provided boiler house, dyehouse and some finishing rooms. Offices on main road frontage (Fig 99). Engine house designed for horizontal engine, but original replaced in 1912, possibly occasioned by expansion of sheds. Rope drive from engine to pulley wheels on central spine wall.

(5) *Flanshaw Mill* (SE 3080 2095) (63625).
Established in early 19th century as steam-powered scribbling and fulling mill. Fragments of first mill survive. Main buildings on site are later warehouses and sheds. Associated buildings: workers' housing, chapel, manufacturer's house.

(6) *Thornes Mill* (SE 327 190) (63766).
Steam-powered worsted mill, probably established in 1837–8. First buildings were shed with corner engine house, with later addition of warehouses, second shed and other buildings. Apparently used mainly for yarn spinning despite adoption of single-storeyed layout normally associated with weaving. Part demolished.

ARMLEY (Leeds), West Yorkshire

(7) *Armley Mills* (SE 2758 3417) (63320).
Established in 16th century as water-powered fulling mill, later working as both fulling and corn mill. Rebuilt 1788 reputedly as the largest fulling mill in the world but only about 44 metres long and of three storeys.

Operated as public scribbling, carding and fulling mill before destruction by fire in 1805. Rebuilt 1805–7 on much larger scale (four storeys, twenty-three bays) by Benjamin Gott as fireproof mill (Fig 36), the earliest known such structure in the woollen branch and the oldest surviving Yorkshire example of the type in all branches; the mill has inverted T-section cast-iron beams, cylindrical cast-iron columns and brick arches (Figs 114, 119d). Other buildings include early 19th-century heated cloth dryhouse of two storeys roofed with elaborate cast-iron trusses (Figs 80, 83), remains of a gas-making plant, and housing for the mill tenant. Steam power added *c*1860.

(8) *Winker Green Mill* (SE 2700 3369) (63324).
Established in early 19th century as woollen scribbling and dyeware mill, later a scribbling and fulling mill. Bought in 1824 by Eyres family, woollen merchants, and rebuilt as large-scale integrated private mill. Earliest surviving building, probably *c*1825–30, is four-storeyed workshop for hand spinning and handloom weaving (Fig 25). Large steam-powered brick mill (four-storeyed, twenty-five bays) of 1833 and 1836 (Fig 45), replacing earlier mill destroyed by fire, has timber internal construction but fireproof willey house on ground floor. One internal engine house, one attached engine house, internal boiler house. Long warehouse range (now curtailed) on street frontage. Workers' housing built nearby.

AUSTONLEY (Holmfirth), West Yorkshire

(9) *Holmbridge Mill, Holmbridge* (SE 120 066) (63194).
Established in mid 1790s as water-powered scribbling and fulling mill. Near-contemporary plan (Fig 38) shows first mill as small three-storeyed building: ground floor had pair of waterwheels and fulling stocks, first floor had scribbling engines and a slubbing billy, together with a single-room dwelling; attic used for wool storage. Later rebuilding on a larger scale, in 1823 and in *c*1840, involved demolition of original mill and addition of steam power. Resulting mill of four storeys and twelve bays with collar-truss roof (Fig 127). Fully integrated working achieved with addition of powerloom weaving shed in late 1850s. Site grew in 20th century with addition of sheds and other buildings.

BAINBRIDGE, North Yorkshire

(10) *Silk Mill, Countersett* (SD 9125 8710) (63823).
Small two-storeyed three-bay building built *c*1800 for waste-silk spinning, combining ground-floor living accommodation and adjacent wheelhouse with chamber over for textile working.

BARKISLAND (Ripponden), West Yorkshire

(11) *Bowers Mills* (SE 0695 2015) (62742).
Water-powered fulling mill, established before the mid 18th century. Site used at different times as corn mill and worsted mill, but principal use was in woollen branch. Development from early small mill was slow: steam-powered timber-floored spinning mill of five storeys and eleven bays built *c*1864 and weaving shed *c*1882 (Fig 69), a surprisingly late date for the achievement of integrated working. Offices, warehouses, finishing buildings and modern manufacturing buildings complete the complex. No substantial remains of the early mill survive. Associated buildings: workers' cottages.

BARNSLEY, South Yorkshire

(12) *Hope Mill, later Hope Works* (SE 3410 0645) (63790).
Built before 1822 as a calender mill for finishing linen cloth but by 1878 also used for cotton spinning and weaving, and printing union cloths. Earliest building a steam-powered three-storeyed mill, partly rebuilt; later, post-1850 buildings include single-storeyed shed, probably of late 1850s, and warehouse. In late 19th century associated with Rob Royd Bleachworks (63803).

(13) *Taylor's Mill, also Peel Street Mill* (SE 3424 0633) (63791).
Steam-powered linen-weaving mill opened in 1845 by Thomas Taylor, fourth generation of a family of Barnsley linen manufacturers. Mill, much enlarged in second half of 19th century, included extensive single-storeyed sheds and warehouses, and incorporated earlier loomshop. Largely demolished.

(14) *Warehouse, St Mary's Place* (SE 343 065) (63808).
Warehouse, stable and coach house (Fig 88) built shortly before 1821 by Samuel Cooper, a Barnsley linen manufacturer, as base for putting-out yarn to domestic weavers. Warehouse, of three storeys and basement, and six bays long, has ground-floor offices; detached pedimented stable and coach house.

BATLEY, West Yorkshire

(15) *Albion Mill* (SE 2449 2277) (63535).
Built in 1831 as steam-powered scribbling, carding and fulling mill by group of eighteen local clothiers. Original complex included a two-storeyed ten-bay mill (Figs 44, 119g) incorporating an internal end engine house, attached boiler house with drying floors over the boilers, chimney, single-storeyed cloth dryhouse and a dyehouse. Rag-grinding shed added before 1850, when mill was fully integrated with both spinning and weaving conducted on site. The complex is typical of the Heavy Woollen area in its inclusion of rag-grinding sheds and is an interesting example of a company mill.

(16) *Blakeridge Mills* (SE 2389 2440) (63485).
Main mill of J, T and J Taylor, the largest woollen manufacturers in Batley (see also Cheapside Mills, Batley (18)). In 1820 site comprised only a house and workshops, but loomshops and press shop soon added, with spinning and fulling undertaken at nearby company mill. After 1845 production concentrated at Blakeridge with enlargement of existing buildings and construction of new steam-powered mills in 1863 (four storeys, fifteen bays), 1870 (four storeys, eight bays), and 1904 (four storeys, four bays). Powerloom weaving located partly in multi-storeyed building and probably partly in sheds. Early 20th-century prosperity evident in construction of very large mill (five storeys, twenty-five bays) in 1912–13 (Figs 59, 118e), probably electrically powered, of large wool warehouse in 1914 (Fig 95), and offices in 1923 (Fig 100g).

(17) *Carlinghow Mills* (SE 238 247) (63484).
Established in 1826 as a private woollen mill by John Nussey, one of a family of prominent manufacturers. In 1834 mill used for scribbling, carding, spinning and fulling; weaving was not undertaken on site, indicating employment of domestic labour. Earliest surviving building, the main mill of 1831 (four and a half storeys, seventeen bays), was steam-powered from a central engine house and was of fireproof construction with cast-iron columns, beams and joists, stone-flagged floors and roof with arched cast-iron trusses (Fig 121a). Further multi-storeyed mills built *c*1860 and *c*1875; time office and cottage built at entrance in 1877 (Fig 105); site developed into a fully integrated woollen mill with addition of weaving sheds *c*1875; further mill built in 1919 (see Fig 118d). In 20th century site used for rag sorting and storage by the firm of J R Burrows, one of largest firms engaged in supplying the local shoddy and mungo industry.

(18) *Cheapside Mills* (SE 2485 2410) (63513).
Established in 1840s as steam-powered fulling, scribbling and spinning mill, but rapidly becoming an integrated woollen mill with construction of powerloom-weaving sheds, finishing and dyeing departments, warehouse and, typical of the Heavy Woollen area, rag-grinding sheds. From 1872 it formed part of the business of J, T and J Taylor, the largest concern in Batley, based at Blakeridge Mills (16). Surviving buildings at time of record included main mill (four storeys, seventeen bays), rebuilt in 1895 after an earlier fire; weaving sheds (one on three levels), rag-grinding sheds (Fig 191), an elaborate warehouse and office building of *c*1865 (Fig 94), and a combined mill and warehouse of *c*1922, the last with a steel frame and concrete floors. A turbine house was built in 1934–5.

(19) *New Ing Mills* (SE 2441 2390) (63516).
Established in 1839 as a woollen-finishing mill by a partnership of local clothiers. By 1859 two partners, Joseph Jubb senior and junior, had acquired control and redeveloped the site as an integrated woollen mill, constructing first a weaving shed (1860) (see Fig 74g) and then a four-storeyed fireproof mill (1863), the latter with a handsome elevation to the street and a corner stair tower with crenellated parapet (Fig 329). Document of 1882 reveals uses of different floors of the mill, with milling, washing, raising and cutting on ground floor and scribbling, carding and spinning on upper floors. Subsequent development included expansion of the sheds and rebuilding of original finishing buildings.

Fig 329 The 1863 multi-storeyed mill at New Ing Mills, Batley (19).

(20) *Victoria Mill* (SE 2375 2478) (63483).
Steam-powered woollen mill, 1860s and later. Early history uncertain, but by 1900 site was a fully integrated mill with production divided between a mill of four and a half storeys (for scribbling and spinning) and sheds

(for weaving, finishing and dyeing). Local concentration on use of recovered wool reflected in construction by 1915 of large rag warehouse and of rag-grinding sheds.

BINGLEY, West Yorkshire

(21) *Ellar Carr Mill, Cullingworth* (SE 0656 3699) (62373).
Water-powered mill established in late 18th century for cotton spinning but by early 19th century used also for worsted spinning. After 1830 used entirely for worsted spinning. Parts of early mill survived a rebuilding of *c*1889, as did engine house added to mill before 1850. Short row of cottages with warehouse in basement built in 1820 (Fig 90). After 1884 two sheds built; mill rebuilt entirely as three-storeyed twelve-bay steam-powered building (designed by J Robertshaw and Son, Bradford); and a crenellated boundary wall with office controlling site access constructed. Power system remodelled 1901 with addition of new engine and rope drive.

(22) *Lees Mill* (SE 0385 3759) (62650).
Built in 1844 as steam-powered worsted-spinning mill by Merrall and Son, later also of Ebor Mill (50) and Lowertown Shed and Mill (52). Lees Mill developed into integrated factory with addition of weaving sheds in *c*1869. Fire and later alterations to main part of site have obscured nature of mill: original multi-storeyed mill was burnt in 1885, its replacement has been demolished, and *c*1869 weaving shed survives only as fragment. On lower part of site, across public road, is weaving shed of two phases, both pre-1892 (see Fig 74m), which drew its power from main site and has offices along the road frontage and two large, round-arched wagon entrances.

BISHOP THORNTON, North Yorkshire

(23) *High Mill, Shaw Mills* (SE 2525 6270) (63838).
Water-powered flax-spinning mill of two storeys and six bays (Fig 41) built *c*1804–5 close to hamlet of Shaw Mills. Heightened by one storey and extended by three bays before 1848–9. Converted to silk spinning by 1871. Associated buildings: millowner's house and terraces of cottages (Fig 305).

(24) *Woodfield Mill, formerly Render Mill* (SE 2359 6339) (63843).
Three-storeyed water-powered mill built in 1831, the lower floors for corn milling, the top floor for flax spinning. The latter ceased shortly after 1850. Unusual example of shared working.

BOWLING (Bradford), West Yorkshire

(25) *Spring Mill* (SE 1645 3195) (62530); *Melange Mills* (SE 1646 3192) (62533); *Springfield Mill* (SE 1646 3182) (62533); *Bowling Mills* (SE 1658 3197) (62534).
Complex of steam-powered mills developed from the mid 1860s as a speculation by Sir Henry Ripley, owner of Bowling Dyeworks. Mills let on a room and power basis, and tenants at different times included worsted spinners and manufacturers, woolcombers and mohair spinners. Ripley's speculation involved the intense development of a block of land, almost entirely built up with mills, warehouses, sheds and ancillary buildings. The Ripleyville estate was developed as workers' housing by the Ripley family: over 200 houses were built, as well as almshouses of 1857 rebuilt in 1871.

BRADFORD, West Yorkshire

(26) *Barkerend Mills* (SE 1745 3345) (62549).
Established in 1815 as steam-powered worsted-spinning mill. Early buildings included mill (timber-floored, four storeys, eight bays with internal end engine house), warehouses on street frontage, and house. Later expansion of warehouses (Fig 140), addition of new mills (1852, four storeys plus basement and attic, twenty-four bays, timber-floored, projecting privy tower (Fig 57b) designed by W Metcalf of Bradford; *c*1870, six storeys, seventeen bays, fireproof); and construction of combing sheds (1864, by Milnes and France of Bradford, replacing earlier provision for combing) (Fig 158). Mill of *c*1870 shows evolution of transmission system from upright shaft in shaft tower to rope race (Fig 265). Late 19th-century partial conversion to room and power mill. Largely demolished.

(27) *Zetland Mill* (SE 1654 3401) (62516).
Steam-powered worsted mill built 1850–1. Complex comprised a double mill of thirty-six bays with centrally sited internal engine house (Fig 51), nearby boiler house, chimney and minor outbuildings. Mill extremely large on plan but of only two storeys with an attic and part basement. Fireproof brick vaults used over basement and ground floors, but flitched timber beams and joists over first floor. Breadth of mill required three rows of columns to support floors and double-span roof with arched cast-iron trusses. Mill appears to have been used originally by two companies, one concentrating on spinning, the other a manufacturing concern. Double-mill plan or the unusual mixed construction may result from this shared occupancy. Demolished.

BRAMLEY (Leeds), West Yorkshire

(28) *Cape Mills, Farsley* (SE 2242 3535) (63266). Early history obscure, but probably originated in late 18th century as water-powered scribbling and fulling mill. From 1813 mill was run by Hainsworth family, woollen manufacturers, but later the related Gaunt family assumed control. Pre-1850 buildings include three-storeyed eight-bay steam-powered mill of *c*1830 (Figs 119c, 227a), and cloth dryhouse of two storeys, formerly attached to gas-making plant (Fig 141). Wheel-pit next to mill end indicates use of water power alongside steam. Mill became integrated only in the mechanised period, for in *c*1864 a three-storeyed twelve-bay spinning mill was added, followed by a weaving shed in 1869. Offices built near site entrance in 1891 to designs by C S Nelson of Leeds (Fig 103), and new boiler house (with drying floors) and dyehouse added in 1901–2 to designs by W D Gill of Stanningley. See also Fig 126.

CARTWORTH (Holmfirth), West Yorkshire

(9) *Holmbridge Mill* (SE 120 066) (63194). See under AUSTONLEY

(149) *Washpit Mill* (SE 1425 0670) (63211). See under WOOLDALE

DEWSBURY, West Yorkshire

(29) *Batley Carr Mills* (SE 2435 2265) (63534). Built in late 1820s and early 1830s as steam-powered woollen mill by the Ellis family. Early buildings included a timber-floored mill (three and a half storeys, seven bays), probably for scribbling, carding and fulling; cloth dryhouse of two storeys; dyehouse; and, by 1832, an L-shaped four-storeyed loomshop. Site expanded with addition of new timber-floored mills in 1838–40 (three and a half storeys, ten bays) and 1845 (six storeys, twelve bays, by James Radcliffe, Huddersfield), the latter and possibly the former signifying introduction of powered spinning, of a new dyehouse, and by 1855 of a weaving shed for powerlooms. Subsequent development principally involved the construction of large new weaving sheds. See Fig 23.

(30) *Calder Bank Mills* (SE 239 211) (63495). Established in 1861 as a steam-powered woollen mill. Site layout suggests that integration was planned, although construction of the main elements – mill, dryhouse, dyehouse (Fig 84), weaving sheds – took place in stages before 1864. After 1872 site was extended with addition of new sheds used for weaving and finishing, and of five-storeyed warehouse (Fig 175; see also Fig 78). Main mill destroyed by fire in 1883, and in 1884 new owners converted factory partly to shoddy and mungo production and partly for room and power letting to tenants. The architects Kirk and Sons of Huddersfield and Dewsbury were responsible for many of the additions to the mill.

(31) *Low Mill* (SE 2265 2195) (63469). Established *c*1850 as steam-powered mill making woollen blankets. Unusual layout, with shed (see Fig 74f) housing both spinning and weaving. Warehouses, small two-storeyed buildings, finishing sheds, office and a cloth dryhouse (1882, designed by B Watson of Batley) complete the grouping. Two streets of workers' housing adjacent to mill may have been erected by millowner, who probably lived in residence sited to one side of complex. Demolished.

(32) *Machells' Warehouse, 128 Bradford Road* (SE 244 224) (63670). Built in 1863 as rag and wool warehouse by R and W Machell, rag and wool merchants, to designs by William and Stead Ellis of Leeds and Heckmondwike. One of a large number of similar warehouses in the area, built 1860–85 to serve the needs of the developing shoddy and mungo industry. Rag merchants were usually men of limited capital, owning or renting a warehouse and employing a small workforce. Machells' warehouse is typical in its size and layout, with an elaborate office frontage and a utilitarian working area used for the sorting, seaming, ripping and cutting of rags (Fig 196). Taking-in doors on four levels in rear range.

(33) *Moor End Mill* (SE 2274 2287) (63467). Built in 1876 as a steam-powered woollen mill to designs by J Kirk and Sons of Huddersfield and Dewsbury. Complex comprised main timber-floored mill building of two storeys and eight bays, engine and boiler houses and chimney, detached willey room, and long cloth dryhouse attached to one side of the mill. With buildings involved in preparatory (willeying) and finishing (cloth drying) stages of production, mill may have functioned as part of a concern also working at another site, for unlikely that main building could have accommodated all intermediate stages of manufacture. The use of a long single-storeyed cloth dryhouse at this date is characteristic of the Heavy Woollen area and appears to be linked to the techniques required in the drying of blankets (see also Low Mill, Dewsbury (31), Calder Bank Mills, Dewsbury (30), and Syke Ing Mill, Soothill (126)). Demolished.

(34) *Spinkwell Mills* (SE 243 220) (63541).
Established probably in the 1790s as a scribbling and carding mill, but developed mainly after 1838 by firm of Mark Oldroyd and Sons. The mill was a fully integrated steam-powered woollen factory by 1850, with power-loom weaving in a shed. A new mill of five storeys and sixteen bays was built for spinning in the early 1860s and the sheds were expanded to cover a wide area (1863 phase designed by J Laycock) (Fig 164). Oldroyds controlled other mills in Dewsbury and *c*1872 bought Hunslet Mills, Hunslet (67). In the early 20th century two multi-storeyed warehouses were built, one replacing the early mill burnt down in 1911; both were designed by Kirk, Sons and Ridgway of Dewsbury. Largely demolished. See also Figs 232, 251.

EAST ARDSLEY (Morley), West Yorkshire

(35) *Ardsley Mills* (SE 2975 2570) (63623).
Steam-powered worsted-spinning mill built 1912 by Thomas Ambler and Sons on relocation from existing Bradford mill in search of labour and better coal supplies. Complex comprised main building of two storeys and basement (by Mouchel and Partners of London) with attached power plant (engine house, boiler house, economiser, chimney) (Fig 62), office block (Fig 100f), and terraces of workers' houses (Fig 306). Main interest and importance of site concerns design and construction of main mill: double-mill plan, with attached central engine house powering rope race; large floor areas provided by great breadth; use of Hennebique system of reinforced-concrete construction; and external appearance with outer walls made up of concrete frame infilled by large windows and red brick; flat roof (Fig 201).

ELLAND CUM GREETLAND (Elland), West Yorkshire

(36) *North Dean Mill, West Vale* (SE 0981 2135) (62805).
Built in 1876–7 as steam-powered woollen mill. Site comprises main mill of 1876–7, designed by Richard Horsfall, architect, of Halifax, of four storeys and thirteen bays with internal end engine house, attached boiler house and chimney (Fig 63), added house and offices (1878; Fig 107), warehouse (1885), and mill extension (1919, by William Hall of Halifax). Original use of main mill not known but since built by a partnership of woollen manufacturers, it is possible that powerlooms were housed on the ground and first floors, utilising the brick-arched ceiling over the ground floor. Extension of 1919 of fireproof construction with floors of steel beams and hollow concrete blocks.

(37) *Victoria Mills, West Vale* (SE 0961 2122) (62807).
Founded in 1850s as room and power mill, burnt down in 1866 and 1893, and then rebuilt as fireproof cotton-spinning mill, to designs by Horsfall and Williams of Halifax, in 1894–5. Four-storeyed thirteen-bay steam-powered mill, incorporating earlier masonry, linked to two-storeyed four-bay warehouse. Only one storey built of second multi-storeyed mill, designed by W C Williams of Halifax in 1898.

(38) *Wellington Mills, Elland* (SE 1110 2115) (62824).
Steam-powered cotton-spinning mills built in 1860 and 1868 and burnt down in 1875 and 1912 respectively. Rebuilt five-storeyed thirteen-bay mill of 1875, and four-storeyed fifteen-bay mill of 1912 designed by Thomas Kershaw, both of fireproof construction (Figs 58, 66). Other buildings include warehouses of 1871 and mid to late 1880s, with stable and cart shed added against former and office against latter.

(39) *West Vale Mills, West Vale* (SE 0949 2110) (62808).
Established in 1850 as steam-powered worsted-spinning mill. First building, a spinning shed, no longer extant. Complex comprises six-storeyed twenty-bay pedimented mill, timber-floored over a fireproof ground floor which includes internal boiler house, attached engine houses (one for a beam engine, a later one for a vertical engine) (Fig 234), storeyed warehouses, single and double-storeyed shed, offices, including time office (Fig 104), and dwellings. Mill run as worsted-spinning factory by John Maude and Co until being taken over *c*1897 by John Horsfall and Sons and converted to manufacture of woollen blankets.

FEWSTON, North Yorkshire

(40) *West House Mill* (SE 168 555) (63849).
Water-powered flax-spinning mill built in 1797, used for cotton spinning from 1850–1 and silk spinning from 1856–64 (Fig 272). Large, five-storeyed mill enlarged before 1816 by addition of warehouse, mill extension, supplementary steam engine, loomshop, bleach house and air drying rooms (Fig 153). Heated dryhouse and new warehouse and bleachworks built between 1820 and 1843. Associated buildings: millowners' houses, workers' cottages and two apprentice houses (Fig 304). Demolished.

FULSTONE (Holmfirth), West Yorkshire

(41) *Sude Hill Mills, New Mill* (SE 1673 0863) (63218).
Woollen mill, obscure origins but certainly in existence by 1848 as a spinning mill, apparently using water power. Buildings, almost entirely of post-1850 date, are two mills, engine and boiler houses and modern sheds (1950). After 1857 mill was occupied by woollen manufacturers and may have been used for both spinning and weaving, despite absence of early weaving sheds. In 1919–20 new owners remodelled power system, building new engine house for a horizontal engine and a rope race. Mill forms part of a closely built up area which includes a number of early 19th-century cottages with loomshops.

GLUSBURN, North Yorkshire

(42) *Midland Mills, Cross Hills* (SE 0095 4536) (62277).
Built as a joinery works in 1899–1900 but largely rebuilt as steam-powered worsted-weaving mill in or shortly before 1919. Single-storeyed shed with minor early extension.

GOLCAR (Colne Valley), West Yorkshire

(43) *Loomshop, Ramsden Mill Lane* (SE 1023 1536) (63185).
Four-storeyed building built *c*1840: storage on ground floor, domestic accommodation on first floor, loomshops on upper two floors (Fig 145). Important surviving example of combined dwelling and workshop showing grouping of workforce outside the factory. Probably built by Ramsden family, owners of nearby Ramsden Mills, Linthwaite (87), and builders of adjacent residence, Bankfield.

(87) *Ramsden Mills* (SE 1045 1546) (63025).
See under LINTHWAITE

(124) *Spa Mills* (SE 0840 1425) (62988).
See under SLAITHWAITE

HALIFAX, West Yorkshire

(44) *Hanson Lane Mill* (SE 0820 2536) (63899).
Steam-powered cotton-spinning mill (Fig 54) of four storeys and basement built in 1868–9 to designs by R Ives and Son. Mill, of fireproof construction, resembles in its considerable depth mills typical of contemporary Lancashire cotton industry. Late 19th-century additions. Demolished.

(45) *Wellington Mills* (SE 0969 2545) (62792).
Built in 1852, to designs by Dixon and Milnes of Bradford, by Samuel Cunliffe Lister of Manningham Mills, Manningham (93). Functioned first as woolcombing works, but in the 1860s changed to silk spinning and weaving. Lister sold the mill in 1873 after a fire, and it was then run as a silk-spinning mill until the mid 20th century. Complex of 1852 included steam-powered four-storeyed mill of seventeen bays, attached combing shed, engine house, boiler house, chimney, warehouse and wash house. Additions relating to the mill's use for silk spinning were a new wash house (1875), sorting sheds (1879), warehouse, by Petty and Ives, Halifax (1884), storerooms, drying rooms, a new power plant (1901), and a new mill (late 1920s). Demolished.

HARTWITH CUM WINSLEY, North Yorkshire

(46) *Knox Mill* (SE 1902 6394) (63842).
Early 19th-century water-powered flax-spinning mill of three storeys and six bays with external end wheelhouse (Fig 138).

HAWES, North Yorkshire

(47) *Gayle Mill, Gayle* (SD 8711 8939) (63829).
Water-powered cotton-spinning mill built in mid 1780s and used in 19th century for flax spinning, then woollen spinning, and finally as saw mill (Figs 137, 212). Three-storeyed six-bay mill with internal waterwheel replaced by turbine in 1879 when long stone and timber headrace evidently replaced original water system.

HAWORTH (Keighley), West Yorkshire

(48) *Charles Mill, Oxenhope* (SE 0348 3468) (62659).
Established early 19th century as water-powered worsted-spinning mill. Steam power added by 1851. Mill largely rebuilt in late 19th century as building of two storeys plus attic and ten bays. Privy tower projects on rear wall. Boiler house and economiser house attached to mill at one end, range of warehouse and offices at other. Mill dam survives to rear.

(49) *Dunkirk Mill* (SE 0200 3519) (62638).
Water-powered worsted-spinning mill, established *c*1800. Main building is a two-storeyed eight-bay mill largely of *c*1870 but incorporating remains of early mill in area of wheelhouse. Cottages, a mill extension used in

the late 19th century for corn milling, remains of added steam power plant, and extensive headrace and mill dam (Fig 217) complete the complex. Waterwheel replaced by a water turbine, still *in situ* (Fig 220).

(50) *Ebor Mill* (SE 0366 3765) (62649).
Worsted mill, established *c*1819 with construction of water-powered spinning mill of three storeys and basement and seven bays. Occupied from *c*1850 by Merrall Brothers, who also worked from Lees Mill, Bingley (22), and Lowertown Shed and Mill, Haworth (52). Ebor Mills expanded with extensions to original mill, addition of large two-phase weaving shed fronted by a warehouse, and construction in 1887 of six-storeyed nineteen-bay mill, timber-floored over a fireproof basement, to designs by W and J B Bailey of Bradford and Keighley (Fig 214). Merralls ran all three of their mills as integrated worsted factories. Associated buildings: row of cottages next to mill, Ebor House and Longlands (Figs 311a, b), and other manufacturers' houses. See also Fig 248.

(51) *Griffe Mill* (SE 0065 3737) (62635).
Water-powered cotton-spinning mill established by 1793, used for worsted spinning from 1820s and from mid 19th century also for worsted weaving. Original three-storeyed six-bay mill extended before third quarter of 19th century when complex grew around mill yard with extra spinning capacity, warehousing, workers' housing and two-phase weaving shed. Separate gasworks. Ruinous.

(22) *Lees Mill* (SE 0385 3759) (62650).
See under BINGLEY

(52) *Lowertown Shed and Mill, Oxenhope* (SE 0340 3485) (62656).
Established 1856 as steam-powered worsted-weaving mill with shed and attached engine and boiler houses. Warehouse added *c*1863. Bought in 1880s by Merrall and Sons of Ebor Mill, Haworth (50), and Lees Mill, Bingley (22), who enlarged the shed, built a new engine house and added a piece room. Converted to integrated working in 1895 with construction of large new spinning mill by W and J B Bailey of Bradford and Keighley. Mill has timber floors, five storeys, sixteen bays and was powered by rope race from attached corner engine house (Figs 264, 330). Demolished.

(53) *Sykes Mill, Leeming* (SE 0405 3435) (62661).
Built *c*1847 as steam-powered worsted-spinning mill. The first mill comprised an eleven-bay timber-floored building of three storeys with attic and part basement; internal end engine house; attached boiler house; and chimney (Fig 155). Mill extended by five bays, and a small shed, probably for combing, was added late 19th century.

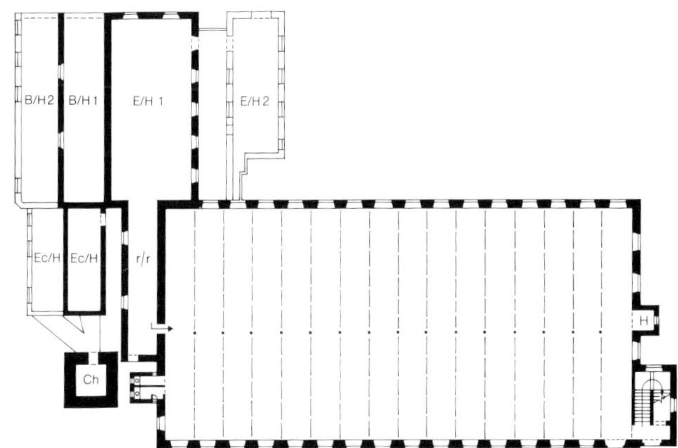

Fig 330 The 1895 multi-storeyed mill and the power plant at Lowertown Shed and Mill, Haworth (52).

HESLINGTON, North Yorkshire

(54) *Heslington Bleach Works* (SE 6210 5055) (63868).
Established *c*1804 and leased by three York linen drapers, one of whom also a partner in Lawrence Street Flax Mill, York (154), from *c*1816. Mill and bleachworks

run jointly until closure of business in early 1850s when bleachworks included bleach house, wash house, sheds, two houses and four closes of grassland. After 1857 sale, land put to agricultural use and farm buildings replaced industrial buildings. Demolished.

HIGH AND LOW BISHOPSIDE, North Yorkshire

(55) *Glasshouses Mill, Glasshouses* (SE 1718 6435) (63831).
Water-powered flax-spinning mill built in 1812 on site of corn mill. Significantly enlarged after purchase in 1835 by Metcalfe family: east and west wings added in late 1830s, warehouse and offices in 1844, warehouse in 1852. Power enhanced by installation in 1850–1 of waterwheel designed by William Fairbairn and Sons of Manchester and fed by 10 million gallon reservoir (Fig 208), steam engine added in 1857, water turbine in 1871 (Fig 219). Gas plant established in 1864 (Fig 109). New boiler house with dryhouse over (Fig 79b) and attached joiners' shop built 1877–8. Mill converted to hemp spinning in 1899, and run from 1912 by Atkinson family. Associated buildings, mostly built between 1850 and 1870, include millowner's mansion of Castlestead, mill manager's house, workers' housing, school and schoolhouse, and chapel (Figs 284–90). Mill extensions and associated buildings of 1860s and 1870s designed by W R Corson of Leeds and later Manchester. See also Figs 119i, 253.

HOLBECK (Leeds), West Yorkshire

(56) *Benyons' Mill* (SE 2990 3256) (63344).
Steam-powered flax-spinning mill built by Benyons and Bage in 1802–3, the multi-storeyed mill and contemporary ?warehouse and hand-heckling block being the first fireproof textile mill buildings in Yorkshire. Integration achieved by addition of weaving shops for handlooms in 1804–5 (Fig 152). Later additions included gas plant of *c*1815. Demolished.

(57) *Marshall's Mill* (SE 2950 3265) (41529).
Foremost flax-spinning mill in England, established in 1791 by John Marshall and also used for many years for linen weaving (Fig 142). Large-scale early growth: by 1795 buildings included two spinning mills, heckling shops, air dryhouse and warehouse. Early 19th-century expansion, all of fireproof construction, included warehouse of 1806 (Figs 92, 101, 119a), slightly later dryhouse and mechanics' shop, and Mills C, D and E built in 1815–16, 1826–7 and 1829–31 (Figs 43, 46, 119b, h, 124a, d). Temple Mill, a top-lit single-storeyed shed of 1838–41 intended for integrated production (Fig 73), and adjacent offices of 1842–3, both have Egyptian-style façades (Figs 73, 100a, 168). Associated buildings: several millowners' mansions built or purchased, some workers' housing, two schools (Fig 316), a church. Partly demolished. See also Figs 222, 226, 260.

HORTON (Bradford), West Yorkshire

(58) *Cannon Mills* (SE 1450 3205) (62450).
Steam-powered worsted mill established in 1826 as a room and power mill. Main surviving buildings are fireproof mill (four storeys, twenty-two bays) of 1855–6 by Andrews and Delaunay of Bradford, incorporating fragments of original mill and of shed of *c*1850, engine house, boiler houses, warehouses (*c*1855 and later), large sheds, built probably for combing and weaving, and stable block (Fig 112). Associated buildings: terraces of workers' housing with corner shops (Fig 327).

(59) *Jesse Street Dyeworks* (SE 1630 3210) (62620).
Built *c*1880 probably as workshops and warehouse by wool and waste dealer, but by 1895 functioning as a dyeworks (Fig 188). Change of use involved conversion of existing buildings and addition of new ones, resulting in small complex of one and two-storeyed buildings including dyehouse, warehouse and office, boiler house with perforated iron floor and drying room over, and small engine house, with horizontal engine *in situ*. Some of these buildings were designed by M Brayshaw, later Brayshaw and Dixon, of Bradford. Site now includes a court of workers' houses, a rare survival from the mid 19th century. The works is of interest in demonstrating how small dyeing concerns, perhaps specialising in one aspect of dyeing, could co-exist with the great Bradford dyeworks like Bowling and Oakwood.

(60) *Legrams Mill* (SE 1495 3285) (62447).
Steam-powered worsted mill, established 1871 by loom manufacturer. Designed by Lockwood and Mawson of Bradford as integrated mill with combing shed, mill, weaving shed and warehouse, but slump in fortunes of traditional Bradford product (cotton-warp worsteds) caused change to spinning mill. Weaving shed never built, mill left as unfinished shell, warehouse converted to act as spinning mill. Original mill building was completed only in 1903, to designs by Moore and Crabtree, Keighley. See Figs 263, 271.

HUDDERSFIELD, West Yorkshire

(61) *Britannia Mills* (SE 1439 1598) (63097).
Room and power mill established in 1860 by engineer as

Fig 331 The enclosed yard at Britannia Mills, Huddersfield (61), has multi-storeyed mills on two sides.

a speculation. First buildings were two five-storeyed fireproof mills of sixteen and eighteen bays (Fig 331), engine house generating power for both mills, boiler house and chimney, warehouse, and small shed. Later addition of warehouses (one, of 1876, by B Stocks, architect, Huddersfield), extension of shed, new engine house (Fig 180). Room and power advertised for let as early as May 1861. Tenants in 1860s included wide range of business concerns, mainly involved in woollen textiles, but cotton and silk branches also represented. Demolished.

(62) *Firth Street Mills* (SE 1475 1609) (63091).
Steam-powered woollen mill, built in 1865–6 (see Frontispiece). Site originally comprised only a mill of five storeys and twenty-one bays with internal engine house, boiler house, chimney, cottage and time office. Mill is of fireproof construction with double-span roof with iron trusses. Boiler house had two wool-drying rooms over, each with a perforated cast-iron floor. By 1866 a tentering place for cloth drying by machine had been added. Not known whether weaving was originally performed on site or elsewhere. After 1886 the mill was bought by a cotton spinner and three years later weaving sheds were added.

(63) *Folly Hall Mills* (SE 1419 1599) (63095).
Room and power mill, established 1825 by Joseph Kaye, a local entrepreneur and builder. By *c*1850 complex included six-storeyed seventeen-bay fireproof mill (Figs 48, 119k), rebuilt in 1844 after fire, two further mills, a 'weaving factory' of loomshop form, 'stoves' (probably heated cloth dryhouses), teasing shops and a gas plant (Fig 178). In 1844 the mill tenants included merchants, manufacturers, cloth finishers and 'country jobbers', and in 1861 twenty-eight businesses operated from the complex (see Table 1). The largest mill, that of 1844, has an elaborate main front with a central pediment and smaller pediments over the end bays; internally the roof has arched cast-iron trusses. The mill, with about 4,300 square metres of working space, was among the largest structures in the woollen branch before 1850.

(64) *Larchfield Mills* (SE 1482 1618) (63090).
Steam-powered woollen mill built in 1865–6 (see Frontispiece). Occupied by fancy woollen manufacturer, possibly as spinning mill but also perhaps for weaving either by handlooms or powerlooms. Site comprised original mill (five storeys, the lower two fireproof, sixteen bays) with internal corner engine house, detached boiler house and chimney (demolished), and long added three-phase range of two storeys plus basement, all under a multi-span gabled roof. One of a group of Huddersfield mills run by woollen manufacturers but originally lacking sheds for weaving (see also Firth Street Mills (62), Albert Mills, Lockwood (89)).

(65) *Starkeys' Mill, later Springdale Mills, Longroyd Bridge* (SE 1376 1615) (63065).
Woollen mill established in 1819 and expanding rapidly to fill island site between River Colne and Huddersfield Canal. By 1835 site included four multi-storeyed mills used for all stages in woollen manufacture, with both powerlooms and handlooms, dyehouses, heated cloth dryhouse, finishing shops, and steam power plant (Fig 170). Very large-scale and early development of mechanically powered integrated working in the woollen branch. Demolished.

HUNSLET (Leeds), West Yorkshire

(66) *Balm Road Mills, formerly Hunslet Flax Mill* (SE 3105 3109) (63396).
Built in 1826 as an integrated flax-spinning and linen-weaving mill, subsequently expanding with addition of warehouses and other buildings. Imposing fireproof Italianate-style mill with attached boiler house (Fig 243) and warehouse built in 1880s, one of last Leeds flax-spinning mills. Largely demolished.

(67) *Hunslet Mills* (SE 314 321) (63376).
Flax-spinning mill built in 1838–40 by John Wilkinson with probable involvement of William Fairbairn, engineer, of Manchester. Multi-storeyed mill and contemporary warehouse both fireproof (Figs 53, 116, 121b,

122); during 1840s, original warehouse heightened and extended and elaborately detailed offices created (Fig 102), and further warehouses and cart shed built (Fig 159). Single-storeyed spinning and carding shed added, probably in 1850s, as well as further warehousing and open sheds. From early 1870s mill used for woollen manufacture, initially by Oldroyds of Spinkwell Mills, Dewsbury (34), who built dyehouse and extended shed, converting it to weaving. Largely demolished.

IDLE, West Yorkshire

(68) *Brackendale Mills, Thackley* (SE 1705 3867) (62542).
Woollen mill, established *c*1800 using water power, with a steam-powered mill built later. Expansion of site involved construction of weaving shed *c*1875 some distance from main buildings. Shed has brick-vaulted part basement and main working floor of eight bays by eight bays. Power provided by vertical engine in corner engine house (Fig 228). See also Fig 255.

KEIGHLEY, West Yorkshire

(69) *Aireworth Mills* (SE 0725 4195) (62297).
Water-powered cotton mill, established in 1787, rebuilt 1808 and converted to worsted spinning in 1813. Conversion from cotton to worsted spinning, common in the Keighley area in the early 19th century, did not involve structural alterations. Mill of 1808, of three storeys and thirteen bays, is timber-floored and has corner wheelhouse (Fig 213) and added circular stair tower. It originally abutted a range including warehouse and cottages. In 1835 powerlooms were introduced to the mill. The complex expanded with the addition of a warehouse (*c*1845), engine and boiler houses (*c*1850), shed for weaving or combing (1870), and later warehouse, sheds, dressing room (1891, by W and J B Bailey of Bradford and Keighley), extension to the mill and new horizontal engine house (1893). See also Fig 216.

(70) *Becks Mill* (SE 0555 4100) (62342).
Built in 1907 as part of expansion of long-established worsted-spinning and manufacturing concern operating from another mill (Grove Mills) in Keighley. Ambitious plans by Moore and Crabtree of Keighley for two large mills and sheds were not followed and the 1907 complex took the form of a single large spinning mill of six storeys and eighteen bays, with attached boiler house and electricity-generating room. The earliest known example of a Yorkshire mill with its own generating plant. The spinning mill, of fireproof con-

Fig 332 Decorative ironwork in New Mill of 1869 at Dalton Mills, Keighley (71).

struction using steel beams and hollow-brick floors, has an angle-iron shed roof (Fig 131).

(71) *Dalton Mills* (SE 0699 4137) (62300).
Large steam-powered worsted mill, begun in 1866 to designs by William Sugden of Leek, Staffordshire, and expanding rapidly over rest of decade. Original scheme comprised three ornate mills (Fig 50) – Tower Mill begun 1866 (four storeys and attic, nine bays), Genappe Mill, begun 1868 (three storeys, thirty-eight bays), and New Mill, begun 1869 (three storeys, thirty-three bays; Fig 332) – a long shed (begun 1866), engine houses, one for Tower Mill and Shed, the other for the two main mills, boiler houses, a chimney and offices. The buildings are grouped around a narrow yard. The mill-owners, I and I Craven, were worsted spinners and manufacturers, but it appears that Dalton Mills was used mainly for spinning. Later alterations included the addition in 1904 of two horizontal engine houses to designs by John Haggas and Sons, Keighley, necessitated by the accidental wrecking of the original pair of beam engines. See also Fig 261e.

(72) *Devonshire Mills* (SE 0565 4117) (62341).
Built in 1909–10 as electrically powered worsted-weaving mill, to designs by John Haggas and Sons, Keighley. Main components were warehouse and attached weaving shed. Original uses of warehouse were yarn storage in basement, offices and piece storage on

ground floor (Fig 97), further storage on first floor, and mending on top-lit second floor. Shed with large bays permitted by use of steel girders (Fig 72). Electricity not generated on site but supplied by public company. Use of mill reflects continuing strength of specialist worsted-weaving sector in early 20th century.

(73) *Knowle Mill* (SE 0600 4035) (62351).
Steam-powered worsted-spinning mill (Fig 64). Planned as double mill by J B Bailey and Sons, Keighley, with first phase of 1906–8 providing a seventeen-bay mill of four storeys and basement with engine house, boiler house, chimney and small shed. Second phase, of 1926, gave nineteen-bay addition to mill, carried out in same style. Engine house and rope race, sited to one end of first mill, became central after addition of extension. See also Fig 119m.

(74) *Low Mill* (SE 0660 4120) (62356).
First cotton-spinning mill built in Yorkshire, begun as speculation by Thomas Ramsden of Halifax and completed in 1780 by Claytons and Walshman who in 1783–4 also built Langcliffe Mill, Langcliffe (81), near Settle. Four-storeyed sixteen-bay water-powered mill, by 1788 with adjoining warehouse and steam engine to pump water back into dam. Extensive sheds and warehouses added after site taken for worsted manufacture *c*1840 by John Craven. Partly demolished.

(75) *Lower Providence Mill, Oakworth* (SE 0340 3827) (62644).
Established in early 19th century as water-powered worsted-spinning mill, but rebuilt as steam-powered mill in 1874–5 and later. Early mill, which survived only in wheelpit area, incorporated into the later mill. Designed by David Whiteoak of Keighley, the 1874–5 mill (see Figs 55, 128e) was of four storeys and attic, thirteen bays long, had timber-floored construction (Fig 55) and was powered by an internal end engine house. Later expansion involved the construction of combing shed (1895, by Judson and Moore, Keighley), wool warehouse (1897, again by Judson and Moore) and warehouse (Fig 128h, i) and shed (pre-1908). Demolished (except chimney) (Fig 328).

(76) *Ponden Mill, Stanbury* (SD 9989 3721) (62159).
Three-storeyed nine-bay water-powered cotton-spinning mill built by Robert Heaton in 1791–2. Mill repaired after fire in 1795; adjoining warehouse and cottage added in 1790s and later enlarged. Engine house and boiler house added in 1850s, shortly after mill converted to worsted spinning; new engine house built in 1893 (Fig 42).

KEXBROUGH (Darton), South Yorkshire

(77) *Swithen Bleachworks* (SE 3019 1139) (63775).
Established in 1826 on site in Dearne valley to serve linen-weaving industry of nearby Barnsley. Additions in late 1830s created plan, little altered by 1895 (Fig 186), with principal buildings around courtyard, steam engine and boiler house at corner, and service buildings, including gas house, beyond. House adjacent; two reservoirs in surrounding grassland. Site closed 1907. Demolished.

KIRKBURTON, West Yorkshire

(78) *Green Grove Mills, Highburton* (SE 1899 1369) (63151).
Established in 1833–4 as two-storeyed six-bay handloom-weaving shop by partnership of two fancy weavers and a dyer. Rare survival of an intermediate stage in transition from domestic production to factory system. Powerlooms apparently not introduced to the mill until the 1870s or later, illustrating predominance of handloom weaving in fancy manufacturing long after the powerloom had become common in rest of woollen branch. Loomshop was heightened and lengthened *c*1850. A tentering shed, dyehouse, warehouse, power plant and cottages complete the complex.

KNARESBOROUGH, North Yorkshire

(79) *Flax-dressing shop, Green Dragon Yard* (SE 350 579) (63865).
Three-storeyed three-bay flax-dressing shop and warehouse built *c*1808 by John Robinson (Fig 24). By 1849 used for handloom weaving of linen.

(80) *Flax-dressing shop, Whiteleys Yard* (SE 350 572) (63863).
Warehouse and flax-dressing shop of three storeys and basement, built in 1825. Ground and first floors of four bays, top floor of seven bays perhaps used for handloom weaving of linen.

LANGCLIFFE, North Yorkshire

(81) *Langcliffe Mill* (SD 8161 6505) (63821) and *Langcliffe Shed* (SD 8175 6435) (63820).
Langcliffe Mill built in 1783–4 as water-powered cotton-spinning mill by Claytons and Walshman who had built Low Mill, Keighley (74), in 1780. Five-storeyed fourteen-bay mill substantially enlarged in early 19th century, when supplementary steam engine also ac-

quired, and in 1868. Firm expanded into weaving in 1820s; powerlooms in due course housed in Langcliffe Shed, a water-powered single-storeyed weaving shed built *c*1840 0.6km south of mill to re-use water supply (Fig 167). Shed successively enlarged in late 19th and very early 20th centuries, and converted to steam power. Associated buildings: Langcliffe Place, manufacturer's house of 1783, and terrace of workers' houses next to mill and shed. Part demolished.

LANGFIELD (Todmorden), North Yorkshire

(82) *Waterside Mill, formerly Laneside Mill, Todmorden* (SD 9345 2380) (38205).
Fielden Brothers, the largest firm in the Yorkshire cotton industry, developed from a domestic cotton-spinning and weaving business established in 1782 by Joshua Fielden. Steam-powered five-storeyed mill soon built and later enlarged; shed (Old Shed) for 800 powerlooms opened in 1829 and another, the New Shed, built for 1,000 powerlooms *c*1840 (Figs 67, 74a, c, 120a). Extensive warehouses, mechanics' and joiners' shops, and gasworks also constructed. Fielden Brothers ran up to thirteen other mills in Todmorden area in 19th century but from 1890 concentrated on Waterside Mill, Robinwood Mill, Todmorden and Walsden (140), and Lumbutts Mill, Langfield (62207). Associated buildings, mainly designed by John Gibson, include the mansions of Stansfield Hall, Dobroyd Castle (Figs 313, 314) and Centre Vale which were respectively extended, built and rebuilt by members of the Fielden family, and various public buildings in Todmorden, including the Unitarian Church (Fig 321), Town Hall (Fig 324) and Centre Vale School (Fig 317). Part demolished.

(83) *Woodhouse Mill* (SD 9515 2444) (62205).
Steam-powered cotton-spinning mill built beside Rochdale Canal in 1832 and, until 1897, run in conjunction with nearby Cinderhill Mill (62203) where powerloom weaving also undertaken. Five-storeyed ten-bay mill of 1832 with detached engine house, boiler house and warehouse, extended in early 1850s (Fig 110); boiler house rebuilt and mill repaired after boiler explosion in 1863. Packing room and cotton warehouse added in 1921 to design of Edward Stott of Todmorden. Boiler house demolished. See also Fig 227b.

LEEDS, West Yorkshire

(84) *Bank Mills* (SE 3099 3301) (63359).
Established in 1791–2 as steam-powered mill for processing cotton and wool, built to design of John Sutcliffe of Halifax. Purchased in 1823 by Hives and Atkinson, former partners in Marshall's Mill, Holbeck (57), becoming one of largest flax-spinning mills in Leeds. Site came to comprise four substantial multi-storeyed mills (A Mill rebuilt 1823, B Mill of 1833, C Mill of *c*1836–9, and D Mill of 1856), all but latest partly or wholly fireproof, specialised warehouses for flax, line, tow (Fig 111) and yarn, and extensive offices. Part demolished. See also Fig 124e.

(85) *Bean Ing Mills, also Park Mills* (SE 290 334) (63389).
Established by Benjamin Gott, woollen merchant, in 1792 as integrated woollen mill. Early complex comprised a large steam-powered mill for scribbling, carding and fulling, spinning rooms, long ranges of loomshops, a dyewood-grinding mill, probably dyehouses, and finishing shops. Later expansion saw rebuilding of dyehouses, construction of heated cloth dryhouses, the first, in 1814, being the earliest known example of the type in the county, extensions to the mill, including work between 1824 and 1829 by William Fairbairn, warehouses, and a gas plant (Fig 108). In terms of organisation of production and of scale, Bean Ing Mills was of great significance. Demolished.

(86) *Wellington Mills* (SE 2885 3357) (79300).
Steam-powered woollen mill, built in and after 1824 as part of industrial development of west Leeds. Mill functioned first as integrated woollen mill, with both mechanically powered and hand-powered processes. Complex comprised a brick five-storeyed fourteen-bay fireproof mill with internal engine house and attached boiler house, two long narrow ranges, probably handloom-weaving shops, a dyehouse and a cloth dryhouse. The mill had an elaborate main front, with giant arches in the wider end bays. In later years the mill concentrated on cloth finishing, a Leeds speciality. Demolished.

LINTHWAITE (Colne Valley), West Yorkshire

(87) *Ramsden Mills* (SE 1045 1546) (63025).
Woollen mill, probably of pre-1770 foundation: in 1789 there were Old and New Mills on the site. Occupied by Ramsden family and later by Ramsden Mill Company. The Ramsden family were variously fulling millers, scribbling and fulling millers and woollen manufacturers, and it is likely that from late 18th century Ramsden Mill provided both public scribbling and fulling services and private services for the family businesses. Early buildings included two water-powered mills; one, of three storeys and attic and five bays, dates probably

from the early 19th century (Fig 39). Later development involved the addition of a five-storeyed fifteen-bay steam-powered mill of *c*1860 (Fig 238). Associated buildings: Bankfield, manufacturer's mansion, of *c*1840, with adjacent loomshop (43). Partially demolished.

LIVERSEDGE, West Yorkshire

(88) *Upper Carr Mills, Littletown* (SE 2012 2432) (63426).
Steam-powered woollen-weaving mill, *c*1875. There were never many specialist woollen-weaving mills, and Upper Carr has an unusual form, with a shed eighteen bays long but only one bay wide with attached engine and boiler houses. Site also included dyehouse and dryhouse. Further sheds added later for worsted spinning.

LOCKWOOD (Huddersfield), West Yorkshire

(89) *Albert Mills* (SE 1405 1555) (63108).
Established in 1853 as steam-powered woollen mill. First buildings included fireproof mill of six storeys and fifteen bays, dyehouse, wash room, and sizing room. Mill has internal end engine house and attached boiler house with drying floors over boilers (Figs 252, 333). New mill, small shed and warehouse (see Fig 74h) added *c*1866, and new range with warehouse and dyehouse (Fig 87), to designs of M Beaumont of Huddersfield, built 1871 on the street front (Fig 176). Chief problem of interpretation lies in use of the mill: operated by woollen manufacturers, it had only a small shed, suggesting either use of main mills for weaving or employment of domestic weavers. Became a room and power mill after failure of original firm in the 1880s. See also Fig 124f.

(90) *Britannia Mills, formerly Firths Mill* (SE 1260 1598) (63060).
Established as a steam-powered woollen mill *c*1830–40. Mill of four storeys and attic, eleven bays, timber-floored. Owners, John Firth and Sons, built extremely large new fireproof mill (six storeys, twenty-seven bays) in 1861 as room and power mill (Fig 179); in 1872, the mill had nine tenants. After *c*1880 mill used mainly for cotton spinning, probably producing warps for the local mixed-fibre manufacture.

LONGWOOD (Huddersfield), West Yorkshire

(91) *Imperial Mills* (SE 1228 1628) (63055).
Built as a paper works in the early 20th century, the buildings were converted to woollen manufacture after 1918. The complex is small and comprises one and two-storeyed structures. Two sheds, one built before and one after conversion to textile use, have Belfast roof trusses (Fig 130). A small engine house accommodated a gas engine, which provided power for the mill.

Fig 333 At Albert Mills, Lockwood (89), the engine house rises through three storeys within the mill. The attached boiler house has drying rooms on the upper floors.

MANNINGHAM (Bradford), West Yorkshire

(92) *Cumberland Works* (SE 1375 3330) (62422).
Woolcombing works, established 1875 (Figs 68, 182). Bradford became the centre of the woolcombing industry, with a number of large establishments. Cumberland Works has typical layout: large sheds form main working areas, with storage basement permitted by the fall of land (Figs 74k, 183, 184). The sheds were probably designed by Thomas Barker, engineer, of Bradford. Addition of large multi-storeyed warehouses (Fig 185), both by Thomas Barker, in 1887 and 1910 reflects changing role of the woolcomber, who came to

act as main supply agency to the worsted industry, holding large stocks of raw wool and despatching it in combed state to local spinners and manufacturers. Site also had grease works and soap-making works.

(93) *Manningham Mills, formerly Lily Croft Mill* (SE 1450 3490) (62439).
Established in 1838 as steam-powered worsted-spinning and combing mill, and under continuing direction of Samuel Cunliffe Lister, created Lord Masham in 1891, converted to silk in 1850s and grew, mainly from 1870 to 1888, into largest silk-spinning and weaving mill in Great Britain (Fig 174). Principal buildings: Green Shed, office (Fig 100d) and dyehouse of 1870, multi-storeyed mill, warehouse and wash house, Lily Shed and Beamsley Shed of 1871–3 (Figs 47, 57c, 74j, 98, 117), and Heaton Shed and Heaton Dyeworks of 1885–8. Architects, all of Bradford: Andrews Son and Pepper in 1870, Andrews and Pepper to 1885, from 1885 James Ledingham and then other architects. Associated buildings: mansions and estates acquired, including Swinton Park and Jervaulx; terraces of workers' housing next to mill; and Cartwright Memorial Hall, built as an art gallery and museum (Fig 326). See also Figs 245, 249b, 257, 267.

(94) *Try Mills* (SE 1524 3341) (62482).
Steam-powered worsted-spinning mill established in 1865 and built to designs of James Ogilvie of Bradford. Small plot, but exploited to full by construction of storeyed buildings around narrow yard. First phase comprised warehouse on street front; timber-floored spinning mill at right angles, of three storeys with basement and attic and of eighteen bays, engine and boiler houses, and a range of buildings giving offices, cottage, coach house and stabling. This first phase immediately supplemented by second phase comprising four-storeyed eleven-bay spinning mill extension and warehouse (Fig 160). Siting of engine house in completed complex – between the two mill phases – suggests the development was planned as a 'double mill', favourable economic circumstances in the boom years of the 1860s perhaps accelerating progress towards completion.

(95) *Whetley Mills* (SE 1475 3365) (62440).
Steam-powered worsted-spinning mill, built in 1863 to designs by Milnes and France of Bradford. Large warehouse (Figs 91, 96, 123), combing shed, engine house, spinning mill, yarn and waste warehouses, offices and foreman's house (Fig 106) were grouped around a small yard which contained boiler house and chimney (Fig 161). Main mill (five storeys, basement and attic, nineteen bays) of fireproof construction. A single engine house provided power to shed and mill: in the latter, drive transmitted by upright shaft in projecting shaft tower. Later additions to combing sheds (1871, 1883, 1912), new power system (Fig 229) and additions to warehouses. An important and architecturally impressive example of a large-scale worsted-spinning mill with its own combing capacity.

(96) *Young Street Mills* (SE 1395 3360) (62423).
Steam-powered worsted mill, designed in 1871 by C H Hargreaves of Bradford as integrated factory with combing and spinning in a multi-storeyed mill and weaving in a large shed (Fig 173). Decline of the Bradford trade after *c*1870, however, caused a change of plans. The shed (see Fig 74i), completed first, was run by a specialist weaving firm, and the main mill, left unfinished and then completed to new designs of 1874 by Hargreaves and Bailey of Bradford, was apparently occupied by a separate firm of spinners. It has four storeys, basement and attic and is eighteen bays long. This change at Young Street reflects the wider trend towards specialised working in the worsted industry after *c*1870. Power transmission in shed was by rope drive along rope alley.

MELTHAM, West Yorkshire

(97) *Bent Ley Mill, Meltham Mills* (SE 1098 1125) (63027).
Steam-powered silk-throwing mill built in 1840 to produce yarn from raw silk, but by 1872 also used for waste-silk spinning. Mill of 1840 a single-storeyed shed with cast-iron roof trusses (Fig 74d) and attached two-storeyed warehouse and office; dyehouse added by 1847. Change of ownership in 1890 led to major expansion of shed area, in particular to building of two sheds and new power plant to designs dated 1901–2 by Stott and Sons of Manchester. Associated buildings: workers' housing (Fig 309).

(98) *Meltham Mills, Meltham Mills* (SE 1090 1085) (63031).
Established by William Brook as woollen mill in late 18th century, converted to cotton spinning by 1805, and developed by Brooks into one of largest cotton mills in Yorkshire, from mid 19th century concentrating on thread manufacture (Fig 157). Site both water and steam powered, with six multi-storeyed mills, up to six storeys high and thirteen bays long, built before 1850. Single-storeyed sheds built after 1850, and five-storeyed mill in 1927–8. Other buildings included gasworks, bleachworks, dyehouse and saw mill. Associated build-

ings: manufacturers' mansions, including Meltham Hall; extensive workers' housing on mill site and elsewhere; public buildings including churches, schools, Convalescent Home, and Carlile Institute and Town Hall in Meltham (Figs 291–8, 325). Largely demolished. See also Fig 249c.

(99) *Scarr Bottom Mill, on site of Scarr Bottom Dyeworks* (SE 1005 1085) (63030).
Cotton-spinning mill designed by Stott and Sons of Oldham and Manchester and built in 1886–7 by Meltham Spinning Company Limited. Five-storeyed steam-powered mill, twelve bays square, of fireproof construction (Fig 118a) with low warehouse and offices to one side and engine house and boiler house at corner (Fig 65). By 1929 small single-storeyed sheds added to two sides and boiler house enlarged. Demolished.

MENWITH WITH DARLEY, North Yorkshire

(100) *Fringill Mill, Fringill* (SE 2063 5924) (63851).
Water-powered flax-spinning mill of five bays and two storeys, attic and part basement, built between 1822 and 1834 by Benson Skaife, a linen manufacturer, who probably built the adjacent pair of cottages with their weaving cellars. In late 19th century mill diversified into spinning rope from hemp, and corn mill built against one corner. Both mills burnt and largely rebuilt in 20th century.

MIDGLEY (Hebden Royd; Sowerby Bridge; Wadsworth), West Yorkshire

(101) *Oats Royd Mills (S/B)* (SE 0395 2655) (62704).
Steam-powered worsted mill, established in 1847 by John Murgatroyd, stuff manufacturer. Mill began as a spinning mill, with handloom and powerloom weavers employed elsewhere, but became fully integrated with introduction of combing and weaving to site, first in multi-storeyed buildings or in small sheds, later in large purpose-built sheds. Massive expansion between 1850 and 1890, with extensive additions to first mill in 1851 and 1855, new warehouse (1857), new mill (1863–4), combing shed (1885) and weaving shed (1887) (Fig 166). Before *c*1880, Murgatroyds used Thomas, then John, Dearden of Halifax as architects. From *c*1884 T Lister Padgett of Halifax received the contracts for building design. Power evolution from beam and vertical engines to horizontal engines (1889, 1894), shaft drive replaced by rope drive. Massive company archive survives. Part demolished. Associated buildings: Oats Royd House (17th century and 19th century) and Broadfold (mansion of 1877; Fig 312a, b); attached terraces of workers' houses (*c*1851, *c*1864) (demolished). See also Figs 119j, 128b–d, g, 169, 242, 246, 266.

MORLEY, West Yorkshire

(102) *Crank Mill* (SE 2685 2823) (63579).
Steam-powered woollen mill built in early 1790s by Lord Dartmouth to provide public scribbling and fulling services. Three-storeyed seven-bay mill powered by engine in attached corner engine house (Fig 139). Engine house contained only cylinder of engine, leaving crank and flywheel exposed on gable wall (Fig 223). Later extensions and addition of dyehouse. Original engine replaced mid 19th century by enclosed beam engine in new engine house.

NORTH BIERLEY, West Yorkshire

(103) *Park View Mills, Wibsey* (SE 1445 3005) (62457).
Built in 1924–5 as electrically powered worsted-weaving mill designed by Moore and Crabtree of Keighley and commissioned by Lee and Foster, manufacturers then renting space in nearby room and power mill. Mill comprised single block on two levels. Basement gave storage space and working area; top-lit main floor had weaving area behind offices, working area for yarn preparation and finishing, and a loading bay (Fig 71). Steel-frame construction independent of outer walls on two sides allowed scope for expansion and freed floor of obstruction, and supported roof (Fig 74n). Lack of generating room indicates power supplied by public company.

(104) *Stadium Mills, Odsal* (SE 1595 2975) (62863).
Built in 1912 to designs by William H Sharp of Bradford as worsted-weaving mill of typical form with small warehouse and attached shed (Fig 202). Mill had fifty-four looms in 1928, less than in the average Bradford weaving mill. Power was supplied first by a gas engine, later by an electric motor.

NORTHOWRAM (Halifax; Queensbury and Shelf), West Yorkshire

(105) *Old Lane Mill, Halifax (H)* (SE 0860 2635) (62765).
Built in 1825–8 as a steam-powered integrated worsted mill by James Akroyd, an innovative worsted manufacturer. Main building was a large fireproof mill,

Fig 334 Single-storeyed sheds provide space for rag storage and sorting at Gedham Mill, Ossett (106).

L-shaped on plan, six storeys high and fifteen bays long, with internal end engine house (Fig 56). Design gave loading passage on ground floor and upper floors with working areas in main range, offices, storerooms and stair in wing, and polygonal privy tower on rear wall. Arched cast-iron roof trusses (Fig 124c). Engine house has decorative window surround (Fig 224) and plaster ceiling and retains beam floor. Detached boiler house with integral chimney. Multi-storeyed mill represents an important experiment, in terms of design and construction, in integrated working in the worsted industry, since it was built in first years of use of the powerloom to house both spinning and weaving.

OSSETT, West Yorkshire

(106) *Gedham Mill* (SE 2776 2065) (63616).
Built as mungo mill in 1897–8. Red brick. Principal buildings included large sheds for storage and sorting (Fig 334), single-storeyed range comprising rag-grinding and scribbling bays (Fig 194), engine and boiler houses, and a block giving carbonising rooms and a dyehouse. Typical small-scale mungo mill with characteristic arrangement of rag-grinding machines.

(107) *Healey New Mill* (SE 2695 1895) (63747).
Built in 1826–7 as steam-powered scribbling and fulling mill by established Ossett clothier and sold in 1836 to a partnership of twenty-nine local clothiers who ran it under the style 'The Healey New Mill Company'. Original mill, of stone and brick, of three storeys with an engine house between main working part (eight bays) and a two-bay narrower end perhaps used for warehousing (Fig 335). The mill is of fireproof construction with cast-iron beams and joists and a stone-flagged floor (Fig 115). Minor buildings included a dyehouse and a single-storeyed heated cloth dryhouse. After 1881 mill was used mainly for the manufacture of shoddy and mungo, and a rag warehouse and a rag-grinding shed built. See also Fig 249a.

(108) *Loomshop, Wesley Street* (SE 2752 2051) (63659).
Loomshop, house and cottages, built 1853–5. Loomshop of two storeys and six bays with stable at one end (Fig 32). After *c*1870 the building was occupied at different times by a rag dealer and mungo manufacturers, the latter apparently using it for storage of rags awaiting processing at nearby mill. Detached two-storeyed house used by tenant of loomshop/warehouse. Terrace of four blind-back cottages occupied mainly by workers in textile industry. Complex is of interest for its original use, for its later use in Ossett's characteristic industry, and for its grouping of buildings of different types.

(109) *Perseverance Mill* (SE 2792 2129) (63613).
Built in 1873–4 as steam-powered mungo and extract mill. Buildings included two-storeyed office, warehouses and rag-sorting building (Fig 192), a rag-grinding shed, attached engine house, boiler house with drying floors, carbonising shed and dyehouse (demolished). Main shed divided into bays, each intended to house a rag-grinding machine. Carbonising sheds housed retorts, furnaces and carbonising chambers.

(110) *Runtlings Mill* (SE 2699 2012) (63603).
Steam-powered shoddy mill, built *c*1907. Brick-built, with buildings arranged around a yard (Fig 195). Carbonising sheds, dyehouse and drying sheds on one

Fig 335 The multi-storeyed mill of 1826–7 at Healey New Mill, Ossett (107).

side. Main range provided shed with six, later seven, bays for rag-grinding machines (Fig 75); attached engine house, with surviving horizontal engine (Fig 221a), boiler house and chimney. Important example of a purpose-built shoddy mill. Part demolished.

(111) *Spedding Oddy's rag warehouse* (SE 2767 2030) (63658).
Built in 1864–5 as combined dwelling and warehouse, the latter for rag storage and grading (Fig 197). One of a number of such rag warehouses in Ossett serving local recovered wool, and especially mungo, manufacturers. The work of a rag merchant involved sorting, seaming, ripping, cutting and packing of rags, and these processes were usually arranged within the warehouse in a sequence starting on the top floor and working down (Fig 198). Firm of Spedding Oddy had occupied this warehouse since the 1930s and continued in business until recent years.

OVENDEN (Halifax), West Yorkshire

(112) *Little Hebble Mill* (SE 0761 2638) (62746).
Built probably in late 18th century as single-storeyed water-powered fulling mill; steam power added *c*1835 and mill heightened to three storeys soon after (Fig 33). Site comprises main mill, attached end engine house, fragmentary remains of chimney, site of boiler house, and attached and detached sheds and cottage. Mill dam infilled but weir survives. Although much altered, mill important in showing small size of some early establishments.

PUDSEY, West Yorkshire

(113) *New Street Mills* (SE 2200 3278) (63273).
Built in 1871 by Pudsey Worsted Mill Company, probably as specialist weaving mill but later functioning as room and power factory: there were eight occupiers in 1910–11. Mill of 1871 comprised a large warehouse (three storeys, nineteen bays), attached weaving shed, corner engine house and boiler house. Narrow yard separates the original mill from a second shed and warehouse block which derived power from 1871 engine house.

SCRIVEN WITH TENTERGATE (Knaresborough), North Yorkshire

(114) *Castle Mill, Knaresborough* (SE 3478 5681) (63850).
Built beside River Nidd and from *c*1847, under Walton family, became principal textile mill in Knaresborough. Originally a corn mill, from 1770 a paper mill, from 1791 a cotton-spinning mill, and from *c*1815 a flax mill, initially for spinning, from late 1840s also for weaving, and from 1860s just linen weaving. Paper mill of three storeys, seven bays by three; attached two-storeyed eleven-bay flax-spinning mill. Adjacent buildings included late 18th and early 19th-century cottages converted to textile use, and warehouse largely rebuilt in 1879. Site water powered until supplementary steam engine added *c*1850. From *c*1860, Walton and Co used Crimple Mill, Scriven with Tentergate (demolished), as their bleachworks and dyeworks. Largely rebuilt.

SETTLE, North Yorkshire

(115) *Runley Bridge Mill* (SD 8110 6230) (63817).
Three-storeyed three-bay water-powered cotton-spinning mill (Fig 34) built *c*1783 on site of corn mill. Single-bay extension built over wheelchamber in early 19th century. Converted to agricultural use shortly after 1850.

SHIPLEY, West Yorkshire

(116) *Saltaire Mills, Saltaire* (SE 142 382) (41553).
Titus Salt's great factory, the main part built 1850–3 with later expansion. Designed by Lockwood and Mawson of Bradford in conjunction with William Fairbairn of Manchester, the original complex provided an integrated worsted mill on a massive scale (Fig 172). Main components were warehouse (Fig 204) and mill (five storeys and basement, sixty bays, Figs 49, 57a, 119n, 125), arranged in a T-plan, combing shed, weaving shed (Figs 74e, 258), offices (100b, c), and power plant (Figs 225, 241). Close to the mill Salt built the village of Saltaire with workers' housing, public buildings and a park (Figs 299–303). Salts dominated the speciality fibre trade and the mills were said to produce eighteen miles of alpaca cloth every day in the late 1850s. Lower part of site between canal and river developed first in the 1850s with construction of gas plant, later by construction of dyehouses and New Mill (1868), with campanile chimney. Further sheds for storage and scouring added to main site. In 20th century, replacement of gas plant by mill buildings. See also Figs 259, 269.

SILSDEN, West Yorkshire

(117) *New Close Shed* (SE 0430 4622) (62291).
Built in 1913 by Waterloo Weaving Company, previously room and power tenants in nearby Waterloo Mills

(118). The firm probably wove mixed worsted and cotton cloth. Mill comprises small weaving shed and engine house, the latter originally with a gas engine. Shed has I-sectioned steel beams and angle-iron roof trusses. Later additions included warehouse, shed extensions, new engine house and a building with Belfast roof trusses.

(118) *Waterloo Mills* (SE 0430 4618) (62292). Steam-powered worsted mill, built *c*1870. Early history obscure, but by early 20th century run as room and power mill. Main buildings include four-storeyed eighteen-bay timber-floored mill of *c*1870, large sheds of various dates, offices, warehouses, and 1916 engine house containing 1905 inverted vertical engine bought second-hand. Original beam engine removed and its internal end engine house subdivided to give rope race connecting with new engine house (Figs 235, 236).

SKIPTON, North Yorkshire

(119) *Belle Vue Mills* (SD 9861 5160) (62117). Founded by John Dewhurst in 1828 as steam-powered worsted-spinning and weaving mill with contemporary warehouse. Mill burnt down and rebuilt in 1831 as four-storeyed fifteen-bay cotton-spinning mill. Major expansion between early 1850s and mid 1880s, when weaving and thread manufacture introduced, led to construction of weaving shed (see Fig 120c), four substantial fireproof multi-storeyed mills, dyehouse and warehouse, all to designs by Wren and Hopkinson of Manchester. Dyehouse rebuilt in 1891; more extensive dyeing and bleaching works built shortly after 1900. New boiler plant, designed by Stott and Sons of Manchester, built in 1901–2 (Fig 249e). Associated buildings: Aireville House, residence of J B Dewhurst (d.1864), who funded chapel and school in Skipton. Dyeing and bleaching works demolished. See also Fig 231.

(120) *Broughton Road Shed* (SD 9770 5145) (62123). Cotton-weaving mill built in 1900–2 by Skipton Room and Power Co Ltd for room and power working. Steam-powered single-storeyed shed with attached three-storeyed warehouse reduced to one storey after fire. Mill housed five weaving firms in 1919.

(121) *Union Mills* (SD 989 511) (62118). Cotton-weaving mill, designed by J Whitehead of Nelson, built in 1867 by Skipton Land and Building Company and run by Skipton Mill Co Ltd on a room and power basis. Steam-powered single-storeyed shed with attached two-storeyed warehouse, later heightened (Fig 163). Weaving shed extension added in 1871, its own warehouse and dyehouse added in 1874. See also Figs 256, 262.

SLAITHWAITE (Colne Valley), West Yorkshire

(122) *Bridge Street Mill* (SE 0820 1398) (62993). Steam-powered woollen mill, probably established in 1875 and occupied by firm of woollen manufacturers. At time of destructive fire in 1902, complex comprised a mill, engine and boiler houses (see Fig 79a), chimney, offices and sheds, the last probably built for weaving. Mill largely rebuilt as five-storeyed building of reinforced concrete construction, powered from earlier engine house. Demolished.

(123) *Globe Mills* (SE 0810 1405) (62992). Established in 1887 as worsted-spinning mill by Globe Worsted Company, a newly formed combination of local manufacturers. Site, divided by a public road, was developed in stages. First mill, detached boiler house, chimney and offices built between road and canal in 1887–8, possibly to designs by Thomas Varley of Slaithwaite, with second mill or warehouse built on other half of plot in 1889. Main mill is fireproof, of five storeys and thirty-three bays, and has central engine house and rope race. Sheds were added to the mill, one at least used for combing. The 1889 mill/warehouse, of five storeys with a basement and of fifteen bays, is of fireproof construction and had a small engine originally. It was connected to main mill from beginning by an overhead walkway. See Fig 119p.

(124) *Spa Mills* (SE 0840 1425) (62988). Established as steam-powered woollen spinning mill in 1860s, single-storeyed weaving sheds added by 1887. Acquired in 1902 by Slaithwaite Spinning Company

Fig 336 The multi-storeyed mill of 1906–7 at Spa Mills, Slaithwaite (124).

which had built three cotton-spinning mills in vicinity, and which in 1906–7 built large five-storeyed fireproof cotton-spinning mill on site, modelled on contemporary Lancashire designs (Fig 336; see also Fig 118c). Low card room along one side; five-storeyed service block at one corner. Existing sheds enlarged and largely rebuilt for winding cotton. Associated buildings: Spa Mill Terrace, 1880.

SOOTHILL (Batley; Dewsbury), West Yorkshire

(125) *Phoenix Mill, Batley (B)* (SE 2478 2400) (63514).
Small mill, reputedly built for machine making *c*1860, but by 1875 in use as a wool, rag, and shoddy and mungo warehouse. Main building of three storeys and seven bays with internal engine and boiler houses, the latter with evidence for a perforated iron floor over to allow air to rise to a drying chamber. Form of building suggests conventional use as woollen mill rather than for engineering or storage purposes. Rag grinding housed in separate range with brick-arched ceiling over ground floor. Interesting example of small-scale mill with typical local association with recovered wool production. Demolished.

(126) *Syke Ing Mill, Earlsheaton (D)* (SE 2615 2135) (63599).
Built *c*1840 by partnership of blanket manufacturers. Operated initially as a steam-powered woollen mill providing public scribbling and fulling services and probably also as base for partnership's (later also the Syke Ing Mill Company's) own business. Surviving buildings included timber-floored main mill (four storeys, eighteen bays) of 1883 on site of earlier mill, attached engine house originally for beam engine (*c*1840), converted 1897 for installation of horizontal engine (Fig 230), and single-storeyed heated cloth dryhouse. See also Fig 119 l.

SOUTH CROSLAND (Huddersfield), West Yorkshire

(127) *Armitage Bridge Mills, Armitage Bridge* (SE 133 135) (63076).
Woollen mill, established *c*1816–17 by Brooke family of Honley, long-established manufacturers and merchants. Built as integrated mill using both hand power (for spinning and weaving) and water power (for preparation and finishing). Substantial remains from this early period include large warehouse (Fig 149), five-storeyed ten-bay fireproof mill (Mill 1) (Fig 146; see also Fig 124b), hand-spinning and weaving shops, and five-storeyed loomshop added *c*1830 (Fig 148). Six-storeyed thirteen-bay mill (Mill 2) built in 1828–9, probably to house machine spinning. Steam power added to supplement waterwheels and in 1834 power provided by three waterwheels (thirty, thirty, and sixty horse power) and two steam engines (thirty-four and forty horse power). Shed for powerloom weaving added in 1838 (Figs 70, 74b), a very early example of the change from hand-looms in the woollen branch, and extended in 1840s (see Fig 120b). Brookes built terraces of cottages on two sides of mill complex, St Paul's Church (1848, by R D Chantrell of Leeds), and Armitage Bridge House. Post-1850 expansion and rebuilding of dyehouses and sheds at lower end of site (Fig 165).

SOWERBY (Sowerby Bridge), West Yorkshire

(128) *Mill House Mill* (SE 0485 2255) (62717).
Established in late 1780s as a water-powered scribbling and fulling mill by the Rawson family, woollen merchants and manufacturers and later bankers. Early buildings included the mill, only perhaps six bays long and probably of three storeys but later extended by five bays, warehouses, and a heated cloth dryhouse of three storeys and thirty bays, lit by small windows (Fig 82). Mill had two waterwheels, from the 1840s supplemented by a steam engine. Later buildings include warehouses (one mid 19th century, Fig 93, one of 1864, one *c*1871–2), offices, dyehouses (mid 19th century and later) and cottage. Original function of the mill was to prepare the wool and finish the cloth otherwise worked up outside the premises by Rawsons' dispersed spinners and weavers.

SOYLAND (Ripponden), West Yorkshire

(129) *Kebroyd Mills* (SE 0415 2130) (62720).
Established as fulling mill *c*1680 but used for cotton spinning from *c*1794 with addition of waste-silk spinning from 1826. Site, decimated by fires, has two main steam-powered mills, Dene Mill, a six-storeyed fifteen-bay cotton-spinning mill rebuilt in 1870, and Kebroyd Mill, a five-storeyed thirty-bay silk-spinning mill of 1905–6 incorporating earlier masonry. Other buildings include 19th-century cottage and office, and warehouse. Associated building: manufacturer's mansion, Dene House. See Figs 119f, 254.

STAINLAND (Elland), West Yorkshire

(130) *Brookroyd Mills, Holywell Green* (SE 0900 1950) (62985).
Established *c*1795 as water-powered woollen scribbling mill by John Shaw, previously a shalloon (worsted)

Fig 337 The New Mill of c1920 at Brookroyd Mills, Stainland (130).

manufacturer. Firm of John Shaw and Sons changed from woollen to worsted manufacturing *c*1866. Additions on a restricted scale before 1850, then massive expansion with construction of five multi-storeyed mills and a weaving shed before 1880. Three mills survived in 1986: B Mill and A Mill of 1860 and 1866, both fireproof, form a single long five-storeyed range of thirty-five bays with central engine house (Fig 52), and New Mill, of *c*1920, a five-storeyed structure of reinforced concrete with brick outer walls (Fig 337; see also Fig 118f, 132). Associated buildings: workers' housing (Fig 310), manufacturer's mansion (Brooklands), Chapel, Mechanics' Institute. Largely demolished.

(131) *Burrwood Mill* (SE 0882 2015) (62786).
Established before 1850 as woollen mill, rebuilt in mid 19th century as steam-powered worsted mill. Main building of five storeys and eleven bays, timber-floored, with projecting stair tower at one end and internal end engine house at other. Low attached building beyond engine house provided boiler house and warehouse, with earlier row of cottages beyond.

STANSFIELD (Todmorden), West Yorkshire

(132) *Bridge Royd Dyeworks, Eastwood* (SD 9615 2490) (62216).
Built in 1868 as steam-powered dyeing and finishing works. Dyehouse, rebuilt after fire in 1878 and recently re-roofed, has attached heated dryhouse. New power source and three-storeyed finishing mill added in mid 1890s; by 1905 further heated dryhouse, warehousing and other buildings added (Fig 189).

(133) *Eastwood Shed, Eastwood* (SD 9618 2585) (62212).
Cotton-weaving shed, initially part of Upper Mill, an integrated cotton mill built on an exposed hillside site between 1833 and 1848. Single-storeyed shed, originally water-powered but by 1848 also steam- powered, subsequently enlarged in two phases. Adjacent warehouse. Shed interior gutted.

(134) *Hare Mill, later Mons Mill, Todmorden* (SD 9310 2495) (62239).
Steam-powered fireproof cotton-spinning mill designed by Stott and Sons of Manchester for Hare Spinning Company Ltd and renamed Mons Mill in 1914 on takeover by Mons Mill Company Ltd. Intended as double mill powered from central power source, but only first half, started 1907, completed in 1911 and opened 1912, of seven storeys and basement, thirty-eight by eighteen bays, completed (Figs 60, 118b). Contemporary detached office block (Fig 100e) with Byzantine detailing originally echoed by top of stair tower of mill. Minor later additions. Associated buildings: adjacent workers' housing. Limited demolition. See also Fig 233.

STEETON WITH EASTBURN, West Yorkshire

(135) *Woodlands Mill, Steeton* (SE 0325 4415) (62288).
Established in early 19th century as water-powered worsted-spinning mill. Early timber-floored mill (six storeys, eleven bays) survives, showing use of two waterwheels. Mill owned by manufacturer performing hand-powered processes (combing and weaving) off the premises. Rapid expansion after *c*1850, with addition of new mill (five storeys and attic, nine bays), combing and weaving sheds and warehouses. Steam power added to supplement waterwheels. After 1860 mill functioned as fully integrated worsted factory.

THORNTON, West Yorkshire

(136) *Prospect Mill* (SE 1017 3262) (62396).
Steam-powered worsted mill. First buildings on site were dwellings of 1831, the base of a family putting-out business. Mill and warehouse built 1849, representing shift away from dispersed working. Mill, of four storeys and attic and eleven bays and with timber floors, had corner engine house probably for vertical engine. Second warehouse built 1855, followed by second mill (*c*1860, three storeys, eleven bays) and six-bay extension to first mill (*c*1865). Occupiers, Joshua Craven and Son, were both spinners and manufacturers, and it is likely that parts of the main mills were used for powerloom weaving. Associated buildings: manufacturer's house, Ashfield House, to east of mills, of *c*1860 (Fig 315); workers' housing, pre-dating mill, in Prospect Street (Fig 307).

TODMORDEN AND WALSDEN, West Yorkshire

(137) *Frostholme Mill, Cornholme* (SD 9075 2625) (62166).
Steam-powered cotton-weaving mill comprising single-storeyed shed and multi-storeyed warehouse built in 1860–1, both subsequently enlarged, the shed in 1884–5 and 1892–3. Original shed and warehousing rebuilt after fire in 1896, latter as four-storeyed building including offices and boiler house (Fig 211). Building of 1884–5 designed by Proctor and Hinnall of Bolton; those of 1892–3 and 1896 by John R Blacka of Todmorden and Littleborough.

(138) *Hollins Mill, Walsden* (SD 9340 2205) (62191).
Steam-powered integrated cotton-spinning and weaving mill built in 1856–8 beside Rochdale Canal. Four-storeyed eighteen-bay mill and attached single-storeyed weaving shed powered from engine house at junction (Fig 171). Contemporary warehouse and mechanics' shop. Further weaving shed and combined office and warehouse added before 1890. Minor demolition.

(139) *Hope Mill, Walsden* (SD 9328 2230) (62189).
Steam-powered cotton-spinning mill built beside Rochdale Canal in 1855–6, from 1879 used for cotton weaving. Original building, unusually for spinning mill, a single-storeyed shed with corner beam-engine house (Fig 162). Two-storeyed warehouse at corner perhaps original, shed enlarged (see Fig 74 l) and offices added before 1890. Minor demolition.

(140) *Robinwood Mill, Lydgate* (SD 9200 2565) (62168).
Steam-powered cotton-spinning mill built in mid to late 1830s by James and John Ramsbotham to designs by William Fairbairn of Manchester. Bought, unused, by John Fielden who added a water-powered single-storeyed carding shed before opening it in 1848 and running it with Waterside Mill, Langfield (82), and other mills in and around Todmorden. Original pedimented mill (Fig 156; see also Fig 119e) is U-shaped on plan, six storeys high and of non-fireproof construction except over engine house; later sheds on two sides, warehouse, rebuilt in 1889, in front. Associated buildings include workers' housing, especially Robinwood Terrace. See also Figs 268, 270 and Waterside Mill, Langfield (82).

WADSWORTH, West Yorkshire

(141) *Pecket Well Shed, Pecket Well* (SD 9975 2969) (62228).
Cotton-weaving mill built in 1858 as speculation by Pecket Well Weaving Shed Co Ltd; tenanted and then purchased in 1862 by John Wilcock and Sons. Steam-powered single-storeyed weaving shed with attached single-beam engine house and warehouse. Shed doubled in size before attached four-storeyed warehouse, office and sizing place rebuilt after fire in 1873 (Fig 181).

WARLEY (Halifax; Sowerby Bridge), West Yorkshire

(142) *Lumb Mill, Wainstalls (H)* (SE 0470 2888) (62712).
Water-powered cotton-spinning mill built *c*1803 and converted to worsted spinning in 1828. Original mill, of two storeys and attics, six bays long, heightened by one storey in late 1850s. Internal end waterwheel replaced between 1859 and 1862 by short-lived steam engine and by large waterwheel (Fig 207) in attached end wheelhouse. Early 19th-century warehouse and cottage joined to mill (Fig 40).

(143) *Sowerby Bridge Mills, Sowerby Bridge* (SE 0609 2360) (8280).
A fulling mill had existed at Sowerby Bridge since the 16th century, utilising water power provided by the confluence of the Calder and Ryburn rivers. Site largely rebuilt in late 18th century (Fig 151) by Greenup family, merchants and manufacturers, and in 1792 operated as integrated woollen mill with fulling, scribbling, dyewood grinding and spinning in a timber-floored main mill building of four storeys and eleven bays (Fig 37), with handloom weaving and finishing in adjacent structures. The early mill survives but the important loomshop (Fig 30) and cloth dryhouse have been demolished. Historically important as the first known integrated woollen mill in Yorkshire. The site developed in 19th century with addition of steam-powered spinning mill (Carlton Mill, *c*1865–70, six storeys, eleven bays) and of further buildings. Part demolished. See also Fig 261d.

WEST ARDSLEY (Morley), West Yorkshire

(144) *Oak Mills, Morley* (SE 2715 2667) (63609).
Steam-powered integrated woollen mill built in 1906 and expanded in 1929. Original complex, possibly by T A Buttery of Morley and Leeds, included office and warehouse range, timber-floored mill of three storeys and seventeen bays used for weaving on ground floor

and carding and spinning on the upper floors, and detached range with engine and boiler houses and rooms for milling, willeying and rag grinding (Fig 203). Siting of buildings allowed room for expansion of mill (never realised) and construction of weaving shed, built in 1929. One of a sizeable group of late 19th and early 20th-century mills in Morley, Oak Mills is typical in both architectural style (red brick) and in its inclusion of rag-grinding capacity. See also Fig 249d.

(145) *Topcliffe Mill, Morley* (SE 272 266) (63610).
Built in 1906 by established rag merchant and used largely as a warehouse. Morley was an important centre of the recovered wool industry and the town had a number of rag dealers, some also involved in the manufacture of shoddy and mungo from rags: David Banks, Topcliffe Mill's builder, appears to have been both merchant and manufacturer. Mill comprised main three-storeyed ten-bay block with attached engine house and offices and open shed and stable. Mill building is typical local style – red brick with mill name and date picked out in white. Engine house originally had gas engine, probably powering rag-shaking machines on ground floor.

WILSDEN (Bingley), West Yorkshire

(146) *Spring Mill* (SE 0915 3645) (62380).
Steam-powered worsted-spinning mill, built in 1832–4 by worsted manufacturers to supply their domestic weavers. In 1837 site comprised mill, adjoining earlier farmhouse, engine and boiler houses, mechanics' shop, wash house, warehouse and reservoir. Mill was of two storeys and seven bays, with internal end engine house. Integrated working achieved probably after 1850 with addition of small weaving shed. Destructive fire of 1905 caused rebuilding of much of mill and early warehouse.

WOOLDALE (Holmfirth), West Yorkshire

(147) *Stoney Bank Mill* (SE 1569 0988) (63212).
Woollen mill, established probably in early 19th century. Site comprises two mills, one with an engine house, a boiler house and chimney, warehouse, dyehouse, other ancillary buildings, including a cart shed (Fig 113), a range of dwellings, and earthworks and mill dam. Little of pre-1850 date survives: original water-powered mill rebuilt *c*1860 incorporating existing wheelhouse, and steam-powered mill of five storeys and thirteen bays was built at approximately same date. Occupation by woollen manufacturers after 1850 raises question of where powerloom weaving was sited, for no sheds were ever built for this purpose. Water power continued in use into 20th century, although steam engine within the larger mill appears to have powered both main buildings.

(148) *Underbank Mill, Holmfirth* (SE 1463 0742) (63208).
Woollen mill, possibly established in late 18th century as water-powered scribbling mill but surviving today as mill of *c*1825 and later. Site comprises two main mills (*c*1825, four storeys, eleven bays, and *c*1875, three storeys and attic, seven bays) with engine and boiler houses and chimney. Early mill incorporates fragments of original structure, with mullioned windows, and has unusual plan with engine house set one bay in from gable.

(149) *Washpit Mill* (SE 1425 0670) (63211).
Woollen mill, origin unclear but certainly in existence by 1834. Earliest substantial building is water-powered mill dated 1840, of four storeys and attic, seven bays long with internal end wheelhouse and timber floors. Post-1850 expansion involved achievement of integrated working with addition of steam-powered weaving sheds *c*1872 and later, and construction of further spinning capacity. Installation in 1909 of Pollit and Wigzell horizontal engine ('Agnes'), still *in situ* (Fig 221b). See also Fig 128a.

WORTLEY (Leeds), West Yorkshire

(150) *Castleton Mill* (SE 2869 3341) (63384).
Steam-powered fireproof flax-spinning mill of four storeys and eighteen bays built in early 1830s (Fig 154). Warehouse and single-storeyed weaving shed added shortly after 1850. After early 1860s used mainly for linen and woollen manufacture: shed enlarged in 1884 to designs of J M Fawcett of Leeds. Part demolished.

(151) *Stone Bridge Mills* (SE 2560 3286) (63308).
Established pre-1805 as steam-powered woollen scribbling and fulling mill. Early history of occupancy obscure, but by 1819 mill was working wholly or in part as integrated woollen factory, with main mill for powered scribbling, carding and fulling, workshops for hand spinning and hand weaving, finishing shops, including a cloth dryhouse, and wool and cloth warehouses. Surviving buildings include original mill (timber-floored, three storeys, nine bays) with attached end engine house, brick workshops of early 19th-century date (Fig 147), cottages, and post-1850 mills and sheds. Early wagon boiler survives, inverted to serve as water tank (Fig 240). See also Fig 261a, b.

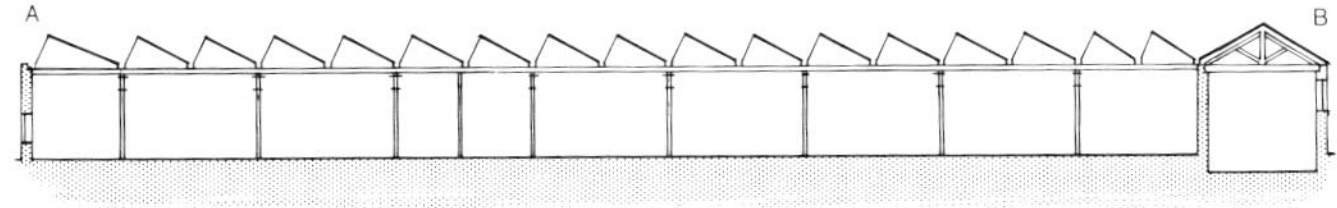

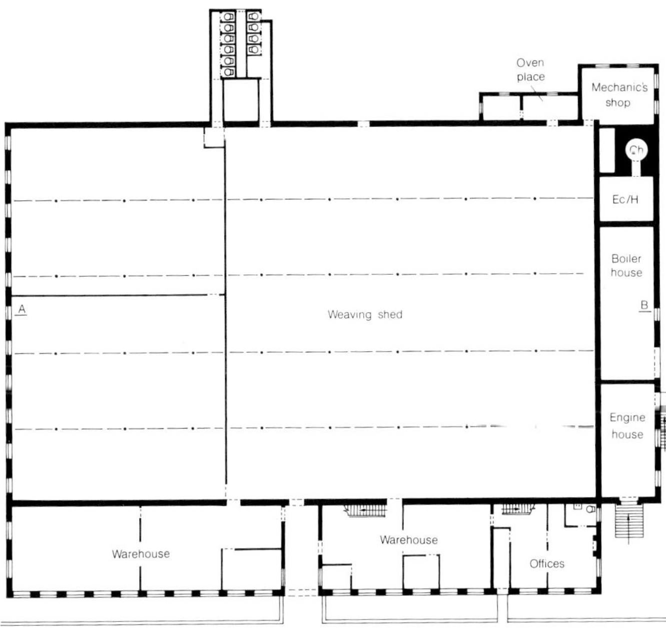

Fig 338 Plan of the original layout of City Shed, Wyke (152) (redrawn from architect's plans).

WYKE, West Yorkshire

(152) *City Shed, later Crown Point Mills* (SE 1550 2735) (62866).
Steam-powered silk-weaving mill built in 1899 to designs by H Fairburn of Wyke. Single-storeyed shed fronted by two-storeyed twenty-two bay office and warehouse block (Fig 338) with free-standing stable and cart shed to rear. Four-bay warehouse extension, with shed to rear, probably built in 1920s.

YEADON (Aireborough), West Yorkshire

(153) *Westfield Mills* (SE 204 409) (63244).
Steam-powered woollen mill built in 1888 by local manufacturer. Unusual single-storeyed layout with all departments in integrated mill housed in two blocks of sheds. Main block had engine house centrally on one side, with preparatory processes (willeying, scribbling and carding), spinning, weaving, and wet and dry finishing processes arranged around it. Dyehouse, warehouse, further willeying space and offices made up smaller shed, sited across a narrow yard from main block. Similar layout to Alverthorpe Mills, Alverthorpe with Thornes (4).

YORK, North Yorkshire

(154) *Lawrence Street Flax Mill* (SE 6113 5133) (60732).
Built as an integrated flax-spinning and linen-weaving mill shortly before 1816, the spinning undertaken in a steam-powered fireproof mill of three storeys and ten bays (Fig 35), hand heckling and weaving in adjacent buildings. Cloth bleached at Heslington Bleach Works, Heslington (54). Warehouse added to mill before *c*1825, when second fireproof mill of four storeys and thirteen bays built with engine house and boiler house powering whole range. After 1872 used by comb makers, then by hide and tallow brokers. Limited demolition.

Gazetteer

This gazetteer lists all sites for which files were created during the survey of textile mills in Yorkshire by the Royal Commission on the Historical Monuments of England, the aims and scope of which are explained in the Introduction. It also contains files on previously demolished sites, some of them recorded as part of the Royal Commission's work on threatened buildings.

The gazetteer is arranged alphabetically by township, the unit of secular administration in use for much of the period under review, and then by mill name. Not all townships lie in a civil parish of the same name, and where they differ the name of the civil parish is given in brackets after that of the township. Where townships lie in more than one civil parish, the names of the relevant civil parishes are given. Although all the sites listed once lay within the historic county of Yorkshire, the county names are those established in 1974. Individual entries contain the following information: mill name; national grid reference; code letter indicating level of archive; National Monuments Record file number. The code letters refer to the following types of record:

A Detailed report, including historical account and architectural description, on part or whole of textile mill site, some with measured surveys, all with photographs (aerial photographs, 35mm and often large format).

B Brief record, usually comprising an initial survey form indicating range of buildings surviving at time of visit, and generally accompanied by aerial photographs and at least one ground photograph. Some published or unpublished text or illustrative material may also be included.

C Records of textile mills already demolished at time of initial survey and comprising various combinations of published and unpublished text and illustrative material.

A and B are equivalent to Levels 3 and 1 as defined in RCHME *Recording Historic Buildings: A Descriptive Specification* (1990). An asterisk following an entry indicates a mill or other site which is described briefly in the Selective Inventory on pages 200–23.

The archive which results from this survey is available for consultation in the National Buildings Record at the Royal Commission on the Historical Monuments of England, which is currently at Fortress House, 23 Savile Row, London W1X 2JQ. Copies of reports on sites in West Yorkshire, and an index to the complete archive, are held by the West Yorkshire Archaeology Service, 14 St John's North, Wakefield WF1 3QA.

ADDINGHAM, West Yorkshire

Breare's Mill SE 0805 4985 (B) 62329
Burnside Mill SE 0758 4979 (B) 62332
High Mill SE 0821 5021 (A) 62271*
High Mill SE 0720 4990 (B) 62334
Loomshop, Chapel Street SE 0756 4986 (A) 62331*
Loomshops, The Rookery SE 0785 4984 (A) 34366*
Low Mills SE 0910 4925 (B) 34368
97 Main Street SE 0758 4983 (B) 62372
Mill SE 0770 4970 (B) 62330
Town End Mill (see High Mill, 62334)
Wolseley Shed SE 0750 4979 (B) 62333

ADEL CUM ECCUP (Leeds), West Yorkshire

Scotland Mill SE 2849 3875 (C) 63421

AIRTON, West Yorkshire

Airton Mill SD 9035 5929 (B) 62114
Bell Busk Mill SD 9051 5629 (C) 62115

ALLERTON (Bradford), West Yorkshire

Allerton Mill SE 1215 3416 (B) 62408
Crossley Hall Dyeworks SE 1325 3310 (B) 62425

Dyeworks SE 1303 3337 (B) 62418
Fairweather Green Mills SE 1350 3335 (B) 62420
Hedge Nook Mill SE 1205 3410 (B) 62409
Napier Works SE 1340 3322 (B) 62421
Prospect Mill SE 1240 3414 (B) 62410
Sydney Works SE 1340 3330 (B) 62419
Top Mill SE 1185 3440 (C) 62406

ALMONDBURY (Huddersfield), West Yorkshire

Bankfield Mills SE 1569 1625 (B) 63126
Birks Mill SE 175 148 (C) 63182
Broadfield Mills SE 1385 1520 (B) 63071
Freehold Mill SE 1396 1387 (B) 63075
King's Mills (part) SE 1489 1597 (B) 63101
King's Mill SE 1486 1586 (B) 63102
Little Royd Mill SE 1438 1582 (C) 63103
Newsome Mills SE 1435 1490 (B) 63110
Northfield Mills SE 1664 1448 (B) 63133
Perseverance Mills (see Broadfield Mills)
Queen's Mill SE 1425 1572 (B) 63105
St Helen's Mill SE 1718 1495 (B) 63141
Scarr Mill SE 1383 1509 (B) 63072
Taylor Hill Mill SE 1350 1456 (B) 63073
Thorpeside Mills (see Taylor Hill Mill)

ALVERTHORPE WITH THORNES (Wakefield), West Yorkshire

Alverthorpe Mills SE 3090 2140 (A) 63624*
Balne Lane Mills SE 3215 2135 (B) 63628
Balne Mill (see Balne Lane Mills)
Bective Mills SE 310 211 (B) 63627
Calder Dyeworks SE 327 187 (B) 63767
Clarkson's Mill SE 3208 2055 (B) 63629
Flanshaw Mill SE 3080 2095 (A) 63625*
Hebble Mill (see Bective Mills)
Oakes Mill (see Flanshaw Mill)
Portobello Mills SE 335 195 (B) 63768
Thornes Mill SE 327 190 (A) 63766*
West Riding Mills (see Calder Dyeworks)
Westgate Common Mill (see Clarkson's Mill)

ARDSLEY (Barnsley), South Yorkshire

Stairfoot Bleachworks SE 3729 0542 (C) 63795
Stairfoot Dyeworks (see Stairfoot Bleachworks)

ARMLEY (Leeds), West Yorkshire

Antwerp Mill SE 2650 3331 (B) 63313
Armley Mills SE 2758 3417 (B) 63320*
Bankfield Mills SE 2755 3380 (B) 63323
Tong Road Mills SE 2730 3305 (C) 63325
Winker Green Mill SE 2700 3369 (A) 63324*

ARNCLIFFE, North Yorkshire

Mill SD 9302 7189 (B) 63824

ASKRIGG, North Yorkshire

Flaxmill Farm SD 9448 9105 (B) 63825

AUSTONLEY (Holmfirth), West Yorkshire

Austonley Mill SE 1165 0685 (C) 63227
Bank End Mill (see Austonley Mill)
Battye Lower Mill SE 1156 0683 (C) 63231
Bilberry Mill SE 104 070 (C) 63229
Black Sike Mill SE 122 080 (C) 63230
Bottoms Mill SE 1315 0745 (B) 63200
Digley Mills SE 1141 0688 (C) 63233
Hinchliffe Mill SE 1275 0709 (B) 63193
Holmbridge Dyeworks SE 1272 0669 (C) 63238
Holmbridge Mill SE 120 066 (A) 63194*
Low Brow Bottoms Mill (see Battye Lower Mill)
Upper Digley Mill SE 109 070 (C) 63234
Yew Tree Mills SE 1255 0714 (B) 63192

AYSGARTH, North Yorkshire

Yore Mill SE 0115 8865 (B) 63828

BAILDON, West Yorkshire

Baildon Mills SE 1545 3980 (B) 62458
Charlestown Mill SE 162 386 (C) 62512
Dyeworks SE 1589 3860 (B) 62461
Lower Holme Mills SE 1530 3810 (B) 62462
Mill SE 1544 3966 (B) 62676
Prospect Works SE 1555 3980 (B) 62459
Sandals Mill SE 1521 3914 (B) 62460

BAINBRIDGE, North Yorkshire

Silk Mill SD 9125 8710 (A) 63823*

BARKISLAND (Ripponden), West Yorkshire

Barkisland Mills SE 0655 1972 (B) 62973
Bowers Mills SE 0695 2015 (A) 62742*

Chapel Field Mill SE 0408 1971 (B) 62961
Firth House Mills SE 0633 1829 (B) 62975
Krumlin Mills SE 0545 1835 (B) 62966
Ripponden Mill SE 0400 1972 (B) 62960

BARNOLDSWICK, Lancashire

Bancroft Mill SD 8745 4610 (B) 62148
Bankfield Shed SD 8815 4715 (B) 62152
Barnoldswick Mill SD 8788 4719 (B) 62150
Butt's Mill SD 8750 4670 (B) 62146
Calf Hall Mill SD 8740 4660 (B) 62147
Coates Mill SD 8824 4742 (B) 62153
Fern Bank Shed SD 8705 4715 (B) 62145
Long Ing Shed SD 8795 4730 (B) 62151
Mill SD 8860 4685 (B) 62154
Mill SD 8840 4690 (B) 62155
Moss Shed SD 8845 4675 (B) 62156
Well House Mill SD 8805 4705 (B) 62149
Westfield Mill SD 8735 4735 (B) 62144

BARNSLEY, South Yorkshire

Beevor Hall Bleachworks SE 3565 0635 (B) 63794
Bleachworks SE 34 07 (C) 63805
Borespring Mill SE 3424 0623 (C) 63800
Dyeworks SE 34 06 (C) 63806
Green Foot Bleachworks SE 3388 0822 (C) 63801
Hope Dyeworks SE 3405 0619 (C) 63799
Hope Mill SE 3410 0645 (A) 63790*
Hope Works (see Hope Mill)
Hoyle Mill Bleachworks SE 3614 0659 (C) 63798
Malton Place, 20–26 Pitt Street SE 3425 0619 (A) 63796
Oak Mill SE 3398 0625 (C) 63788
Old Mill SE 3499 0720 (C) 63793
Old Mill Bleachworks SE 348 072 (C) 63792
Peel Street Mill (see Taylor's Mill)
Pinder Oaks Bleachworks SE 35 05 (C) 63804
Rob Royd Bleachworks SE 3308 0433 (C) 63803
Rodney Row SE 3501 0600 (C) 63797
Shaw Mill SE 3390 0600 (C) 63789
Taylor's Mill SE 3424 0633 (B) 63791*
Union Mill SE 3405 0635 (C) 63811
Utilitas Works SE 3398 0640 (C) 63812
Warehouse, Eastgate SE 3447 0659 (B) 63809
Warehouse, St Mary's Place SE 343 065 (A) 63808*

BARUGH (Darton), South Yorkshire

Red Brook Bleachworks SE 3215 0770 (B) 63787

BATLEY, West Yorkshire

Albert Mills SE 2442 2274 (B) 63532
Albion Mill SE 2449 2277 (A) 63535*
Blakeridge Mills SE 2389 2440 (A) 63485*
Bottoms Mill (part) SE 2475 2374 (C) 63520
Bottoms Mill SE 2475 2384 (B) 63519
Bradford Road, 203 SE 244 227 (B) 63681
Bradford Road, 209 SE 244 228 (B) 63682
Branch Road Mills SE 2425 2445 (C) 63668
Brights Mill SE 2469 2340 (B) 63524
Brookroyd Mill SE 2299 2560 (B) 63459
Bullrush Mills SE 2355 2512 (B) 63481
Carlinghow Mill SE 2348 2525 (B) 63480
Carlinghow Mills SE 238 247 (A) 63484*
Carr Bridge Mills SE 2455 2283 (B) 63530
Carr Dyke Mill SE 2441 2272 (B) 63533
Carr Top Mills SE 2376 2286 (C) 63492
Cheapside Mills SE 2485 2410 (A) 63513*
Clerk Green Mill SE 2392 2395 (B) 63488
Clothing Factory SE 2475 2391 (B) 63643
Commercial Mill SE 2455 2417 (C) 63512
Dock Ing Mill SE 2360 2495 (B) 63482
Fountain Mill SE 2383 2477 (B) 63645
Healey Lane Mill SE 2329 2405 (B) 63487
Hick Lane Mills SE 246 240 (C) 63662
Hick Well Mill SE 2460 2396 (B) 63515
Highfield Mills SE 2275 2340 (B) 63465
Ings Mill SE 2458 2298 (B) 63527
Little Orm Mill SE 2392 2410 (B) 63486
Livingstone Mills SE 2449 2313 (B) 63525
Mill SE 2455 2390 (B) 63647
Mill SE 2285 2559 (B) 63650
New Ing Mills SE 2441 2390 (A) 63516*
Old Mill SE 244 242 (C) 63661
Park Mills SE 2402 2460 (C) 63509
Park Works (see Carlinghow Mill)
Perseverance Mill SE 2449 2431 (C) 63511
Perseverance Mill SE 2440 2285 (B) 63671
Prospect Mill SE 2401 2468 (B) 63508
Providence Mill SE 2259 2564 (B) 63457
Providence Mill SE 2412 2457 (C) 63510
Providence Street Mills SE 2418 2410 (C) 63666
Providence Works SE 2461 2421 (C) 63667
Purlwell Mills SE 2419 2378 (B) 63518
Ridings Mill SE 2231 2479 (B) 63460
Spa Field Mills SE 2391 2286 (B) 63493
Spring Mill SE 2314 2319 (B) 63490
Spring Mill SE 231 248 (C) 63870
Springwell Mills SE 2449 2295 (B) 63528
Staincliffe Low Mills SE 2331 2300 (B) 63491
Staincliffe Mills SE 2303 2327 (B) 63489
Station Road, 10-14 SE 248 238 (B) 63708

Valley Mills SE 2439 2398 (B) 63517
Victoria Mill SE 2375 2478 (A) 63483*
Victoria Mills SE 2455 2287 (B) 63529
Warehouse, Carr Street SE 244 228 (B) 63683
Warehouse, Station Road SE 2477 2329 (B) 63707
Warehouse, Station Road SE 2473 2392 (B) 63706
Warwick Road Mills SE 2445 2303 (B) 63526
Wensleydale Mills SE 2272 2565 (B) 63458
Wheatcroft Mills SE 2440 2280 (B) 63531
Wilton Mills SE 2375 2489 (B) 63646
Warehouse, Firths Yard SE 24 22 (B) 63684

BEESTON (Leeds), West Yorkshire

Grove Hall Mills SE 2900 2995 (B) 63622

BENTHAM, North Yorkshire

High Bentham Mill SD 6660 6875 (B) 63814
Low Mill SD 6490 6929 (B) 63813

BEWERLEY, North Yorkshire

Foster Beck Mill SE 1478 6641 (B) 63841
Hollin House Mill SE 1708 6391 (C) 63830
Riggs Mill SE 1557 6533 (B) 63845

BILTON WITH HARROGATE, North Yorkshire

Bleach Green SE 310 565 (C) 63860
Bleach Yard SE 317 575 (C) 63861

BINGLEY, West Yorkshire

Airedale Mills SE 1035 4077 (B) 62304
Angora Mill SE 1130 3890 (B) 62403
Argyll Mill SE 1105 3928 (B) 62632
Beckfoot Mill SE 1031 3849 (B) 62394
Bingley Mills SE 1085 3955 (B) 62389
Bowling Green Mills SE 1077 3945 (B) 62390
Britannia Mills SE 1125 3912 (B) 62399
Britannia Works (see Britannia Mills)
Castlefields Mill SE 0992 4030 (B) 62301
Cottingley Mill SE 1180 3744 (B) 62404
Cross Roads Mill SE 0480 3800 (B) 62678
Crossflatts Mill SE 1035 4060 (B) 62306
Cullingworth Mills SE 0685 3670 (B) 43595
Dubb Mill SE 1115 3912 (B) 62400
Ebor Mill SE 1120 3910 (B) 62401
Eldwick Beck Mill SE 1260 4050 (C) 62307
Eldwick Moulding Mill SE 1210 4015 (B) 62308
Ellar Carr Mill SE 0656 3699 (A) 62373*
Harden Mill SE 0851 3835 (B) 62376
Holroyd Mill SE 1010 4160 (B) 62303
Lees Mill SE 0385 3759 (A) 62650*
Lily Croft Mills SE 1099 3909 (B) 62393
Limefield Mill SE 1040 4065 (B) 62305
Monarch Mills SE 1110 3920 (B) 62398
Park Road Mills SE 1096 3930 (B) 62391
Stanley Mill SE 1090 3925 (B) 62392
Tannery SE 0659 3621 (B) 62605
Vale Mill SE 0380 3822 (B) 62645
Victoria Mills SE 1125 3899 (B) 62402
Woodfield Mill SE 0714 3711 (B) 62606

BIRSTWITH, North Yorkshire

Wreaks Mill SE 2440 5965 (B) 63859

BISHOP THORNTON, North Yorkshire

High Mill SE 2525 6270 (A) 63838*
Low Mill SE 2552 6245 (B) 63840
Render Mill (see Woodfield Mill)
Woodfield Mill SE 2359 6339 (A) 63843*

BOLTON (Bradford), West Yorkshire

Bolton Woods Mill SE 1595 3620 (B) 62473
Mill SE 1615 3415 (B) 62514
Oswin Mills SE 1565 3590 (B) 62475

BOWLING (Bradford), West Yorkshire

Albion Dyeworks SE 1795 3085 (B) 62560
Albion Mill SE 1798 3080 (B) 62562
Alma Mill SE 1855 3158 (B) 62586
Bowling Dyeworks SE 167 315 (B) 62536
Bowling Mills SE 1658 3197 (B) 62534*
Broad Lane Mill SE 1860 3205 (B) 62584
Cabinet Works, former SE 1700 3220 (B) 62622
Central Mills SE 1619 3079 (B) 62539
Duiness Street Mill SE 1659 3225 (B) 62525
Globe Mills SE 1698 3225 (B) 62528
Harold Mills SE 1755 3215 (B) 62559
Holroyd Mills SE 1542 3042 (B) 62508
Ivy Mills SE 1655 3219 (B) 62526
Ladywell Mills SE 1690 3220 (B) 62527
Laundry SE 1712 3211 (B) 62623
Marshfield Dyeworks SE 1585 3108 (B) 62504
Marshfield Mills SE 1580 3100 (B) 62505

Melange Mills SE 1646 3192 (B) 62533*
Mill SE 1671 3239 (B) 62524
Mill SE 1732 3221 (B) 62625
Mill SE 1819 3099 (B) 62626
Moorside Mill SE 1725 3204 (B) 62624
New Industry Mill SE 1975 3085 (B) 62588
New Mill (see Albion Mill)
Parkside Mill SE 1620 3082 (B) 62538
Peace Mills SE 1645 3096 (B) 62537
Prospect Mills SE 1715 3225 (C) 62557
Recta Mill SE 1800 3092 (B) 62561
Spring Mill SE 1645 3195 (B) 62530*
Springfield Mill SE 1646 3182 (B) 62533*
Springhead Mills SE 1636 3192 (B) 62532
Terry's Mill SE 1820 3118 (B) 62587
Upper Croft Mills SE 1835 3232 (B) 62583
Victoria Mills SE 1739 3219 (B) 62558
West Bowling Shed SE 1611 3070 (B) 62540

BRADFORD, West Yorkshire

Albion Works SE 1865 3263 (B) 62580
Barkerend Mills SE 1745 3345 (A) 62549*
Bower Green Shed SE 1829 3280 (B) 62575
Bradford Moor Mill SE 1870 3320 (B) 62571
Carlisle Mills SE 15 33 (C) 62674
Cashmere Works SE 1789 3266 (B) 62556
City Paper Mills SE 1686 3348 (B) 62631
College Mill SE 1690 3331 (B) 62669
Conditioning House SE 1648 3390 (B) 62682
Croft Boiler Works SE 1822 3275 (B) 62574
Dyeworks SE 166 331 (C) 62679
Eastbrook Mills SE 1700 3295 (B) 62552
Exchange Mills SE 167 327 (C) 62672
Garden Mill SE 1587 3301 (B) 62614
Greenhill Mill SE 1840 3280 (B) 62576
Greystone Mill SE 1772 3340 (B) 62551
Harris Mills SE 1714 3328 (B) 62630
Harris Street Works SE 1709 3327 (B) 62548
High Street Mills (see Barkerend Mills)
Hillside Mills SE 1790 3275 (B) 62555
Holling's Mill SE 15 33 (C) 62673
Hollings Mill SE 1580 3315 (B) 62492
Holme Mill SE 1590 3300 (B) 62612
Hope Mills SE 185 328 (C) 62577
Hubert Shed SE 1802 3272 (B) 62572
Industry Mill SE 1548 3336 (B) 62485
Junction Mill SE 1870 3284 (B) 62579
Junction Mill SE 1582 3302 (B) 62613
Kyme Mill (see Bradford Moor Mill)
Lonsdale Works (see Hillside Mills)
Midland Mills SE 1649 3380 (B) 62518
Mill SE 1588 3301 (B) 62491
Mill SE 1605 3310 (B) 62495
Mill SE 1596 3303 (B) 62496
Mill SE 1530 3348 (B) 62608
Mill SE 1761 3249 (B) 62621
Mill SE 1695 3329 (B) 62670
Moorside Mill (see Bradford Moor Mill)
Mount Street Mills SE 1743 3278 (B) 62553
Norcroft Dyeworks SE 1545 3330 (B) 62604
North Brook Mills SE 1649 3372 (C) 62519
North Vale Mills SE 1645 3398 (B) 62517
Onward Works SE 1753 3285 (B) 62629
Penny Oaks Mill SE 1770 3282 (C) 62554
Pit Lane Mills SE 1749 3325 (B) 62550
Priestley's Warehouse SE 167 331 (B) 62686
Providence Mills SE 1590 3311 (B) 62493
Raglan Foundry SE 1812 3279 (B) 62628
Raglan Mills SE 1809 3272 (B) 62573
Rock Mills SE 1710 3330 (B) 62547
Soho Mills SE 1589 3308 (B) 62610
The Wool Exchange SE 1640 3311 (B) 62684
Thompson Shed SE 1599 3319 (B) 62494
Vicuna Works SE 1876 3291 (B) 62578
Wapping Works SE 1690 3375 (B) 62520
Warehouse SE 1589 3301 (B) 62611
Warehouse: Quebec Street SE 1615 3294 (B) 62683
Wool Warehouse SE 167 331 (B) 62685
Woolston Warehouses SE 1596 3316 (B) 62615
Zetland Mill SE 1654 3401 (A) 62516*

BRAMLEY (Leeds), West Yorkshire

Aire Vale Dyeworks SE 239 367 (B) 63281
Airedale Mills SE 2290 3610 (B) 63262
Allen Brigg Mill SE 2283 3362 (B) 63270
Arrowvale Mill (see Aire Vale Dyeworks)
Bath Lane Mill SE 2429 3453 (B) 63300
Bramley Mill SE 2315 3485 (B) 63285
Britannia Mill SE 2342 3421 (C) 63288
Broad Lane Mill (see Bramley Mill)
Cape Mills SE 2242 3535 (A) 63266*
Catherine Mills SE 2488 3570 (B) 63297
Craven Mills SE 2474 3449 (B) 63302
Elmfield Mill SE 2485 3435 (B) 63304
Empire Mills SE 2335 3515 (C) 63283
Hough End Mills SE 244 336 (C) 63393
Low Mill SE 2215 3449 (B) 63267
Mill SE 2486 3349 (B) 63388
Moss Bridge Works (see Airedale Mills)
Prospect Works SE 2314 3493 (B) 63284
Ross Mills SE 2365 3589 (B) 63282
St Catherine's Mill (see Catherine Mills)
Spring Valley Mills (see Low Mill)
Springfield Mill SE 2482 3449 (A) 63303

Swinnow Grange Mill SE 2322 3461 (B) 63287
Swinnow Lane Mill (see Bramley Mill)
Town End Mills SE 2512 3441 (B) 63306
Victoria Mill SE 2409 3441 (B) 63301
Waterloo Mill SE 2473 3540 (C) 63299
Wellington Mill SE 2473 3555 (C) 63298
West Field Mills SE 2337 3495 (B) 63286

BREARTON, North Yorkshire

Scotton Mill SE 3150 5857 (B) 63852

BURLEY-IN-WHARFEDALE (Ilkley), West Yorkshire

Greenholme Mills SE 1685 4680 (B) 62310
Rombalds Moor Bleachworks SE 1594 4450 (C) 62309

CALVERLEY WITH FARSLEY (Pudsey), West Yorkshire

Calverley Mills SE 2206 3695 (C) 63261
Bank Bottom Mill SE 2229 3560 (B) 63264
Broom Mill SE 2230 3540 (B) 63265
Burlington Works SE 1930 3405 (B) 62596
Clover Greaves Mill SE 202 370 (C) 63871
Farsley Beck Bottom Mill (see Broom Mill)
Holly Park Mills SE 2035 3655 (B) 63251
Lydgate Mill SE 2015 3700 (C) 63250
Mill SE 1912 3388 (B) 62598
Providence Mill SE 2183 3429 (B) 63256
Ravenscliffe Mills SE 1950 3675 (B) 62595
Rushton Mills SE 1915 3390 (B) 62597
Springfield Mills SE 2210 3570 (B) 63263
Sunny Banks Mill SE 2170 3535 (B) 63255
Thornbury Shed SE 1919 3385 (B) 62599

CARLETON, North Yorkshire

Carleton Mill SD 9720 4970 (B) 62142
Mill SD 9735 4964 (B) 62143
The Wend, Carleton SD 9710 4960 (B) 62158

CARTWORTH (Holmfirth), West Yorkshire

Dob Mill SE 1240 0669 (B) 63226
Dover Mill SE 1450 0699 (B) 63209
Green Lane Mill SE 1443 0682 (B) 63210
Hinchliffe Mill SE 1275 0709 (B) 63193
Holmbridge Mill SE 120 066 (A) 63194*
Jane Wood Dyehouse SE 144 071 (C) 63235
Lower Mills SE 1393 0800 (B) 63195
Perseverance Mills SE 1358 0775 (C) 63197
Ribbleden Mill SE 1428 0810 (B) 63206
Swan Bank Mill SE 1450 0775 (B) 63207
Washpit Mill SE 1425 0670 (A) 63211*

CHURWELL (Morley), West Yorkshire

Gelderd Road Dyeworks SE 2626 3010 (B) 63316
Laneside Mills SE 265 290 (B) 63572

CLAYTON, West Yorkshire

Beck Mills SE 1186 3148 (B) 62407
Highgate Mills SE 1214 3072 (B) 62414
Oak Mills SE 1205 3160 (B) 62412

CLAYTON WEST, West Yorkshire

Kaye's Mill SE 2608 1078 (B) 63749
Park Mills SE 2610 1159 (B) 63748
Spring Grove Mill SE 2525 1070 (B) 63745

CLECKHEATON, West Yorkshire

Albert Mill SE 1672 2570 (B) 62870
Brook Mill SE 1875 2510 (B) 62882
Brookhouse Mills SE 18 25 (C) 62941
Butts Mills SE 1866 2529 (C) 62881
Central Mill SE 1915 2575 (B) 62894
Clarence Mill SE 1865 2507 (C) 62883
Exchange Mills SE 1865 2625 (B) 62876
Mill SE 1819 2559 (B) 62925
Moor End Mill SE 1909 2576 (B) 62893
Moorland Mills SE 1885 2605 (B) 62877
Netherfield Mills SE 1925 2549 (B) 62895
Northgate Mills SE 1891 2549 (B) 62923
Old Robin Mill SE 19 25 (B) 62951
Prospect Mill SE 1669 2554 (B) 62871
Prospect Mills SE 1870 2547 (B) 62880
Scandinavia Mills SE 1865 2635 (B) 62875
St Peg Mills SE 1949 2528 (B) 62897
Victoria Mills (see Moor End Mill)
Water Lane Mill SE 1890 2593 (B) 62879
Waterfield Mill SE 1899 2599 (B) 62878
West End Mills SE 1815 2503 (C) 62885
Westcliffe Mill SE 1828 2540 (B) 62924
Wharfe Works SE 1840 2495 (B) 62884
Woodroyd Mills (see Westcliffe Mill)

CLIFFORD, West Yorkshire

Clifford Mill SE 4328 4421 (B) 63867

CLIFTON (Brighouse), West Yorkshire

Bailliff Bridge Mill SE 149 251 (B) 62847
Clifton Mills (see Bailliff Bridge Mill)
Grove Mills SE 1499 2275 (B) 62861
Kirklees Mills SE 1699 2195 (B) 62943
Little John Mill SE 1498 2295 (B) 62920

CLIVIGER (Todmorden), West Yorkshire

Caldervale Mill SD 9080 2635 (B) 62163
Cornholme Mills SD 9070 2635 (C) 62164
Glen Dye Works SD 9081 2661 (B) 62162
Portsmouth Mill SD 8995 2635 (B) 62161

CONONLEY, North Yorkshire

Station Mills SD 9936 4685 (B) 62124

COWGILL (Dent), Cumbria

Loomshop SD 7580 8692 (B) 63816

COWLING, North Yorkshire

Acre Shed SD 9729 4305 (B) 62133
Carr Mills SD 9731 4279 (B) 62134
Croft Mill SD 9750 4335 (B) 62131
Freegate Mill SD 9640 4290 (B) 62135
Ickornshaw Mill SD 9685 4230 (B) 62129
Lumb Mill SD 9878 4448 (B) 62126
Mill SD 9800 4380 (B) 62130
Royd Mill SD 9739 4320 (B) 62132

CUDWORTH, South Yorkshire

Midland Bleachworks SE 3810 0890 (C) 63807

CUMBERWORTH, West Yorkshire

Elm Mills SE 2305 1081 (B) 63739
Greenside Mills SE 2339 1092 (B) 63738
High Bridge Mill SE 2470 1010 (B) 63742
Ings Dyeworks SE 2481 1015 (B) 63744
Ings Mill (see Ings Dyeworks)
Nortonthorpe Mills (see High Bridge Mill)
Tenter Croft Mills SE 2332 1078 (B) 63740
Twin Mills SE 2479 1020 (B) 63743

DACRE, North Yorkshire

Banks Mill SE 1999 6235 (B) 63836
Dacre Banks Mill (see Banks Mill)

DALTON (Huddersfield), West Yorkshire

Bankfield Mills SE 1569 1625 (B) 63126
Bradley Mills SE 1560 1773 (B) 63118
Dalton Dyeworks SE 1575 1690 (B) 63123
Dalton Mills SE 1701 1725 (B) 63136
Fearnheads Dyeworks (see Dalton Dyeworks)
Green Lea Mill SE 1720 1675 (B) 63137
Greenside Mills SE 1695 1640 (B) 63138
Minerva Works SE 1740 1740 (B) 63135
Rookery Mills SE 1560 1625 (B) 63125
Storth's Mill SE 1535 1638 (B) 63124
Upper Bankfield Mill SE 15 16 (C) 63186
Water Royd Mill SE 1519 1695 (B) 63119
Westfield Mills SE 1590 1698 (B) 63172

DENBY (Denby Dale), West Yorkshire

Birds Edge Mill SE 2021 0792 (B) 63776
Cuttlehurst Mill SE 2465 0994 (B) 63782
Dearnside Mill SE 2279 0833 (B) 63779
Hartcliffe Mills SE 2230 0830 (B) 63777
Inkerman Mill SE 2310 0807 (C) 63781
Lower Putting Mill SE 2391 0923 (C) 63780
Pudding Mill (see Lower Putting Mill)
Springfield Mill SE 2282 0842 (B) 63778

DEWSBURY, West Yorkshire

Albert Mills SE 2286 2297 (B) 63466
Aldams Mill SE 2411 2149 (C) 63544
Anchor Mill (see Aldams Mill)
Batley Carr Mills SE 2435 2265 (A) 63534*
Batley Carr Old Mill SE 2434 2253 (B) 63537
Britannia Mill SE 2445 2145 (A) 63549
Calder Bank Mills SE 239 211 (A) 63495*
Calder Mills SE 2470 2132 (C) 63550
Calder Steam Mill SE 2370 2071 (B) 63640
Calder Works (see Calder Steam Mill)
Carlton Mill SE 2430 2232 (B) 63539
Carr Mills SE 2449 2265 (B) 63536
Cloth Hall Mills SE 2455 2205 (B) 63542
Crown Mills SE 2295 2245 (B) 63468
Dewsbury Mills SE 2405 2050 (B) 63556
Dyeware Mills (see Calder Steam Mill)
Eastfield Mills SE 2502 2129 (B) 63568
Ellis's Mill (see Batley Carr Mills)
Hirstland Mill SE 2426 2233 (B) 63538
Kiln Mill SE 2400 2135 (B) 63545
Low Mill SE 2265 2195 (A) 63469*
Machells' Warehouse, 128 Bradford Road
SE 244 224 (A) 63670*
Meadow Mill SE 2436 2235 (B) 63540

Moor End Mill SE 2274 2287 (A) 63467*
New Wakefield Mill SE 2475 2205 (B) 63543
Old Mill (see Batley Carr Old Mill)
Providènce Mill SE 2399 2120 (B) 63494
Providence Mills SE 2447 2211 (B) 63641
Rag Warehouse SE 2448 2262 (B) 63642
Ratcliffe Mill SE 2393 2020 (B) 63500
Ravenswharf Mills SE 2315 2057 (B) 63497
Sands Mill SE 2539 2056 (B) 63570
Scout Hill Mills SE 2350 2082 (B) 63660
Shoddy Mill SE 2330 2062 (B) 63496
Spinkwell Mills SE 243 220 (A) 63541*
Victoria Works (see Kiln Mill)
Warehouse, 23 Bond Street SE 244 217 (B) 63718
Warehouse, 23 Bradford Road SE 2442 2218 (B) 63672
Warehouse, 25 Bradford Road SE 244 221 (B) 63673
Warehouse, 27 Bradford Road SE 2442 2220 (B) 63674
Warehouse, 29 Bradford Road SE 244 222 (B) 63675
Warehouse, 39–41 Bradford Road SE 244 223 (B) 63676
Warehouse, 40 Bradford Road SE 244 221 (B) 63704
Warehouse, 42 Bradford Road SE 244 221 (B) 63703
Warehouse, 44–46 Bradford Road SE 244 221 (B) 63702
Warehouse, 52 Bradford Road SE 2447 2220 (B) 63701
Warehouse, 55–57 Bradford Road SE 2441 2231 (B) 63677
Warehouse, 62–64 Bradford Road SE 244 222 (B) 63699
Warehouse behind 64 Bradford Road SE 244 222 (B) 63700
Warehouse, 86 Bradford Road SE 244 223 (B) 63697
Warehouse, 88–90 Bradford Road SE 2444 2235 (B) 63694
Warehouse, 89 Bradford Road SE 244 224 (B) 63679
Warehouse, 100 Bradford Road SE 2445 2239 (B) 63693
Warehouse, 102 Bradford Road SE 244 224 (B) 63691
Warehouse, 103 Bradford Road SE 243 225 (B) 63680
Warehouse, 130 Bradford Road SE 244 224 (B) 63689
Warehouse, 138 Bradford Road SE 2445 2250 (B) 63688
Warehouse, 146–150 Bradford Road SE 224 226 (B) 63687
Warehouse, 152 Bradford Road SE 224 226 (B) 63686
Warehouse, 166 Bradford Road SE 244 226 (B) 63685
Warehouse, Carlton Road SE 243 223 (B) 63678
Warehouse, Lower Peel Street SE 2449 2230 (B) 63698
Warehouse, North Street SE 244 224 (B) 63690
Warehouse, 5 Upper South Street SE 2448 2337 (B) 63696
Warehouse, 12 Upper South Street SE 2447 2235 (B) 63695
Warehouse, Ward Street SE 244 224 (B) 63692
Warehouse, 3 Wellington Road SE 244 218 (B) 63720
Warehouse, 7 Wellington Road SE 244 218 (B) 63721
Warehouse, 9 Wellington Road SE 244 218 (B) 63722
Warehouse, 15 Wellington Road SE 2440 2178 (B) 63723
Warehouse, 23–25 Wellington Road SE 243 216 (B) 63705
Warehouse, 26 Wellington Road SE 243 216 (B) 63724
Warehouse, 28 Wellington Road SE 243 216 (B) 63725
Warehouse, 13 Wellington Street SE 2442 2181 (B) 63719
West End Mills SE 2397 2129 (C) 63669

DODWORTH, South Yorkshire

Weaver's cottage SE 31 05 (B) 63810

DRIGHLINGTON (Morley), West Yorkshire

Greystone Mill SE 2379 2837 (B) 63479
Moorland Mill SE 2229 2870 (B) 63448
New Mill SE 2205 2855 (B) 63449
Valley Mills SE 2350 2990 (B) 63477

EARBY, Lancashire

Albion Mill SD 9060 4675 (B) 62140
Brook Shed SD 9070 4640 (B) 62137
Dotcliffe Mill SD 9060 4459 (B) 62127
Grove Mill SD 9076 4695 (B) 62139
Spring Mill SD 9100 4655 (B) 62141
Victoria Mill SD 9065 4660 (B) 62138

EAST ARDSLEY (Morley), West Yorkshire

Ardsley Mills SE 2975 2570 (A) 63623*
Perseverance Mill SE 3115 2578 (B) 63626

ECCLESHILL, West Yorkshire

Albion Mills SE 1869 3740 (B) 62566
Apperdale Mills SE 1919 3765 (B) 62634
Apperley Brook Mill SE 1920 3771 (B) 62590
Canal Mills SE 1930 3765 (B) 62591
Dyehouse Mills (see Apperley Brook Mill)
Holybrook Mill SE 1910 3710 (B) 62594
Moorside Mill SE 1849 3501 (B) 62570
Oaklea Mills (see Apperley Brook Mill)
Old Mill SE 1841 3581 (B) 62568
Providence Dyeworks (see Apperdale Mills)

Stone Hall Shed SE 1799 3605 (B) 62546
Stylo House SE 1945 3765 (B) 62592
Tunwell Mills SE 1825 3590 (B) 62567
Union Mills SE 1870 3570 (B) 62569
Valley Mills SE 1921 3756 (B) 62593

ELLAND CUM GREETLAND (Elland), West Yorkshire

Albert Mills SE 1035 2108 (B) 62820
Bank Bottom Mills SE 1022 2104 (B) 62821
Bridgefield Mill SE 1059 2131 (B) 62816
Broad Carr Mill SE 0965 1980 (B) 63000
Broad Lea Mill SE 1133 2084 (B) 62829
Brow Bridge Mill SE 0960 2135 (B) 62804
Bryanroyd Mill SE 0795 2104 (B) 62760
Calder Mill SE 1065 2125 (B) 62818
Calder Works SE 1058 2119 (B) 62819
Castle Mills (see Calder Works)
Century Dyeworks SE 1080 2130 (B) 62937
Ellistones Mill SE 0825 2065 (B) 62785
Exchange Mill (see Calder Mill)
Exchange Mill (see Calder Works)
Greetland Dyeworks (see Ellistones Mill)
Hollyns Mill SE 0940 2137 (B) 62803
Ing Wood Mill SE 0928 2091 (C) 62811
James Street Mill SE 1105 2070 (B) 62830
Lower Ellistones Mill SE 0840 2099 (B) 62784
Marshall Hall Mills SE 1122 2119 (B) 62916
Marshfield Mill SE 1130 2090 (B) 62827
Mill SE 1115 2090 (B) 62917
Mill SE 1100 2055 (B) 62918
North Dean Mill SE 0981 2135 (A) 62805*
Park Road Mills SE 1095 2185 (B) 62814
Pendleton Mills SE 1101 2066 (B) 62831
Perseverance Mill SE 1119 2091 (B) 62826
Prospect Mill SE 0986 2136 (B) 62806
Scarbottom Mill SE 07766 2128 (B) 62759
Smithfield Mill SE 1102 2049 (B) 62833
South Lane Mills SE 1105 2062 (B) 62832
Spa Field Mills SE 1130 2085 (B) 62828
Springwood Mills SE 0905 1995 (B) 62997
Springwood Mills SE 0928 1989 (B) 62998
Sunnyside Dyeworks SE 0920 2105 (B) 62809
Tag Cut Mill SE 10 21 (C) 62939
Valley Mills SE 1080 2162 (B) 62815
Victoria Mills SE 0961 2122 (A) 62807*
Wellington Mills SE 1110 2115 (A) 62824*
West Vale Mills SE 0949 2110 (A) 62808*
Westbury Mills SE 1119 2115 (B) 62825
Whitwell Mill SE 1099 2136 (B) 62817
Woodfield Mill SE 0900 2102 (C) 62810

EMBSAY WITH EASTBY, North Yorkshire

Crown Spindle Works SE 0025 5430 (B) 62276
Loomshop SE 0080 5381 (B) 62274
Loomshop SE 00 53 (B) 62275
Millholme Shed SE 0065 5345 (B) 62272
Primrose Mill SE 0060 5375 (B) 62273

ERRINGDEN (Hebden Royd), West Yorkshire

Cragg Mill SE 004 237 (C) 62693
Hebble End Dyeworks SD 9903 2712 (B) 62237
Holme End Dyeworks SE 0039 2640 (B) 62689
Hoo Hole Mill Dyeworks SE 0085 2535 (B) 62692
Mill SD 9895 2715 (B) 62242
Rudclough Mill SD 9975 2320 (C) 62260
Vale Mill (see Rudclough Mill)

ESHOLT (Aireborough), West Yorkshire

Esholt Mill SE 1721 3989 (B) 62541

FARNHILL, North Yorkshire

Aireside Mills SD 9970 4682 (B) 62125

FARNLEY (Leeds), West Yorkshire

Britannia Mill SE 2389 3179 (B) 63292
Butterbowl Mill SE 2575 3253 (C) 63309
Farnley Low Mills SE 2645 3175 (B) 63314
Farnley Mill SE 2395 3239 (C) 63291
Providence Dye Works SE 268 318 (C) 63872
Upper Mill (see Britannia Mill)

FARNLEY TYAS (Kirkburton), West Yorkshire

Farnley Mill SE 1665 1239 (B) 63134

FEWSTON, North Yorkshire

West House Mill SE 168 555 (C) 63849*

FULSTONE (Holmfirth), West Yorkshire

Holme Bottom Mill SE 1620 0910 (C) 63215
Moorbrook Mills SE 1619 0880 (B) 63216
Sude Hill Mills SE 1673 0863 (A) 63218*

GARGRAVE, North Yorkshire

Goffa Mill SD 9330 5395 (B) 62116
Low Mill (see Goffa Mill)

GILDERSOME (Morley), West Yorkshire

Allied Mills SE 2481 2884 (C) 63505
Deanhurst Mill SE 2490 2890 (B) 63504
Highfield Mills SE 2499 2910 (B) 63503
Maiden Mills SE 2457 2926 (B) 63502
Moorhead Mill SE 2385 2985 (B) 63478
St Bernard's Mill SE 2585 2995 (C) 63557
Springfield Mills SE 2442 2930 (C) 63501
Union Mill (see Moorhead Mill)

GLUSBURN, North Yorkshire

Hayfield Mills SE 0010 4470 (B) 62278
Junction Mills SE 0140 4500 (B) 62282
Midland Mills SE 0095 4536 (A) 62277*
Standard Mills SE 0125 4535 (B) 62281

GOLCAR (Colne Valley; Huddersfield), West Yorkshire

Albion Mills (CV) SE 0965 1551 (B) 63003
Brook Mills (CV) SE 0825 1440 (B) 62987
Clough Road Mills (CV) SE 0815 1455 (B) 62986
Commercial Mill (H) SE 1154 1616 (B) 63042
Dale Street Mills (H) SE 1125 1633 (B) 63040
Heath House Mill (CV) SE 0905 1560 (B) 63002
Holme Mill (CV) SE 1050 1555 (B) 63024
Lees Mill (CV) SE 0895 1436 (B) 62994
Loomshop, Ramsden Mill Lane (CV) SE 1023 1536 (A) 63185*
Low West Woods Mills (CV) SE 0950 1458 (B) 63005
Low West Woods Upper Mill (see Low West Woods Mills)
Mill (CV) SE 0999 1579 (B) 63184
Milnsbridge Bottom Dyeworks (H) SE 1099 1580 (B) 63021
Milnsbridge Iron Works (H) SE 1195 1595 (B) 63174
New Mill (CV; H) SE 1035 1685 (B) 63016
Parkwood Mills (see New Mill)
Ramsden Mills (CV) SE 1045 1546 (A) 63025*
Scarbottom Mills (H) SE 1079 1570 (B) 63022
Spa Mills (CV) SE 0840 1425 (A) 62988*
Stanley Mills (CV) SE 1070 1575 (B) 63023
Titanic Mill (CV) SE 0975 1465 (B) 63004
Victoria Mills (CV) SE 0945 1565 (B) 63001
Weavers Cottage (CV) SE 0956 1585 (B) 37049

GOMERSAL (Batley; Gomersal), West Yorkshire

Brier Mill (B) SE 2218 2598 (C) 63454
Britannia Mills (G) SE 2277 2655 (B) 63450
Carr Mill (B) SE 2225 2602 (B) 63453
Cloth Hall Mill (G) SE 204 260 (B) 63424
Clough Mill (G) SE 2050 2722 (B) 63423
College Mill (B) SE 2215 2605 (B) 63452
Dyeworks (G) SE 2191 2624 (B) 63435
Flock House (B) SE 2218 2613 (B) 63451
Gomersal Mill (see Cloth Hall Mill)
Grove Mills (B) SE 2240 2590 (B) 63455
Howden Clough Mill (B) SE 2406 2708 (B) 63506
Mill (G) SE 1956 2530 (B) 62922
Nellroyd Mills (G) SE 1965 2490 (B) 62901
Popeley Mills (C) SE 2140 2580 (B) 63653
Providence Mills (G) SE 1955 2505 (B) 62898
Quarry Mill (G) SE 2095 2520 (B) 63425
Round Hill Mill (G) SE 1967 2605 (B) 62892
Smithies Mill (B) SE 2252 2577 (B) 63456
Spen Mills (G) SE 1955 2534 (B) 62896
Union Mills (G) SE 2105 2515 (B) 63436

GRASSINGTON, North Yorkshire

Low Mill SE 0068 6322 (B) 63827

GUISELEY (Aireborough), West Yorkshire

Albion Dyeworks SE 1949 4220 (B) 62321
Cassfield Works SE 1905 4187 (B) 62323
Cotton Processing Works SE 1858 4197 (B) 62318
Gordon Mills SE 1855 4271 (B) 62315
Green Bottom Dyeworks SE 1920 4175 (B) 62324
Green Bottom Mill (see Green Bottom Dyeworks)
Guiseley Low Mill SE 1940 4110 (B) 62326
High Croft Works SE 1945 4240 (B) 62320
Liberty Mills SE 1850 4220 (B) 62317
Netherfield Mill SE 1875 4235 (B) 62316
Nunroyd Mills SE 1955 4150 (B) 62325
Spring Head Mill SE 1930 4205 (B) 62322

HALIFAX, West Yorkshire

Albany Works SE 0765 2579 (B) 62747
Albion Mills SE 0976 2485 (B) 62795
Albion Mills SE 0985 2504 (B) 62913
Arden Works SE 0769 2441 (B) 62753
Beech Hill Mills SE 0853 2555 (B) 62769
Billinghay Mills SE 0768 2462 (B) 62751
Bowling Dyke Dyeworks SE 0925 2572 (B) 62790
Brunswick Mills SE 0880 2470 (B) 62781
Bull Close Lane Works SE 090 249 (C) 62944
Clarence Mills SE 0808 2555 (B) 62768
Clark Bridge Mills SE 0991 2525 (B) 62794
Clay Pits Mills SE 0748 2561 (B) 62748
Craven Edge Mills SE 0814 2497 (B) 62776
Dunkirk Mills SE 0745 2450 (B) 62752
Eagle Mills SE 0969 2535 (B) 62793

Fenton Road Works SE 0775 2445 (B) 62754
Fenton Works SE 0776 2440 (B) 62755
Hanson Lane Mill SE 0820 2536 (C) 63899*
Keighley Mill SE 0889 2535 (B) 62778
Lee Mills SE 0865 2585 (B) 62766
Livingstone Mills SE 0800 2526 (B) 62771
Miall Street Mills SE 0808 2565 (B) 62768
Mill SE 0933 2563 (B) 62791
Mill SE 0800 2520 (B) 62772
Mill SE 0805 2505 (B) 62775
Pellon Lane Mills SE 0885 2549 (B) 62777
Queen's Road Mills SE 0791 2510 (B) 62773
Raglan Works SE 0850 2541 (B) 62770
Riding Hall (see Clark Bridge Mills)
Royal Mills SE 0875 2509 (B) 62779
Ryburne Mill SE 0782 2535 (B) 62749
Scarborough Mill SE 0811 2429 (B) 62782
Spring Hall Works SE 0720 2495 (B) 62750
Stone Dam Mill SE 0969 2538 (A) 62947
Trafalgar Works (see Scarborough Mill)
Wellington Mills SE 0969 2545 (A) 62792*
West End Dyeworks SE 0800 2501 (B) 62774
West Grove Mill SE 0880 2500 (B) 62780

HARTLINGTON, North Yorkshire

Hartlington Mill SE 0417 6096 (B) 42907

HARTWITH CUM WINSLEY, North Yorkshire

High Mill SE 1915 6329 (C) 63833
Knox Mill SE 1902 6394 (A) 63842*
Low Mill SE 1890 6355 (B) 63832
New York Dyeworks (see New York Mills)
New York Mills SE 1955 6285 (B) 63835

HAWES, North Yorkshire

Gayle Mill SD 8711 8939 (A) 63829*

HAWKSWORTH (Aireborough), West Yorkshire

Tong Park Mills SE 1695 4015 (B) 62311

HAWORTH (Bingley; Keighley), West Yorkshire

Ashmount Mills (K) SE 0305 3746 (B) 62648
Bridge Mill/Lowertown Mill (K) SE 0343 3475 (B) 62657
Bridgehouse Mills (K) SE 0350 3685 (B) 62651
Brooks Meeting Mill (K) SE 0250 3508 (B) 62641
Charles Mill (K) SE 0348 3468 (A) 62659*
Dunkirk Mill (K) SE 0200 3519 (A) 62638*
Ebor Mill (K) SE 0366 3765 (A) 62649*
Fisher's Lodge Mill (K) SE 0282 3528 (B) 62668
Forks House Mill (K) SD 9936 3574 (C) 62160
Griffe Mill (K) SE 0065 3737 (A) 62635*
Hollins Mill (K) SE 0208 3742 (B) 62640
Holme Mill (K) SE 0342 3491 (B) 62655
Ivy Bank Mill (K) SE 0341 3676 (B) 62652
Lees Mill (B) SE 0385 3759 (A) 62650*
Lower Town Mill (K) (see Holme Mill)
Lowertown Shed and Mill (K) SE 0340 3485 (A) 62656*
Lumb Foot Mill (K) SE 0149 3759 (B) 62637
Mill (K) SE 0298 3741 (B) 62647
Mytholmes Mill (K) SE 0335 3795 (B) 62671
New Mill (K) SE 007 367 (C) 62681
Oxenhope Mill (K) SE 0332 3541 (B) 62654
Perseverance Mill (K) SE 0350 3472 (B) 62658
Royd House Mill (K) SE 0390 3581 (B) 62653
Spring Row Mill (K) SE 0412 3438 (B) 62666
Sykes Mill (K) SE 0405 3435 (A) 62661*
Wadsworth Mill (K) SE 0342 3450 (B) 62660

HEADINGLEY CUM BURLEY (Leeds), West Yorkshire

Abbey (Kirkstall) Mills SE 2625 3571 (B) 8279
Burley Bridge Mills SE 2799 3413 (B) 63322
Burley Mill SE 2695 3477 (B) 63312
Burley Vale Mills SE 2784 3416 (B) 63321
Cardigan Clothing Factory SE 2765 3435 (B) 63318
Cardigan Mills SE 2770 3425 (B) 63319
Haddon Mill SE 2730 3462 (B) 63317
St Annes Mill SE 2637 3524 (B) 63311
Savins Mill SE 2620 3545 (B) 63310

HEALEY WITH SUTTON (Healey), North Yorkshire

Healey Corn Mill SE 1855 8014 (B) 63844
Healey Saw Mill (see Healey Corn Mill)

HEATON (Bradford), West Yorkshire

Dumb Mill SE 1530 3635 (B) 62470
Frizinghall Works SE 1525 3630 (B) 62471
Showers Mill SE 1530 3595 (B) 62474
Springfield Mills SE 1119 3560 (B) 62405

HECKMONDWIKE, West Yorkshire

Beehive Mills SE 2150 2281 (B) 63443
Brighton Mills SE 2145 2435 (B) 63437

Brunswick Mill SE 2175 2328 (B) 63655
Croft Mills SE 2145 2336 (B) 63441
Flush Mill SE 211 236 (B) 63438
Grove Mill SE 2200 2375 (B) 63464
Longfield Mills SE 2202 2398 (B) 63463
Low Mill SE 2172 2279 (B) 63445
Lower Mill (see Low Mill)
Mill SE 2202 2362 (B) 63656
Moorfield Mills SE 2215 2409 (B) 63462
Orchard Dyeworks SE 2167 2285 (B) 63444
Spen Vale Mills SE 2155 2295 (B) 63442
Spen Vale Works (see Orchard Dyeworks)
Walkley Mills SE 2180 2280 (B) 63446
Westfield Mills (see Brighton Mills)
William Royd Mills SE 2215 2419 (B) 63461

HEPTONSTALL (Hebden Royd; Heptonstall), West Yorkshire

Beehive Works (HR) SD 9889 2715 (B) 62226
Bob Mill (H) SD 974 282 (C) 62258
Bridge Mill (H) SD 988 290 (C) 62222
Brunswick Mill (HR) SD 989 271 (C) 62268
Calder Mill (HR) SD 9875 2719 (B) 62225
Everest Works (HR) SD 9895 2725 (B) 62247
Hanging Royd Mill (HR) SD 9932 2760 (C) 62246
Hanging Royd Works (see Hanging Royd Mill)
Hebden Works (HR) SD 9936 2755 (B) 62235
Higher Lumb Mill (H) SD 9765 2821 (C) 62219
Hudson's Mill (H) SD 9650 2819 (C) 62259
Jack Bridge Mill (H) SD 9625 2825 (C) 62208
Lee Mill (H) SD 9922 2842 (C) 62230
Linden Works (HR) SD 9919 2755 (B) 62234
Lower Lumb Mill (H) SD 977 282 (C) 62220
Lower Slater Ing Mill (see Lower Lumb Mill)
Melbourne Works (HR) SD 9901 2729 (B) 62265
Regent Works (HR) SD 9920 2749 (A) 62267
Royds Mill (HR) SD 9920 2740 (B) 62236
Salem Mills (HR) SD 9896 2719 (C) 62227
Salem Mills (HR) SD 9901 2712 (B) 62264
Salford Works (see Melbourne Works)
Slater Ing Mill (see Higher Lumb Mill)
Waterside Mill (H) SD 986 272 (C) 62224

HEPWORTH (Holmfirth), West Yorkshire

Dobroyd Mill SE 1639 0720 (B) 63222
Hepworth Mill SE 1649 0650 (C) 63223

HESLINGTON, North Yorkshire

Heslington Bleach Works SE 6210 5055 (C) 63868*

HIGH AND LOW BISHOPSIDE (High and Low Bishopside; Hartwith cum Winsley), North Yorkshire

Fell Beck Mill (HLB) SE 1961 6531 (B) 63846
Glasshouses Mill (HLB) SE 1718 6435 (A) 63831*
Smelt House Mill (HLB) SE 1920 6340 (C) 63834

HIPPERHOLME CUM BRIGHOUSE (Brighouse), West Yorkshire

Albert Mills SE 1475 2275 (B) 62855
Alexandra Mill SE 1459 2262 (C) 62949
Bailiff Bridge Mill SE 147 253 (B) 62846
Bridge Road Works SE 1439 2269 (B) 62853
Britannia Mills (see Albert Mills)
Broad Holme Mill SE 1465 2265 (B) 62854
Canal Mills SE 1 2 (C) 62942
Cranbrook Mills SE 1449 2669 (B) 62843
Ganny Mill SE 1420 2281 (B) 62851
Mill SE 1425 2281 (B) 62921
Millroyd Mills SE 1475 2269 (B) 62857
Mytholme Mills SE 1155 2552 (B) 62823
North Vale Mills SE 1482 2500 (B) 62848
Norwood Green Mill SE 1429 2667 (B) 62844
Owler Ings Mill SE 1430 2275 (B) 62852
Perseverance Mill SE 1467 2274 (B) 62919
Phoenix Mills SE 1488 2287 (B) 62856
Rookes Mill SE 1450 2660 (B) 62845
Slead Sike Mill SE 1345 2355 (B) 62838
Stott's Mill SE 1465 2260 (C) 62950
Thornhill Bridge Dyeworks SE 1465 2365 (B) 62849
Thornhill Briggs Mill (see Thornhill Bridge Dyeworks)
Upper Mill (see Bridge Road Works)
Victoria Mill (see Bailiff Bridge Mill)
Victoria Mills (see Albert Mills)
Wilkin Royd Mills SE 1490 2280 (B) 62860
Woodvale Mills SE 1475 2355 (B) 62850

HOLBECK (Leeds), West Yorkshire

Benyons' Mill SE 2990 3256 (C) 63344*
Clothing Factory (see Marshall's Mill)
Clothing Works SE 2959 3285 (B) 63340
Clyde Works SE 2885 3215 (B) 63331
Flax Mill SE 2960 3275 (C) 63401
Globe Foundry SE 2960 3300 (B) 63338
Globe Mill SE 2949 3304 (B) 63337
Globe Mills SE 2985 3279 (B) 63341
Holbeck Clothing Works SE 2925 3270 (B) 63343
Holbeck Mills SE 2895 3258 (C) 63417
Holbeck Mills (see Benyons' Mill)
Hope Mills SE 2985 3295 (C) 63400
Low Hall Mills SE 2904 3259 (B) 63342

Manor Mills SE 297 327 (C) 63873
Manor Road Mills SE 2985 3270 (C) 63394
Marshall's Mill SE 2950 3265 (A) 41529*
Round Foundry Estate (see Flax Mill)
Saville Works (see Clyde Works)
Soho Foundry Flax Mill SE 2979 3249 (C) 63405
Temple Mill (see Marshall's Mill)
The People's Mill (see Flax Mill)
Tower Works (see Globe Foundry)
Union Mills SE 3008 3256 (B) 63361
Water Lane Mills (see Hope Mills)

HOLME (Holmfirth), West Yorkshire

Brownhill Mills SE 114 061 (C) 63232
Rake Mill SE 1059 0555 (C) 63228

HONLEY (Holmfirth), West Yorkshire

Bridge Dyeworks SE 1415 1198 (B) 63115
Cocking Steps Mill SE 1255 1235 (B) 63062
Crossley Mills SE 1435 1180 (B) 63116
Dean House Mills SE 1400 0995 (B) 63201
Grove Mills SE 1443 1210 (B) 63114
Honley Mill SE 1408 1108 (B) 63155
Lord's Mill SE 1292 1218 (B) 63063
Lower Mytholm Bridge Mills SE 1525 1045 (C) 63128
Moll Springs Dyeworks SE 1306 1209 (B) 63078
Neiley Mills (see Crossley Mills)
Queen's Mill SE 1352 1155 (B) 63154
Reins Mill SE 1402 1241 (B) 63113
Smithy Place Mills SE 1502 1109 (B) 63127
Thirstin Dyeworks SE 1355 1232 (B) 63077
Thirstin Mills SE 1345 1210 (B) 63079
Victoria Mill (see Queen's Mill)

HORBURY, West Yorkshire

Addingford Mills SE 2915 1767 (B) 63764
Albert Mill SE 2875 1792 (B) 63760
Albion Mills SE 2845 1799 (B) 63757
Dudfleet Mill SE 2995 1735 (B) 63765
Ford Mill SE 2872 1798 (B) 63759
Horbury Bridge Mill SE 2789 1820 (B) 63752
Manor Mills SE 2890 1930 (C) 63756
Navigation Mill SE 2815 1798 (B) 63771
New Mill (see Horbury Bridge Mill)
Peel Mills SE 2942 1809 (B) 63763
Terry Mills SE 2885 1860 (B) 63773
Victoria Mill SE 2850 1797 (B) 63758

HORSFORTH, West Yorkshire

Brookfoot Mills SE 2450 3870 (B) 63295
Clough Mill SE 2200 3775 (B) 63260
Horsforth Mill SE 2525 3770 (B) 63305
Troy Mill SE 2440 3884 (B) 63294
Woodbottom Mill (see Clough Mill)
Woodside Dyeworks SE 2491 3840 (B) 63296

HORTON (Bradford), West Yorkshire

Albert Mills SE 1550 3310 (C) 62487
Albion Mills SE 1585 3156 (B) 62501
Albion Works (see Albion Mills)
Ashfield Mills SE 1525 3330 (B) 62484
Aslan House SE 1559 3310 (B) 62617
Atlas Mills SE 1560 3300 (B) 62488
Bank Top Mills SE 1270 3065 (B) 62415
Beckside Dyeworks SE 1399 3198 (B) 62426
Beckside Mills SE 1405 3185 (B) 62451
Beehive Mills SE 1566 3309 (B) 62489
Bentley Mills SE 1410 3275 (C) 62448
Bowling Mill SE 1625 3195 (B) 62531
Briggella Mills SE 1551 3140 (B) 62502
Britannia Mills SE 1650 3255 (B) 62522
Caledonia Works SE 1651 3241 (B) 62523
Cannon Mills SE 1450 3205 (A) 62450*
Carrara Mill SE 1631 3207 (B) 62529
Cartwright Mills SE 1445 3292 (B) 62444
Cliff Mills SE 1370 3130 (B) 62428
Cross Lane Mills SE 1453 3175 (B) 62452
Cusson's Mill (see Cross Lane Mills)
Douglas Mills SE 1620 3185 (B) 62619
Fieldhead Mills SE 1514 3330 (C) 62483
Grange Shed SE 1455 3220 (B) 62449
Harris Court Mill SE 1420 3140 (B) 62453
Haycliffe Hill Mill SE 1438 3091 (B) 62455
Haycliffe Shed SE 1455 3105 (B) 62454
Holme Top Mills SE 1568 3165 (C) 62500
Jesse Street Dyeworks SE 1630 3210 (A) 62620*
Kelwood Mill (see Grange Shed)
Lane Close Mills SE 1395 3138 (B) 62427
Legrams Mill SE 1495 3285 (A) 62447*
Manchester Road Mill (see Bowling Mill)
Marshall's Mill SE 163 326 (C) 62521
Mill SE 1539 3120 (B) 62503
Mill SE 1476 3279 (B) 62607
Mill SE 1549 3299 (B) 62616
New Mill (see Beckside Mills)
Northside Mill SE 14 32 (C) 62680
Paddock Dyeworks SE 1274 3165 (B) 62413
Pakington Street Shed SE 1594 3183 (B) 62499
Phoenix Mill SE 1530 3274 (B) 62497

Phoenix Works SE 1570 3300 (B) 62490
Richmond Mills SE 1542 3310 (B) 62486
St Andrew's Mills SE 1472 3285 (B) 62446
St Stephen's Shed SE 1600 3165 (B) 62535
Shearbridge Mills SE 1525 3245 (B) 62498
Star Mills (see Beehive Mills)
West Brook Mills (see Phoenix Mill)
West End Mills SE 1553 3299 (C) 62609
Westcroft Mill SE 1410 3165 (B) 62618
Westfield Mill SE 1450 3286 (B) 62415

HUDDERSFIELD, West Yorkshire

Albany Mills SE 1490 1635 (B) 63088
Albion Mill SE 1440 1605 (B) 63094
Ash Brow Mills SE 1465 1930 (B) 63080
Ash Brow Print Works (see Ash Brow Mills)
Aspley Dyeware Mills SE 1510 1645 (B) 63122
Aspley Mills SE 1515 1670 (B) 63121
Bay Hall Mills SE 1415 1799 (B) 63081
Bay Hall Works SE 1411 1790 (B) 63176
Britannia Mills SE 1439 1598 (A) 63097*
Chapel Hill Mills SE 14 16 (C) 63187
Colne Bridge Mill SE 1772 2030 (B) 62873
Colne Road Mills SE 1445 1595 (B) 63098
Commercial Mills SE 1470 1600 (B) 63163
Crescent Mills SE 1319 1611 (B) 63068
Deighton Mills SE 1662 1907 (B) 63130
Engine Bridge Mills SE 1430 1597 (C) 63096
Fairfield Mills SE 1447 1602 (B) 63093
Fern Street Mills SE 1506 1655 (B) 63165
Field Mills SE 1545 1825 (B) 63117
Firth Street Mills SE 1475 1609 (A) 63091*
Folly Hall Mills SE 1419 1599 (A) 63095*
Gledholt Works SE 1338 1625 (B) 63175
Granville Mills SE 1311 1612 (B) 63066
Grove Mills SE 1490 1744 (B) 63083
Holme Mills SE 1745 2085 (B) 62872
Larchfield Mills SE 1482 1618 (A) 63090*
Mill SE 1320 1611 (B) 63067
Mill SE 1438 1600 (B) 63162
Mill SE 1482 1611 (B) 63164
Mill SE 1495 1680 (B) 63166
Mill SE 1490 1679 (B) 63167
Mill, Salendine Nook SE 1046 1811 (B) 63188
Paddock Mills SE 1328 1614 (C) 63069
Phoenix Mills SE 1502 1745 (B) 63082
Priest Royd Mills SE 1456 1595 (B) 63099
Richmond Mills SE 1475 1726 (B) 63085
Riverside Mills SE 1475 1598 (B) 63100
Springdale Mills (see Starkeys' Mill)
Stanley Mills SE 1272 1719 (C) 63053
Starkeys' Mill SE 1376 1615 (C) 63065*
Tan Field Mills (see Grove Mills)
Tower Mills SE 1509 1687 (B) 63120
Trafalgar Mills SE 1625 1845 (B) 63132
Turnbridge Mills SE 1490 1685 (B) 63087
Union Dyeware Mills SE 1356 1620 (B) 63064
Upper Aspley Mills SE 1495 1626 (B) 63089
Victoria Mills SE 1480 1730 (B) 63084
Waterloo Mills SE 1488 1709 (B) 63086
Woodhouse Carr Mills SE 1665 1900 (C) 63131
Zetland Mills SE 1460 1608 (B) 63092

HUNSLET (Leeds), West Yorkshire

Airedale Works SE 3115 3249 (B) 63374
Balm Road Mills SE 3105 3109 (A) 63396*
Calf Garth Mill SE 3115 3155 (C) 63407
Clothing Factory SE 3065 3166 (B) 63362
Highfield Mills SE 2987 3137 (B) 63345
Hunslet Flax Mill (see Balm Road Mills)
Hunslet Linen Works SE 3135 3205 (B) 63378
Hunslet Mills SE 314 321 (A) 63376*
Hunslet Old Mill SE 3155 3170 (C) 63399
Joseph Street Mill SE 3101 3179 (C) 63379
Larchfield Mills SE 3105 3220 (C) 63375
Low Road Mill SE 3160 3145 (C) 63408
Potterdale Mills SE 3015 3239 (C) 63419
Quebec Works SE 2978 3217 (C) 63402
Robert Busk's Flax Mill SE 3031 3149 (C) 63406
Temple Works (see Joseph Street Mill)
Victoria Mill SE 313 321 (B) 63377

HUNSWORTH (Cleckheaton), West Yorkshire

Balme Mill SE 1900 2610 (B) 62890
Brookhouse Mills SE 1908 2610 (B) 62891
Crosses Works SE 1985 2904 (B) 62889
Hunsworth Ironworks (see Brookhouse Mills)
Hunsworth Mill SE 1845 2693 (B) 62874

IDLE, West Yorkshire

Ashfield Mills SE 1800 3825 (B) 62563
Bowling Green Mills SE 1752 3870 (B) 62543
Brackendale Mills SE 1705 3867 (A) 62542*
Buck Mill SE 169 391 (C) 62511
Castle Mills SE 1816 3781 (B) 62564
Dock Mill SE 1540 3800 (B) 62463
Dockfield Mills SE 1532 3785 (B) 62466
Dyeworks SE 1553 3631 (B) 62472
Greenside Mill SE 1875 3755 (B) 62565
Junction Mill SE 1525 3785 (B) 62465
Midland Dyeworks SE 1496 3715 (B) 62436

Mill SE 1777 3728 (B) 62633
New Mills SE 1795 3780 (B) 62544
Perseverance Mill SE 1514 3741 (B) 62468
Springfield Mill SE 1770 3721 (B) 62545
Water Pits Mill SE 1510 3735 (B) 62469

INGLETON, North Yorkshire

Ingleton Mill SD 6942 7328 (B) 63815

KEIGHLEY, West Yorkshire

Acres Mill SE 0577 4058 (B) 62347
Aireworth Mills SE 0725 4195 (A) 62297*
Alexandra Mill SE 0642 4115 (B) 62357
Alexandra Shed (see Alexandra Mill)
Becks Mill SE 0555 4100 (A) 62342*
Beech Mill SE 0585 4015 (B) 62352
Botany Buildings SE 0699 4149 (B) 62295
Burlington Mills SE 0678 4134 (B) 62296
Cabbage Mill SE 0650 4079 (B) 62363
Calversyke Mill SE 0525 4115 (B) 62340
Castle Mill SE 0519 4092 (B) 62368
Cavendish Mill SE 0624 4125 (B) 62353
Coney Lane Works SE 0629 4100 (B) 62359
Crown Saw Mills SE 0645 4093 (B) 62360
Cyclops Works, Marley Street SE 0612 4070 (B) 62366
Dalton Mills SE 0699 4137 (A) 62300*
Damems Mill SE 0510 3879 (B) 62665
Devonshire Mills SE 0565 4117 (A) 62341*
Dyeworks SE 0708 4165 (B) 62299
Eastwood Mill SE 0735 4170 (B) 62298
Fleece Mill SE 0630 4125 (B) 62355
Goodley Works SE 0309 3889 (B) 62642
Goose Eye Mill SE 0280 4056 (B) 62336
Greengate Mills SE 0605 4049 (B) 62367
Grove Mill SE 0545 3960 (B) 62664
Hanover Mill SE 0625 4120 (B) 62354
High Mill, Newsholme SE 0187 3963 (B) 62636
Higher Holme Mill SE 0230 4022 (B) 62335
Holme Mill SE 0471 4090 (B) 62338
Holme Mill (see Higher Holme Mill)
Hope Mill SE 0596 4045 (B) 62350
Ingrow Mill SE 0555 3972 (B) 62663
Kensington Sheds SE 0558 4070 (B) 62345
Knowle Mill SE 0600 4035 (A) 62351*
Low Bridge Mill SE 0629 4085 (B) 62361
Low Mill SE 0660 4120 (B) 62356*
Low Mill, Newsholme SE 0209 3963 (B) 62639
Low Street Mill SE 0635 4110 (B) 62358
Lower Holme Mill SE 0476 4091 (B) 62339
Lower Providence Mill SE 0340 3827 (A) 62644*
Marley Street Mill SE 0610 4073 (B) 62365
Melbourne Mills SE 0699 4154 (B) 62295
Mill SE 0640 4202 (B) 62294
North Beck Mill SE 0545 4095 (B) 62343
Oakworth Mill SE 0305 3875 (B) 62643
Peel Mills SE 0595 4070 (B) 62349
Ponden Mill SD 9989 3721 (A) 62159*
Prospect Mill SE 0575 3998 (B) 62662
Rhone Mill SE 0647 4079 (B) 62362
Royal Works, Goulbourne Street SE 0585 4070 (B) 62346
Royd Works SE 0600 4255 (B) 62370
Springfield Mills SE 0570 4094 (B) 62344
Springhead Mill SE 0301 3780 (B) 62646
Strong Close Mill (see Dalton Mills)
Stubbing House Mill (see Aireworth Mills)
Turkey Mill SE 0295 4061 (B) 37153
Upper Providence Mill SE 0330 3838 (C) 62675
Walk Mill SE 0625 4070 (B) 62364
West Lane Mill (see Calversyke Mill)
Wood Mill SE 0332 4069 (B) 62337
Worsted Mill, Goulbourne Street SE 0573 4068 (B) 62369

KELBROOK (Earby), Lancashire

Sough Bridge Works SD 9025 4540 (B) 62136

KEXBROUGH (Darton), West Yorkshire

Swithen Bleachworks SE 3019 1139 (C) 63775*

KIRKBURTON, West Yorkshire

Brookfield Mill SE 1895 1300 (B) 63147
Dogley Lane Mill SE 1869 1405 (B) 63146
Green Grove Mills SE 1899 1369 (A) 63151*
Linfit Mill SE 2042 1372 (B) 63772
Moxon's Mill SE 1945 1325 (B) 63161
Springfield Mills SE 1915 1305 (B) 63152

KIRKBY MALHAM, North Yorkshire

Scalegill Mill SD 8991 6168 (B) 63822

KIRKHEATON (Kirkburton), West Yorkshire

Gawthorpe Green Dyeworks SE 1935 1675 (B) 63149
Kirkheaton Mills SE 1805 1785 (B) 63142
Levi Mill SE 1919 1689 (C) 63148

KNARESBOROUGH, North Yorkshire

Flax-dressing shop, Green Dragon Yard SE 350 579 (A) 63865*
Flax-dressing shop, Whiteleys Yard SE 350 572 (A) 63863*
High Street, 25 SE 3499 5709 (B) 63870
Kirkgate, 15 SE 3492 5703 (B) 63864
Linen Mill SE 3471 5739 (B) 63854
Raw Gap, weaving shop SE 3495 5720 (B) 63862
The Old Tannery, York Place SE 352 569 (B) 63866

LANGCLIFFE, North Yorkshire

Langcliffe Mill SD 8161 6505 (B) 63821*
Langcliffe Shed SD 8175 6435 (A) 63820*

LANGFIELD (Todmorden), West Yorkshire

Albion Mills SD 9394 2415 (B) 62183
Anchor Mill SD 9415 2440 (B) 62198
Canal Street Works SD 9400 2415 (B) 62197
Causeway Wood Mill SD 9520 2379 (C) 62254
Der Street Mill SD 9420 2415 (B) 62199
Derdale Mill SD 9430 2417 (B) 62200
Jumb Mill SD 9555 2349 (C) 62206
Laneside Mill (see Waterside Mill)
Lumbutts Mill SD 9565 2345 (B) 62207
Nanholme Mill SD 9600 2475 (B) 62217
Old Royd Mill SD 9512 2398 (C) 62255
Sandholme Mill SD 9440 2420 (B) 62201
Stoodley Bridge Mill SD 9630 2500 (B) 62215
Waterside Mill SD 9345 2380 (A) 38205*
Woodhouse Mill SD 9515 2444 (A) 62205*

LEEDS, West Yorkshire

Aire Place Mills SE 2826 3397 (B) 63328
Bank Low Mills SE 3111 3325 (C) 63368
Bank Mills SE 3099 3301 (A) 63359*
Bank Top Mill SE 3119 3327 (C) 63410
Bean Ing Mills SE 290 334 (C) 63389*
Black Dog Mills SE 3132 3290 (B) 63371
Bowman Lane Dyeworks SE 3065 3313 (B) 63357
Buslingthorpe Mills SE 3035 3525 (B) 63347
Byron Street Mills SE 3090 3405 (B) 63353
Camp Hall SE 2997 3295 (C) 63403
Carlton Cross Mills SE 301 346 (C) 63398
Carr Mills SE 3001 3561 (B) 63385
Clothing Factory SE 2955 3356 (B) 37582
Clothing Factory SE 2935 3389 (B) 63335
Clothing Factory SE 3125 3474 (B) 63363
Clothing Manufactory SE 2880 3444 (B) 63326
Clothing Works SE 3069 3421 (B) 63351
Clothing Works SE 3051 3401 (B) 63354
Clothing Works SE 3050 3397 (B) 63355
Crown Point Dyeworks SE 3085 3316 (C) 63422
Drying House, Saxton Lane SE 3095 3339 (C) 63418
East Street Mills SE 3105 3309 (B) 63369
Ellerby Lane Mills SE 3145 3280 (B) 63372
Ellerby Road Mills (see Ellerby Lane Mills)
Elmwood Mill SE 3041 3439 (B) 63350
Elmwood Works (see Elmwood Mill)
Empire Shoe Works SE 3100 3435 (B) 63364
Grove Works SE 3033 3440 (B) 63349
Harcourt Mills SE 2902 3375 (C) 63391
Hill House Mills SE 3145 3303 (C) 63370
Hope Foundry SE 3095 3411 (B) 63387
Hudson Road Mills (Clothing) SE 321 344 (B) 63383
Isles Lane Mills SE 29 32 (C) 63395
Lady Bridge Mills SE 3048 3373 (C) 63414
Land Court Mill SE 3015 3295 (C) 63360
Little Top Mill SE 3120 3321 (C) 63411
London Works SE 3115 3410 (B) 63365
Low Fold Mill SE 3130 3275 (B) 63373
Mabgate Mill SE 3110 3417 (B) 63386
Marsh Lane Mill SE 3088 3335 (C) 63412
Millgarth Mills SE 3061 3356 (C) 63392
Millgarth Street Mills SE 3065 3362 (C) 63413
Nether Mills SE 3089 3315 (C) 63358
Park Mills (see Bean Ing Mills)
Perseverance Mill SE 2871 3365 (C) 63390
Perseverance Mills SE 2996 3538 (B) 63334
Prospect Mills SE 3150 3350 (B) 63366
Providence Street Mill SE 3126 3330 (C) 63367
Providence Works SE 3010 3430 (B) 63348
Ridge Mills SE 2998 3570 (B) 63333
Shannon Street Mills SE 3128 3362 (B) 63415
Sheepscar Works SE 3032 3530 (B) 63346
Spring Hill Dyeworks (see Buslingthorpe Mills)
Steander Mills SE 3100 3322 (C) 63409
Templar Works SE 3046 3375 (B) 63356
Trafalgar Mill SE 3023 3290 (C) 63397
Valley Mills SE 2980 3582 (B) 63332
Victoria Mill (see Shannon Street Mills)
Victoria Mills SE 2891 3349 (C) 63420
Virginia Mills SE 3075 3421 (B) 63352
Water Hall Mills SE 2975 3298 (B) 63339
Wellington Dyeworks SE 2820 3415 (B) 63327
Wellington Mills SE 2885 3357 (A) 79300*
Whitehall Mills SE 2931 3315 (B) 63336
Wilson Street Mill SE 3012 3290 (C) 63404
York Road Linen Factory SE 3145 3366 (C) 63416
Yorkshire Dyeworks SE 3215 3455 (B) 63382

LEPTON (Kirkburton), West Yorkshire

Cowmes Mill SE 1800 1608 (B) 63143
Fenay Mills SE 1823 1541 (B) 63144
Rowley Mills SE 1880 1430 (B) 63145
Spa Mill (see Cowmes Mill)
Vale Mills SE 1785 1645 (B) 63140
Waterloo Bridge Works SE 1772 1660 (B) 63139
Whitley Willows Mill SE 1958 1663 (B) 63150

LINDLEY CUM QUARMBY (Huddersfield), West Yorkshire

Acre Mills SE 1195 1770 (B) 63034
Hollin's Mill SE 1266 1721 (B) 63052
Marsh Mill SE 1262 1709 (B) 63054
Oakes Mill SE 1185 1745 (B) 63037
Plover Mill SE 1180 1775 (B) 63033
Quarmby Mills SE 1146 1742 (B) 63036
Temple Street Mill SE 1170 1825 (B) 63032
Wellington Mills SE 115 176 (B) 63035

LINGARDS (Colne), West Yorkshire

Britannia Mills SE 0805 1390 (B) 62995
Colne Mills SE 0790 1390 (B) 62984

LINTHWAITE (Colne Valley; Huddersfield), West Yorkshire

Black Rock Mills (CV) SE 0965 1380 (B) 63009
Bridge Croft Mills (H) SE 1172 1587 (B) 63048
Burdett Mill (H) SE 1203 1578 (B) 63173
Colne Vale Mill (H) SE 1123 1579 (C) 63050
Elm Ing Mills (H) SE 1186 1582 (B) 63046
Hoyle Ing Dyeworks (CV) SE 0982 1455 (B) 63006
Longfield Dyeworks (CV) SE 0914 1412 (B) 63008
Ramsden Mills (CV) SE 1045 1546 (A) 63025*
Spring Garden Mill (H) SE 1165 1575 (B) 63049
Spring Grove Mills (CV) SE 0955 1430 (B) 63007
Spring Mills (H) SE 1210 1588 (B) 63059
Stanley Mills (H) SE 1205 1595 (B) 63058
Stonefield Mills (H) SE 1198 1582 (B) 63044
Union Mills (H) SE 1195 1585 (B) 63045
Union Mills (H) SE 1195 1577 (B) 63047

LINTON (Threshfield), West Yorkshire

Linton Mill SE 0011 6328 (C) 63826

LIVERSEDGE, West Yorkshire

Balm Mills SE 1973 2256 (B) 62905
Broomfield Mills SE 1805 2502 (B) 62886
Crystal Mill SE 2132 2337 (B) 63440
Greenfield Mill (see Crystal Mill)
Hare Park Mills SE 1866 2367 (B) 62926
Lower Rawfolds Mill SE 1975 2460 (B) 62903
Marsh Works SE 1950 2495 (B) 62899
Mill SE 2079 2373 (B) 63430
Mill SE 2022 2426 (B) 63654
Providence Mills SE 2091 2355 (B) 63433
Pyenot Works SE 1935 2494 (B) 62900
Rawfolds Dyeworks SE 1980 2465 (B) 62902
Rayner's Mill SE 1842 2401 (B) 62888
Spen Valley Carpet Works SE 2085 2365 (B) 63431
Stanley Mill SE 2009 2427 (B) 63427
Tanhouse Mill SE 1985 2354 (B) 62904
Upper Carr Mills SE 2012 2432 (A) 63426*
Valley Mills SE 2125 2339 (B) 63439
Valley Works (see Tanhouse Mill)
Victoria Dyeworks SE 1830 2410 (B) 62887
Victoria Mill SE 2031 2420 (B) 63428
Watergate Mill SE 2042 2419 (B) 63429
Wellington Mills SE 2075 2352 (C) 63432
Woodfield Mill (see Tanhouse Mill)

LOCKWOOD (Huddersfield), West Yorkshire

Albert Mills SE 1405 1555 (A) 63108*
Bath Mills SE 1397 1545 (B) 63109
Britannia Mills SE 1260 1598 (A) 63060*
Broadfield Mills SE 1385 1530 (B) 63169
Crosland Moor Mill SE 1305 1593 (B) 63070
Croslands Mill (see Crosland Moor Mill)
Firths Mill (see Britannia Mills)
Mark Bottom's Mill SE 1270 1599 (B) 63061
Melbourne Mills SE 1376 1519 (B) 63168
Mill SE 1378 1530 (B) 63170
Rashcliffe Brass/Iron Works SE 1415 1570 (B) 63171
Rashcliffe Mills SE 1420 1580 (B) 63104
Victoria Mills SE 1405 1559 (B) 63107
Woollen Mill SE 1401 1565 (B) 63106

LONGWOOD (Colne Valley; Huddersfield), West Yorkshire

Bank House Mill (H) SE 1210 1604 (C) 63056
Cliff End Mills (H) SE 1140 1634 (B) 63041
Clough Mills (H) SE 1065 1672 (B) 63017
George Street Mill (H) SE 1185 1595 (B) 63043
Grove Mill (H) SE 1085 1666 (B) 63019
Imperial Mills (H) SE 1228 1628 (A) 63055*
New Mill (CV; H) SE 1035 1685 (B) 63016
Parkwood Mills (see New Mill)
Prospect Mills (H) SE 1080 1680 (B) 63018
Quarmby Clough Mill (H) SE 1149 1670 (C) 63038

Quarmby Mill (see George Street Mill)
Stafford Mills (H) SE 1219 1600 (B) 63057
Sunny Bank Mills (H) SE 1098 1663 (B) 63020
Woodland Mills (H) SE 1115 1640 (B) 63039

LOTHERSDALE, North Yorkshire

Dale End Mill SD 9595 4590 (B) 62128

MANNINGHAM (Bradford), West Yorkshire

Alston Works SE 1445 3315 (C) 62443
Brick Lane Mill SE 1505 3365 (B) 62480
Brown Royd Dyeworks SE 1460 3355 (B) 62441
Bullroyd Mill SE 1345 3371 (B) 62417
Cumberland Works SE 1375 3330 (A) 62422*
Globe Mills SE 1520 3375 (B) 62478
Lily Croft Mill (see Manningham Mills)
Low Globe Mill (see Globe Mills)
Low Royd Dyeworks SE 1459 3343 (B) 62442
Lumb Lane Mills SE 1565 3385 (B) 62477
Manningham Dyeworks SE 1515 3445 (B) 62476
Manningham Mills SE 1450 3490 (A) 62439*
Oakwood Dyeworks SE 1515 3365 (B) 62479
Parkinsons Buildings SE 1520 3355 (B) 62481
Try Mills SE 1524 3341 (A) 62482*
Valley Dyeworks SE 1620 3430 (B) 62515
Valley Mills SE 1605 3465 (B) 62513
Whetley Mills SE 1475 3365 (A) 62440*
Whitehead's Mill SE 1399 3360 (B) 62424
Young Street Mills SE 1395 3360 (A) 62423*
Young Street Sheds (see Whitehead's Mill)

MARSDEN (Colne Valley), West Yorkshire

Bank Bottom Mills SE 047 111 (B) 62965
Cellars Clough Mills SE 0585 1254 (B) 62968
Clough Lee Mill SE 0460 1165 (B) 62962
Clough Lee Mill SE 0466 1172 (B) 63157
Fall Lane Mills SE 0475 1135 (B) 62963
Holme Mills SE 0630 1300 (B) 62979
Kiln Croft Mill (see Fall Lane Mills)
Middle Mill (see Clough Lee Mill, 63157)
New Mills SE 0505 1170 (B) 62971
Ottiwells Mill (see Bank Bottom Mills)
Reedy Carr Mills SE 0495 1130 (B) 62964
Upper End Mill SE 0518 1179 (B) 62970
Warehouse Hill Mills (see Upper End Mill)
Wood Bottom Mill SE 0537 1200 (B) 62969

MELTHAM, West Yorkshire

Albion Mill SE 0940 1067 (B) 63013
Bent Ley Mill SE 1098 1125 (A) 63027*
Brigg Mill SE 1013 1090 (B) 63029
Brighouse Mill (see Brigg Mill)
Lane End Dyeworks SE 1033 1016 (B) 63153
Lower Sunny Bank Mill SE 0925 1080 (B) 63011
Meltham Mills SE 1090 1085 (A) 63031*
Mill SE 0953 1077 (B) 63180
Moor Road Mills SE 0957 1065 (B) 63014
New Bridge Mill SE 0885 1063 (B) 62996
Old Mill (see Brigg Mill)
Owler Bars Mill SE 0939 1069 (C) 63012
Royd Edge Dyeworks SE 1002 0995 (B) 63190
Royd Edge Mill (see Royd Edge Dyeworks)
Scarr Bottom Dyeworks (see Scarr Bottom Mill)
Scarr Bottom Mill SE 1005 1085 (A) 63030*
Sefton Mills SE 0969 1072 (C) 63015
Shoe Broads Mill SE 1049 1090 (B) 63183
Spinks Mire Mill SE 1085 1115 (B) 63028
Upper Sunny Bank Mill SE 0914 1085 (B) 63010
Wilshaw Mill SE 1161 0967 (B) 63191

MENWITH WITH DARLEY, North Yorkshire

Darley High Mill SE 1947 5988 (B) 63858
Fringill Mill SE 2063 5924 (A) 63851*

MICKLEY (Azerley), North Yorkshire

Mickley Mill SE 2531 7702 (B) 63839

MIDGLEY (Hebden Royd; Sowerby Bridge; Wadsworth), West Yorkshire

Albert Mills (HR) SE 0170 2585 (B) 62698
Brearley Lower Mills (HR) SE 0270 2594 (B) 62700
Clough Mill (HR) SE 0140 2605 (B) 62697
Dean Mill (SB) SE 0430 2731 (C) 62934
Oats Royd Mills (SB) SE 0395 2655 (A) 62704*
Stoney Springs Mills (HR) SE 0283 2597 (B) 62701
White Lee Mill (HR) SE 0159 2615 (B) 62696

MIRFIELD, West Yorkshire

Bank Mills SE 1952 2014 (B) 62909
Bankfield Mills (see Bank Mills)
Branch Mill SE 2247 2005 (B) 63473
Britannia Mill SE 2045 1955 (B) 63730
Brooklyn Mills SE 2271 2018 (B) 63474
Butt End Mill SE 2001 1968 (B) 63727

Calder Vale Mills SE 2275 2020 (B) 63475
Clive Mills SE 1962 2013 (B) 62910
Crossley Mills SE 2008 2166 (B) 63434
Fold Head Mill SE 2015 1979 (B) 63726
Holme Bank Mills SE 206 192 (B) 63731
Hopton Mills SE 2120 1860 (B) 63736
Ledgard Bridge Mills SE 2018 1950 (B) 63728
Low Mills SE 2189 1980 (B) 63735
Netherfield Mills SE 2249 2018 (C) 63471
Newtown Mill SE 2280 2022 (B) 63476
Oaklands Mill SE 2232 2010 (B) 63472
Perseverance Mill SE 1915 2035 (B) 62907
Ravens Ing Mill SE 2308 2045 (B) 63498
Raventhorpe Mills SE 225 202 (B) 63470
Roe Head Mill SE 1931 2199 (B) 62906
Sands Mill SE 1925 2026 (B) 62908
South Brook Mills SE 2026 1945 (B) 63729
Spring Place Mill SE 2170 2065 (B) 63447
Wellington Mill SE 1925 2023 (B) 62911
Wharf Mill SE 2302 2042 (B) 63499

MONK BRETTON (Barnsley), West Yorkshire

Newbridge Bleachworks SE 3705 0766 (C) 63802

MORLEY, West Yorkshire

Albion Mill SE 2650 2838 (C) 63577
Alexandra Mill SE 2611 2734 (B) 63590
Asda House SE 2597 2674 (B) 63652
Bantam Grove Dyehouse SE 2785 2765 (B) 63607
Brunswick Mill SE 2685 2799 (B) 63581
City Mill SE 2677 2782 (B) 63582
Cliffe Mill SE 250 273 (C) 63874
Commercial Street Mills SE 2652 2780 (B) 63585
Crank Mill SE 2685 2823 (A) 63579*
Daisy Hill Mills SE 271 285 (C) 63604
Dean Hall Mills SE 2564 2809 (B) 63559
Deanfield Mills SE 2569 2860 (B) 63558
Field Mill SE 2605 2756 (B) 63588
Fountain Street Mills SE 2629 2741 (B) 63589
Gillroyd Mills SE 2740 2766 (B) 63606
Grove Mill (see Bantam Grove Dyehouse)
Hembrigg Mill SE 2645 2705 (B) 63595
Highcliffe Mill SE 2551 2805 (B) 63560
Hollow Top Mill SE 2660 2702 (B) 63596
Low Moor Mill SE 2681 2805 (B) 63580
Lower Mill SE 2499 2503 (B) 63507
Melbourne Mills SE 2670 2756 (B) 63584
Mill SE 2642 2767 (B) 63587
Mill SE 2655 2730 (B) 63591
Mill SE 2645 2829 (B) 63651
Park Mills SE 2681 2765 (B) 63657
Parkfield Mills SE 2589 2736 (B) 63561
Peel Mill SE 2665 2760 (B) 63583
Peel Street Mills SE 2651 2769 (B) 63586
Perseverance Mill SE 2650 2818 (B) 63578
Prospect Mills SE 2629 2834 (B) 63574
Providence Mill SE 2620 2829 (C) 63575
Quarry Mills SE 2635 2709 (B) 63594
Queen Mills SE 2629 2775 (C) 63664
Rods Mill SE 2681 2731 (C) 63592
Springfield Mill SE 260 288 (B) 63573
Tingley Mills SE 2692 2670 (B) 63597
Valley Mills SE 2737 2829 (C) 63605
Victoria Mills SE 2618 2819 (B) 63576
Wellington Mills SE 2649 2719 (B) 63593

MORTON (Keighley), West Yorkshire

Botany Mills SE 1010 4255 (C) 62302
New Woodhead Worsted Mill SE 0680 4340 (C) 62371

NETHERTHONG (Holmfirth), West Yorkshire

Alma Mill SE 1475 0983 (C) 63236
Thongsbridge Mills SE 1479 0970 (B) 63202

NORLAND (Sowerby Bridge), West Yorkshire

Belmont Mill SE 0533 2283 (B) 62730
Lock Hill Mills SE 0625 2355 (B) 62740
Meirclough Mills SE 0695 2368 (B) 62915
Old House Mill (see Belmont Mill)
Valley Mills SE 0610 2352 (B) 62739
Watson Mills SE 0550 2290 (B) 62729

NORTH BIERLEY, West Yorkshire

Acre Mills SE 1510 3046 (B) 62506
Bankfoot Mill SE 1565 3020 (B) 62509
Blackshaw Mill SE 1319 2910 (B) 62837
Buttershaw Mill SE 138 292 (B) 62836
Carr Lane Mill SE 1560 2814 (B) 62865
Carrwood Mills SE 1535 3048 (B) 62507
Denham's Shed SE 1320 3030 (B) 62429
Mill SE 1585 2901 (B) 62864
Park House Wire Mills SE 1625 2895 (B) 62869
Park View Mills SE 1445 3005 (A) 62457*
Perseverance Mill SE 1425 3028 (B) 62456
Prospect Mills SE 1541 3010 (C) 62510
Stadium Mills SE 1595 2975 (A) 62863*
Victoria Mills SE 153 289 (C) 62940

NORTHOWRAM (Halifax; Queensbury and Shelf), West Yorkshire

Bankfield Mill (H) SE 0901 2598 (B) 62787
Black Dyke Mills (QS) SE 104 302 (B) 62397
Bowling Dyke Dyeworks (H) SE 0925 2572 (B) 62790
Bowling Dyke Mills (H) SE 0920 2578 (B) 62789
Crossleys Dyeworks (H) SE 084 265 (C) 62946
Dean Clough Mills (H) SE 089 258 (A) 62767
Eastfield Mill (H) SE 1015 2590 (B) 62813
Garden Street Mills (H) SE 0965 2570 (B) 62912
Haley Hill Mills (H) SE 0195 2585 (B) 62788
Haley Hill Mill (see Bankfield Mill)
Haley Hill Shed (see Bankfield Mill)
Ladyship Mills (H) SE 0850 2679 (B) 62764
Mill (H) SE 1005 2590 (B) 62812
New Bank Mills (see Garden Street Mills)
Old Lane Dyeworks (H) SE 0851 2642 (C) 62945
Old Lane Mill (H) SE 0860 2635 (A) 62765*

OSSETT, West Yorkshire

Bottomfield Mill SE 2809 2120 (B) 63618
Calder Vale Dyeworks SE 2710 1910 (B) 63751
Cockcroft Mills SE 2785 1980 (B) 63750
Field Lane Mill SE 2775 2079 (B) 63614
Foster's Mill SE 2711 2192 (B) 63636
Gedham Mill SE 2776 2065 (A) 63616*
Guildford Street Mills (see Cockcroft Mills)
Healey Low Mill SE 272 189 (C) 63774
Healey New Mill SE 2695 1895 (A) 63747*
Healey Old Mill SE 2690 1935 (C) 63746
Highfield Mill SE 2768 2135 (B) 63612
Ings Mill SE 2805 2077 (B) 63620
Loomshop, Wesley Street SE 2752 2051 (A) 63659*
Mill SE 2950 1980 (B) 63761
North Field Mill (see Field Lane Mill)
Ossett Mill (see Healey Old Mill)
Perseverance Mill SE 2792 2129 (A) 63613*
Pildacre Mill SE 2665 2090 (B) 63602
Queen Street Mills SE 2778 2016 (B) 63634
Rag Warehouse SE 2767 2048 (B) 63633
Rag Warehouse SE 2751 2006 (B) 63635
Royds Mill (see Foster's Mill)
Runtlings Mill SE 2699 2012 (A) 63603*
Spedding Oddy's rag warehouse SE 2767 2030 (A) 63658*
Spring End Mill SE 2973 1936 (B) 63762
Spring Field Mills (see Spring End Mill)
Storrs Hill Mill SE 2822 1934 (B) 63755
Sunnydale Mills SE 2830 2026 (B) 63621
Temperance Mill SE 2778 2074 (B) 63615
Victoria Mill SE 2805 1940 (B) 63754
Westfield Mill SE 2740 2050 (C) 63617
Whitley Spring Mill SE 2879 2096 (C) 63619

OTLEY (Aireborough; Otley), West Yorkshire

Ackroyd Mill (O) SE 1930 4520 (B) 62319
Eller Ghyll Mill (O) SE 1780 4445 (B) 62313
Gill Mill (O) SE 1775 4450 (B) 62312
Middle Mill (O) SE 1796 4448 (B) 62314
Otley Mills (see Ackroyd Mill)
Silver Hill Mill (A) SE 208 448 (C) 63249

OVENDEN (Halifax), West Yorkshire

Beechwood Mills SE 0819 2790 (B) 62763
Beechwood Works SE 0765 2779 (B) 62743
Box Trees Mill SE 0676 2705 (B) 62732
Bradshaw Mill SE 0785 3010 (C) 41508
Dapper Mill SE 0695 2672 (B) 62733
Farcroft Mill SE 0816 3047 (B) 62378
Forest Mill SE 0765 2750 (B) 62744
Holmfield Mills SE 0845 2850 (B) 62762
Illingworth Mills SE 071 282 (C) 62936
Jumples Mills SE 0646 2798 (B) 62731
Lee Bank Mills SE 086 261 (C) 62938
Little Hebble Mill SE 0761 2638 (A) 62746*
Lower Jack Royd Mill SE 0759 2649 (B) 62745
Mixenden Works SE 0552 2829 (B) 62722
Old Lane Mills (see Lee Bank Mills)
Providence Mills (see Farcroft Mill)
Wheatley Dyeworks (see Dapper Mill)
Wire Mill (see Lower Jack Royd Mill)
Clifby Works SE 0692 2589 (B) 62734

OXSPRING, South Yorkshire

Kirkwood Mill SE 2595 0293 (B) 63786

PLOMPTON, North Yorkshire

Plompton Mill SE 3610 5598 (B) 63853

POOL, West Yorkshire

Pool Mill SE 2465 4538 (C) 63247
Pool Walk Mill (see Pool Mill)

POTTER NEWTON (Leeds), West Yorkshire

Clothing Works SE 3205 3520 (B) 63381
Crestona Works SE 3205 3535 (B) 63380

PUDSEY, West Yorkshire

Albert Mill SE 2255 3274 (B) 63277
Alexandra Shed SE 1879 3220 (B) 62585
Brick Mills SE 2255 3286 (B) 63275
Cliffe Mill SE 2245 3265 (B) 63276
Crawshaw Mill SE 2245 3319 (B) 63272
Dick Lane Mills SE 1900 3238 (B) 62600
Firland Mill SE 2236 3283 (B) 63274
Gibraltar Mill SE 2079 3323 (C) 63252
Grangefield Mill SE 2242 3435 (B) 63268
Leigh Mills SE 2185 3412 (B) 63257
New Lane Mills SE 1900 3280 (B) 62582
New Street Mills SE 2200 3278 (A) 63273*
Priestley Mill SE 2295 3400 (B) 63269
Prospect Mill SE 2175 3345 (B) 63258
South Park Mills SE 2260 3160 (B) 63280
Southroyd Mill SE 2257 3218 (B) 63279
Troydale Mills SE 2390 3250 (B) 63290
Try Mill SE 2238 3329 (B) 63271
Union Bridge Mill SE 2370 3159 (B) 63293
Union Mill SE 2290 3267 (C) 63278
Valley Mills SE 2305 3275 (B) 63289
Waterloo Mills SE 2105 3320 (B) 63259
Wellington Mills SE 1875 3267 (B) 62581

RASTRICK (Brighouse), West Yorkshire

Calder Bank Mill SE 1476 2255 (B) 62858
Prince of Wales Mill SE 1481 2250 (C) 62948
Rosemary Dyeworks SE 1415 2200 (B) 62862
Slade Lane Mill SE 1352 2071 (B) 62841
Snake Hill Mill SE 1481 2255 (B) 62859
Spout Mill SE 1335 2100 (B) 62840

RAWDON (Aireborough), West Yorkshire

Airedale Park Mills SE 2192 3875 (B) 63253
Green Lane Dyeworks SE 2085 4035 (B) 63245
Green Lane Mill (see Green Lane Dyeworks)
Low Mills SE 2175 3765 (B) 63254

RISHWORTH (Ripponden), West Yorkshire

Rishworth Mills SE 0365 1795 (B) 62958
Slithero Mills SE 0347 1876 (B) 62957
Spring Mill SE 0355 1689 (B) 62959

SALTERFORTH, Lancashire

Salterforth Shed SD 8900 4540 (B) 62157

SCAMMONDEN (Colne Valley; Elland), West Yorkshire

Old House Mill (CV) SE 052 164 (C) 63178
Scammonden Mill (CV) SE 04 15 (C) 63189
Upper Firth House Mills (E) SE 0602 1767 (B) 62976

SCRIVEN WITH TENTERGATE (Harrogate; Knaresborough), North Yorkshire

Castle Mill (K) SE 3478 5681 (A) 63850*
Crimple Mill (H) SE 3305 5377 (B) 63855

SETTLE, North Yorkshire

Bridge End Mill SD 8170 6411 (B) 63819
Kings Mill SD 8142 6388 (B) 63818
Runley Bridge Mill SD 8110 6230 (A) 63817*
Snift Mill (see Kings Mill)

SHELF (Queensbury and Shelf), West Yorkshire

Clough Mill SE 1185 2795 (B) 62822
Lumbrook Mills SE 1205 2705 (B) 62835
Shelf Mill SE 1239 2865 (B) 62834
Victoria Mill (see Shelf Mill)

SHELLEY (Kirkburton), West Yorkshire

Woodhouse Mills SE 2189 1082 (B) 63737

SHEPLEY (Kirkburton), West Yorkshire

Barncliffe Mills SE 2080 1054 (B) 63734
Shepley New Mills SE 2002 1075 (C) 63732
Victoria Mills SE 1986 0985 (B) 63224
Whitby Mill SE 2001 1046 (B) 63733

SHIPLEY, West Yorkshire

Airedale Mills SE 1490 3785 (B) 62433
Airedale Works SE 1508 3790 (B) 62464
Ashley Mills SE 1455 3780 (B) 62432
Hirst Mill SE 1306 3837 (B) 62416
Orbic Works SE 1445 3785 (B) 62431
Park Works SE 1471 3768 (B) 62434
Providence Mill (see Airedale Mills)
Red Beck Mill SE 1499 3668 (B) 62438
Red Beck Mill SE 1492 3670 (B) 62437
Rosse Street Mills SE 1460 3760 (B) 62435
Saltaire Mills SE 142 382 (A) 41553*
Spring Dyeworks (see Red Beck Mill, 62437)

Union Mill SE 1515 3760 (B) 62467
Victoria Works SE 1470 3800 (B) 62430

SHITLINGTON, West Yorkshire

Coxley Mill SE 2776 1724 (B) 63753

SILSDEN, West Yorkshire

Airedale Shed SE 0410 4635 (B) 62290
Becks Mill SE 0402 4585 (B) 62293
Canal Mills SE 0405 4620 (B) 62328
Canal Mills SE 0412 4619 (B) 62327
Elliott Street Mills SE 0398 4616 (B) 62285
Harwal Works (see Canal Mills, 62327)
New Close Shed SE 0430 4622 (A) 62291*
North Street Mills SE 0425 4671 (B) 62289
Riverside Works SE 0392 4575 (B) 62286
Waterloo Mills SE 0430 4618 (A) 62292*

SKIPTON, North Yorkshire

Belle Vue Mills SD 9861 5160 (A) 62117*
Broughton Road Shed SD 9770 5145 (A) 62123*
Firth Sheds SD 9905 5105 (B) 62120
High Mill SD 9919 5214 (C) 62121
Low Mill SD 9905 5125 (B) 62119
New Mill (see Low Mill)
Park Mill SD 9939 5161 (B) 62122
Union Mills SD 989 511 (A) 62118*
Victoria Mill SD 9869 5170 (B) 44101

SKIRCOAT (Halifax), West Yorkshire

Albert Mills SE 0635 2405 (B) 62737
Canal Mills SE 0735 2365 (B) 62757
Clough Mill SE 0642 2385 (B) 62738
Copley Mill SE 0825 2250 (C) 62932
Farrar Mills SE 0975 2355 (B) 62800
Haugh Shaw Mills SE 0830 2421 (B) 62783
Kings Mill (see Albert Mills)
Lower Willow Hall Mills SE 0641 2419 (B) 62736
Moorfield Mills (see Haugh Shaw Mills)
Salterhebble Mill SE 0972 2288 (B) 62802
Sedburgh Mills SE 0970 2434 (B) 62797
Shaw Lodge Mills SE 0968 2408 (B) 62798
Sterne Mills SE 0775 2325 (B) 62758
Washer Lane Dyeworks SE 0770 2385 (B) 62756

SLAITHWAITE (Colne Valley), West Yorkshire

Bank Gate Mill SE 0764 1418 (B) 62981
Bridge Street Mill SE 0820 1398 (A) 62993*
Clough House Mills SE 0685 1435 (C) 62977
Commercial Mills SE 0770 1385 (B) 62983
Globe Mills SE 0810 1405 (A) 62992*
Merrydale Mill SE 0595 1435 (C) 62967
Mill SE 0819 1420 (B) 63160
Mill SE 082 141 (B) 62990
Mill SE 0769 1408 (B) 63159
Platt Mills SE 0831 1416 (B) 62989
Shaw Carr Wood Mill SE 0680 1334 (C) 62978
Spa Mills SE 0840 1425 (A) 62988*
Upper Mill SE 0762 1382 (B) 62982
Water Side Mill SE 0825 1405 (B) 62991

SOOTHILL (Batley; Dewsbury), West Yorkshire

Alexandra Mills (B) SE 2485 2355 (B) 63521
Chickenley Mill (D) SE 2622 2118 (B) 63600
Culvert Mills (B) SE 2510 2451 (B) 63563
Greengates Mill (D) SE 2683 2164 (B) 63598
Greenhill Dyeworks (B) SE 2518 2360 (B) 63648
Greenhill Mills (see Greenhill Dyeworks)
Hoyle Head Mills (D) SE 2562 2129 (B) 63566
Jilling Ing Mills (D) SE 2610 2110 (B) 63601
Lady Ann Mill (B) SE 2505 2467 (B) 63562
Little Royd Mill (D) SE 2534 2110 (B) 63567
Mill (B) SE 2485 2370 (B) 63644
Mill (B) SE 2490 2387 (B) 63649
Phoenix Mill (B) SE 2478 2400 (A) 63514*
Providence Mill (D) SE 2583 2137 (B) 63565
Savile Mill (B) SE 2484 2350 (B) 63522
Scar End Mill (D) SE 2553 2029 (B) 63571
Station Road, 16–18 (B) SE 248 238 (B) 63709
Station Road, 20–22 (B) SE 248 238 (B) 63710
Station Road, 24–26 (B) SE 248 238 (B) 63711
Station Road, 25 (B) SE 2482 2392 (B) 63717
Station Road, 31–33 (B) SE 2485 2389 (B) 63716
Station Road, 32–40 (B) SE 2489 2378 (B) 63712
Station Road, 35–37 (B) SE 248 238 (B) 63715
Station Road, 39 (B) SE 248 238 (B) 63714
Station Road, 47–51 (B) SE 2491 2381 (B) 63713
Syke Ing Mill (D) SE 2615 2135 (A) 63599*
Sykeing Mills (D) SE 2598 2140 (B) 63564
Union Mill (B) SE 2490 2348 (B) 63523
Warehouse (D) SE 2555 2121 (B) 63637

SOUTH CROSLAND (Huddersfield; Meltham), West Yorkshire

Armitage Bridge Mills (H) SE 133 135 (A) 63076*
Crosland Mills (M) SE 1175 1215 (B) 63051
Dungeon Mill (H) SE 1305 1430 (B) 63074
Park Valley Mills (see Dungeon Mill)

Queen's Square Mill (H) SE 1413 1265 (B) 63112
Steps Mill (H) SE 1401 1281 (B) 63111
Steps Mill (see Queen's Square Mill)
Tolson Dyeworks (H) SE 1310 1380 (B) 63158
Upper Steps Mill (H) SE 1399 1262 (B) 63156

SOUTHOWRAM (Brighouse; Halifax), West Yorkshire

Bailey Hall Mill (H) SE 0990 2508 (B) 62914
Bottoms Mill (H) SE 0999 2321 (B) 62801
Boys Mill (H) SE 0969 2380 (B) 62799
Brookfoot Mills (H) SE 1360 2285 (B) 62839
Clark Bridge Mills (H) SE 0991 2525 (B) 62794
Phoebe Lane Mills (see Boys Mill)
Riding Hall (see Clark Bridge Mills)
Stoney Road Mills (H) SE 0980 2455 (B) 62796

SOWERBY (Hebden Royd; Sowerby Bridge), West Yorkshire

Asquith Bottom Dyeworks (SB) SE 0575 2315 (B) 62728
Asquith Bottom Mills (SB) SE 0581 2317 (B) 62727
Asquith Bottom Shed (see Asquith Bottom Dyeworks)
Brockwell Mill (SB) SE 0490 2290 (B) 62716
Fairlea Mill (SB) SE 0385 2460 (B) 62708
Holme Royd Mill (SB) SE 0380 2470 (B) 62707
Mill House Mill (SB) SE 0485 2255 (A) 62717*
Scar Bottom Mill (HR) SE 0101 2575 (B) 62691
Square Shed (HR) SE 0129 2575 (B) 62699
Stansfield Mill (SB) SE 0445 2210 (B) 62718
Thorpe Mill (SB) SE 0450 2150 (B) 62931
West End Mills (SB) SE 0580 2334 (B) 62726
West Mills (SB) SE 0584 2339 (B) 62725

SOYLAND (Ripponden; Sowerby Bridge), West Yorkshire

Beeston Hall Mill (R) SE 0179 1911 (B) 62952
Clough Mill (SB) SE 0252 2039 (C) 62702
Commercial Mills (R) SE 0355 1906 (B) 62955
Dean Mill (R) SE 0413 2132 (B) 62719
Excelsior Mills (R) SE 0355 1900 (B) 63177
Hollins Mill (see Excelsior Mills)
Kebroyd Mills (R) SE 0415 2130 (A) 62720*
Lower Soyland Mill (R) SE 0351 2119 (B) 62930
Mill (SB) SE 0346 2118 (B) 62710
Ryburndale Paper Mill (R) SE 0260 1868 (B) 62953
Small Lees Mills (R) SE 0378 1950 (B) 62954
Stones Mill (R) SE 0328 1870 (B) 62956
Thrum Hall Mill (see Beeston Hall Mill)
Upper Soyland Mill (R) SE 034 211 (C) 62935
Upper Swift Place Mill (see Ryburndale Paper Mill)
Victoria Mills (R) SE 0430 2015 (B) 62721

STAINLAND (Elland), West Yorkshire

Bankhouse Mill SE 0669 1992 (B) 62972
Brookroyd Mills SE 0900 1950 (A) 62985*
Burrwood Mill SE 0882 2015 (A) 62786*
Dog Lane Mill SE 0695 1890 (B) 62974
Gatehead Mill SE 0767 2051 (B) 62761
Greave Mill SE 0929 1979 (B) 62999
New Mill SE 063 171 (C) 63179
Town Ings Mill SE 0799 1946 (B) 62980

STANLEY CUM WRENTHORPE (Stanley), West Yorkshire

Stanley Mills SE 3408 2472 (B) 63632

STANSFIELD (Blackshaw; Todmorden), West Yorkshire

Adamroyd Mill (T) SD 9354 2465 (B) 62177
Bridge Royd Dyeworks (T) SD 9615 2490 (A) 62216*
Calais Mill (B) SD 9740 2660 (B) 62221
Calderside Dyeworks (B) SD 9806 2706 (C) 62223
Caldervale Mill (T) SD 9080 2635 (B) 62163
Callis Mill (see Calais Mill)
Canteen Shed (T) SD 9220 2555 (B) 62169
Carr Mill (T) SD 9384 2450 (B) 62181
Cinderhill Mills (T) SD 9520 2465 (B) 62203
Cockden Mill (T) SD 9644 2554 (C) 62214
Cornholme Mills (T) SD 9070 2635 (C) 62164
Cowbridge Mill (T) SD 9659 2667 (C) 62209
Crow Carr Ings Mill (T) SD 9380 2433 (B) 62179
Eastwood Dyeworks (see Cockden Mill)
Eastwood Shed (T) SD 9618 2585 (A) 62212*
Glen Dyeworks (T) SD 9081 2661 (B) 62162
Hare Mill (T) SD 9310 2495 (A) 62239*
Harley House Mill (T) SD 9360 2470 (B) 62178
Hope Mill Size Works (T) SD 9378 2444 (B) 62180
Jumble Hole Mill (B) SD 9685 2640 (B) 62211
Land Mill (B) SD 9549 2895 (C) 62202
Lydgate Mill (T) SD 9211 2566 (B) 62263
Millsteads Mill (T) SD 9519 2465 (B) 62204
Mons Mill (see Hare Mill)
Mytholm Mill (B) SD 9830 2730 (B) 62240
Phoenix Punch and Shear Works SD 9467 2449 (B) 62196
Portsmouth Mill (T) SD 8995 2635 (B) 62161
Ridgefoot Mill (T) SD 9368 2430 (C) 62270
Spa Hole Mill (B) SD 9669 2641 (C) 62210
Spaw Mill (see Spa Hole Mill)
Spring Wood Mill (T) SD 9085 2631 (B) 62165
Stamps Mill (B) SD 962 269 (C) 62256
Underbank Dyeworks (see Jumble Hole Mill)
Underbank Mill (see Jumble Hole Mill)
Vale Mill (T) SD 9388 2446 (C) 62182

Winters Mill (B) SD 973 271 (C) 62257
Wood Mill (T) SD 9665 2580 (B) 62213

STEETON WITH EASTBURN, West Yorkshire

Bobbin Mill SE 0335 4421 (B) 62287
Eastburn Mill SE 0190 4455 (B) 62284
Woodlands Mill SE 0325 4415 (A) 62288*

SUTTON IN CRAVEN (Sutton), North Yorkshire

Croft Shed SE 0055 4395 (B) 62280
Greenroyd Mills SE 0060 4405 (B) 62279
Sutton Mills SE 0100 4440 (B) 62283
Sutton Old Mill (see Greenroyd Mills)

THORNHILL (Dewsbury), West Yorkshire

Albert Mills SE 2435 2135 (B) 63546
Bridge Mill SE 2441 2135 (B) 63547
Cut End Mills SE 2479 2122 (B) 63551
Headfield Mills SE 241 206 (B) 63555
Hebble Mill SE 2465 1969 (B) 63741
King's Mill SE 2503 2109 (B) 63569
Midland Mills SE 2428 2138 (B) 63639
Mill SE 2495 2102 (B) 63638
Queen's Mill SE 2489 2115 (B) 63552
Savile Mills SE 2460 2115 (B) 63553
Slaithwaite Mill (see Hebble Mill)
Thornton's Rag Warehouse SE 2449 2126 (B) 63548
Victoria Mills SE 2478 2111 (B) 63554

THORNTHWAITE WITH PADSIDE, North Yorkshire

Folly Gill Flax Mill SE 1814 5895 (B) 63857

THORNTON (Denholme; Thornton), West Yorkshire

Albion Mill (T) SE 0905 3285 (C) 62386
Denholme Mills (D) SE 067 337 (B) 62374
Dole Mill (T) SE 1011 3261 (C) 62395
Excelsior Mills (T) SE 0865 3275 (B) 62377
Foreside Works (D) SE 0700 3225 (B) 62375
Leventhorpe Mill (T) SE 1251 3289 (B) 62411
New Mill (T) SE 0969 3295 (B) 62387
Prospect Mill (T) SE 1017 3262 (A) 62396*
Thornton Mills (see New Mill)
West Scholes Mill (T) SE 0985 3140 (B) 62388

THRUSCROSS, North Yorkshire

High Mill SE 137 581 (C) 63847
High Mill SE 146 580 (C) 63856
Little Mill SE 143 580 (C) 63848
Low Mill, West End SE 1510 5784 (B) 37899
Patrick's Mill (see High Mill, 63856)

THURLSTONE (Penistone), South Yorkshire

Hoyle Mill SE 2378 0361 (B) 63785
Oil Mill (see Hoyle Mill)
Plumpton Mill SE 2292 0330 (B) 63784
The Old Mill SE 2181 0304 (B) 63783

THURSTONLAND (Holmfirth), West Yorkshire

Rock Mills SE 151 108 (C) 63181

TODMORDEN AND WALSDEN (Todmorden), West Yorkshire

Alma Mills SD 9330 2220 (B) 62190
Asia Mill SD 905 278 (C) 62250
Birks Mill SD 9358 2190 (B) 62193
Bottoms Mill SD 9335 2145 (B) 62194
Carrfield Mill SD 9020 2615 (B) 62167
Clough Mill SD 9302 2260 (B) 62261
Copperas House Mill SD 9305 2281 (B) 62262
Dancroft Mill SD 9299 2315 (B) 62174
Friths Mill SD 9265 2314 (B) 62172
Frostholme Mill SD 9075 2625 (A) 62166*
Gauxholme Mill SD 929 232 (C) 62173
Gorpley Mill SD 918 235 (C) 62249
Hollins Mill SD 9340 2205 (A) 62191*
Hope Mill SD 9328 2230 (A) 62189*
Inchfield Picker Works SD 9332 2192 (B) 62192
Italy Mill SD 902 237 (C) 62248
Jubilee Mill SD 9330 2145 (B) 62195
Lacy Mill SD 932 223 (C) 62188
Lineholme Mill SD 9236 2549 (B) 62170
Mill, Jumps SD 921 261 (B) 62269
Owler Carr Mill SD 9111 2380 (B) 62251
Portsmouth Mill SD 8980 2630 (B) 62241
Ramsden Mill SD 9291 2122 (B) 62176
Robinwood Mill SD 9200 2565 (A) 62168*
Salford Mill SD 9340 2395 (B) 62184
Smithy Holme Mill SD 9307 2275 (B) 62186
Spring Dyeworks SD 9281 2130 (B) 62175
Spring Mill (see Ramsden Mill)
Stones Wood Mill SD 9221 2331 (B) 62252
Stoneswood Mill SD 9224 2331 (B) 62171
Wadsworth Mill SD 932 234 (C) 62185
Waterstalls Mill SD 943 212 (C) 62253
Wood Bottom Mill SD 9320 2261 (B) 62187

TONG, West Yorkshire

Dyeworks SE 1834 3060 (B) 62627
Perseverance Mills SE 1830 3069 (C) 62589
Prospect Mill SE 1925 3032 (B) 62602
Stanley Mills SE 1902 3019 (B) 62603
Tyresal Mills SE 1950 3190 (B) 62601

UPPERTHONG (Holmfirth), West Yorkshire

Albert Mills SE 1438 0849 (B) 63205
Bridge Mill SE 1430 0880 (B) 63204
Prickleden Mills SE 1382 0795 (B) 63196
Riverholme Works (see Bridge Mill)
Spring Lane Mill SE 1321 0774 (B) 63198
Upper Mill (see Prickleden Mills)
Victoria Mill SE 1343 0776 (B) 63199

WADSWORTH (Hebden Royd; Wadsworth), West Yorkshire

Acre Mill (W) SE 0045 2825 (B) 62687
Alexandra Shed (W) SE 0075 2639 (B) 62690
Bridge Mill (HR) SD 9932 2736 (B) 62245
Canal Wharf Saw Mills (HR) SE 0032 2649 (B) 62927
Crimsworth Dyeworks (W) SD 9920 2899 (B) 62229
Croft Mill (HR) SD 9939 2716 (B) 62243
Crossley Mill (HR) SD 9940 2710 (B) 62238
Foster Mill (HR) SD 9925 2779 (C) 62232
Gibson Mill (W) SD 9731 2985 (B) 62218
Hawks Clough Shed (see Alexandra Shed)
Hawksclough Mill (HR) SE 0090 2624 (B) 62933
Lord Holme Mill (see Gibson Mill)
Martin Mill (W) SE 0025 2798 (C) 62688
Mayroyd Mill (HR) SD 9958 2690 (B) 62266
Mill (HR) SD 9939 2719 (B) 62244
Mount Pleasant Mill (W) SE 0145 2620 (B) 62695
Nutclough Mill (HR) SD 9945 2755 (B) 8277
Old Town Mill (W) SD 9985 2840 (B) 62231
Pecket Well Shed (W) SD 9975 2969 (A) 62228*
Upper Midge Hole Mill (see Crimsworth Dyeworks)
Victoria Shed (HR) SD 9925 2770 (B) 62233
Westfield Mill (W) SE 0119 2615 (B) 62694
Windsor Shed/Works (see Victoria Shed)

WAKEFIELD, West Yorkshire

Albion Mills SE 3275 2050 (B) 63630
Calder Mill SE 3375 1930 (B) 63770
Castle Bank Mill SE 3375 1940 (B) 63769
Chald Mill SE 3 2 (C) 63663
Providence Mills SE 3265 2040 (B) 63631
Westgate New Mills SE 3 2 (C) 63665
Whiteoak Mills (see Providence Mills)

WARLEY (Halifax; Sowerby Bridge), West Yorkshire

Carlton Mills (see Sowerby Bridge Mills)
Cooperhouse Mills (SB) SE 0391 2440 (C) 62709
Corporation Mill (SB) SE 0590 2361 (B) 62724
Denholme Mill (SB) SE 0391 2471 (B) 62706
Hole Bottom Mill (H) SE 0482 2921 (B) 62711
Holme House Mill (H) SE 0398 2801 (B) 62703
Holme Mill (SB) SE 055 237 (C) 62723
Hoyle Bottom Mill (see Hole Bottom Mill)
Jowler Mill (see Holme House Mill)
Lock Hill Mills (SB) SE 0625 2365 (B) 62740
Longbottom Mill (SB) SE 0419 2405 (B) 62715
Luddenden Clothing Factory (H) SE 0415 2590 (B) 62929
Luddenden Foot Mill (SB) SE 0380 2510 (B) 62705
Luddenden Mills (see Luddenden Clothing Factory)
Lumb Mill (H) SE 0470 2888 (A) 62712*
Peel House Mill (H) SE 0425 2674 (C) 62714
Sowerby Bridge Mills (SB) SE 0609 2360 (A) 8280*
Square Mill (see Hole Bottom Mill)
Wainstalls Mill (H) SE 0440 2865 (B) 62713
Wainstalls New Mill (H) SE 0467 2855 (B) 62928
Warley Springs Dyeworks (H) SE 0626 2478 (B) 62735
Wharf Mill (SB) SE 0640 2368 (C) 62741

WEST ARDSLEY (Morley), West Yorkshire

Glen Mills SE 2728 2685 (B) 63608
Oak Mills SE 2715 2667 (A) 63609*
Southfield Mills SE 2716 2659 (B) 63611
Topcliffe Mill SE 272 266 (A) 63610*

WILSDEN (Bingley), West Yorkshire

Albion Mills SE 0930 3635 (B) 62381
Bents Mill SE 0777 3643 (B) 62677
Birkshead Mill SE 0975 3610 (B) 62382
Hewenden Mill SE 0778 3608 (B) 62667
Lingbob Mill SE 0950 3570 (B) 62385
Prospect Mill SE 0939 3570 (B) 62384
Providence Mill SE 0903 3665 (B) 62379
Spring Mill SE 0915 3645 (A) 62380*
Well House Mill SE 0942 3515 (B) 62383

WINKSLEY, North Yorkshire

Millhouse Farm SE 2479 7116 (B) 63837

WOOLDALE (Holmfirth), West Yorkshire

Albion Mill SE 1485 0973 (B) 63203
Choppards Mill SE 141 064 (C) 63225
Ford Mill SE 1555 0845 (B) 63214
Glendale Mills SE 1628 0866 (B) 63217
Ing Nook Mills (see Glendale Mills)
Kirkbridge Mill SE 1589 0929 (C) 63213
Lee Mills SE 1600 0755 (B) 63221
Midge on Wood Bottom Mill SE 1628 0777 (B) 63220
Moorbrook Mills SE 1619 0880 (B) 63216
Scholes Mill (see Midge on Wood Bottom Mill)
Stoney Bank Mill SE 1569 0988 (A) 63212*
Town Mill SE 1429 0829 (C) 63237
Underbank Mill SE 1463 0742 (A) 63208*
Upper Mytholm Bridge Mills SE 1529 1019 (B) 63129
Washpit Mill SE 1425 0670 (A) 63211*
Wildspur Mill SE 1680 0815 (B) 63219

WORTLEY (Leeds), West Yorkshire

Canal Mills SE 2860 3346 (B) 63329
Castleton Mill SE 2869 3341 (A) 63384*
Junction Mills SE 2874 3293 (C) 63330
Stone Bridge Mills SE 2560 3286 (A) 63308*
Swallow Hill Mills SE 2599 3299 (B) 63307
Upper Mill SE 2671 3181 (B) 63315
Wortley Low Mills (see Upper Mill)

WYKE (Brighouse; Wyke), West Yorkshire

Bailliff Bridge Mill (B) SE 149 251 (B) 62847
City Shed (W) SE 1550 2735 (A) 62866*
Clifton Mills (see Bailliff Bridge Mill)
Crown Point Mills (see City Shed)
New Mill (W) SE 1545 2698 (B) 62868
Station Mills (W) SE 1490 2685 (B) 62842
Wyke Mills (W) SE 1503 2690 (B) 62867

YEADON (Aireborough), West Yorkshire

Albert Mills SE 2129 4120 (C) 63246
Bankfield Dyeworks SE 2075 4150 (B) 63239
Green Lane Dyeworks SE 2085 4035 (B) 63245
Green Lane Mill (see Green Lane Dyeworks)
Kirk Lane Mills SE 2030 4105 (B) 63242
Leafield Mills SE 2015 4110 (C) 63241
Manor Mills SE 2055 4116 (C) 63240
Moorfield Mills SE 2150 4097 (C) 63248
Westfield Mills SE 204 409 (A) 63244*
Yeadon Old Mills SE 2056 4107 (B) 63243

YORK, North Yorkshire

Lawrence Street Flax Mill SE 6113 5133 (A) 60732*
Providence Place Linen Manufactory SE 609 516 (C) 63869

Notes

Introduction

1 Giles and Goodall 1986–7.

1 The Yorkshire textile industry 1770–1930

1 Material for this chapter has been drawn from many published and unpublished sources. Nineteenth-century descriptions of particular value include Abraham Rees *Cyclopaedia* (1819–20, the entries on Manufacturing Industry reprinted in Cossons 1972); Edward Baines *History of the Cotton Manufacture in Great Britain* (1835); A Ure, *The Cotton Manufacture of Great Britain* (1836); Charles Tomlinson's mid 19th-century *The Useful Arts and Manufactures of Great Britain*; and Edward Baines' *An Account of the Woollen Manufacture of England* (published in 1875, but taken from a paper read in 1858, and reprinted in Ponting 1970). More recent historical surveys and accounts of processes within the different branches of the textile industry include, for the woollen and worsted branches: Sigsworth 1958, Jenkins 1972, Jenkins 1975, Aspin 1982, Jenkins and Ponting 1982, Hudson 1986; for the recovered wool branch: Malin 1979, Jenkins and Ponting 1982; for the cotton branch: Farnie 1979, Jenkins 1979, Ingle 1980, Aspin 1981; for the flax and linen branch: Rimmer 1960, Jennings 1970, Kaijage 1975, Goodchild 1982, Jennings 1983, Baines 1985; for the silk branch: Warner 1921, Bush 1987. Technological progress is studied in Singer *et al* 1958*a*, 1958*b*, English 1969, Benson 1983, and Benson and Warburton 1986.
2 Crossley 1989, 14.
3 Carpet works were recorded in RCHME's survey and are included among the sites listed in the Gazetteer.
4 Parliamentary Papers, *Returns of Mills and Factories*, 1833–1905.
5 Worrall 1919–20; supplemented for the Todmorden area by Worrall 1930, 351–3.
6 Defoe 1724–6, 500.
7 See Thornes 1981, Introduction and Chapters 1 and 4 for more details of the evolution of the industrial landscape in West Yorkshire before the mid 19th century.
8 McCutcheon 1980, 251.

2 The buildings of the textile mill

1 Jennings 1983, 178–9.
2 Brown 1821, 4.
3 Connell 1975, site 178.
4 Tann 1970, 133.
5 Sigsworth 1958, 7–9, 38–43, 177-200.
6 Cudworth 1891, 314–15 and plate facing p314; illustration also in Sheeran 1986, 86.
7 Aspin 1974, 19.
8 Sigsworth 1951–2, 61.
9 Aireworth Mills: Guildhall Library, Royal Exchange, MS 7253, Vol 32a, Policy no. 157479, 14 July 1797; Greengate Mills: Guildhall Library, Sun CR, Ms 11937, Vol 127, Policy no. 955629, 19 May 1819; Ingle 1974, 51–3.
10 Ingle 1974, 53.
11 Ingle 1980, 58–61.
12 Tann 1970, 34.
13 Jennings 1983, 356–9; RCHME 1986*b*, 127–31, 152–5; RCHME 1987, 97–8.
14 Bythell 1969, 36; Smith 1977; Timmins 1979.
15 Goodchild 1982, 251–4.
16 Kaijage 1975, 104.
17 Ranger 1852, frontispiece, 18–19.
18 Thornes 1981, 19–20, figs 18–20; Caffyn 1986, 9–15.
19 Bodey 1971.
20 Tann 1970, 4, 7; Jones 1985, 16–17, fig 3.
21 Jenkins 1975, 6–8.
22 Tann 1970, 149.
23 Jones 1985, 23–5, 46–7.
24 Nussey 1984, 6–9, fig 11; Jones 1985, 32, fig 16.
25 Tann 1970, 151.
26 Chapman 1981–2.
27 Chapman 1981–2, 10.
28 Tann 1970, 8, 13, 15; Chapman 1981–2, 15, fig 2.
29 Jenkins 1975, 56, fig 7.
30 The Old Mill at Congleton in Cheshire, a water-powered silk-throwing mill erected in 1753, was probably the first

textile mill built to this plan (Calladine and Fricker forthcoming); early 19th-century examples include Greg and Ewart's mill in Manchester (Tann 1970, 132) and Barracks Mill, Whitehaven, Cumbria (Falconer and Thornes 1986–7, 28, figs 1, 2, pls 2, 3).

31 Fitzgerald 1987–8*b*, 216.

32 Ibid, 209–15.

33 Ure 1836, Vol 1, 294–308, fig 21, pls I, II.

34 RCHME 1986*a*, 11.

35 The Byzantine-style office at Hare Mill survives (Fig 100e), but the turrets and detailing around the water tank over the corner stair tower of the spinning mill have been removed.

36 Jones 1985, 173.

37 Sington 1897, 1.

38 Saxonhouse and Wright 1984, 507.

39 Parliamentary Papers, *Returns of Mills and Factories*, 1901.

40 *Institution of Civil Engineers, Minutes of Proceedings*, 1842, 142–5; Hume 1977, 268–9; Moss and Hume 1981, pl 13.

41 Guildhall Library, Sun CR, MS 11937, Vol 18, Policy no. 663500, 6 January 1797.

42 Guildhall Library, Sun CR, MS 11937, Vol 116, Policy no. 924754, 10 December 1816.

43 Walton and Co Ltd, Harrogate, Utensil Ledger, *c*1872.

44 Rogers 1976, 58–9.

45 Hargrave and Crump 1931, 90–4.

46 Ibid, 94, 102.

47 Fitzgerald 1987–8*a*, 133, pl 4.

48 Tann 1970, 44; Macleod *et al* 1988, 44.

49 Brown 1821, 5.

50 Tann 1970, 133; Rogers 1976, 62.

51 Guildhall Library, Sun CR, MS 11937, Vol 127, Policy no. 952490, 11 March 1819.

52 Rogers 1976, 62, 93.

53 Glover 1959, 384.

54 Ibid.

55 Ibid.

56 William Partridge, a dyer with experience of Gloucestershire and New England dyeworks, recommended in 1823 that dyehouses 'should be built of stone or brick, and the wall thick, to keep it warm during winter, and cool in the summer. The roof should be high, with capacious air holes in it, over the furnaces, to let out the steam as fast as it rises. The part containing the blue vats should be separated by a partition, and the floor should be higher than the other, to prevent any of the liquor from the furnaces running among the blue wool . . . Over each vat there should be one good light' (Partridge 1823, 124–5).

57 Roberts 1977.

58 Ibid, 10.

59 Ibid, 14–16, 28–9.

60 Falkus 1967; Tann 1970, 123–31; Falkus 1982.

61 Tann 1970, 127 and information kindly supplied by Dr H Nabb.

62 For details of Gott's provision of gas at Bean Ing Mills, Armley Mills and Burley Mills see Crump 1931*c*, 258–60, 265–8, pls VII, X–XII and Tann 1970, 129, 134. The new gas plant at Bean Ing Mills is not shown on Fowler's map of Leeds of 1826 but is included on his plan of 1831 and his Western Panoramic View of Leeds, published in 1832 (Fig 273).

63 Pike 1896, 18.

64 Coad 1973, 89, pl XIV.

65 Tann 1970, 137.

66 Peters 1974, 46–52, figs 18–24. NB The plates are iron, not tin; Calladine and Fricker forthcoming.

67 Brears nd, 6.

68 Guildhall Library, Sun CR, MS 11937, Vol 156, Policy no. 1040865, 12 January 1826.

69 Johnson and Skempton 1955–7, 179–93.

70 Also called Castle Foregate Mill; see Skempton and Johnson 1962 and Macleod *et al* 1988.

71 Fitzgerald 1987–8*a*.

72 Ibid, 129.

73 Ibid, 133, pl 4.

74 Ibid, 134–5, pl 5.

75 Ibid, 136–43.

76 Jones 1985, 162; Holden 1987–8, 163, fig 2a.

77 Holden 1987–8, 163, fig 2b; Patent No. 1967 of 1885; information from Dr R N Holden.

78 Jones 1985, 175, fig 89.

79 Bannister 1950, 235.

80 Fitzgerald 1987–8*a*, 128–9.

81 Textile mills, including some in Yorkshire, were in the forefront of early developments. Cast-iron trusses were used in such early 19th-century mills as North Mill, Belper, Ditherington Mill, Shrewsbury and Barracks Mill, Whitehaven, while trusses combining cast and wrought iron were used at Boar's Head Mill, Darley Abbey and Chepstow Street Mill, Manchester. Naval architects also made use of trusses combining the two types of iron, as in the roofs of the spinning house in the ropeyard at Devonport dockyard, and a forge at Woolwich dockyard (Information from Keith Falconer).

82 Arched cast-iron trusses were used in other mid 19th-century textile mills, among them Douglas Mill, Verdant Mill and Camperdown Works in Dundee, and Bennochy Works, Kirkcaldy (Watson 1987–8; Watson 1990, 44–9, 138–58).

83 Fitzgerald 1987–8*a*, 133, pl 4.

84 Ibid, 143–4, pl 7.

85 Fitzgerald 1979, 61, 66.

86 University of Leeds, Brotherton Library: Special Collections, Gott MSS 193/170, letter from W Fairbairn to Messrs B Gott and Sons, 19 February 1829.

3 The development of the textile mill complex

1 Borthwick Institute of Historical Research, University of York, Exchequer Probate Records, Deanery of Pontefract, May 1714; see also RCHME 1986*b*, 129.

2 Atkinson 1956, 1–18; Dickenson 1974, 134; for a recent

discussion of the organisation of production before 1770, see Hudson 1986, 30–9.
3 Jenkins 1975, 9.
4 Jennings 1983, 176–81; Goodchild 1982, 250–1, 263–4.
5 RCHME 1986*b*, 152–5.
6 Goodchild 1981, 26–9.
7 Jennings 1983, 180; Goodchild 1982, 250, 254–5.
8 Jenkins 1975, 8, 10; Crossley 1989, 14–15.
9 Jenkins and Ponting 1982, 28–9; Jenkins 1979, 81; Jennings 1983, 209–10.
10 Beresford 1988, 215–16.
11 Jenkins 1975, 191–205; Jenkins 1979, 78–81; Jennings 1983, 210–11; Beresford 1988, 215–16; Hudson 1986, 30–41, 70–81, 86–7; Rimmer 1960, 36–7.
12 Parliamentary Papers (House of Commons) 1834 (167), *Employment of Children in Factories*, xx, C1, Part 2, Mill no. 136.
13 Jenkins 1979, 80–3; Rimmer 1960, 124–30.
14 The best account of the workings of a public mill is contained in the diary of Joseph Rogerson, scribbling and fulling miller of Bramley, near Leeds, dating from the period 1808 to 1814; see Hargrave and Crump 1931.
15 Jenkins 1975, 8–9.
16 Cossons 1972, 493–4.
17 Hargrave and Crump 1931, 82, 95.
18 Hartley and Ingilby 1976, pl 42.
19 *The Penny Magazine* Vol 12, 503, 30 December 1843.
20 Baines 1822, 110; White 1853, 253–6.
21 Parliamentary Papers (House of Commons) 1834 (167), *Employment of Children in Factories*, xx, C1, Part 1, Mill no. 32.
22 Baines 1822, 107–8.
23 West Yorkshire Archive Service, Leeds: Acc 1715; Guildhall Library, Sun CR, MS 11937, Vol 193, Policy no. 1131689, 9 November 1831.
24 Guildhall Library, Royal Exchange, MS 7352, Vol 7, Policy no. 86734, 6 June 1783.
25 Anon 1806, 28.
26 Cossons 1972, Vol 5, 468.
27 Jenkins 1975, Appendix iv; Jenkins 1979, 90–2.
28 Crump 1931*b*, 33–5.
29 Aikin 1795, 560.
30 Parliamentary Papers (House of Commons) 1806 (268), III, *State of the Woollen Manufacture of England*, quoted in Crump and Ghorbal 1935, 92.
31 Glover 1959, 378.
32 Crump 1931*c*, 263.
33 Ibid.
34 Jenkins 1975, 68.
35 Jenkins and Ponting 1982, 78, 80.
36 Goodchild 1982, 264; Jenkins and Ponting 1982, 116–17.
37 Ingle 1974, 107–8.
38 Parliamentary Papers, *Returns of Mills and Factories* 1861, 1889.
39 Farnie 1979, 284–8.
40 Parliamentary Papers, *Returns of Mills and Factories* 1871.
41 Ibid, 1871, 1874, 1878.
42 Sigsworth 1958, Chapter 3.
43 Parliamentary Papers (House of Commons) 1834 (167), *Employment of Children in Factories*, xx, C1, Part 1, Mill no. 16.
44 Tann 1970, 41.
45 Jenkins 1975, 133.
46 Fairbairn 1863, 172–81, pls V, VI.
47 Information regarding Manchester mills kindly supplied by Michael Williams.
48 Hudson 1986, 72–3, 137.
49 Parliamentary Papers (House of Commons) 1833 (690) *Report . . . [on] the present state of Manufactures, Commerce and Shipping*, vi, 82.
50 Sigsworth 1958, 154–7.
51 Information kindly given by Mr A J Brooke.
52 See Farnie 1979, 289–95 for a discussion of the organisation of room and power in the Lancashire weaving industry.
53 Travis 1901, 52.
54 Feather 1972, 91.
55 White 1853, 411, 483.
56 Kelly 1893, 1335; this number excludes any woolcombers in Leeds not covered in this directory.
57 *Illustrated Weekly Telegraph*, 10 October 1885.
58 City of Bradford 1947, 47–9, 59 etc.
59 Sigsworth 1958, 183.
60 Ibid, 124–9.
61 Jenkins and Ponting 1982, 241–2.
62 Walton and Co Ltd, Harrogate; Utensil Ledger, *c*1872.
63 James 1857, 474.
64 *The Warehouseman and Draper*, 30 September 1899.
65 *Illustrated Weekly Telegraph*, 12 May 1888.
66 Parliamentary Papers (House of Commons) 1873 (C347-I), *Report . . . on the Best Means of Preventing Pollution of Rivers*, 126, 100.
67 Malin 1979, 214–18.
68 Kelly 1889, 1566, 1615, 1628.
69 Malin 1979, 250–2, 259, 265–71.
70 Ibid, 250; Smith 1866, 61.
71 Malin 1979, 273–4.
72 Jennings 1983, 259–65.
73 Jenkins 1979, 88–90.
74 Pafford and Pafford 1974, 60–5.
75 Jenkins and Ponting 1982, Chapters 8, 9.
76 Worrall 1919–20, 77–123.

4 Power and power transmission

1 Fairbairn 1861, 66.
2 von Tunzelmann 1978, 117–18.
3 Jenkins 1975, 71–4.
4 Ingle 1980, 59–60.
5 Hills 1970, 89–90.
6 Ibid.
7 Parliamentary Papers (House of Commons) 1834 (167), *Employment of Children in Factories*, xx, C1, Part 1, Mill No. 13.

8 Ibid, C1, Part 2, Mill No. 212.
9 Crump 1931*b*, 9.
10 Stowers 1958*a*, 199–200.
11 Jenkins 1975, 8.
12 Tann 1970, 60–1.
13 Ibid, 67.
14 Parliamentary Papers (House of Commons) 1834 (167), *Employment of Children in Factories*, xx, C1, Parts 1 and 2.
15 Wild 1972, 209.
16 Shutt 1979, 108–13.
17 Holroyde 1980, 71; Ingle 1974, 102–3.
18 Shutt 1979, 108–18; Jennings 1983, 231–4, 246.
19 von Tunzelmann 1978, 166–7.
20 Chapman 1971; von Tunzelmann 1978, 129–38.
21 Chapman 1971, 1–2; Jenkins 1975, 77–8.
22 Binns 1972, 74–5.
23 Parliamentary Papers (House of Commons) 1834 (167), *Employment of Children in Factories*, xx, C1, Part 1, Mill No. 20; C1, Part 2, Mill No. 292.
24 Ibid, C1, Part 1, Mill No. 17.
25 Ibid, C1, Part 2, Mill No. 267.
26 Ibid, C1, Part 2, Mill No. 79.
27 Tann 1965.
28 Jennings 1983, 246.
29 Ibid, 232–5.
30 Jenkins 1975, 80.
31 Garnett 1951, 3; West Yorkshire Archive Service, Calderdale: Misc 221; HXT 675, 676.
32 Fairbairn 1861, 173–4; Allen 1958, 528–34.
33 von Tunzelmann 1978, 166–7.
34 Dickinson 1958, 168–81.
35 Tann 1970, 75, 91; Connell 1990, 193; Holroyde 1980, 67; Trigg 1933, 146–9.
36 For an illustration of a colliery pumping engine and its engine house, see Dickinson 1958, 180.
37 See Hills 1970, 134–64 and Hills 1989 for a discussion of the development of the rotative steam engine.
38 Tann 1970, 79; Hills 1970, 160–1.
39 Parliamentary Papers (House of Commons) 1834 (167), *Employment of Children in Factories*, xx, C1, Parts 1 and 2.
40 von Tunzelmann 1978, 87, 221.
41 Fairbairn 1861, 237–9, 243–5.
42 Stowers 1958*b*, 130–3.
43 *Engineering*, 23 March 1866.
44 Hills 1970, 152–8.
45 Lists of Sun and Planet and Crank Engines, Boulton and Watt Collection, Birmingham Library Services.
46 Jenkins 1975, 82–5, 90.
47 University of Leeds, Brotherton Library: Brotherton Collection, MS 18.
48 Jenkins 1975, 93–5; Dr Jenkins' findings for the wool textile industry are substantiated by the evidence of the Factory Returns relating to other branches.
49 Brown 1821, 2.
50 Tann 1970, 84–7; Hills 1970, Chapter 9.
51 Parliamentary Papers (House of Commons) 1873 (C347-I), *Report . . . on the Best Means of Preventing Pollution of Rivers*, 95.
52 Boulton and Watt Collection, Birmingham Library Services: cf Portfolios 96 (wooden frame) and 126 (lever wall).
53 See Watkins 1970, 44, for other Yorkshire mills with vertical engines.
54 Details of boiler design are derived from Fairbairn 1864, 259–62, and Buchanan and Watkins 1976, 103–7.
55 Brown 1821.
56 Boulton and Watt Collection, Portfolios 91–2, 105, 496, Birmingham Library Services.
57 Fairbairn 1864, 264
58 Ingle 1974, 58.
59 Fowler 1895, 1–17; Green 1956, 46–7.
60 Buchanan 1980, 193–6.
61 Fairbairn 1863, 7.
62 Fairbairn 1861, 248–9; 1863, 100.
63 *Textile Manufacturer*, 15 June 1876, 151–2.
64 *Building News*, 12 April 1882, 476.
65 Nasmith and Nasmith 1909, 338.
66 Field 1958, 157–60.
67 Dickinson 1938, 194–5.
68 Du Boff 1967, 512.
69 Emmott and Company 1919, 196.
70 Nasmith and Nasmith 1909, 275–7.
71 Emmott and Company 1919, 196.

5 The impact of the textile industry on the landscape

1 Defoe 1724–6, 479–505.
2 For details of these and other cloth halls see Linstrum 1978, 281–9; Burt and Grady 1987, 9–11; Smithies 1988; Grady 1989.
3 Mason 1989, 29.
4 A local writer felt it worthwhile to note in 1860 that 'manufacturers have lately erected stately groups of warehouses, in part of the town convenient to the railway; and this they have done for the purpose of facilitating the disposal of their goods' (Jubb 1860, 118–20).
5 Roberts 1977.
6 Kelly 1893, 312.
7 White 1858, 351–2.
8 Kelly 1893, 103; Linstrum 1978, 306–9.
9 See Darley 1975; Hay and Stell 1986, 76–83; Pevsner, revised Williamson 1978, 157–60; Peters 1974; Rose 1986.
10 Jowitt 1986*b*.
11 For information about Wilshaw, Copley, Akroydon, Ripleyville and West Hill Park see Linstrum 1978, 133–45; Caffyn 1986, esp. 58–68; Taylor 1961; Pearce 1979–80*a*; Pearce 1986; Jowitt 1986*c*; *The Bradford Observer*, 11 November 1882; Fieldhouse 1981, 151–2; Girouard 1979, 205–12. For Glasshouses, Meltham Mills and Saltaire, see pp172–83 and references.
12 For the fullest published account of Glasshouses Mill see

Jennings 1983.
13 Wilson 1937, 40–77; Linstrum 1978, 375.
14 See Hughes 1866; Linstrum 1978, 105, 143; Pearce 1979–80*b*; Pearce 1986.
15 Sheeran 1990, 217–18.
16 Hughes 1866, 198.
17 Kelly 1877, 710.
18 See Balgarnie 1877; Suddards 1976; Reynolds 1983, 1985 and 1986.
19 Balgarnie 1877, 118–19.
20 *The Builder*, 30 October 1852, 694.
21 Reynolds 1983, 265.
22 Reynolds 1986, 55.
23 Linstrum 1978, 80.
24 Girouard 1979, 414, pl 407.
25 Sigsworth 1951–2, 70.
26 *Leeds Intelligencer*, 19 November 1804.
27 Rose 1986, 28–33, 105–11.
28 Allen 1986, 4–8.
29 Shutt 1979, 231.
30 Ingle 1980, 118; Shutt 1979, 232–3.
31 Rose 1986, 56, quoting *Report on the state of children employed in cotton mills and factories*, PP 1816 (397) III, 133.
32 Rimmer 1957–60, 65, 67; Macleod *et al* 1988, 36–7, fig 23.
33 Pevsner, revised Williamson 1978, 49, 87–8, 281–2.
34 Ibid, 49, 193; Peters 1974.
35 Calladine and Fricker forthcoming.
36 For a general survey of the provision of workers' housing in West Yorkshire, see Caffyn 1986, esp. 73–106.
37 Brayshaw and Robinson 1932, 210–11. NB For 1794 read 1784.
38 *Leeds Intelligencer*, 10 April 1787.
39 Taylor 1961; Pearce 1979–80*b*; Pearce 1986.
40 Hughes 1866, 209.
41 Brayshaw and Robinson 1932, 210; Settle and District Civic Society 1975, 56.
42 Linstrum 1978, 81–2, pl 44.
43 Marshall had ventured into London society in 1821 and initially rented a house. He leased 4 Grosvenor Square from 1825 to 1832 and then acquired 34 Hill Street, Berkeley Square (Rimmer 1960, 104).
44 Ibid, 98–9, 113–17, pl II.
45 Linstrum 1978, 84, pl 47; Girouard 1979, 403–4, pl 394; Worsley 1986, 303–4, pls 3–5.
46 Linstrum 1978, 104–24.
47 For an overall view of the buildings erected for educational purposes in West Yorkshire, see Linstrum 1978, 237–68. For a study of Leeds see Stephens 1980.
48 Rimmer 1960, 68, 105–9.
49 Shutt 1979, 231.
50 Holden 1912, 201.
51 Ibid.
52 Jowitt 1986*c*, 78–82.
53 *Bradford Observer*, 11 November 1882; Kelly 1893, 104.
54 James 1986, 113.
55 Almond 1919, 26–7.
56 *Bradford Observer*, 11 November 1882; Jowitt 1982, 48. Ripley gave the site of St Bartholomew's Church in Ripleyville, which was built in 1871–2.
57 White 1853, 649.
58 Linstrum 1978, 226–8, pls 178, 181.
59 Jennings 1983, 405–43.
60 James 1986, 112.
61 Kelly 1893, 105.
62 *Bradford Observer*, 11 November 1882.
63 Almond 1919, 39.
64 Ayers 1972, 72, pls 138–9.
65 Taylor 1961, 42–3; Pearce 1986, 68, 99–100.
66 Rimmer 1960, 100–2, 110–13.
67 Linstrum 1978, 354–5, pl 286; Cunningham 1981, 77, pl 38.
68 Jowitt 1986*c*, 82.
69 James 1986, 112; Kelly 1893, 604.
70 Hodgson 1879, 77–81; Dewhirst 1972.
71 James 1986, 112.
72 Robinson 1972; Linstrum 1978, 360, pl 293; Bradford Art Galleries and Museums 1987.
73 Caffyn 1986, 99, pl 118; Jowitt 1986*c*, 78.

Bibliography

Aikin, J 1795. *A Description of the Country from Thirty to Forty Miles around Manchester*

Allen, J 1958. Hydraulic engineering. In Singer *et al* 1958*b*, 522–51

Allen, N 1986. *David Dale, Robert Owen and the Story of New Lanark*

Almond, A 1919. *Biography of James Ickringill Esquire*

Anon 1806. *The Leeds Guide*

Anon 1893. *The Century's Progress*

Aspin, C 1981. *The Cotton Industry*

1982. *The Woollen Industry*

Aspin, C (ed) 1974. *Angus Bethune Reach. The Yorkshire Textile Districts in 1849*

Atkinson, F (ed) 1956. *Some Aspects of the Eighteenth Century Woollen and Worsted Trade in Halifax*

Ayers, J 1972. *Architecture in Bradford*

Baines, E 1822. *History, Directory and Gazetteer of the County of York*

1835. *History of the Cotton Manufacture in Great Britain*

Baines, P 1985. *Flax and Linen*

Balgarnie, R 1877. *Sir Titus Salt*

Bannister, T 1950. The first iron-framed buildings. *Architectural Rev* **107**, 231–46

Benson, A P 1983. *Textile Machines*

Benson, A and Warburton, N 1986. *Looms and Weaving*

Beresford, M 1988. East End, West End: the face of Leeds during urbanisation, 1684–1842. *Publ Thoresby Soc* **60**, **61** (for 1985 and 1986)

Binney, M *et al* 1979. *Satanic Mills. Industrial Architecture in the Pennines*

Binns, G R 1972. Water wheels in the upper Calder valley. *Trans Halifax Antiq Soc*, 51–76

Bodey, H A 1971. Coffin Row, Linthwaite. *Ind Archaeol* **8**, 381–91

Bradford Art Galleries and Museums 1987. *Cartwright Hall. A Guide to the Building and its Architecture*

Brayshaw, T and Robinson, R M 1932. *The History of the Ancient Parish of Giggleswick*

Brears, P C D nd. *Armley Mills. The Leeds Industrial Museum*

Brown, W 1821. Information regarding flax spinning in Leeds. Typescript in Leeds City Library

Buchanan, R A 1980. *Industrial Archaeology in Britain*. 2nd edn

Buchanan, R A and Watkins, G 1976. *The Industrial Archaeology of the Stationary Steam Engine*

Burt, S and Grady, K 1987. *The Merchants' Golden Age. Leeds 1700–1790*

Bush, S 1987. *The Silk Industry*

Bythell, D 1969. *The Handloom Weavers. A Study in the English Cotton Industry during the Industrial Revolution*

Caffyn, L 1986. *Workers' Housing in West Yorkshire, 1750–1920*

Calladine, A and Fricker, J forthcoming. *The Textile Mills of East Cheshire*
Calvert, R K (ed) 1910. *Commercial Year Book of the Leeds Incorporated Chamber of Commerce*
Chapman S D 1971. The cost of power in the Industrial Revolution in Britain: the case of the textile industry. *Midland Hist* **1**, 1–23
1981–2. The Arkwright mills – Colquhoun's Census of 1788 and archaeological evidence. *Ind Archaeol Rev* **6**, 5–27
City of Bradford 1947. *Sewage Disposal 1870–1947*. 4th edn
Coad, J G 1973. Two early attempts at fire-proofing in Royal Dockyards. *Post-Medieval Archaeol* **7**, 88–90
Connell, E J 1975. Industrial development in South Leeds, 1790–1914. Unpublished PhD thesis, University of Leeds. 2 vols
1990. The supply of water as a factor in the location of industry. *Yorkshire Archaeol J* **62**, 191–4
Cossons, N (ed) 1972. *Rees's Manufacturing Industry (1819–20)*. 5 vols
Crossley, D 1989. *Water Power on the Sheffield Rivers*
Crump, W B (ed) 1931*a*. The Leeds woollen industry 1780–1820. *Publ Thoresby Soc* **32**
Crump, W B 1931*b*. The Leeds woollen industry 1780–1820, general introduction. In Crump 1931*a*, 1–58
1931*c*. The history of Gott's mill. In Crump 1931*a*, 254–71
Crump, W and Ghorbal, G 1935. *History of the Huddersfield Woollen Industry*
Cudworth, W 1891. *Histories of Bolton and Bowling*
Cunningham, C 1981. *Victorian and Edwardian Town Halls*
Darley, G 1975. *Villages of Vision*
Defoe, D 1724–6. *A Tour through the Whole Island of Great Britain*. Abridged and edited by P Rogers, 1971
Dewhirst, I 1972. *Old Keighley in Photographs*
Dickenson, M 1974. The West Riding woollen and worsted industries, 1689–1770. An analysis of probate inventories and insurance policies. Unpublished PhD thesis, University of Nottingham
Dickinson, H W 1938. *A Short History of the Steam Engine*
1958. The steam engine to 1830. In Singer *et al* 1958*a*, 168–98
Du Boff, R B 1967. The introduction of electric power in American manufacturing. *Econ Hist Rev*, 2nd series **20**, 509–18
Emmott and Company 1919. *Textile Manufacturer Year Book*
English, W 1969. *The Textile Industry. An Account of the Early Innovations of Spinning, Weaving and Knitting Machines*
Fairbairn, W 1854. *On the Application of Cast and Wrought Iron to Building Purposes*
1861. *Treatise on Mills and Millwork. Part 1. On the Principles of Mechanism and on Prime Movers*
1863. *Treatise on Mills and Millwork. Part 2. On Machinery of Transmission and the Construction and Arrangement of Mills*
1864. *Treatise on Mills and Millwork. Part 2. On Machinery of Transmission and the Construction and Arrangement of Mills*. 2nd edn
Falconer, K and Thornes, R 1986–7. Industrial archaeology and the RCHME. *Ind Archaeol Rev* **9**, 24–36
Falkus, M E 1967. The British gas industry before 1850. *Econ Hist Rev*, 2nd series **20**, 494–508
1982. The early development of the British gas industry, 1790–1815. *Econ Hist Rev*, 2nd series **35**, 217–34
Farnie, D A 1979. *The English Cotton Industry and the World Market, 1815–1896*

Feather, G A 1972. A Pennine worsted community in the mid-nineteenth century. *Textile Hist* **3**, 64–91

Field, D C 1958. Internal combustion engines. In Singer *et al* 1958*b*, 157–76

Fieldhouse, J 1981. *Bradford*. 2nd edn

Fitzgerald, R 1979. Structural development. In Binney *et al* 1979, 60–7

1987–8*a*. The development of the cast iron frame in textile mills to 1850. *Ind Archaeol Rev* **10**, 127–45

1987–8*b*. Albion Mill, Manchester. *Ind Archaeol Rev* **10**, 204–30

Fowler, W H (ed) 1895. *Fifty Years' History of the Development of Green's Economiser*

Fraser, D (ed) 1980. *A History of Modern Leeds*

Garnett, W O 1951. *Wainstalls Mills. The History of I & I Calvert Ltd, 1821–1951*

Giles, C and Goodall, I H 1986–7. Framing a survey of textile mills: RCHME's West Riding experience. *Ind Archaeol Rev* **9**, 71–81

Girouard, M 1979. *The Victorian Country House*. Revised and enlarged edition

Glover, F J 1959. Dewsbury Mills. A history of Messrs Wormalds and Walker Ltd, blanket manufacturers, Dewsbury. Unpublished PhD thesis, University of Leeds

Goodchild, J 1981. *Wakefield and Wool*

1982. Enterprise in the Barnsley linen industry in the eighteenth and nineteenth century. *Textile Hist* **13**, 249–69

Grady, K 1989. The Georgian public buildings of Leeds and the West Riding. *Publ Thoresby Soc* **62** (for 1987)

Green, E and Son Ltd 1956. *Waste Not: The Story of Green's Economiser*

Hargrave, E and Crump, W B 1931. The diary of Joseph Rogerson, scribbling miller of Bramley, 1808–14. In Crump 1931*a*, 59–166

Hartley, M and Ingilby, J 1976. *Life and Tradition in West Yorkshire*

Hay, G D and Stell, G P 1986. *Monuments of Industry. An Illustrated Historical Record*

Hills, R L 1970. *Power in the Industrial Revolution*

1989. *Power from Steam: A History of the Stationary Steam Engine*

Hodgson, J 1879. *Textile Manufacture and Other Industries in Keighley*

Holden, J 1912. *A Short History of Todmorden*

Holden, R N 1987–8. Pear Mill, Stockport: An Edwardian cotton spinning mill. *Ind Archaeol Rev* **10**, 162–74

Hole, J 1886. *The Homes of the Working Classes, with Suggestions for their Improvement*

Holroyde, H 1980. Power technology in the Halifax textile industry, 1770–1850. *Trans Halifax Antiq Soc*, 63–75

Hudson, P 1986. *The Genesis of Industrial Capital. A Study of the West Riding Wool Textile Industry c1750–1850*

Hughes, J 1866. *The History of the Township of Meltham*

Hume, J R 1977. *The Industrial Archaeology of Scotland. II. The Highlands and Islands*

Ingle, G 1974. History of R V Marriner Ltd, worsted spinners, Keighley. Unpublished MPhil thesis, University of Leeds

1980. The West Riding Cotton Industry, 1780–1835. Unpublished PhD thesis, University of Bradford

James, D 1986. Paternalism in Keighley. In Jowitt 1986*a*, 104–19

James, J 1857. *History of the Worsted Manufacture in England*

Jenkins, D T 1975. *The West Riding Wool Textile Industry, 1770–1835. A Study of Fixed Capital Formation*

1979. The cotton industry in Yorkshire, 1780–1900. *Textile Hist* **10**, 75–95

Jenkins, D T and Ponting, K G 1982. *The British Wool Textile Industry, 1770–1914*

Jenkins, J G (ed) 1972. *The Wool Textile Industry in Great Britain*

Jennings, B (ed) 1970. *A History of Harrogate and Knaresborough*
1983. *A History of Nidderdale*. 2nd edn
Johnson, H R and Skempton, A W 1955–7. William Strutt's cotton mills, 1793–1850. *Trans Newcomen Soc* **30**, 179–205
Jones, E 1985. *Industrial Architecture in Britain 1750–1939*
Jowitt, J A 1982. The Pattern of Religion in Victorian Bradford. In Wright and Jowitt (eds) 1982, 37–61
Jowitt, J A (ed) 1986*a*. *Model Industrial Communities in Mid-Nineteenth Century Yorkshire*
1986*b*. Introduction. In Jowitt 1986*a*, 5–16
1986*c*. Copley, Akroydon and West Hill Park: moral reform and social improvement in Halifax. In Jowitt 1986*a*, 73–88
Jubb, S 1860. *The History of the Shoddy Trade*
Kaijage, F J 1975. Labouring Barnsley, 1816–1856. A social and economic history. Unpublished DPhil thesis, University of Warwick
Kelly 1877. *Directory of the West Riding of Yorkshire*
1889. *Directory of the West Riding of Yorkshire*
1893. *Directory of the West Riding of Yorkshire*
Linstrum, D 1978. *West Yorkshire Architects and Architecture*
McCutcheon, W A 1980. *The Industrial Archaeology of Northern Ireland*
Macleod, M *et al* 1988. *The Ditherington Flax Mill, Shrewsbury. A Survey and Historical Evaluation*. The Ironbridge Institute Research Paper No 30
Malin, J C 1979. The West Riding Recovered Wool Textile Industry, *c*1813–1939. Unpublished PhD thesis, University of York
Mason, K M 1989. *Woolcombers, Worsteds and Watermills. Addingham's Industrial Revolution*
Moss, M and Hume, J 1981. *The Making of Scotch Whisky*
Nasmith, J and F 1909. *Recent Cotton Mill Construction and Engineering*
Nussey, J 1984. *Smithies Mill, Birstall. The Life and Times of an 18th-Century Steam-Driven Scribbling and Fulling Mill in the Yorkshire Heavy Woollen District*
Pafford, E R and J H P 1974. *Employer and Employed: Ford, Ayrton & Co Ltd, Silk Spinners with Worker Participation, Leeds and Low Bentham 1870–1970*
Partridge, W 1823. *A Practical Treatise on Dying*. Reprinted with an introduction by J de L Mann and technical notes by K G Ponting, 1973
Pearce, C 1979–80*a*. A model example. *Pennine Magazine* **1**, no 3, 20–1
1979–80*b*. A community sewn up. *Pennine Magazine* **1**, no 5, 20–1
1986. Paternalism and the industrial village — the cases of Wilshaw and Meltham Mills. In Jowitt 1986*a*, 89–103
Peters, D 1974. *Darley Abbey: From Monastery to Industrial Community*
Pevsner, N, revised Williamson, E 1978. *The Buildings of England. Derbyshire*. 2nd edn
Pike, W T and Co 1895. *A Descriptive Account of Dewsbury*
1896. *Views and Reviews. Special Edition. Todmorden*
Ponting, K G 1970. *Baines's Account of the Woollen Manufacture of England*. New edition with introduction by K G Ponting
Ranger, W 1852. *Report to the General Board of Health on a Preliminary Inquiry into the Sewerage, Drainage, and Supply of Water, and the Sanitary Conditions of the Inhabitants of the Town of Barnsley, in the County of York*
Reynolds, J 1983. *The Great Paternalist: Titus Salt and the Growth of Nineteenth-Century Bradford*
1985. *Saltaire. An Introduction to the Village of Sir Titus Salt*
1986. Reflections on Saltaire. In Jowitt 1986*a*, 43–61

Rimmer, W G 1957–60. Castle Foregate Flax Mill, Shrewsbury (1797–1886). *Trans Shropshire Archaeol Soc* **56**, 49–68

1960. *Marshalls of Leeds Flax Spinners 1788–1886*

Roberts, J S 1977. *Little Germany*

Robinson, A H 1972. *Bradford's Public Statues*

Rogers, K H 1976. *Wiltshire and Somerset Woollen Mills*

Rose, M B 1986. *The Gregs of Quarry Bank Mill. The Rise and Decline of a Family Firm, 1750–1914*

RCHME 1986*a*. *Annual Review 1985–6*

RCHME 1986*b*. *Rural Houses of West Yorkshire 1400–1830*

RCHME 1987. *Houses of the North York Moors*

RCHME 1990. *Recording Historic Buildings: A Descriptive Specification*

Saxonhouse, G R and Wright, G 1984. New evidence on the stubborn English mule and the cotton industry, 1878–1920. *Econ Hist Rev*, 2nd series **37**, 507–19

Schofield, J and J C 1927. *Cloth Finishing: Woollen and Worsted*

Settle and District Civic Society 1975. *The Ancient Parish of Giggleswick*

Sheeran, G 1986. *Good Houses Built of Stone*

1990. *Landscape Gardens in West Yorkshire 1680–1880*

Shutt, G 1979. Wharfedale water mills. Unpublished MPhil thesis, University of Leeds

Sigsworth, E M 1951–2. William Greenwood and Robert Heaton. Two eighteenth-century worsted manufacturers. *J Bradford Textile Soc*, 61–72

1958. *Black Dyke Mills*

Singer, C *et al* (eds) 1958*a*. *A History of Technology. Vol IV. The Industrial Revolution c1750 to c1850*

1958*b*. *A History of Technology. Vol V. The Late Nineteenth Century c1850 to c1900*

Sington, T 1897. *Cotton Mill Planning and Construction*

Skempton, A W and Johnson, H R 1962. The first iron frames. *Architect Rev* **131**, 175–86

Smith, W 1866. *Rambles about Morley*

Smith, W J 1977. The cost of building Lancashire loomhouses and weavers' workshops: the Account Book of James Brandwood of Turton, 1794–1814. *Textile Hist* **8**, 56–76

Smithies, P 1988. *The Architecture of the Halifax Piece Hall 1775–1779*

Stephens, W B 1980. Elementary education and literacy, 1770–1870. In Fraser 1980, 223–49

Stowers, A 1958*a*. Watermills, *c*1500–*c*1850. In Singer *et al* 1958*a*, 199–213

1958*b*. The stationary steam engine, 1830–1900. In Singer *et al* 1958*b*, 124–40

Suddards, R W (ed) 1976. *Titus of Salts*

Tann, J 1965. Some problems of water power: a study of mill siting in Gloucestershire. *Trans Bristol Gloucs Archaeol Soc* **84**, 53–77

1970. *The Development of the Factory*

Taylor, A 1961. *The History of Wilshaw*

Thornes, R C N 1981. *West Yorkshire: 'A Noble Scene of Industry'. The Development of the County 1500 to 1830*

Timmins, J G 1979. Handloom weavers' cottages in central Lancashire: some problems of recognition. *Post-Medieval Archaeol* **13**, 251–72

Tomlinson, C nd. *The Useful Arts and Manufactures of Great Britain. First Series, Textile Fibres, etc*

Travis, J 1901. *Chapters in Todmorden History*

Trigg, W B 1933. The industrial water supply of Ovenden. *Trans Halifax Antiq Soc*, 135–64

Tunzelmann, G N von 1978. *Steam Power and British Industrialization to 1860*
Ure, A 1836. *The Cotton Manufacture of Great Britain*. 2 vols
Walker, G 1814. *The Costume of Yorkshire*
Warner, F 1921. *The Silk Industry of the United Kingdom – its origins and development*
Watkins, G 1970. *The Textile Mill Engine. Vol 1*
Watson, M 1987–8. Jute manufacturing: a study of Camperdown Works, Dundee. *Ind Archaeol Rev* **10**, 175–92
1990. *Jute and Flax Mills in Dundee*
White, W 1853. *Directory and Gazetteer of Leeds, Bradford and the Clothing Districts of the West Riding of Yorkshire*
1858. *A Month in Yorkshire*
Wild, M T 1972. The Yorkshire wool textile industry. In Jenkins 1972, 185–234
Wilson, T B 1937. *Two Leeds Architects. Cuthbert Brodrick and George Corson*
Worrall, J 1919–20. *The Yorkshire Textile Directory*
1930. *The Cotton Spinners and Manufacturers Directory*
Worsley, G 1986. One family, one architect. John Gibson and the Fieldens of Todmorden. *Country Life* 6 February 1986, 302–5
Wright, D G and Jowitt, J A (eds) 1982. *Victorian Bradford. Essays in Honour of Jack Reynolds*

Index

References in **bold** are to illustrations